ALL
THE
STARS
IN HEAVEN

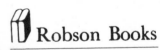
Robson Books

ALL
THE
STARS
IN HEAVEN

Louis B. Mayer's
M-G-M

Gary Carey

ALSO BY GARY CAREY

Lost Films
Cukor & Co.
Brando!
Lenny, Janis & Jimi
Katharine Hepburn
Doug & Mary

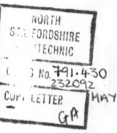
FIRST PUBLISHED IN GREAT BRITAIN IN 1982 BY ROBSON BOOKS LTD.,
BOLSOVER HOUSE, 5-6 CLIPSTONE STREET, LONDON W1P 7EB
COPYRIGHT © 1981 BY GARY CAREY

British Library Cataloguing in Publication Data
Carey, Gary
   All the stars in heaven: the story of Louis B. Mayer and MGM.
   1. Mayer, Louis Burt   2. Moving-picture producers
   and directors — United States — Biography
   I. Title
   791.43'0232'0924   PN1998.A2
   ISBN 0-86051-164-2

Designed by Nicola Mazzella.

All photographs courtesy of the Museum of Modern Art Film Stills Archive.
Reprinted with permission.

Printed and bound in Great Britain by R. J. Acford, Chichester.

For
Carol Estelle Koshinskie Carey
my own kapusta świeża na kwaśno

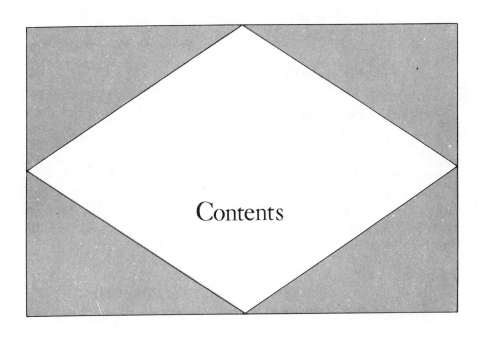

Contents

List
of Illustrations

An 18-page photo gallery follows page 172.

William Powell and Jean Harlow
Jean Harlow
Clark Gable, Tully Marshall and Jean Harlow
Clark Gable with Mayer and others
Robert Montgomery, Clark Gable and Robert Taylor
Clark Gable and Margaret O'Brien
Clark Gable and Greer Garson
Joan Crawford and Wallace Beery rehearsing a scene for *Grand Hotel*
Thalberg and Norma Shearer, 1933
Jean Howard
Thalberg and Shearer with Mayer
Groucho Marx and Margaret Dumont
Mayer with Greer Garson
Judy Garland and Mickey Rooney
Judy Garland and Vincente Minnelli with Mayer
Helen Hayes
Tracy and Hepburn
Lana Turner
Actors from *Battleground*
M-G-M studio

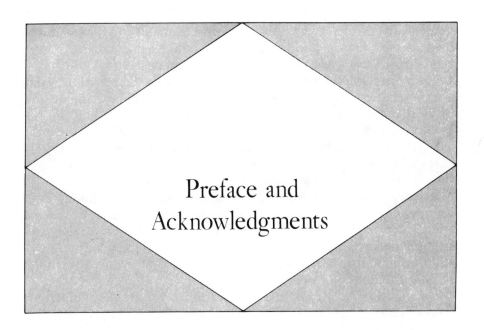

Preface and Acknowledgments

"I'll go down on my knees and kiss the ground talent walks on." Louis B. Mayer—otherwise known as Mr. Mayer or L.B. or just plain Louie—who was never an innovator, but knew a good one-liner when he heard it, picked up this old saw and made it a staple of his conversational repertoire. It was a pet phrase he trotted out in conferences and interviews or during his notorious pep talks with the M-G-M stars. His admirers—those who still call him Mr. Mayer and bite their tongues when they make a slip and mention L.B. or Louie —repeat the phrase as though it were a final summation, an epitaph that says all that needs to be said about old man Mayer.

And, as epitaphs go, this one is not so inappropriate. Mayer was, after all, the creator of M-G-M, the studio that once boasted (with good-natured, almost self-parodistic, hyperbole) of having "more stars than there are in heaven." Today that slogan, like Mayer's avowed humility before the talent he employed, seems corny, a bit overblown and old-fashioned, but then, so was the man. Mayer had a knack for self-dramatization; he enjoyed presenting himself as bigger than life; he had a personal style, and idiosyncratic kind of flamboyance. He was a showman in the tradition of Barnum and Belasco and the Frohmans.

But like these earlier theatrical producers (all of whom speech-
ified, at one time or another, of genuflecting before talent), Mayer
stepped on a lot of toes, crushed a lot of delicate psyches, as he forged
ahead in pursuit of getting his show on the road. He racked up a slew
of enemies along the way. "He put it all in reverse," says one former
M-G-M screenwriter. "It was the talent that got down and did the
kissing . . . and what they were expected to kiss wasn't the ground."

Hypocrite is hardly the worst thing Mayer has ever been called.
There's barely a nasty adjective in any thesaurus that hasn't at one
time or another been applied to him. He was described as vain,
mercenary, bombastic, hot-headed, semi-illiterate, reactionary, ty-
rannical, Tartuffish, a dummkopf whose peacock reign at M-G-M
would have been impossible without the brains and steady hands of
Irving Thalberg, his chief lieutenant, and Nick Schenck, his "boss"
and president of Loew's, Inc., the parent company which controlled
the Metro-Goldwyn-Mayer studios.

A fair share of these descriptions of Mayer are admissible, but
the line must be drawn at dummkopf, and yet this is precisely the
image of Mayer which has endured as part of the Hollywood legend:
he is remembered as an outspoken incompetent with no taste, no
understanding of "cinematic" art; a man who cramped the vision of
directors by insisting on glamour, happy endings and sentimental
uplift; a little Caesar who envisioned himself as a latter-day Sun
King.

The first sketch for this caricatured, yet seemingly indelible,
portrait was drawn by Bosley Crowther, the former film critic of *The
New York Times,* whose biography of Mayer, *Hollywood Rajah,* appeared in 1960, three years after the death of M-G-M's one time czar.
Crowther placed Mayer in the tradition of the old-time robber bar-
ons, a tradition he did not especially admire. A staunch liberal, the
biographer was not in sympathy with "that phalanx of men of aggressive bent who seized on the opportunities that an expounding
civilization exposed," and while he tried and wanted to be fair to his
subject, his distaste shows through on nearly every page. His pen is
dipped not so much in acid as in a peculiar kind of good-natured
ridicule, and his L. B. Mayer emerges as more buffoon than robber
baron, a power-hungry opportunist with little integrity and less
vision.

Crowther merely opened the gates. After *Hollywood Rajah* came
the real deluge of Mayerphobia. It was the early 1960s; the era of
movie nostalgia was beginning to blossom; and the stars and personalities of Hollywood either courted or were courted by publishers
with promises of or requests for tell-all memoirs. The day of ven-

geance was at hand. The film and theatre biographies of the next decade were filled with anecdotes that cast Mayer and the other studio bosses in a vicious or ridiculous light. Grievances, petty or otherwise, were hauled out of mothballs, aired, laundered and often exaggerated. Even the most spurious and ill-documented of these reminiscences were taken as truth, partly because they were so amusing that people wanted to believe them, partly because the American public had been primed to believe that anything and everything was possible in Hollywood.

But however diverting they may be, many of the Mayer stories don't hold up under close examination. Why, for instance, if Thalberg was the genius behind Mayer's throne, do so many of the films he personally supervised or supported (*Hallelujah!, The Sin of Madelon Claudet, The Barretts of Wimpole Street, Romeo and Juliet, The Good Earth*) seem so dated and stultifyingly pompous today, while Mayer's favorites (*San Francisco, Ziegfeld Girl,* the Arthur Freed musicals, even the best of the Hardy pictures and the better Garland-Rooney puppy-love comedies) are still passable entertainments? If Thalberg was the genius, then how did Mayer manage to steer the company smoothly and successfully during the decade following his protégé's premature death in 1936? And if Mayer was such an incompetent studio boss, why did Nick Schenck (who was never an L.B. aficionado) put up with him for over twenty-five years?

The only way of answering these questions is to reevaluate Mayer's career, and the end result of such an evaluation suggests that, purposefully or inadvertently, Mayer has been maligned and deprived of his rightful position as one of the key figures of Hollywood history. To say this is not to deny or diminish Thalberg's and Schenck's contribution to M-G-M's success, only to put it in its proper perspective. Thalberg (who needed little push in this direction) was told by Mayer to "think big," but he couldn't have thought as big as he did without Mayer around to provide the foundation to make his dreams a reality. Mayer, on the other hand, would have been hard put to provide that foundation without Schenck and Loew's, Inc. It was a three-man chain of power, but Mayer was the central, controlling link.

In the past, M-G-M was often called the Tiffany's of Hollywood studios; today it is still remembered as the studio of studios, the poshest and most glamorous, the one with the most incandescent stars. When writing about M-G-M, it is all too easy to slip into superlatives or hyperbole, but that is what M-G-M was all about; that was the way Mayer built it. Again, he wasn't an innovator—the ground plans for the star and studio systems had been drawn up long before he arrived on the film scene—but still he was the chief architect of what has been called the Hollywood Dream Factory.

The subsequent pages of this book present a reevaluation of Mayer's life and career; they represent an attempt to separate fact from the myth and apocryphal anecdotage that has clotted earlier accounts of the man and his achievements. This task would have been impossible to achieve without the aid, advice and recollections of many people to whom I am deeply indebted. Those with whom I talked or corresponded include Howard Strickling and his late wife, Gail, who entertained me several times at their ranch in Chino and allowed me to examine their collection of M-G-M records and memorabilia; Irene, Jeffrey and Daniel Selznick; the late Myron Fox; J. J. Cohn; Robert Vogel; Arnold Gillespie; Robert Hoag; Emily Torchia; Ann Straus; Esmée Chandlee; Alan Jay Lerner; Katharine Hepburn; Bessie Love; Maureen O' Sullivan; Carmel Myers; Clarence Brown; Steve Reid; Anita Loos; the late George Oppenheimer and Sara Mankiewicz. For past projects, I had spoken with Joseph Mankiewicz, George Cukor, Leatrice Joy and the late Josef von Sternberg, and I have drawn on material from these interviews for this book.

Secondary research was done mainly at the Lincoln Center Library for the Performing Arts and The Film Study Center of The Museum of Modern Art in New York, and at The Margaret Herrick Library of The Academy of Motion Picture Arts and Sciences. I wish to thank the staff at each of these institutions, particularly my friends Mary Corliss and Charles Silver at The Museum of Modern Art.

I am also indebted to John Greenleaf, Selma Herbert, Beverly Walker, Jerry Mickey and Stacey Graham for various courtesies during my stays in California. Finally, a deep bow of thanks to my agent, Ray Pierre Corsini, a true pillar of support and understanding, and to my editors, Bill Whitehead and Paul De Angelis. Without their help and expert advice, I doubt whether the book would ever have been completed.

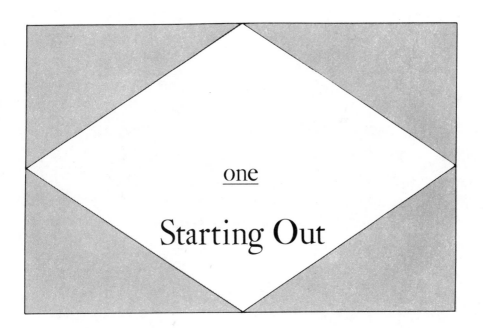

one

Starting Out

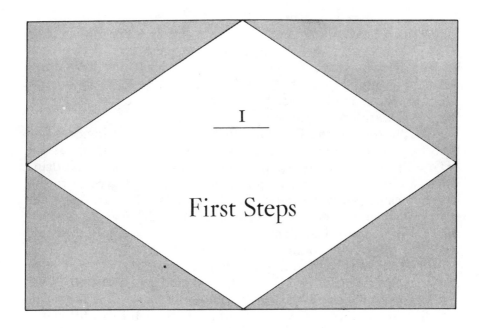

I

First Steps

One blustery autumn afternoon in the late 1940s, Louis B. Mayer and
the elder of his two grandsons, Jeffrey Selznick, were having lunch
in one of Manhattan's better restaurants, Le Pavillon. There was
nothing unusual about the event—eating together was the most satisfying form of sociability, as far as Mayer was concerned, and many
of Jeffrey's early memories of his grandfather have a breakfast or
dinner table as their background. So there was nothing unusual
about this lunch except the locale—a chilly, prewintry New York,
not palmy Southern California.

Mayer had come east on business, and Jeffrey, who was then
attending Deerfield Academy in New England, had traveled to Manhattan specifically for this lunch. The conversation that day—at least
as much of it as Jeffrey can remember—ran along familiar lines.
There was probably a lecture—"Grandpa gave a lot of lectures, most
of which I managed to ignore"—and there was probably some talk
about horses and cars, two mutual enthusiasms. Something that
wasn't discussed was the movies, a subject Jeffrey had learned to
avoid. Months before in California, driving home after a disastrous
preview of the M-G-M version of *The Three Musketeers*, Jeffrey had
told Mayer that he agreed with the audience, the picture was lousy.

Mayer made no comment, but afterwards, Jeffrey was banished from all M-G-M previews until *Musketeers* had opened to good reviews and big business. By then, Mayer had made his point and Jeffrey had learned a lesson. "My mother said that if Grandpa ever really became angry at me, he might never forgive me. Maybe she was exaggerating, but I wasn't going to find out."

By the time of the Pavillon lunch, the *Musketeers* incident had been forgotten, and over a cup of boiling hot coffee—"that was one of Grandpa's idiosyncracies," Jeffrey remembers, "he wouldn't drink coffee unless it was hot enough to cause second-degree burns"— Mayer became expansive and invited his grandson to share one of the most private moments of his personal life. That day was the anniversary of his mother's death, and he asked Jeffrey to join him as he said Kaddish in a service commemorating her yahrzeit.

"I knew next to nothing about Kaddish or the yahrzeit ceremony," Jeffrey recalls, "but I thought I should, so I accepted." Outside Le Pavillon, he and his grandfather got into a waiting limousine and drove south and then west, out of the fashionable east fifties and into the heart of the Garment District, where Mayer stopped the car in front of a modest, somewhat dilapidated synagogue that was Middle European in appearance and ambience.

Once inside, Mayer put on a yarmulke and prayer shawl, and for over an hour, "with tears streaming down his cheeks," he sobbed and recited Kaddish and other prayers. Afterwards, he had to walk several blocks to compose himself; then he pressed a fifty-dollar bill into Jeffrey's palm, hailed the trailing limousine and drove off into the thick of New York rush-hour traffic. Left behind, Jeffrey waved at the car, then glanced at the bill in his hand. It was sometime before he felt he had both feet on the ground.

If young Selznick experienced "something like cultural shock" as he watched the scene in the synagogue, it was because he had been allowed a rare glimpse of his grandfather acting out a part of his ancestral heritage. Usually Mayer was extremely reticent about his family history. Fiercely proud of his American citizenship, he was never keen on discussing his foreign background or his boyhood years as an immigrant in this country, and since his recollections of that period were probably not pleasant, who's to blame him? Only the biographer, who is faced with a large number of blank spots in the record of Mayer's early life and who can answer a large number of important questions only with suppositions.

One of these questions concerns the family name. Originally it might have been Meyer, as it often appears erroneously in newspaper accounts of the young Louis B. Mayer's activities, but just as possibly it could have been something far more remote, something that bore no resemblance to the name the family finally accepted as their own. Over the years, as they fled Russian persecution of the Jews, his ancestors had changed identities so frequently that no one seemed to remember what they had originally been called. As Irene Mayer Selznick points out, most immigrant families accepted the name given them by immigration authorities who rarely understood the native language of their guests.

Nor is there any certainty about Mayer's date of birth. His mother said he was born during a period of famine, so it was probably 1882 or 1885, years in which there were devastating crop failures throughout Russia. As to the month and day, she was equally vague; sometime in midsummer, she thought. For a long time, Mayer wavered between 1882 and 1885, but finally, when applying for naturalization papers in 1912, he settled on July 4, 1885, as his birthday, a choice that suggests strong emotional identification with his adopted country.

There is also confusion about precisely where he was born. Sources vary between Minsk and Vilna, and it is also possible that the event occurred in Dmra, a small village situated midway between these two cities. Sarah (or Chaye), his mother, was of peasant stock; Jacob, his father, was a laborer and sometime tradesman or peddler. Louis (or Lazar) was the second of their children; the first-born was Yetta, and two years after Louis's birth came another daughter, Ida. Providing them with food and shelter was a constant struggle for Jacob, and later Mayer claimed that he could remember nothing of his Russian childhood except that he was always hungry.

The rest of the story can easily be imagined. Mayer's early years coincide with one of the cruelest periods of Russian history. In 1881, Czar Alexander II, "the kindliest prince who ever ruled Russia," was assassinated by revolutionary terrorists, and his death dashed the hopes of Russian Jews that an enlightened autocracy might someday grant them equal rights as citizens. The new czar, Alexander III, was in the thrall of his minister of religion, the violently anti-Semitic Constantine Pobyedonostzev, who declared that the Jewish problem would be solved only when one-third of Russia's Jews had emigrated, one-third had been converted to Christianity, and one-third had "disappeared." Once Alexander III was in power, pogroms broke out all over Russia. The worst of them were over by the time of Mayer's birth, but they were to continue sporadically throughout the 1880s, the decade that saw the first great exodus of Russian Jews to America. As Irving Howe has written in *World of Our Fathers*, they left for a variety of reasons: "yearnings for riches, for land, for change, for tranquillity." Most, however, went to ease lives that had become intolerable because of persecution and deprivation.

Getting out was not easy. A one-way, steerage-class ticket from Europe to New York then cost about thirty dollars. Saving that much money meant years of scrimping for people who were living a hand-to-mouth existence, but somehow, in 1888, Jacob Mayer managed to squeeze himself and his family aboard a transatlantic steamer. Probably they sailed from one of the Baltic ports—this, at least, was the traditional route—but which one is not known. On reaching America, they first settled in New York City and stayed there long enough for Sarah to give birth to two more sons—Jerome (Jerry) and Rudolph (Rudy). Then, for unknown reasons, they gathered up their meager belongings and moved to Canada.

There is a vague but persistent rumor that the Mayers fled New York because of an embarrassing incident involving a fire for which they were held responsible. The story has never been substantiated, but it is entirely possible that the Mayers may have caused some minor accident or had some slight brush with the law that frightened them. Because of their past experience, Jewish immigrants had a great suspicion and fear of the police. The mere mention of the words *police, law* and *prison* terrified them, and out of self-protection, they became evasive and secretive. They had been taught to feel guilty, whether they were or not, and rather than face interrogation, they were always ready to pull up stakes and vanish, as they had so often in the past.

Whether this pattern of behavior fits the Mayers is, however, open to question. Louis B. Mayer had a far simpler explanation for his family's decision to leave New York. Years later he told a friend, "We just weren't making any headway."

Why they decided to settle in Saint John, New Brunswick, is yet another mystery. This small city on the Bay of Fundy, well sheltered from Atlantic storms by its location on the inland side of the peninsula, was a thriving maritime port, with prosperous lumber mills and iron founderies dotting the adjacent countryside. The population of Saint John was predominately of English, Scotch and Irish heritage, but in the early 1880s there was a small influx of Jewish settlers who had come to learn that ghetto subsistence was not confined to Europe, but was also flourishing in the big cities of the New World. Saint John wasn't paradise—the main streets were mud and wood planks—but compared to the Lower East Side of New York, it was just this side of Eden. The first Jewish settlers were roughed up by the townspeople, but they endured and eventually made a place for themselves in the daily life of Saint John.

By 1895, even Jacob Mayer was getting ahead. He had established himself as a peddler, going from door to door with a stock of petty household supplies—needles, soup greens, dress goods, buttons, anything a housewife might have forgotten to pick up at the local store. He prospered well enough to progress to the junk business and then to the scrap metal trade.

Jacob had drive and ambition, but these qualities were dirt cheap in the new world. Short, stooped in posture, uncomfortable when talking with strangers, he was just another door-to-door salesman as far as most of Saint John was concerned, but within his own circle of friends, he was considered a Hebrew scholar. His reputation was not based on extensive education—at most, he spent no more than a few years at an Orthodox yeshiva where the curriculum was restricted to an exhausting study of the Talmud and the proper performance of rituals. But the traditional Jewish idea of scholarship was based not on breadth of knowledge but on a style of life. Through his constant studies, the scholar was trying to reach God, and was demonstrating his preference for "the Sabbath" over "the week," for God's world over the workaday world of human commerce.

From all reports, Jacob was bookish and otherworldly, qualities that his son suspected as hypocritical. Louis accepted the values of the commercial world his father seemingly rejected. In this way, he was closer to his mother, a peasant-smart woman who could take a bunch of herbs, some cabbage and a stringy fowl, stew them together and come up with three or four nourishing dinners for her family. And Sarah nourished her children, especially "Louie," in other ways. She was practical; she never forgot that Sabbath was only one of seven days of the week, though like Jacob, she had her otherworldly side. But for Sarah, it was the world of the imagination. After supper, she led the family in singing folk songs and transcriptions of the holy music they heard at services; or like Scheherazade, she recited the old, traditional tales or read aloud, as best she could, new stories from periodicals. Louis was the most appreciative member of her audience —his favorite was an 1898 song called "The Rosary" which became so popular that it was novelized and later dramatized. (A sentimental variation of Schnitzler's *Reigen,* it is about a rosary which passes from hand to hand until it ends where it started—in the possession of the chaste young lady who originally gave it away.)

This was Louis's first brush with art, and it was decisive. From then on, he was hooked on the pleasures of music and storytelling of any kind. About his only other entertainment was watching the neighborhood kids play baseball in a vacant lot adjacent to his parents' home. Several times he tried to join the team, but the other kids told him baseball wasn't "a Yid's game," and anyway, he didn't own a glove. So for weeks he ferreted away pennies until he collected a couple of dollars. Then he marched into the local hardware store and bought the best baseball mitt that could be had. When he left the shop, the glove was strapped to his belt in the best professional manner, and he swaggered down the street and past the baseball field, pointedly ignoring the admiring glances of his former tormenters.

As this story suggests, the Mayers were regarded as outsiders by most of the Saint John's townspeople. Jew-baiting was an accepted pastime, and it was not unusual for Louis and his brothers to have to fight their way home after school. Mayer never grew accustomed to the ugly names or the sneering voices that spoke them, but in time he came to enjoy the physical sensation of fighting. He was good with his fists, and found these rough-and-tumble brawls a convenient way to work off his frustrations and anxieties.

One of the greatest trials of young Mayer's life was the New World educational system. Neither in elementary school nor in junior high did he distinguish himself as a promising scholar. He wasn't much of a reader, and his grammar was poor—not surprising, since Yiddish was the common language at home. His instructors pushed and prodded but Louis remained unresponsive, seemingly content to coast along until his term of trial had ended. Only once did he show any real interest in his daily lessons. This happened when his teacher asked each pupil in the class, "If you had a thousand dollars, what would you do with it?"

One boy said, "I'd build a house." Another answered, "I'd buy a boat." Louis was more practical. "I'd put it into a business." Why? the teacher asked. "Because then I'd get a return on my investment."

This story, which comes from an M-G-M press release, may well be apocryphal, but there is nonetheless something that can be learned from it. As Irving Howe points out in *World of Our Fathers,* many immigrant boys were poor students because the kind of information they were seeking was not to be found in a McGuffey reader. What they wanted to learn was how to make money and get out of the slums; what they were taught was how to parse a sentence.

Often the boys who were the worst students were the ones, like Louis Mayer, who had Hebrew "scholars" as fathers. They did not have to search very far to find an example of the impracticality of pursuing knowledge for the sake of knowledge. Many of the boys, like Mayer, developed a distrust of abstract or higher education that was difficult for them to shake even when they reached maturity. And again like Mayer, most of them left school as soon as they could.

Mayer's departure, according to an M-G-M press release, happened like this:

> There was that day, after long and Spartan saving of pennies, when the juvenile Mayer rattled home with his surprise on wheels, a red wagon. His mother thought it was a very nice wagon, indeed, all new and shiny, yet she wondered what her son intended doing with it. "Put it to work, Mother," he announced. "When?" was her indulgent inquiry. "Tomorrow," came the prompt decision.

The authenticity of this anecdote, like all press releases, is dubious—it smacks too much of George Washington and the cherry tree to be taken literally—but again, there is an element of truth to it. Shortly after his twelfth birthday, Louis quit school and went to work for his father. His first assignment was to take a wagon (or old potato sack) and walk around Saint John, collecting any bits of metal —a rusty nail, a piece of pipe, a discarded tool—that he saw in the streets. These he carted back to his father's office in the front of the rickety, one-story building in which the family lived.

Two years later, Jacob placed a new sign above his office: J. MAYER & SON. Louis had been accepted into the business as a full partner. Years later, Jacob told a friend that he had always considered Rudy to be the brightest of his boys, but, he added, Rudy was too much of a "get-rich-quick-Wellington"; he was forever coming up with devious schemes to make a fast buck. Louis, on the other hand, was steady, sensible and reliable, fully prepared to work, not dream his way to success.

But the young Louis Mayer was not above taking shortcuts, and on one occasion he was caught in an embarrassing situation. He was found loitering outside a tin foundry, and the night watchman, thinking he had cornered a thief, had the boy arrested. The next day, Louis told his side of the story to the owner of the tin business, a shrewd and serious Scot named John Wilson, who listened attentively and then decided to drop charges. Maybe he believed Mayer, maybe he admired his enterprise; whatever the reason, he thought the lad should have a second chance.

Mayer never forgot this incident, and frequently cited it as an illustration of his belief in democratic fair play. Nor was he ever to forget Wilson, who was to become his friend and mentor, someone he frequently turned to for advice and understanding. Despite the barrier of age and social class, a true bond developed between the men, one that Mayer came to depend on and was to try to duplicate as he worked his way to the top.

Very quickly, the son of Mayer & Son established himself as the more important member of the partnership. While still in his teens, Louis urged his father to move on to the more ambitious enterprise of salvaging materials from ships that had been wrecked along the coast. The younger Mayer directed these ventures, which called for the employment of as many as two hundred men, and required a good head for management and capital. It was hard work, and since the overhead was enormous it wasn't terribly profitable, but the returns were large enough to allow the Mayers to move to a bigger house in a better neighborhood. More importantly, the salvage business took Louis Mayer out of Saint John and allowed him to test his abilities in a more demanding sphere of the business world.

Around 1900, Mayer & Son became the northeastern representatives of a national salvaging corporation, and as his father's deputy, Mayer traveled extensively through New England, often ending up in Boston, which became a second home. When these journeys started, Louis was short and stocky, with thick black hair and a powerful upper torso that was the by-product of his work as a salvager. Daily contact with longshoremen had provided him with a colorful vocabulary and a man's way of looking at life. And in his own eyes he was an adult—he was then using 1882 as a birth date because it made him older—but to his mother, he was still her *boychik*.

Whenever he left home, Sarah made sure he was wearing his best suit, hid his money in a small bag sewn inside the lining of his jacket, and as a final precaution encharged him to the care of a train conductor named Sandy Brown, a family friend. At first Louis resented this slur on his maturity, but soon he and "Brownie" became close friends, and years later, out of gratitude, Mayer gave him a job as an M-G-M night watchman.

Before every one of these trips, Jacob told his son, "Be sure to go to synagogue each Sabbath." Louis dutifully fulfilled his religious obligation, but that still left six days of the week to follow more worldly pursuits. When he wasn't working, he was exploring the various kinds of entertainment each town had to offer. Plays, concerts, variety shows, amateur musicales, the little films that were shown in the nickelodeons that were then beginning to pop up all over the United States—whatever he could afford, he went to see. And by hanging around the theatres once the show had ended, he struck up acquaintances with men who shared his enthusiasm, even with some who made money from peddling and packaging entertainment.

Returning to Saint John was always a letdown, and Mayer soon resolved to leave the town for good. There was no sound reason for him to hang around—Jerry and Rudy were now old enough to help Jacob with the family business. Finally, on New Year's Day, 1904, he moved to Boston permanently. He would continue to act as his father's business representative whenever needed, but otherwise he was on his own.

He rented a room in a boardinghouse in Boston's South End, a neighborhood much like New York's Lower East Side: tenements and shops were piled together, pushcarts lined the streets, pavements teemed with *shaytl*-crowned matrons and old men in beaver hats or yarmulkes. The South End, as described in a 1906 Boston playbill (in a column entitled "Parts of the City You've Never Seen"), was "quaint . . . and old worldly . . . exuding the strange aromas of exotic foods . . . filled with the noises of foreign tongues. . . ." One wonders whether the author of this piece had ever visited that part of Boston: certainly the South End didn't seem so glamorous to its inhabitants or to Mayer, who spent his first days there wondering how he would pay for his next exotic meal, maybe a bowl of matzoh-ball soup or a slice of stuffed derma.

Things got a little better once he wangled a job with a local scrap metal merchant, and then improved immeasurably after he found a wife. He first spotted her while attending services at the Knesseth Israel synagogue on Emerald Street, just a few blocks from his boardinghouse. She was in her early twenties, had a porcelain complexion, thick black hair, bright eyes and a warm smile; she had a pleasing figure and was very pretty. Her name was Margaret ("Maggie") Shenberg and her father was the cantor at Knesseth Israel.

Cantor Shenberg had come to the South End from Pittsburgh, but he wasn't, according to Irene Mayer Selznick, "one of your big-city, fancy cantors; he was strictly small-time." In other words, his profession didn't earn him much money, and to support his family, he performed other duties, including acting as the mohel at *bris* (circumcision) ceremonies. There is also a story that Shenberg moonlighted as a butcher, but this appears to be untrue. "I don't know how that rumor started," says Mrs. Selznick, "unless some people consider circumcision a form of butchery."

The Shenbergs did not discourage Mayer's attention to their daughter, though they thought she deserved a suitor of more substance. But Margaret knew what she wanted, and on June 14, 1904, became Mrs. Louis B. Mayer. (To bolster his growing sense of self-importance, Mayer had added a middle initial to his name—later he was to say it stood for Burton or Burt.) At the end of the ceremony, the Shenbergs hadn't lost a daughter, they had gained a son-in-law. The Mayers immediately moved into the Shenbergs' already cramped five-room apartment. Fourteen months later, there was a new addition to the household, Edith ("Edie") Mayer, Maggie and Louis's first child.

A few months after her birth, Mayer was offered an opportunity to buy into a scrap metal business in New York and moved his family to the Greenpoint section of Brooklyn, then known as the Polish capital of America. There, in April 1907, Margaret gave birth to their second child, Irene. Mayer had been hoping for a son, but he accepted a daughter gratefully: her birth was, in fact, to be the Mayers' only happy memory of their stay in Brooklyn. Shortly after their arrival, a financial recession swept the country, wiping out many small businesses and bringing Mayer to the point of bankruptcy. His prospects vanished, and by the end of 1907 they had returned to Boston and were again living with the Shenbergs.

This setback left Mayer disillusioned about his chances of advancing himself through the salvage or scrap metal trades. He was discouraged, but not defeated. John Wilson had told him there might come a time when he felt he had reached the end of his rope; if that happened, Wilson had advised, he "should tie a knot at the end of the rope and hang on."

Mayer did more than just hang on; he also started exploring other routes to success. He circulated around Boston, keeping his eye open for any promising opportunity, and one day, when he had an hour to kill, he dropped in at a nickelodeon called the Hub on Dover Street. After the show, he struck up a conversation with the theatre owner, an ex-vaudevillian named Joe Mack. How was business? Mayer asked. Booming, Mack replied. He had opened the Hub only a year ago, but he had done so well that he was now the Massachusetts agent for the Miles Brothers' Exchange, a distributor for many of the country's leading film producers.

Across the United States, Mack went on to say, there were now more than three thousand nickelodeons, almost twice as many as the year before. The little silent dramas and "actualities" shown in these theatres were one of the few forms of entertainment the non-English-speaking immigrant population could understand, and just about the only kind of amusement that the working class could afford. The nickelodeons had not been adversely affected by the recent recession; instead, they had benefited from it. Of all the various branches of the entertainment business, film was the one that showed the greatest potential for growth and expansion.

Impressed by these facts, Mayer started hanging around the Hub, and occasionally helped out by selling or taking tickets. He asked lots of questions and carefully studied the short films that made up the Hub's programs, soon becoming adept at picking out those that would please Mack's clientele. He read the trade papers, and one day spotted an advertisement for a theatre that was for rent in Haverhill, Massachusetts, some thirty miles north of Boston. Mack said it didn't sound too promising, but still it might be worth a look. So the next day he and Mayer got on a train and went up to investigate.

The theatre was named the Gem, but the locals called it the Germ. Built in 1900, in a disreputable part of the city known as the Bowery, it had once served as a home for traveling burlesque shows. Never very glamorous, the six-hundred-seat house had declined into a state of filthy and foul-smelling disrepair: the walls were stained with tobacco juice; many of the rickety auditorium seats had lost their backs or armrests; the floor was covered with an inch of gummy sawdust.

Mack shook his head, but Mayer wasn't so easily put off. He thought the Gem had possibilities, the most important of which was its location. Haverhill, a bustling city of forty-five thousand, was the center of the American shoe industry. And two neighboring communities, Lowell and Lawrence, were equally commercial—the whole area was dotted with mills and factories and other manufacturing concerns, both large and small. There was, then, a large population of workers, many earning no more than subsistence wages, who needed the kind of cheap and simple entertainment that only the nickelodeon could provide.

After inspecting the premises, Mayer and Mack visited the owner of the Gem, a Haverhill real estate agent named Charlie Chase. A flinty and hard-bargaining New Englander, Chase asked six hundred and fifty dollars for a year's lease on the Gem, figuring he'd probably wind up with five hundred—if he got lucky. But Mayer was too excited to haggle. He gave Chase a fifty-dollar cash down payment and promised to produce the remaining six hundred within three days.

Returning to Boston, he broke the news to Margaret, who encouraged him to go ahead; she shared his ambition and was ready to make any sacrifice to help him along. That left the problem of raising six hundred dollars in three days. Mack had promised to chip in a hundred or so, provided Mayer rented films from the Miles Brothers' Exchange. Other friends made small contributions and the balance was supplied by members of Mayer's family.

Once the lease was signed, Mayer started cleaning and renovating the theatre: the walls and floor were scrubbed and painted; seats were repaired; a projector and movie screen were rented and set in place. Rechristened the Orpheum, the theatre opened on Thanksgiving Day, 1907, with a bill of Miles Brothers' films. Besides Mayer, there was a staff of three. Margaret, an experienced bookkeeper before her marriage, sold tickets and looked after the accounts. A lady pianist provided background music and accompaniment for the illustrated song slides that were a part of every program. "Bodger" Flynn, a former bouncer and policeman, patrolled the aisles, cautioning customers that spitting, urinating and other indecorous behavior was strictly forbidden.

The opening of the Orpheum got a one-paragraph mention in the Haverhill *Evening Gazette,* but otherwise the event was something less than auspicious. The Orpheum was still the Germ to most Haverhill citizens, and few of them were willing to risk public disgrace by passing through its doors. Business was bad the first week, and showed little improvement after a month. Several times, after checking receipts, Mrs. Mayer warned her husband that there might not be enough money to cover Bodger and the lady piano player's salaries.

The Orpheum's unsavory past was only one of the problems facing Mayer as he tried to build up a respectable clientele. At this time, there was widespread public distrust of the nickelodeons. Many were unsanitary firetraps, and the films they presented, according to the standardbearers of American morality, were often suggestive and sometimes pornographic. One of the most salacious of these dramas, claimed the public do-gooders, featured a popular stage comedian, John Rice, kissing a matronly soubrette named May Irwin. Imagine, one outraged commentator asked, what would happen when this scene was shown to men and women sitting in a pitch-black theatre: a knee presses a knee, a hand reaches for a hand, and another innocent girl is on her way down the primrose path.

Mayer decided to meet the problem head on. He introduced himself to the city leaders and, through them, got the chance to speak at businessmen's luncheons and the meetings of various clubs and fraternal organizations. He urged his audience to support the film medium, which had the potential of becoming a purveyor of high moral standards as well as the twentieth century's newest and most appealing form of entertainment. He did not deny that some nickelodeons catered to the prurient tastes of their patrons, but his theatre was different. Everything about the Orpheum—exterior, interior and the images on the screen—was clean.

Proving that he meant what he said, Mayer booked a film version of the Oberammergau *Passion Play* for Christmas week, 1907. The film had been produced by a French company, Pathé, and was three reels (over half an hour) in length, which made it an epic since most films of this period ran no more than twelve minutes. The Pathé *Passion Play* was four years old, but it was new to Haverhill, and the townspeople flocked to see it. One of the local papers praised Mayer for bringing "one of the monuments of European culture to our community."

The people who came to the Orpheum to see the *Passion Play* returned the following weeks to see such risqué-titled, but harmless, fare as *Bluebeard, the Man with Many Wives* and *My Husband Comes.* By March of 1908, the Orpheum was doing so well that Mayer could afford to hire Harry Houdini for a night of magic, and by the end of the year, he had made a gross profit of $25,000. Charlie Chase was very impressed. When it came time to renew the lease and Mayer asked the theatre owner to share the costs of renovating the theatre along grander lines, Chase told him to go ahead.

The theatre was closed for alterations for two months. When it reopened in the fall of 1908, the Haverhill *Sunday Record* welcomed it with a front-page tribute:

> At last!
>
> [Tomorrow], the doors of the New Orpheum Theatre . . . will be thrown open to the public and the season of 1908–1909 will have started.
>
> Since the close of the theatre early in the summer of the present year, much has been done getting out plans and the details for the theatre which has been completely changed, and yesterday when the final fixture was set in its place, a grand piece of work had been accomplished of which the city as well as manager Mayer may justly feel proud. . . . Finished in the finest product of the great woods of the far West, adorned with the best fixtures that are obtainable, and cosy and homelike in every detail, the New Orpheum has no peer.
>
> From the front, the first thing that attracts the eye is the scroll work which is of the Gothic style of architecture. . . . The side balcony has been done away with and in its place, retiring rooms have been added with all the latest and best comforts found at any of the large metropolitan theatres. . . . The walls have been adorned with new tapestry while the ceiling has been tinted in beautiful colors. . . .

The *Record* went on to mention that Mayer had planned a surprise for the premiere. So the opening-night guests were expecting something special as they took their seats, and after enduring the usual dedicatory speeches, they got their reward. The curtain rose to reveal an all-woman orchestra, which played Ponchielli's "Dance of the Hours" and "The Meditation" from *Thaïs;* then their soloist,

Miss Maude Neilson, sang "some of the latest sentimental ballads." Finally the film program began—a series of Miles Brothers' comedies plus a dramatization of one of the greatest historical controversies of the time, Pathé's *The Dreyfus Affair.*

The Haverhill *Record* ended its report on the opening of the New Orpheum by saying, "Louis B. Mayer has the good wishes of no small amount of friends and acquaintances in this city." There was more than journalese behind these congratulations—Mayer had found a place for himself in a city that prided itself on its ongoing growth and sophistication. New England society was then notorious for its insularity, but many of Haverhill's leading citizens welcomed Mayer into their homes. One of the first was lawyer Charles Poore, president of the Haverhill Water Board and a leading member of the Masonic fraternity. Through Poore, Mayer met the even more aristocratic George Elliott, a sixty-year-old, independently wealthy bachelor, noted for his philanthropy and regular attendance at the Pentucket Country Club (which ran its flag at half-mast at his death in 1916).

Elliott's home was one of the showplaces of Haverhill. "The day my mother first walked through the door of that house, she thought she'd arrived," recalls Irene Mayer Selznick. "This was the top—she never expected to see anything better."

Mayer halfheartedly agreed: yes, they had arrived, but there was still a long way to go. The New Orpheum was just a beginning. He was content to rest on his laurels for a while, but soon he began to dream of a new and better theatre which would follow the latest trend of alternating (or combining) film shows with vaudeville, at an elevated ticket price of ten to twenty-five cents. At the end of 1909, he leased a theatre in nearby Lawrence—the Broadway—and began to refurbish it according to the blueprint in his mind.

Before the Broadway was ready to open, Mayer decided that Haverhill's Academy of Music, the local showcase for concerts and legitimate plays, was too old-fashioned for the city's burgeoning cultural awareness. Something more elegant was needed, but since most of his capital had been invested in the Lawrence enterprise, he couldn't handle it alone. So he talked to Poore and Elliott, who formed a syndicate to build a theatre which Mayer would manage. At a cost of $30,000, the partners purchased one of Haverhill's derelict landmarks—the dilapidated Eagle Hotel—with the intention of razing it and building on the site "a great amusement palace, the equal of any seen in Boston or New York."

Things looked good at the beginning of 1910, but suddenly everything went wrong. The Lawrence theatre, located in one of the worst sections of the city, turned out to be a white elephant, and Mayer lost most of his investment before he was rid of it. Even more serious was the status of the Eagle Hotel property. Shortly after Poore's and Elliott's syndicate had bought it, a rival group of businessmen announced they were planning to build a theatre on Merrimack Street, the main thoroughfare of the Haverhill business district. This was too much of a defeat for Mayer's ego to accept: he convinced his syndicate to buy out the rival concern. The Eagle Hotel site was later sold (according to the Haverhill *Gazette*) for a business block at $40,000, and construction started on Merrimack Street for "a $150,000 theatre."

The new theatre was called the Colonial. So many people wanted to attend its opening on December 12, 1911, that two premieres were scheduled—one for the afternoon and another for the evening. At both performances, all 2,500 seats were filled, with standees clogging the back and side aisles. This was, the Haverhill *Evening Gazette* proclaimed, "a landmark in the city's progress in the entertainment field":

> The Colonial is one of the largest theatres in New England . . . each seat is as conveniently located as the others. . . . The portico is not a deep one, but it is prettily conceived in faced and colored brick. . . . It is lighted by a cluster of frosted tungstens. . . . Among the notable features are swinging glass doors . . . walls finished in old rose with frescoes of green . . . pilastered ceilings . . . carpeted floors . . . marble fireplaces . . . a painting of the lioness in her den . . . a superb portrait of art from the brush of Mrs. Essex S. Abbot, an illuminated Cleo, supporting a wreath of tiny electric bulbs . . . a grand staircase to the balcony . . . windows of grand glass. . . .

Festivities got under way with the "theatre's resident orchestra" playing "The Colonial March," written especially for the occasion by Will E. Brown, Haverhill's leading composer. Mayor Edwin H. Moulton spoke of the city's industrial and commercial development during the past few years, pausing to pay tribute to "the zeal of Louis B. Mayer, a man who is giving Haverhill a theatre that is a pride to everyone who beholds it." Then ten-year-old Pauline Gertrude Cummings christened the theatre, "strewing the stage and the front of the auditorium with roses from a cornucopia handed her by Mr. Mayer."

"The huge oration that greeted Mayer seemed to overwhelm him," noted the *Gazette*. "At first, he could only bow and smile, but once the applause had subsided he found the words to express his gratitude. The Colonial, he stated, represented the zenith of his ambitions. . . ."

Then, without commenting on what was an obvious contradiction, the *Gazette* went on to note that Mayer had hired a general manager for the Colonial so that he could "look after the other enterprises in which he is interested."

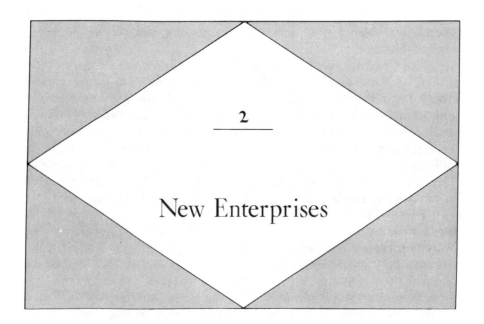

2

New Enterprises

"Louie was a worker," George Elliott told an interviewer. "He never slept, you know, at least not much. And he rarely ate without talking business at the same time. He was always scheming up something."

In 1912 most of Mayer's schemes centered on monopolizing the entertainment trade of Haverhill. Early that year he had taken a lease on the Bijou Nickelodeon in the business district of the city, and by March, he was also managing the Academy of Music. It was a clean sweep—he had taken control of all Haverhill's theatres.

Under his management, each of these houses had its own personality. As in the past, the Academy of Music continued to offer concerts and other types of musical entertainment, but no longer were the presentations in the hands of the Canobie Lake Opera Company, a choral society that usually performed at fairs and amusement parks. In March 1912, for a single performance, Mayer imported the Boston Opera Company, featuring Alice Neilsen in *Madama Butterfly*. He was warned that he would never recoup his investment, but twenty-four hours before the opening, fifty Haverhill music-lovers were already lined up outside the Academy. The performance was a sell-out, and in the next months, the Boston Opera and the Boston Symphony Orchestra played several one-night engagements at the Academy of Music.

The Colonial specialized in what were known as "combination shows," a mixture of vaudeville and short films. (The films usually closed the bill—they were called chasers because they cleared the auditorium for the next show.) The acts that appeared at the Colonial were of various types, but magic shows and escape artists were particularly popular. One of the biggest draws was Hardeen, the Handcuff King, who could, wrote a reviewer for the Haverhill *Gazette,* "get out of anything"—a chained packing case, "the crazy crib used in famous lunatic asylums," even "a convict punishment suit."

The two remaining houses were both film theatres, but the Bijou was a nickelodeon, while the New Orpheum had long outgrown that humble category both in price range and in the elegance of its architecture. As further diversification, in the spring of 1912 Mayer expanded the Orpheum's policy to live theatre presentations. He formed his own stock company with such resident "artists" as Frank Elliott ("formerly connected with the Keith Stock Company of Woonsocket, Rhode Island"), Miss Marione Francis ("an ingenue with wide experience with prominent road productions") and the alluringly named Valerie Valaire, a femme fatale "who has recently played *Sapho* and *ZaZa* to great applause in some of the greater metropolitan centers").

The Mayer Stock Company's first production was *East Lynne,* one of the standbys of the provincial repertory, and then each week for three months the troupe presented a different melodrama or comedy, some old, some recently performed on Broadway. The season ended with *A Festival of Song,* a minstrel show featuring Jack Murray and Clara Lane with their famous sextet and, as interlocutor, Louis B. Mayer. As the world would soon learn, there was the makings of a great ham actor locked up inside Mayer, but this was the only occasion when he took part in a theatrical production.

By the end of 1912, he had expanded his managerial enterprises to neighboring towns, and eventually would hold leases on theatres in Lynn, Brockton, Manchester and Lowell. He was constantly traveling, not only around the local vicinity but often to Boston and New York, in search of films, vaudeville acts or plays for the Orpheum Stock Company. Margaret Mayer sometimes longed for the kind of husband who left for work at eight in the morning, came home at six, read the newspapers, ate dinner and went to bed, but that was not and would never be Mayer's style. Though a conscientious father and loving husband, he did not fit the pattern of the typical American family man.

Many years later, while vacationing with friends, he sat down before dinner and made a great show of reading the evening newspaper. The sense of drama he brought to this simple activity was the cue for someone to ask, "Louie, what *are* you doing?" Peering over his glasses, he answered smugly, "I'm doing what six million American men do every night: I'm relaxing with the paper."

After dinner, he settled into an easy chair and looked around vacantly. "Well," he asked, "what do I do now?" The truth was that Mayer really didn't know what the average family man did once dinner was over and the papers had been read. He had to be taught the art of relaxation, and the teaching wasn't undertaken until he was well into middle age. In the earlier part of his life, his only diversions from business were pinochle and an occasional outing with his wife and daughters.

On arriving in Haverhill, the Mayer family had taken rooms in a boardinghouse in one of the poorer sections of the city. Then, after the opening of the renovated Orpheum, they moved to a small house in Bradford, a quiet residential town on the Merrimack River. By the summer of 1912, they had settled in a substantial house on Hamilton Avenue in one of Haverhill's best neighborhoods, not far from where Charles Poore and George Elliott lived.

The Mayers were now able to afford a few luxuries, including a cook, a maid and their first automobile, an open-topped traveling car. Whenever Mayer traveled, he went first class. In New York City, he always stayed at the Knickerbocker, a hotel located in the heart of the theatre district which catered to the tastes and idiosyncrasies of show people. Mary Pickford and her first husband, Owen Moore, had one of their many marital squabbles in its lobby, and Broadway celebrities such as George M. Cohan, Nat C. Goodwin and the Frohman brothers ate or drank their lunches in the Knickerbocker Grill. Mayer wasn't a drinker—he could get tipsy on a glass of red wine— but by being gregarious, he struck up casual friendships with several of the Knickerbocker Grill habitués. One of his acquaintances was Ben Stern, formerly the general manager for Henry B. Harris, a prominent producer who had gone down with the *Titanic.*

Stern was then thinking of striking out on his own, but he needed a partner with cash; Mayer was interested in expanding his "live theatre" activities, but needed the guidance of someone with experience in that area. The outcome of their meeting was that in November 1912 they formed a partnership, rented office space in the Fitzgerald Building in the Broadway district and announced plans to produce "three big attractions with major stars."

At about the same time, Mayer and another neophyte producer,

Adolph Mayer—their kinship was of name only—teamed up to finance the tour of a repertory company headed by Nance O'Neil, a highly regarded "tragedienne" who alternated Shakespeare and Ibsen with such up-to-date modern "classics" as *Camille* and Benavente's *The Passion Flower.* Miss O'Neil's tour for the Messrs. Mayer opened in Portland, Maine, went up to Canada, then down through most of New England, winding up at the Colonial in Haverhill on the first anniversary of the theatre's opening.

A month later, January 1913, the Mayer and Stern company became active, although along different lines than had been originally announced. Instead of three major attractions, Stern and Mayer offered touring editions of several recent Broadway hits, many featuring a major theatrical star. As a starting point for these tours, they leased the Walnut Street Theatre in Philadelphia, originally built in 1809, one of the oldest and most historic of American theatres. The Walnut was then in a state of disrepair, and the lessees had to spend over six thousand dollars in refurbishing it. After a week's engagement in Philadelphia, the Mayer/Stern productions toured up and down the eastern seaboard, always stopping for a few days at either the Colonial or the Orpheum in Haverhill.

The first season was a success, so much so that the owner of the Walnut increased the rent for the next year. What he was asking was more than traffic would allow, and Mayer and Stern went to court to recover the six thousand dollars they had spent on modernizing the theatre. For reasons that aren't entirely clear, this marked the end of their partnership and the end of Mayer's interests in legitimate theatre production.

But it was not the end of live theatre for Haverhill. The Orpheum Stock Company went on, and the Colonial became a standard two- or three-night stopover for most road companies. The list of stars who appeared at Mayer's theatres between 1913 and 1916 is virtually a who's who of Broadway and the vaudeville circuit at that time: Laurette Taylor in *Peg O' My Heart,* Maude Adams *(Peter Pan),* George Arliss *(Disraeli),* George M. Cohan, Ina Claire, John Drew, Raymond Hitchcock, Billie Burke, Gus Edwards, Mrs. Fiske, Dustin Farnum, Frances Starr, Evelyn Nesbit Thaw, Harry Lauder and, for a while, the very young Eddie Dowling who acted as master of ceremonies for the Colonial's vaudeville presentations. Mayer also booked some of the great concert artists of the day—Luisa Tetrazzini, Fritz Schumann and John Philip Sousa all appeared at one of the Haverhill theatres.

Interspersed with the live programs at the Colonial and the Orpheum were such films as *Cabiria, The Count of Monte Cristo* with

James O'Neill (Eugene's father) and *Queen Elizabeth* and *Camille*, both starring Sarah Bernhardt. These pictures represented a revolutionary form of screen entertainment. First, they were "features," meaning they were four or five reels (or about sixty minutes) in length, more than double the running time of the average film. Second and more important, they presented a direct challenge to the cultural preeminence of the stage. By appearing in screen versions of their greatest triumphs, Bernhardt and O'Neil were raising the tone of the photodrama—they were helping to make movies a respectable form of entertainment for the middle and upper classes.

The concept of filming great stage actors in their best-known roles originated in France around 1909, and was brought to this country by Adolph Zukor, a Hungarian immigrant who, like Mayer, started out in show business as a nickelodeon entrepreneur. In 1912 he imported the French-made *Queen Elizabeth* and then went off to form his own company, Famous Players, which produced a series of feature films starring Broadway stars. (His first production was the O'Neill *Monte Cristo*.) Like their European models, the Zukor films were static, clumsily photographed and poorly acted. Nonetheless, they garnered critical praise and attracted a large audience, one composed of both regular moviegoers and the kind of patron who normally turned out only for cultural events.

Many exhibitors thought the success of the Famous Players pictures was a fluke, but Mayer disagreed. Poor as they were, these films had shown that the motion picture had the potential of reaching all segments of the public eager for entertainment. In diversifying the policies of his theatres, Mayer had been trying to provide something for everybody, but now he realized that this had been doing things the hard way; through the movies, the same objective could be achieved with less effort—and more profit.

By 1913 Mayer was convinced that his future lay in the motion-picture business. But what part of the business? was the question that puzzled him. At this time the three branches of the industry—production, exhibition and distribution—were separate entities, and while there had been some attempts to link them together, they had failed because of poor management. The result was a constant jockeying for top position, with the exhibitor nearly always coming out low man on the totem pole: the theatre owner had no say about what kinds of films were made and almost no bargaining power when it came to determining the charges for film rentals. He was being bled white by the producers and exhibitors, who kept raising the prices and asking for ever greater chunks of the box-office profits.

The distribution and exhibition of films was then organized on a franchise system known as the states-rights plan, which operated in the following way: producers leased their films to distributors, who thereby gained the rights to rent those films to exhibitors within a specified geographical area. Since there were many distributors in any one of these districts, there was also a lot of nasty, cutthroat competition to obtain the franchises for the best pictures. This was definitely a seller's market, and while the producer had the controlling hand, the distributor came next, in that he could pass along his expenses to the exhibitor in the form of increased rental fees.

Mulling this over, Mayer decided to take one step up the ladder and move into the field of distribution. On his trips to New York, he started attending the sales conferences held by producers for exchange men (distributors) and theatre owners, and at one of these meetings, struck up a conversation with Hiram Abrams, who then held the East Coast franchise of Zukor's Famous Players films. He confessed that he wanted to go into distribution, but needed someone to guide him as he learned the business. Abrams suggested Fanny Mittenthal, who had worked for several New England film exchanges and knew just about all there was to know about that phase of the industry.

Later Mayer arranged to meet Abrams and Fanny, a profession-proud and smart-talking lady, at a Sunday afternoon baseball game. While his companions ate frankfurters and watched the game, Mayer rambled on about his ambitions, finally reaching a point where he felt secure about offering a job to the experienced and worldly Miss Mittenthal. Her response was short and not so sweet. What he was offering, she pointed out, was less than half her current salary.

Mayer was taken aback, but not for long. A week later, he made another appointment with Fanny and offered her five dollars more than she was earning—forty dollars a week. She accepted. They rented a one-room office on Tremont Street in Boston, bought some chairs and a desk and painted a sign on the door: THE LOUIS B. MAYER FILM COMPANY. Fanny sent out to all exhibitors in the New England area a circular letter promising that the Mayer Company would soon be offering the best in new, quality motion pictures. The response was surprisingly good. But as yet there were no films—quality or otherwise—to meet the demand.

Mayer went to New York and bought the franchise for a series of comedies starring Stan Lupino, a popular British music-hall comedian (and father of Ida Lupino). These three-reel comedies were not the type of quality film making that Mayer had promised his patrons, but they rented well anyway. Still something more was needed, and one day, just as Fanny was shutting up shop, a man named Sam Goldfish walked into the office.

A former glove manufacturer, Goldfish (soon to become Goldwyn) had gone into motion-picture production with his brother-in-law, ex-vaudevillian Jesse Lasky, and a mutual, ne'er-do-well friend, a minor actor and playwright named Cecil Blount De Mille. The Jesse Lasky Feature Film Company, they called themselves, Lasky being the only one of the trio who had any reputation in the entertainment world. Their company was a copy of Adolph Zukor's Famous Players in Famous Plays: they were going to produce feature-length film versions of recent stage successes starring Broadway actors.

Lasky's famous players weren't quite so famous as Zukor's, and Goldfish, Lasky and De Mille didn't know much about film making —but then, a year or so earlier, Zukor hadn't either. Fanny was impressed enough by Goldfish/Goldwyn's spiel to ask him to return the next day and talk to Mayer. Mayer was equally impressed, and by the end of his conversation with Goldwyn, he bought a franchise for the first two Lasky pictures at four thousand dollars—two thousand down and the rest to be paid on delivery of the films.

Years later, Goldwyn openly accused Mayer of never paying the second installment, and since Mayer never denied the allegation, it may well be true. It was an ungentlemanly but fairly common practice for distributors to shortchange producers in this way. It is also possible that Mayer thought he had overpaid the Lasky company. Its first release, *The Squaw Man* (directed by De Mille and starring Dustin Farnum), was no great shakes and the second, *Brewster's Millions* (with Edward Abeles), didn't look very promising either. But for some reason—certainly it wasn't quality—the second film was a runaway hit and played an important part in establishing Mayer as a leading distributor. From then on, one imagines, he was prompt and exact in his payments; at any rate, he was to distribute several Lasky films over the next two years.

Just at this time, when his business interests were prospering so nicely, there came a setback in Mayer's personal life. In the early fall of 1913, he received word that his mother was seriously ill. He rushed to Saint John where he learned that Sarah had undergone a routine operation, after which serious complications had set in. Two weeks later, she was dead.

Her death was a great blow to Mayer. He had adored his mother and was to cherish her memory in many ways. Nothing, nobody was ever able to shake his belief in the sanctity of motherhood; anyone taking the name of Mother in vain was sure to feel the full force of his wrath. As production chief at M-G-M, Mayer kept careful check over the studio's output to see that motherliness was honored as being next to godliness, and that the sanctity of the family, another of Sarah's ideals, was similarly respected.

Sarah was buried in a Jewish cemetery not far from her home in Saint John. Her death brought a close to one chapter in the Mayer family's life—soon they were all to follow brother Louie by wandering far from New Brunswick. Mayer, who had recently become an American citizen, claimed Haverhill as home, and Haverhill had adopted him as a native son, but this bond, like the earlier one with Saint John, was no more than temporary, and around this time Mayer began to show signs of wanting to move on.

Early in 1914, he handed over the management of the Colonial to an outsider, an arrangement that aroused "considerable curiosity" among Haverhill businessmen. "Yes, I have decided to give up the management of the Colonial," Mayer told the *Gazette*. "I want to devote more of my time to my other enterprises. Of course, this does not mean that I will relinquish all interests in my theatres." Nor was he planning to leave Haverhill. "I have no intention of giving up my home," he continued, "although a greater part of my time will necessarily have to be spent away from the city."

What Mayer was really saying was that in the future he intended to concentrate on his distribution interests rather than his theatre enterprises. He was looking for possible ways to expand the activities of the Louis B. Mayer Film Company, and his opportunity came in the spring of 1914 when a snappily dressed stranger dropped by his office for a chat. His name was Alexander ("Al") Lichtman, and up to a few months before, he had been Adolph Zukor's right-hand man. Now he was working on a plan which he thought might interest Mayer.

In his years in the business, Lichtman had noticed that many small producers often didn't get as much as they should for films sold outright to distributors on the states-rights plan. At the same time, he knew that distributors and exhibitors were hungry for more and better films. His proposal was that some of the country's leading theatre owners and exchange men should form an organization that would put up part of the financing for the best of these minor producers; in return, they would receive a steady flow of good pictures as well as a share of the producers' profits.

Lichtman had already talked to several leading figures of the film business—Richard Rowland and James C. Clark of Pittsburgh; the Mastbaum brothers of Philadelphia; William Sievers, a leading St.

Louis theatre owner; George Grumbacher of Oregon; several New York exhibitors and distributors. They were all ready to participate. Now Lichtman was inviting Mayer to represent the New England branch of the company. He accepted immediately.

Lichtman called his organization Alco—an abbreviation of "Al's Company." Walter Hoff Seeley, a former newspaperman who had flittered in and out of several key positions in the industry, was appointed president. From the founding members, Lichtman collected $150,000, parceling this out in $15,000 advances to several producers who were ready to start work on the first Alco releases. Profits were to be shared in the following manner: 50 percent (minus the advance) for the producer, 30 percent to be divided among the Alco members, 20 percent for the company till as a source for future capitalization.

Alco's first releases included Ethel Barrymore's first film, *The Nightingale;* Charles Chaplin and Marie Dressler in *Tillie's Puncture Romance; Michael Strogoff* with Jacob Adler, one of the great stars of the Yiddish theatre; Olga Petrova in *The Vampire;* and *Salomy Jane,* a screen adaptation of a once popular melodrama starring the soon-to-be-forgotten actress Beatriz Michelena. Overall the pictures were mediocre in quality, but they returned a substantial profit, and for a while it looked as though Alco might become an important force in the industry.

But something went wrong. The details are vague, but apparently either Lichtman or Seeley—the latter seems the more likely culprit—got mixed up with a shady financier who took control of the company's resources, and through speculation, depleted them so thoroughly that Alco was soon forced into receivership.

It was an unpleasant experience, but many Alco members still believed Lichtman's plan was basically sound. In early 1915, a group of them got together in Parlor B of the Claridge Hotel in New York and formed a new organization named Metro. Richard Rowland was elected president. George Grumbacher and James Clark were made vice-presidents. The secretary was Mayer.

Though Metro was organized along the same lines as Alco, there was one important difference: while the former group had contracted with various producers for its supply of films, Metro planned to produce most of the twenty-four pictures it released each year. The company started to build up a roster of contract players which included Mabel Taliaferro, Ethel and Lionel Barrymore, Olga Petrova, Mary Miles Minter and the movies' first matinée idol, Francis X. Bushman.

Mayer was not impressed by the first Metro pictures, which

were at best pedestrian in quality. Richard Rowland shrugged off his criticisms and pointed out that the films were making money—that was the important thing, wasn't it? Mayer couldn't argue with that, but he felt there were long-range factors to be considered: how could the public be expected to build up any appetite for films when the bill of fare was nothing but slops? People didn't go to the movies just to see stars; they wanted good stories, too.

As time passed and Mayer's carping continued, Rowland began to wonder whether the company might not be able to find a more amenable secretary. Mayer, on his part, had started to think he had made a mistake in coming into the Metro organization. He was not yet prepared to sever the relationship—his position as secretary of a nationally known production company was too prestigious to be cast aside lightly—but neither was he about to make a total commitment to Metro. He continued to operate as an independent distributor, and it was through his work in this area that he was finally to earn the kind of money he needed to fulfill his ambitions.

His chance came when D. W. Griffith's *The Birth of a Nation* was placed on the states-rights market after playing advanced-price "special engagements" in Los Angeles, New York, Boston and Chicago. Mayer immediately got in touch with Harry Aitken of Mutual, the company that had financed Griffith, and inquired how much was being asked for the New England franchise. The price quoted by Aitken was staggering for that period—$50,000 plus 10 percent of the net profits—but Mayer accepted the deal without hesitation.

He had put aside a few thousand dollars for investment, and Fanny Mittenthal, who knew a good thing when she saw it, offered a thousand from her savings. The bulk of the money came from some of Mayer's friends who became partners in a new corporation, Master Photoplays, of which Mayer was president and major shareholder —he owned 25 percent of it. The company had been established to separate *Birth of a Nation* from Mayer's other distribution interests, and to underline this autonomy, Master Photoplays maintained offices separate from those of the Louis B. Mayer Film Company.

The Birth of a Nation opened its general-release New England run at the Colonial Theatre in Haverhill on September 3, 1915. Two years later Mayer boasted that his company had made over $1 million from the film, but probably he was exaggerating—the records of the Mutual Company suggest that Master Photoplays made no more than $665,000. Minus the advance and the producer's percentage, this means Master Photoplays cleared about $600,000, of which Mayer's share would have been $150,000, a very tidy sum for a time when income tax was low.

All Mayer's partners did well, too, except Fanny Mittenthal, who, it turned out, wasn't a partner at all. A month or so after she had given him a check for a thousand dollars, Mayer returned it, saying the stockholders of Master Photoplays had voted against the contributions of petty investors. Fanny thought she had received a raw deal. She never really forgave Mayer, and her reminiscences of her former boss were invariably tinged with contempt. She taught him everything he knew, she implied; she was responsible for the Lasky contract; she had urged him to go after *Birth of a Nation*. He hadn't absorbed much, but she had also given him lessons on gentlemanly conduct: she had built up his vocabulary and smoothed the rough edges of his social deportment.

If Fanny's testimony is suspect, it is not only because her bitterness is so transparent. If he were nothing more than the pushy little greenhorn she portrays, Mayer wouldn't have been accepted by Poor, Elliott and the other prominent families of Haverhill. Of course, then (and later) he had many traits that could be easily ridiculed: he was emotional and easily excitable, and when provoked, was capable of flying into blistering rages. His apparel—chesterfield coats, derby hats, diamond stickpins, a pince-nez—was fastidious almost to a fault: he looked like a fashion plate from a gentlemen's magazine. At times his lack of formal education showed, as he was well aware. He always asked Fanny for the definition of a word he hadn't heard before, and he soon was using that word in his own conversations.

Fanny was the first of a number of people who felt they were the power behind Mayer's throne and decided because of imaginary or real insults, to reveal their true position of importance when talking to interviewers. This was to become a common pattern as Mayer became more successful. "Whenever M-G-M turned out a good film, everyone rushed forward to claim credit," remembers a long-term studio employee. "But every bomb and every mistake was nobody's fault but Mayer's. He rarely got the credit and always took the blame."

There can be no question that Fanny played a small though important role in Mayer's early career. But by 1915–16, he was turning toward other, more experienced and worldly figures for guidance. At the top of the list was J. Robert Rubin, whom Irene Mayer Selznick remembers as one of her father's role-models, as well as a figure of the romantic fascination for herself and her sister, Edith.

Born to a well-to-do family in Syracuse, the tall, handsome, Waspish-looking Rubin had worked for a leading Wall Street law firm before accepting an appointment as assistant district attorney of

New York County. Later he became deputy police commissioner, and was thinking of making a career in politics when, in the line of duty, he was asked to look into the Alco receivership case. Rubin was fascinated by what he learned, and once the Alco members regrouped to form Metro, he stayed on as their counsel.

Rubin was something of an anomaly in these surroundings. He was well educated, debonair, a connoisseur of music and theatre—in a word, he had class. Mayer respected Rubin's friendship, retained him as his personal attorney and, in many small ways, tried to emulate his savoir faire. A true friendship grew between the men, and Rubin was to become, in the words of one M-G-M executive, "next to his wife, Mayer's greatest asset."

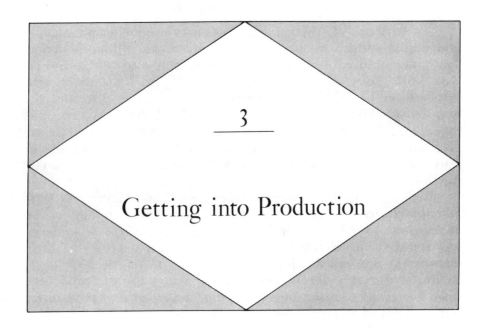

3

Getting into Production

With the profits of *Birth of a Nation* behind him, Mayer was ready to push onward. In 1916 he started selling his interests in his Haverhill theatres and consolidated his various distributing enterprises into one corporation, the American Feature Film Company. Then he moved his family to Brookline, a fashionable suburb of Boston. "I am leaving Haverhill with regret," he told the *Gazette*. "This is my home; wherever I go, wherever I am interviewed I will always point out Haverhill as my home."

There was genuine sentiment behind this speech, and after a fashion Mayer lived up to it: he rarely failed to mention Haverhill in interviews that touched on his early life. But by 1916 the time had come for him to break his ties with Haverhill and the world of small-time distribution and exhibition; it was time for him to take the next inevitable step and move into production. This was the route taken by most of the bright young men who wanted to get ahead in the film business. Lots of money could be made in exhibition and distribution, but of the three branches of the industry, production was far and away the most prestigious and potentially the most powerful. These were qualities that had strong appeal for Mayer, but there was another, perhaps more fundamental reason why he was drawn in this direction: he was a born showman.

As early as 1913, Mayer had spoken of producing pictures in Haverhill, but this was no more than a pipe dream. Film production was not centralized in those days—movies were made in California, New York, Texas, New Orleans, Chicago, Philadelphia, practically any location that boasted a sufficient number of actors, directors and technicians. Haverhill didn't fit that category. Probably Mayer could have found the personnel he needed in Boston, but in 1913 he lacked capital and experience, and was wise enough to proceed cautiously, learning thoroughly one branch of the business before moving on to the next.

Before taking the plunge into picture making, Mayer gave serious thought to the kind of film his first production should be. He decided on a serial. Ever since 1912, when *What Happened to Mary?* was released episodically, a new "chapter" each week for three months, th.se so-called cliff-hangers had been one of the most popular forms of screen entertainment. They were a boon to producers since they could be made on a shoestring, and when successful, often returned ten to twenty times their cost.

Through his position at Metro, Mayer had come to know virile Francis X. Bushman, perhaps the most popular screen actor of the period, and his attractive leading lady (and offscreen mistress), Beverly Bayne. They had formed their own company, Quality Pictures (a real misnomer), which turned out twelve films a year for Metro release. Though neither Bushman nor Bayne was endowed with exceptional talent, they had their aspirations, and in 1915 had won wide acclaim for their screen appearances as a noticeably superannuated Romeo and Juliet.

Consequently, Bushman was horrified when Mayer invited him and Miss Bayne to star in the serial he was planning to produce. Serials were a profitable but not particularly reputable form of picture making, and few actors would consent to appear in them except as a final resort. True, the cliff-hangers had produced such screen favorites as Pearl White, Helen Holmes and Kathlyn Williams, but no established star was about to sacrifice his dignity by strapping himself to a railway track or by squirming with terror as a buzzsaw threatened to slice him in two.

"No," Bushman told Mayer, "absolutely no!" Mayer explained that his film wouldn't employ the cruder sort of last-minute-rescue high jinks that were a staple of all the earliest serials. "No!" Bushman repeated. Mayer went right on arguing and cajoling until Bushman finally said yes.

By this time Mayer could have financed the film out of his own pocket—the major expense was Bushman and Bayne's $15,000 salary

—but instead, he played safe and sought outside investors to form a new corporation, the Serial Producing Company. Colman Levin, a rug merchant, was president, but Mayer had total artistic control; he hired veteran serial writer Fred de Gresac to prepare the script and Christy Cabanne—one of D. W. Griffith's assistants—as director. Called *The Great Secret*, the film traveled along a very familiar plot line: it was little more than the standard story of an heiress and the dastardly relatives who try to do her out of her fortune.

On January 8, 1917, *The Great Secret* opened in Boston in a novel fashion. Mayer booked it in several theatres, each showing a different one of the first four episodes—"The Whirlpool of Destiny," "The Casket of Tainted Treasure," "The Hidden Hand," "From Sunshine to Shadow"—so that serial buffs could get well into the story by rushing from one theatre to the next. The gimmick helped the box office take in Boston, but once the serial went into national release, it failed to live up to expectations. Even as serials go, this one wasn't very good, and it barely managed to recoup its production costs. Francis X. Bushman never really forgave Mayer for persuading him to make it.

But Mayer wasn't discouraged—he hadn't made much on *The Great Secret*, but he hadn't lost anything either. And besides, he had thoroughly enjoyed his first brush with production. He was ready to push ahead in this direction, but to do so, he decided he would have to find a star or stars (preferably the latter) and sign them up, not for a one-picture deal like that with Bushman and Bayne, but under an exclusive contract for a series of films. The big obstacle was, of course, finding stars who were willing to hitch up with an unknown producer.

In the spring of 1917, Mayer got wind of a leading screen actress who just might be interested. This piece of news came to him through a Damon Runyonesque Broadway character, a hunchbacked dwarf named Toby who ran a newspaper and shoeshine stand around the corner from the Knickerbocker Hotel. The denizens of the entertainment world had adopted Toby as a mascot, and as they bought their papers or had their shoes shined, they chattered and occasionally passed along the latest bit of Broadway gossip. Pretty soon, Toby was a treasure chest of privileged information—he knew who was doing what with whom, both professionally and privately. One of his favorite clients was Louis Mayer, who always dropped by the stand whenever he was in Manhattan. Like everyone else, Mayer confided in Toby and in 1917, he mentioned that he was going into production as soon as he found the right star.

Well, it so happened that Toby knew a star. Her name was Anita

Stewart and he was her number-one fan. Every so often, he was invited to her home in Brooklyn, and during his last visit, Miss Stewart had dropped a few remarks suggesting that she wasn't very happy about the way her career was being handled by the Vitagraph Company. Mayer's ears perked up, so Toby proceeded to tell him the rest of the story.

Anita Stewart had been a student at Erasmus High School in the Flatbush section of Brooklyn when, in 1911, she had answered a casting call at the Vitagraph Studios, also located in Brooklyn. Starting out as a bit player, she had swiftly progressed to leading roles, and by 1915, often ranked just below Mary Pickford in popularity polls. But then something went wrong. Anita's sister, Lucille Lee, was married to Ralph Ince, one of Vitagraph's top directors, and Lucille, it appears, had decided that she and not Anita should be Vitagraph's crowning star.

Suddenly Anita discovered she wasn't getting the caliber of script, direction and photography to which she had become accustomed. And she depended heavily upon the kindness of her cameramen. Though admired for her "patrician quality," she possessed a very prominent nose that could look ungainly in profile or low-angle shots. "Please," she pleaded, *"please* be careful of my nose."

Mayer said he would like to talk to Miss Stewart, and within a few days Toby had arranged a meeting. He had given his friend a big buildup, and Anita received Mayer warmly, eagerly listening to what he had to propose. Yes, she admitted, she was unhappy at Vitagraph, but no, she didn't see how she could sign on with a new producer at this time. Her contract with Vitagraph didn't expire until January 1918, several months away.

Mayer consulted J. Robert Rubin, who felt there would be no trouble about breaking the contract, and Dennis O'Brien, Miss Stewart's distinguished attorney—he also represented Mary Pickford and Douglas Fairbanks—agreed. But Anita was still uncertain, so Mayer employed a strategem he was to use many times in the future: he became extravagantly attentive to the actress's mother, plying her with flowers, gifts and such shameless flattery that she soon became his staunchest supporter in the campaign to lure her daughter away from Vitagraph.

Anita, however, continued to waver until she got everything she wanted. Eventually, Mayer promised to match her current Vitagraph salary—$1,000 a week plus 10 percent of the net profits, with a guarantee of $127,000 a year. On signing the contract, she was to be awarded a bonus of $10,000. And to bring her up to the status of Pickford, Clara Kimball Young and the other prominent photoplay stars of the period, Mayer agreed that credit for all her films should go to "Anita Stewart Pictures, Inc." This sounded impressive, but all it really meant was that Anita, like Pickford and Young, was to be consulted about scripts, directors, photographers and supporting players, and that her choices would be honored—within reason. According to the screen credits, she was her own producer, but in reality she was an employee of Louis B. Mayer.

After these terms had been agreed upon, Stewart hesitantly asked for one final favor. Recently she had wed one of her Vitagraph leading men, Rudolph Cameron, and this marriage was still a closely guarded secret. In most of her films, she played heroines who were as pure as they were patrician, and Vitagraph had repeatedly warned her that her popularity might decline if the public learned she was not as virginal as the heroines she portrayed. Consequently, Anita had reluctantly agreed to keep Cameron under wraps, but, as she confessed to Mayer, this subterfuge was turning their marriage into a clandestine charade. She then went on to say that Adolph Zukor had approached her about joining Famous Players, and that he thought he could find a place for Cameron as well. Picking up the cue, Mayer answered that he saw no reason why she shouldn't acknowledge her husband, and that he was sure there was a place for Cameron on the board of directors of Anita Stewart Pictures, Inc.

Once this problem was resolved, Stewart was ready to risk breaking with her old company. In the spring of 1917, she informed Vitagraph that her doctor had ordered her to take a rest cure at a Connecticut sanitarium. A few weeks later, she wrote Albert E. Smith, president of Vitagraph, and informed him that she was severing relations with the company on the grounds of contractual violations. Smith wrote back, asking her to be more specific. Vitagraph, she replied, had failed to present proper financial statements, had foisted unsuitable directors and story material on her and had perpetrated "other abuses" that had brought her to her current state of nervous collapse.

Nothing else happened until Mayer announced he had signed Anita Stewart to a three-year contract. Then Vitagraph immediately obtained an injunction restraining Miss Stewart from working for Mayer or any other producer. The action could not have been unexpected. Star raiding—the practice of stealing stars from a rival producer—was fairly common at this time, and nearly always led to some kind of legal battle. These entanglements were costly and time-consuming, but also valuable in providing plenty of publicity for the usurping producer, who invariably looked smarter and sharper than his rival. This was particularly true in the case of Mayer. Most star raiders were established producers like Adolph Zukor of Famous Players, who was something of a specialist in this area. For someone as green as Mayer to take on Vitagraph—well, that took real chutzpah.

Of course not everyone in the industry admired Mayer's boldness. One of the holdouts was Richard Rowland of Metro. Not that he had any qualms about the secretary of his company stealing a star from a competitor, but, as he pointed out to Mayer, it seemed only proper that the star be brought into the Metro fold. Mayer didn't see it that way: Miss Stewart was under personal contract to him, though he might be willing, provided the terms were right, to release her pictures through Metro. The simmering animosity between the two men now reached the boiling point and Mayer abruptly, perhaps rashly, decided to pull out of the company.

The injunction against Stewart was upheld by a New York judge, and soon thereafter, Vitagraph initiated two suits. One, filed in New York, asked that Miss Stewart be ordered back to work; the other, filed in Boston, sought $250,000 in damages from Mayer. There were numerous delays, but finally in April 1918, the New York Supreme Court ruled that Stewart must honor her Vitagraph commitment. Since her contract had expired during the intervening months, the court ruled that it be extended to cover every day she had failed to report for work—meaning she would not be free to leave Vitagraph until September 1918.

This decision did not augur well for the Boston suit, so Mayer and Rubin conferred with the Vitagraph attorneys and tried to reach an out-of-court settlement. The opponents held all the trumps, but Mayer still managed to win the hand. His victory was pure luck, or better, a quirky combination of good and bad luck since the outcome was determined by an accident that befell Anita Stewart.

Following the court's orders, she had returned to Vitagraph and started filming *The "Mind-the-Paint" Girl,* a trifle by Sir Arthur Wing Pinero about a saucy chorus girl who is nearly decapitated when a stagehand drops a bucket of paint within inches of her head. "Mind the paint!" she yells (with a pout and admonishing finger), and from then on, she is known as the you-know-what girl. It wasn't exactly the kind of role actresses dream about, but Billie Burke had played it with great success on Broadway in 1912, and Anita, miscast though she was, valiantly and vainly tried to be as gay and fluttery as her stage predecessor.

She was miscast, she knew, and she suspected that Vitagraph had probably straddled her with this role because of her defection to Mayer. The only thing that made her work bearable was the kindness of her co-workers, especially director Wilfred North, who often drove her home after work.

One day, as they were leaving the Vitagraph studio in Brooklyn, at about six P.M., North's car ran headlong into a speeding truck. No one was seriously hurt, but Anita came out of the accident so bruised and bandaged that production on the film was halted for over two weeks. Vitagraph made some hasty calculations: *"Mind the Paint"* could easily be completed before the expiration of Stewart's extended contract, but a second feature, *Human Desire*, already in the planning stages, would be left half-finished at best. The time had come, the Vitagraph lawyers proposed, to strike a more accommodating note in the talks with Mr. Mayer.

Within a couple of weeks, there was an out-of-court settlement: Mayer was to pay Vitagraph $75,000 in exchange for Miss Stewart's services and the distribution rights for *"Mind-the-Paint" Girl* and the yet unfinished *Human Desire*. This was no bargain—Mayer was aware that Stewart's final films for Vitagraph were pretty shoddy, intentionally so—and through perseverance, he was able to wangle a few more concessions from Vitagraph. The company agreed to release Stewart a few weeks early and also promised to rent Mayer space in its Brooklyn studio for the production of his first feature film.

Mayer had already found a property for this production. Months earlier, Fanny Mittenthal had read the serialization of a novel called *Virtuous Wives* in *Cosmopolitan* magazine. She mentioned it to Mayer, who asked for a description of the plot. Well, Fanny explained, it was the story of a young wife who almost destroys her marriage by becoming a social butterfly; it was sleek and sophisticated, yet staunchly supportive of marital traditions, a combination of values that Mayer found highly attractive. He asked Fanny to inquire about the film rights. The author, Owen Johnson, was asking ten thousand dollars, and no bargaining was advisable since five other producers were bidding on the novel, including Cecil B. De Mille, who was a specialist in this kind of haute couture drama. Mayer had no intention of haggling—he promptly paid Johnson the ten thousand.

While Stewart was finishing her Vitagraph commitment, Mayer had busied himself with arranging financing and distribution for *Virtuous Wives* and the other films he hoped to produce in the future. After leaving Metro, he had formed an alliance with Lewis J. Selznick's Select Picture Corporation, but this was of short duration—Selznick and he didn't see eye to eye. Then, in the summer of 1918, he formed a partnership with Nathan Gordon, a Boston exhibitor who controlled the Olympic Theatre Circuit in New England. The Gordon-Mayer Film Exchange, their company was called, and its primary assets were Mayer's various distribution enterprises and Gordon's large chain of movie and "combination" houses.

Mayer had made an astute choice in picking Nat Gordon for his partner. Gordon was one of the founders of First National, a recently organized production corporation that was built along Metro lines, except that its original membership was formed exclusively of exhibitors. There were other important differences: First National was intelligently managed, and with such stars as Mary Pickford and Charles Chaplin under contract, it carried far more prestige than Metro.

While there were certainly other reasons for the partnership, by teaming up with Gordon, Mayer had provided himself with an immediate entrée into the First National organization as a contributing producer. This meant that the company would advance him $125,000 for each picture he produced and that he would receive 50 percent of the gross profits, minus the advance. It was a good deal, made more attractive by the fact that his films would have an immediate exhibition outlet through the circuits controlled by Gordon and the other First National theatre owners.

By the time Anita Stewart was free to start work on *Virtuous Wives,* Mayer had reached an agreement with First National. The company put up the money for this picture and a substantial part of the financing for all Mayer productions made in the next two years.

At the beginning of 1919, close to the starting date of production for *Virtuous Wives,* Mayer had seemingly tied up all the loose ends— he had his star, a story, financing and distribution; he had chosen most of the supporting cast and the director, up-and-coming George Loane Tucker, who was also adapting Owen Johnson's novel for the screen. Then a ticklish matter of diplomacy arose. Anita Stewart didn't like Johnson's book or Tucker's adaptation, and was generally peevish in her reactions to Mayer's selection of the cast and crew.

Apparently she felt she had been left out of too many of the important artistic decisions concerning *Virtuous Wives,* the first Anita Stewart Inc. production, and to soothe her discontent, Mayer asked her to select the actress for the second female role, a meaty part that offered infinite possibilities for upstaging the leading lady.

Mayer's choice for the role was Hedda Hopper, the handsome actress-wife of a leading Broadway comedian, De Wolfe Hopper, who was noted for her elegant and expensive wardrobe. But for this interview, Mrs. Hopper dressed herself in the kind of rags she would normally have passed along to her maid. "Splendid," cried Anita Stewart, "you're exactly what I want for this role."

Once she had signed a contract, Hedda went out and bought an entire wardrobe from Lucile, the smartest New York couturier of the day. On the first day of shooting, she waltzed onto the set, wearing one of Lucile's masterpieces, "a handkerchief tea gown of mauve and lilac chiffon." Anita told Mayer she was not going to be upstaged by an overdressed "bit player," and Hedda, overhearing the comment, retorted that nothing she wore could possibly outshine Miss Stewart's "little frocks run up at home by loving hands."

Mayer mustered up all his tact and managed to keep the two actresses on the job, one wearing her Lucile gowns, the other dressed in her homemade finery. They worked together peacefully, but off camera, they kept their distance and never spoke. Hedda, who had more than a streak of the feline in her nature, rather enjoyed the feud, even stoking it a bit whenever it was about to die out. Once when Stewart was clowning around with the extras, Hopper commented loudly, "My, my, would you look at the dignity of our star!"

But these temperamental outbursts never upset the shooting plan, and *Virtuous Wives* finished on schedule, exactly eight weeks after it had gone into production. This was about a month longer than it took to shoot most feature-length pictures, but *Virtuous Wives* was intended as a "quality production," and Mayer planned to launch it with equivalent showmanship: the picture would be sold through a glamorous, yet highly dignified advertising campaign. Possibly because Vitagraph was then promoting Corinne Griffith, its replacement for Stewart, as "The Orchid Lady," Mayer issued a series of photographs of Anita peeking out coyly from the center of a huge calla lily: she was, read a caption, "L. B. Mayer's Prize Lily." The flower symbolism succeeded in capturing the attention of the press. "Merrie Olde England had a war of the roses," noted one trade columnist, "and now Movieland is waging its own battle of the flowers: it's the orchids against the lilies."

Mayer's advertising campaign suggested that *Virtuous Wives* was naughty but nice: the film was billed as "A View of High Society With a Moral." Not all critics agreed. *The New York Times,* for example, wrote that the only discernible moral was "the impunity with which American citizens can break as many middle-class commandments as they please without injury to their characters." Overall the press notices were lukewarm, but the public flocked to see the picture when it opened at the Strand theatre on Broadway in December 1918. A substantial hit, it assured Mayer's future as a producer.

But he hadn't waited to see the box office returns. Well before *Virtuous Wives* had opened, he was working on plans for his next two pictures for Anita Stewart, both of which were to be made on a more elaborate scale than the inaugural production. Much of the added expense was due to a shift in locale—instead of shooting these films at the Vitagraph studio in Brooklyn, Mayer was moving operations to California. Shortly after Armistice Day in 1918, he and his wife left for the West Coast, where a few weeks later they were joined by Anita Stewart and her husband.

The film industry's mass decampment from the East Coast to Southern California had started around 1907. At that time, in hopes of luring winter vacationists westward, the Los Angeles Chamber of Commerce had launched a massive publicity campaign extolling the area's climate, varied scenery and monotonous sunshine—on an average, there were rarely more than six rainy or overcast days a year. Some of the promotional literature reached the desks of eastern film producers who were looking for just this kind of Eden to solve their winter shooting problems: they couldn't work on location because of the unpredictable weather conditions, and they couldn't always work indoors since most studios still depended on the sun (filtered through glass or muslin roofs) as their main source of lighting.

As part of their search for a winter haven, the East Coast producers started sending exploratory troupes out west for brief visits. All reports came back favorable, so one by one, the producers started to make a practice of sending small companies to the Los Angeles area for three or four months of the year. Then gradually they began establishing facilities that were active on a year-round basis.

By 1918, nearly every major company or producer had a studio somewhere in the environs of Los Angeles. Many were no more than barnlike structures, surrounded by what looked like wooden or concrete outhouses, on a plot of land just big enough to hold a few flimsy outdoor sets. Fox had a lot on Western Avenue. Zukor's Famous Players and Lasky Feature Films (which had merged in 1916) shared facilities at Sunset and Vine. Goldwyn, who had left Lasky to form his own company, had taken over the impressive Triangle studios in Culver City. Universal was out in the San Fernando Valley on Lankersheim Boulevard. Metro had recently built a studio at Santa Monica and Cahuenga (presently the site of the Technicolor laboratories).

Mr. and Mrs. Mayer came to Los Angeles by train and stayed at the fashionable Garden Court Apartments on Hollywood Boulevard. The landscape they viewed looked less an Eden than a wilderness or a tangled wildwood. Los Angeles was then a dusty, sundrenched and disorganized cluster of neighborhoods that were poking along toward becoming a community—as late as the 1940s, it was considered witty to refer to Los Angeles as "six suburbs in search of a city." Nestled among the groves of citrus, avocado, oleander and eucalyptus trees were small ethnic settlements and enclaves of brilliantly hued bungalows. Everywhere there were patios—this was the land of al fresco living—and everyone moved at a languid pace; an atmosphere of tropical indolence hung heavy in the air. Many areas were still undeveloped—Beverly Hills was an uncharted territory of briars, brambles and bridle paths, inhabited only by deer, coyotes, rattlers, an occasional wildcat and Douglas Fairbanks, who had recently bought one of the few houses in the area, a hunting lodge that was soon to be known as Pickfair.

The famous and much abused sign that spells out H O L L Y W O O D in gigantic white letters at the top of one of the hills that form the Los Angeles basin wasn't constructed until 1926, but Hollywood—or Hollywoodland, as the neighborhood was originally called—was a thriving community at the time of the Mayers' arrival. And even then it was connected with the film business, since most actors and industry personnel lived there—until they had earned enough money to move elsewhere.

The liveliest cross-section of the transient film population was to be found at the Hollywood Hotel, a sprawling, dun-colored caravansary at the corner of Hollywood and Highland avenues. The American-plan rates were cheap, the rooms were clean and comfortable, but the major attraction was the proprietress, a Mrs. Hershey who claimed to be a member of the Pennsylvania chocolate family. A motherly type alternately described as buxom and gaunt, loving and dictatorial, Mrs. Hershey had one attribute about which everyone agrees: she loved to dance.

The social highlight of every week was the Thursday night cotillion in the lobby of the Hollywood Hotel. The music was provided by a three-piece ensemble and Mrs. Hershey, though no Irene Castle, was always the belle of the ball. Her gentlemen lodgers knew their hands would be slapped every time they reached for a second helping of chicken fricassee unless they partnered their landlady at least once every Thursday.

Across the street from the Hollywood Hotel, there was a row of shops that catered to the professional needs of a show-business clientele. Among them were Hellman's barbershop, which specialized in pomades and razor-cut sideburns, and a makeup studio run by a man called Max Factor. A half-block north was the Montmartre restaurant, where the stars ate lunch when they weren't working, and in a year or so there would be a couple of other fashionable restaurants —the Brown Derby and the West Coast version of Sardi's and the Algonquin Round Table, Musso and Frank's Grill on Hollywood Boulevard. There were also a few country clubs, but their boards of directors looked down on movie people and discouraged them from seeking membership.

Socially and culturally, not much was going on in Hollywood or

Los Angeles—people had to create their own amusements, a challenge that pricked the imagination of the picture colony. "They had fun in those days," says one long-standing observer. "But . . . well . . . some of the fun was pretty quirky."

Well, Los Angeles could be pretty quirky too, especially the abrupt way the scenery shifted from one block to the next. For example, just a few blocks from the Hollywood Hotel shop area was Franklin Avenue, then one of the city's most pleasant residential districts. It was here that Mayer established his first home in California—6615 Franklin Avenue. He chose to rent rather than buy the house, a modest stucco bungalow, because he was not yet ready to make a permanent commitment to the West Coast.

The main reason he had come to California was that the next Anita Stewart picture required a lot of outdoor shooting. Called *In Old Kentucky,* it was based on a once popular melodrama by Charles T. Dazey, a kind of bluegrass precursor of *National Velvet:* a young, feisty orphan saves the life of the man she loves, and later, disguised as a jockey, rides his horse to victory in the derby.

Dazey's play was a particular favorite of Mayer's—he had produced it during his management of the Walnut Street Theatre in Philadelphia—and while old-fashioned by the stage standards of the late 1910s, it was no more sentimental or farfetched than many Mary Pickford pictures. In fact, Mayer may have selected it primarily for that reason—Pickford was then at the peak of her popularity, and many actors and producers were trying to duplicate her success through slavish imitation. Stewart had her own style, which was not at all like Pickford's, and she was too well known to be considered an imitator, but there were indications that her aristocratic image was losing popularity with the public, and that Mayer had decided she needed a more accessible screen personality.

Before leaving Boston, he had made arrangements to rent space in the Selig Polyscope studios on Mission Road in East Los Angeles. The founder of the studio was Colonel William Selig, one of the more colorful figures of Hollywood history. His military title was of doubtful authenticity, but he had definitely led the life of a soldier of fortune, doing battle with any kind of job that came his way—he had been a magician, a scab, the manager of a health spa, a photographer and a minstrel man before drifting into film production in Chicago around 1907. One of his first productions was *Big Game Hunting in Africa,* a film purporting to show actual footage of Teddy Roosevelt's 1908 safari, though "Teddy" was a down-and-out vaudevillian and the animals he stalked were rented from a broken-down menagerie on the outskirts of Milwaukee. But the footage looked passably authentic and this was all that mattered. The picture was a resounding success, and Colonel Bill Selig realized that at long last he had found his true métier.

He moved to Los Angeles in 1910, and six years later built the studio on Mission Road. It was known throughout Hollywood as the Zoo on account of the menagerie the colonel maintained for the animal and wildlife pictures that were his specialty. Selig Polyscope was not one of the industry's glamour studios, but it served Mayer's purposes. It had several permanent outdoor sets, including an African village, a cave, a jungle and a vast eucalyptus grove which served as background for less exotic pictures. The buildings that housed the animals, Selig's pride and joy, were more spacious than those used for indoor shooting, but on the whole the facilities were adequate for the filming of any standard production.

As supervisor of *In Old Kentucky*, Mayer had hired Lois Weber, the first woman director in American film history. Weber's most notable achievements had been a series of birth-control propaganda films, including the 1914 *Hypocrites*, which scandalized audiences because it featured a naked lady, representing Truth, who wandered allegorically in and out of the main story. Nothing Weber had done in the past suggested she was ideally suited to overseeing an outdoor picture, but she was a quality director, and quality was something Mayer hankered after. In a letter to his director, he outlined the ingredients that went into the making of any topnotch film: "Great star, great director, great play, great cast."

In his enthusiasm, he encouraged Weber to "spare no expense," but actually he was in no position to disregard his cost sheets. The $125,000 advance from First National would have been enough for the budget of any average production, but since Mayer wanted his pictures to be "special," he often had to dig into his own pocket for added production expenditures. At this time, any picture grossing $250,000 was considered to have done well, so Mayer's share of the profits, after the advance had been subtracted, was rarely more than $75,000, often a good deal less, and this money could come dribbling in over a period of many months. Consequently, in the next two years, Mayer was occasionally hard pressed for ready cash.

Other problems arose almost as soon as Mayer arrived at the Selig studio. *In Old Kentucky* had to be delayed because of script and casting problems, and since Mayer couldn't afford to pay Weber and Stewart for doing nothing, he rushed them into production of two potboilers, *Midnight Romance* and *Mary Regan*. Anita Stewart disliked both. In fact, there wasn't much she did like about her current work. She had arrived in Hollywood during a torrential rainfall which lasted for more than a week and understandably, she formed a low opinion of the Southern California climate. The roaring of Colonel Selig's lions unnerved her, and she was distressed to discover that the studio had no glass-roofed stages. Like many film stars, she considered reflected sunlight to be the most flattering form of lighting, and so once again she started worrying about her nose.

Her spirits improved when work began on *In Old Kentucky,* most of which was shot outdoors. Since Lois Weber's contract with Mayer had expired, the direction of the picture was taken over by Marshall ("Mickey") Neilan, a flamboyant, hard-drinking Irishman who had been a child actor and leading man to Mary Pickford before launching a highly successful career as director in 1916. (Just prior to *Old Kentucky,* he had directed two of Pickford's best films, *Rebecca of Sunnybrook Farm* and *Stella Maris.*) Neilan had a way with the ladies, which endeared him to Stewart, but his relations with Mayer were not so happy.

By *Kentucky* time, Mayer was bubbling with enthusiasm and excitement about the whole crazy business of picture making. He was all over the studio, poking his nose into everything, asking endless questions as he crashed his way through a self-taught course in production technique. Some onlookers were amused by his thirst for knowledge, but Neilan was not among them. One day, after finishing a take, the director turned peremptorily to Mayer and snapped, "And now what is your question about *that,* Mr. *Producer?*" From then on, Mayer kept his distance from Neilan, but continued to hover around the sidelines of the set, watching and learning.

He was now completely infatuated with the production end of the business, and had also become attached to Southern California. In the summer of 1919, as soon as *In Old Kentucky* was completed, he returned to the East Coast for a visit, the main purpose of which was to wind up or sell his business interests there and his Brookline home so he could settle permanently in Hollywood. And just a few weeks prior to the trip, he had completed arrangements to build his own studio on a lot adjacent to the Selig Zoo at 3800 Mission Road in East Los Angeles.

He and his wife returned to California by train with their daughters. The family car was driven across country by a chauffeur, George, who had as a traveling companion, Irene and Edie's dog, Teddie. The family settled in at 6615 Franklin Avenue, but soon moved to another, bigger house on Franklin near La Brea, and then again to a more comfortable home on North Cherokee. Despite all the upheaval in living quarters, it was clear that the Mayer family had come to California to stay.

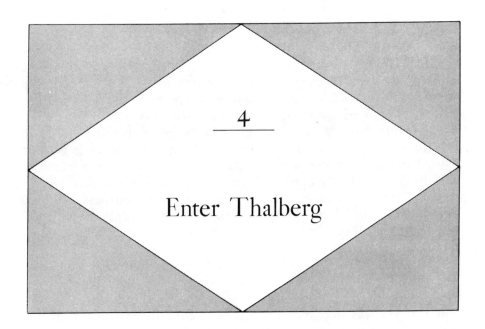

4

Enter Thalberg

The Mayer studio was finished in January 1920. By necessity it was modest in scope, but there were as many touches of Hollywood splendor as money would allow. The main office building was designed to resemble a doll-sized château of Chenonceaux. There were four stages, all larger than those at Selig, and two dressing-room bungalows, one for Anita Stewart, the other for Mayer's newest star —Mildred Harris Chaplin.

Signing Mrs. Charlie Chaplin was something of a coup for Mayer—at least at the outset. Initially the alliance brought Mayer a lot of publicity, which was good, but not all the publicity was favorable, and in the long run, Mildred Harris Chaplin proved to be more trouble than she was worth. At age ten, Mildred had made her movie debut at Triangle studios where her mother was wardrobe mistress. A few years later, she starred in a couple of substandard Lois Weber pictures, and her career was pretty much at a standstill when, just before her eighteenth birthday, she met Charlie Chaplin at a Sam Goldwyn beach party. Mildred then had a crush on Elliott Dexter, who was married to "adorable" Marie Doro, who had once been admired by Charlie—it was a classic case of *La Ronde*, Hollywood style. Despite her attraction to Dexter, Mildred started "dating"

Chaplin, and on October 23, 1918, they were married—mainly, it seems, because Mildred believed (incorrectly) that she was pregnant.

If Chaplin's autobiography is to be trusted, Mayer approached Mildred the day after the wedding with the offer of a $50,000 contract for six pictures. (This is highly questionable, since Mayer was then still in New York working on *Virtuous Wives*—Chaplin may have Mayer confused with Adolph Zukor, who did approach Mildred at this time.) Chaplin was furious; he told Mildred that he could get her $50,000 for *one* picture if he wanted to, which he didn't. He was certain she was being exploited because of his name, and of course he was right. Besides youth, vivacity and a plump prettiness, Mildred Harris had nothing to offer that suggested she might become an important star, but Mildred Harris Chaplin was a marketable commodity.

Mildred signed with Mayer just before his trip to the East Coast. She was then unmistakably pregnant—a few months later she gave birth to an internally malformed baby who lived only three days—and Charlie was enraged that she was thinking of resuming her career. One night when Mildred invited her new boss for dinner, Chaplin locked himself in the conservatory of their house and refused to come out until Mayer left. The marriage was clearly nearing its final chapter, and shortly after Harris had settled into her bungalow on the Mayer lot, the couple separated.

A few months later, April 8, 1920, Mayer and a party of twelve including Mrs. Mayer, Anita Stewart and her husband were having dinner at the Alexandria Hotel when Chaplin entered with a small group including Jack Pickford (Mary's fast-living brother). The Chaplin party was seated at a table close by the Mayer party. Almost immediately, an argument broke out. First nasty looks, then nasty remarks and finally nasty notes were exchanged; Mayer and Chaplin agreed to settle matters away from the ladies on the great oval carpet in the Alexandria lobby. The gist of the quarrel was that Chaplin had offered Mildred a divorce settlement which Mayer considered niggardly. Chaplin thought it was none of Mayer's business, but Mayer was already beginning to think of his employees as members of his family. He felt entitled to uphold his surrogate patriarchal rights.

"Take off your glasses," Chaplin demanded. Mayer complied and Charlie hit him in the face. Mayer retaliated and Chaplin keeled over backward. Jack Pickford rushed forward, got Charlie to his feet and pushed him outside and into a waiting limousine. By then, a large crowd had gathered, including a couple of reporters. "I only did what any man would have done," Mayer told them. Unfortunately, not many members of the press agreed.

Anita Stewart got caught up in the aftermath of this battle. Mildred had confided that she wanted to keep Chaplin as a husband, and to help her out, Anita had devised a plot to lure Charlie back through jealousy. The "other man" was her brother George, who started dining at Mildred's house two or three times a week. This bit of Hollywood melodrama backfired—Charlie never became jealous, but he did start keeping tabs on Mildred in hopes of finding her in flagrant violation of her marriage vows. He failed—Mildred was a paragon of chastity during this period—but he did persuade her to petition for divorce in the fall of 1920. Mildred Harris Chaplin was then reduced to plain Mildred Harris, not so marketable a commodity, and none of the five films she made for Mayer was more than modestly successful. Her contract was not renewed for the next year.

At about the same time, Mayer parted company with Anita Stewart. She had continued to be unhappy about the stories she was asked to film, and despite her friendship with Harris, she was not overjoyed when Mayer started bringing other actresses into the studio, some of whom, she felt, he favored over her. The truth was that she was now well past the peak of her popularity—she had never quite regained the ground she had lost just before leaving Vitagraph. Mayer offered to renew her contract, but she decided to accept a more lucrative offer from William Randolph Hearst's Cosmopolitan Company, although in doing so, as she must have known, she was definitely going to be eclipsed by Hearst's protégée, Marion Davies. As it turned out, Stewart was to continue to play leading roles until 1928, but her days as a major star were over once she left the Mayer studio.

By and large, the films produced by Mayer during his so-called Mission Road period, the years between 1918 and 1923, exist only as titles known to a handful of hard-core film buffs—prints of most of them have long ago disintegrated or been discarded as worthless. Judging from the plot synopses, they tended to be comedies or melodramas constructed to exhibit the limited talents of Mayer's leading ladies to optimum advantage. The vast majority are the stories of a woman who must make a fateful decision which will either save or destroy herself and the man she loves.

In *Harriett and the Piper* (1920), for example, Anita Stewart plays a former artist's model who must decide whether she should tell her socialite husband of her bohemian past. *The Inferior Sex* (also 1920) has Mildred Harris Chaplin as a neglected wife flirting with the idea of an extramarital dalliance, while Renée Adorée in *The Eternal Struggle* (1924) runs the rapids in a canoe rather than submit to that fate-worse-than-death. And Barbara LaMarr—the most beautiful of Mayer's early stars, indeed, one of the most stunning women in American film history—plays a variation of Carmen in the 1924 *Thy Name Is Woman:* she is Guerita, a Spanish gypsy who is ready to accept dishonor rather than reveal the whereabouts of her smuggler husband.

According to reviews, most of these films were pleasant time-passers; few were below average in quality and the majority were well directed, decently acted and handsomely mounted. But none of them broke new ground—Mayer wasn't then, and never would be, much of an innovator—and none made any important contribution to film history. These films were pure entertainment, pictures with handsome people, strong story values and a staunch affirmation of traditional American morality.

Some of the films offer glimpses of a naughty nonconformism, but they all end with adultery routed, cosmopolitanism condemned, fidelity enshrined, the family exalted and true love conquering all. There has been a lot of comment on the puritanical provincialism of Mayer's early films, but most of it comes from critics who fail to realize that the same could be said of most films of the late 1910s and early 1920s. Even Cecil B. De Mille's social comedies, then considered the ultimate in raciness, ended on a stern moralistic note; the message was implicit in their titles—*Old Wives for New; Don't Change Your Husband; Why Change Your Wife?*

American movies reflected, but did not condone, the shifting moral climate of the post-World War I era. In taking a condemnatory view of such modern issues as free love, flaming youth, divorce and the disintegration of the family unit, American film makers were conforming with the values of its largely middle-class audience. A bit of titillation was acceptable, but there must be nothing that was lewd or blasphemous, nothing that abused the sanctity of marriage and motherhood, nothing that challenged the virtues of wholesome living. "I've got one rule to guide me in the kind of pictures I make," Mayer told an interviewer. "I'll never make anything that I wouldn't take my daughters to see."

With the departure of Anita Stewart and Mildred Harris, Mayer was temporarily bereft of star names to carry his films. So he went in a new direction, one inaugurated by Cecil B. De Mille. This was the "all-star production," a euphemism for a type of film that featured a group of second-rank actors instead of a genuine box office attraction like Pickford or Fairbanks or Chaplin. Mayer never referred to his films as all-star productions, but obviously they were patterned after the De Mille pictures, which were ostensibly designed as showcases for the talents of promising new players. (In reality, they were a showcase for De Mille's ambition to be the star of his own films.)

Among the actresses who appeared frequently in Mayer's films during this period were Hedda Hopper, Claire Windsor, Barbara LaMarr and Renée Adorée, a French circus performer who had recently scored a success on Broadway in *The Dancers.* His leading men included Milton Sills, Wallace Beery and Lewis Stone, who was later to become one of Mayer's favorite contract players. Stone was to have a noteworthy career as a character actor, and Beery was to make it to the top, but the majority of Mayer's Mission Road stars never became major ones. (LaMarr and Adorée might have gone farther had they not been plagued by illness and personal problems.)

Mayer had more luck in building up a roster of talented directors. In this area he knew exactly what he wanted, or rather what he didn't want, which was the Mickey Neilan type of director. During his second production for Mayer (another Anita Stewart vehicle called *Her Kingdom of Desire*), Neilan started going off on periodic benders, sometimes not showing up at the studio for several days in succession. Harsh words were exchanged. Neilan's drinking didn't upset Mayer—that was a private matter—but his absence from the set was a clear-cut case of unprofessionalism, and that was something Mayer wouldn't abide.

Mayer's ideal director was reliable, versatile and free of prima donna attitudes. He was looking for able craftsmen rather than star personalities or master artists like Cecil B. De Mille and D. W. Griffith. The best known of the directors who worked at the Mission Road studio was Fred Niblo, who had just supervised the making of the first Douglas Fairbanks swashbuckler, *The Three Musketeers.* Next in rank of prestige came Edward José, who had directed Enrico Caruso's first film, *My Cousin;* then Reginald Barker and John M. Stahl. Each had his specialty—Niblo was adept at torrid romances and spectacles, Barker liked action pictures, Stahl had a penchant for the sob sister type of film—but each was dexterous enough to handle any sort of story that came his way.

Unquestionably Mayer would have liked to add other directors and actors to his list of contract employees, but this was financially not feasible. The policy of having many people under exclusive contract was advantageous to a producer only if he could keep them working steadily enough to absorb their weekly salaries. Mayer did not as yet belong to that exalted category of producers. If he were to increase his payroll, then he would have to increase production, but his contract with First National called for only six to eight films a year. And there was no way the contract could be renegotiated—the company couldn't accept any more pictures from Mayer because of its commitments with other independent producers.

There was only one possible route of escape from this vicious circle: Mayer had to find another outlet for his films. In the fall of 1920 he had found a partial solution to this problem by signing a second contract with Metro, the company he had left to join First National. Since then Metro had undergone a major upheaval in its organization. Richard Rowland, Mayer's nemesis, had been ousted as president and the company had been bought by Marcus Loew, a pioneer exhibitor with a large chain of East Coast theatres.

The legal technicalities of the takeover were handled by J. Robert Rubin, the attorney who represented both Metro and Mayer, and who soon won the trust of the genial and highly regarded Loew. One of the first matters they discussed was how the poor quality of Metro films could be improved. Rubin recommended that the company bolster its program through the acquisition of a small number of films from some of the better independent producers, men like his friend and client, Louis B. Mayer. Loew readily agreed.

The contract between Metro and Mayer called for four films a year. The terms of the agreement were basically the same as those with First National, only the advance money was more generous, and generally the classiest of Mayer's Mission Road pictures were released through Metro. Otherwise the Metro connection did not immediately alter Mayer's status in any dramatic way. The scale on which he was forced to operate was still too small to fit his ambitions.

But the scale was becoming just a little too big for one man to carry alone. Ten to twelve pictures wasn't much compared to the yearly output of Fox or Universal or Famous Players–Lasky, but it was a pretty heavy load for Mayer who was, on the executive level, running what amounted to a one-man operation. By 1922 the burden had become so great that Mayer told his friends he was looking for an assistant or associate, preferably someone with creative production experience, an area in which Mayer felt insecure. Several recommendations were forthcoming, but it was not until the end of the year that he found the person he was looking for.

Irving Thalberg was born in a middle-class Brooklyn neighborhood in May 1899. His father, William, a German immigrant, ran a lace importing company in Manhattan and his mother, Henrietta, was the daughter of the owner of a prosperous department store, Heyman and Sons. Irving was their first child—later would come a daughter, Sylvia—and his birth, so eagerly anticipated, was the occasion for the first real sorrow the couple had known in their married life. The child was born with cyanosis or imperfectly oxygenated blood, a condition which usually indicates a congenital heart or lung disorder. He would survive, the doctors told Henrietta, but he could not be expected to live a long life.

After the initial shock subsided, Henrietta accepted the prognosis as a challenge. Though her son's life might be short, that did not mean it could not be productive and fulfilling. Henrietta had suffered one disappointment—she had come to realize she had married an affable but bland and complacent man—and she was not about to accept another. In time she convinced herself that Irving's cyanosis was a sign that he had some special quality that set him apart from the ordinary run of mankind.

As far as possible, she treated Irving as though he were a normally healthy child. He attended P.S. 85, and then in February 1913 transferred to Boys' High School where he remained for six terms. Henrietta enforced a rigorous routine of schoolwork, but there was always time for street sports, including stickball, which Irving played enthusiastically and sometimes incautiously. Every so often he overextended himself and would be forced to spend days in bed to recover his health. During these periods of convalescence, he read voraciously anything that came to hand—novels, plays, biographies, philosophy, magazines, newspapers. He discovered socialism through Upton Sinclair and George Bernard Shaw, and pragmatism through William James, whose writings were to leave a strong impression on young Thalberg.

Henrietta had decided Irving should be a lawyer, but shortly after his sixteenth birthday, he contracted rheumatic fever, and was forced to spend six months in bed. The doctors warned Henrietta that Irving's heart had been severely damaged and that he could not be expected to live much beyond early middle age. The arduous preparation for a law career was now out of the question, so Thalberg enrolled in a business course at New York University and took additional courses in shorthand and Spanish at a secretarial school.

Six months later, he obtained a position as a bilingual secretary with a small trading company. Within a year he had been promoted to assistant manager, but the work was tedious and there were no immediate opportunities for further advancement. Someday, something might open up, but patience was required, and that was a virtue Thalberg couldn't afford to cultivate.

During his months in bed, he had drawn up a list of maxims that would guide him through life:

Never take any one man's opinion as final.
Never think your own opinion is unassailable.
Never expect help from anyone but yourself.

Good, pragmatic self-advice, perhaps, but the first of these rules was one that Thalberg had trouble in following. The medical estimate of his life expectancy was one opinion that, at least unconsciously, he did accept as final. His feverish activity, the way he drove himself, the incredible work load he imposed upon himself in the years ahead—all this is understandable only in light of Thalberg's knowledge that he had to pack the accomplishments of a lifetime into a period that might be less than half the average life expectancy.

After about a year, Thalberg resigned from the trading company and took a short vacation before looking for a new job. Part of this time he spent with his maternal grandmother, who owned a cottage on Long Island just next door to the summer home of Carl Laemmle, the head of Universal Pictures. Often Laemmle strung a sheet across the front veranda and projected movies for his family and neighbors, always taking note of their comments and criticisms. He was continually impressed by the perspicacity of young Thalberg's remarks, and at the end of the summer, egged on by Irving's grandmother, he offered the boy a job as his executive secretary.

Laemmle spent most of his time at his offices in New York, but every so often he paid a visit to his California studio, and on one occasion, he asked his secretary to accompany him. Thalberg immediately realized that the studio was in a state of chaos. Laemmle had the irritating habit of hiring people without defining the precise nature of their duties, a practice that created widespread confusion about the demarcations of authority. Nearly every department had its share of deadbeats, most of them kept on the payroll because they were distantly related to "Uncle Carl," as Laemmle was known throughout the industry. As far as Thalberg could ascertain, there was no organization to speak of, no awareness that things could and should be run in a more methodical and productive fashion.

When Laemmle returned to New York, he left his secretary behind, but typically, he neglected to tell Thalberg what he should do in his absence. Left to his own devices, Thalberg read through the scenarios of upcoming productions and wandered around the studio, taking notes on how conditions could be improved. When Laemmle returned, Thalberg confronted him with a list of his proposals. "The very first thing you have to do," he said, "is to establish a new job of general manager and give him total responsibility for supervising day-to-day operations." Laemmle thought for a moment. "Okay," he replied, "you're it." Thalberg was then twenty years old.

Thalberg's promotion was a typical example of the way Laemmle handed out jobs without defining the responsibilities those jobs entailed—he liked to watch his employees fight for their rights. There were three other men at Universal who thought they outranked Thalberg in authority—and two of them were related to Uncle Carl. This made for difficulties, but within a matter of months, Irving had established his command so thoroughly that two of his rivals resigned and the third was demoted to a figurehead position. Thalberg proved his worth through his no-nonsense handling of Erich von Stroheim, one of Universal's problem directors, and through his development of the studio's first superproduction, *The Hunchback of Notre Dame*. It was his idea to film the Victor Hugo novel, and he was responsible for casting Lon Chaney, then a minor character actor best known for his portrayal of Fagin in a 1922 film version of *Oliver Twist*, as the hunchbacked Quasimodo, the role that would establish Chaney as a master of Grand Guignol characterization.

Thalberg envisioned *The Hunchback* as a spectacle as well as a horror film. He ordered the construction of a huge set which slavishly duplicated the façade and the courtyard of Notre Dame as it was in the mid-nineteenth century. This made for a costly film, especially for Universal which wasn't noted for lavish expenditures, but when Thalberg saw the assembled footage, he decided it wasn't big enough. He was certain the film would establish Chaney as a major star, but not if Universal dumped it into their regular programming schedule —it needed special handling if it were to receive the attention it deserved. And the only way to assure that it would get distinctive treatment, Thalberg reasoned, was to make it even bigger and more costly.

At this point Thalberg initiated a policy that he was to employ many times in the future: he ordered the picture back into production. New scenes were added and others were reshot to enhance their pictorial values—one night scene required every arc lamp in Hollywood before it was properly lit. Laemmle didn't know what was going on—he was in Europe at the time—and when he learned that Thalberg had added $150,000 to the cost of a picture that was already extravagantly expensive, he was stunned. But short of firing Thalberg—an action he was not prepared to take—there was little he could do besides giving the picture the biggest sendoff possible. The gamble paid off. *The Hunchback of Notre Dame* became Universal's most profitable film to that date.

It also made Thalberg the most talked about figure in Hollywood. He was the "wonder boy," "the baby genius," the kid who had stolen some of the spotlight from the middle-aged moguls who ruled the industry. It was astonishing that anyone so young and seemingly frail could possess the daring, self-assurance and know-how that brought Thalberg to the top of his profession at such an early age. (As a point of comparison, Mayer was then thirty-eight, Goldwyn was forty-one, De Mille was forty-two, Griffith was forty-eight, Zukor was fifty-one and Laemmle was nearing his fifty-sixth birthday.)

Thalberg was five feet, six inches tall, and rarely in his adult life did he weigh more than a hundred and twenty pounds. He had a long, ascetic nose, melting eyes, broad shoulders and a well-formed chest, but his legs and arms were underdeveloped, almost puny—one woman friend recalls that she never thought about Irving's "condition" until she saw him in a bathing suit. He dressed conservatively and cultivated the mannerisms of a mature and worldly executive. Whenever a visitor entered his office, he was seated at his desk, leafing through a screenplay or drafting a letter in longhand. After a few seconds, he would look up with a startled expression, as though caught unawares; then, with a nod or a smile, he gave full attention to his guest. It was a successful ploy, but it really wasn't necessary, since Thalberg had a natural poise and magnetism that attracted people, particularly people of the opposite sex.

One of the first ladies to be captivated by Thalberg's charm was Carl Laemmle's daughter, Rosabelle. A bright, but not very attractive girl, she had been polished at the best finishing schools and had traveled extensively through Europe, an education that had taught her that Pickfair was definitely not the Versailles of the modern world. She tended to sneer at the pretensions of Hollywood, but both there and in New York she frequently acted as her father's hostess, and her tact and social graces more than compensated for Laemmle's occasional lapses into boorishness. Rosabelle was a girl practically any mother might have considered a good catch for her son, but not Henrietta Thalberg. She thought Irving could do better.

Laemmle also disapproved of the growing attachment between Rosabelle and Thalberg for reasons that are in dispute. According to some reports, Laemmle did not learn of Irving's precarious health until the romance had become serious. Angry that Thalberg had withheld this information and upset at the prospect of his daughter marrying an invalid, he began to think he should encourage his production manager to look for another job.

A second version of the story opens as Thalberg begins to lose interest in Rosabelle. The girl became so distraught that Laemmle asked Henrietta to speak to Irving on his daughter's behalf. Henrietta did so halfheartedly, but her mission was a failure. Enraged at the slight to Rosabelle, Laemmle hinted broadly to his attorney, Edwin Loeb, that he wanted someone to take Thalberg off his hands. He did not, however, mention Rosabelle. Thalberg had taken on too much, he told Loeb, and therefore there could be "terrible consequences" for Universal if he ever suffered a heart attack. That at least was the way Loeb later reconstructed the conversation, though in light of subsequent events, it seems possible that he may have given too much importance to what Laemmle intended as no more than an offhand observation.

This much is certain: by the fall of 1922, there were strained relations between Laemmle and Thalberg. But the source of the friction, according to a third version of the story, was money, not Rosabelle. During his stay at Universal, Thalberg's salary had jumped from thirty-five dollars a week to four hundred and fifty, a handsome increase, but he thought he deserved more. He asked for a raise and Laemmle refused.

Perhaps Laemmle's refusal was a reflection of the Rosabelle affair; perhaps it was just another example of his chronic stinginess; possibly he thought he could hold on to Thalberg without boosting his salary. If so, he was wrong. It was a point of honor with Thalberg to be paid precisely what he thought he was worth—and he did not hold himself cheap. He decided it was time to leave Universal.

At this point, Edwin Loeb again enters the story. Thalberg confided to him that he was unhappy at Universal, and Loeb, thinking he was acting in the best interests of everyone concerned, promised to scout around for possible openings. First he approached Joseph Schenck, then head of First National, but Schenck wasn't encouraging. "You take care of the legal stuff," he told Loeb, "I'll run the studio."

On his own, Thalberg made overtures to Cecil B. De Mille, who was ready to pay the boy genius whatever he wanted. His partner, Jesse Lasky, wasn't so obliging. "Geniuses we have all we need," he shouted. "Tell him no, Cecil, definitely no!"

Next Thalberg talked to Hal Roach, one of Hollywood's leading comedy producers, and they had almost reached an agreement when Roach selected a last-minute applicant who had worked with Mack Sennett. It was a logical decision—Thalberg had little practical experience in this area of comedy, and in the years ahead, it was often said that Thalberg's major deficiency as a studio supervisor was his apparent disinterest in slapstick.

Once the Roach deal collapsed, Edwin Loeb offered to introduce Thalberg to Mayer. A year or so before, at a banquet at the Alexandria Hotel, Loeb had nudged Thalberg and said, "There's Louis B. Mayer. He's just become one of my clients and he's going to be very important someday." At the end of 1922, Mayer still wasn't as important as Laemmle, Zukor, Roach, Schenck or De Mille, but nonetheless, Loeb reasoned, the time was ripe for Mayer and Thalberg to have an exploratory conversation.

At first glance, Thalberg and Mayer would seem to have had little in common. Thalberg was widely and well read and was capable of scoring points in any literary or learned discussion. Mayer was frequently ill at ease with intellectuals, at least with those who were smug about their academic superiority. But Thalberg never flaunted his knowledge and never took a high-flown approach to film making. "A good picture," he said, "has to touch the audience here [he pointed to his head] and here [he tapped his heart] and here [he gestured toward his genitals]." It might seem as though Mayer would have looked askance at the brain and crotch sides of this theory, but of course Thalberg wasn't referring to the cerebral or direct-arousal type of movie.

In the fall of 1922, Thalberg spent several evenings at Mayer's home, and the pair talked about the film business far into the night. From the first conversation, they got along beautifully. Thalberg showed great respect for Mayer's experience and Mayer was impressed by Thalberg's devotion to his mother and his total absorption in picture making. Here was a young man of exceptional ability, someone who understood the complexities of the creative process and yet also possessed a sound business mind. "Good people make me look good," Mayer often said. "I'll go down on my knees to talent." Thalberg possessed these requirements of the good employee—he had talent and he would definitely make Mayer look good.

On February 15, 1923, Thalberg assumed the position of vice-president and production assistant of the Louis B. Mayer Company. The news of his appointment created a considerable stir in the industry. In leaving Universal for the second-rank Mayer Company, Thalberg was taking a backward step—or so many people thought, including Carl Laemmle. If he had ever truly wanted to be rid of Thalberg, he now had an abrupt change of heart. For years to come, he held a grudge against Mayer for "stealing" Thalberg from Universal.

From the outset, Mayer and Thalberg complemented each other superbly. Business was Mayer's bailiwick—he had few peers when it came to closing a deal or working out the most advantageous terms for a contract. On the other hand, he recognized—and frequently acknowledged—his limitations as a creative producer. He realized that he needed someone who could develop picture properties and see them through every phase of production, someone who could spot script problems and find ways of solving them, who had the diplomacy and perseverance to deal with the vagaries of the star temperament. This was the area in which Thalberg was supreme—this was his specialty.

A close bond developed between them, and before long it was a commonplace around Hollywood to say that Mayer regarded Thalberg as the son he had always wanted but had never had. An alternative supposition was that Mayer intended Thalberg as a husband for one of his daughters. But this was not true. If anything, the exact reverse was the case. The girls were warned not to get any notions about Irving and were never left alone with him for more than five minutes.

Both Mayer girls had been told about Thalberg's delicate health. "My father was fully informed about his condition—he knew he had a bad heart before he hired him," recalls Irene. "Just about everybody who worked closely with Irving knew. Believe me, any time he looked a little pale, we all panicked."

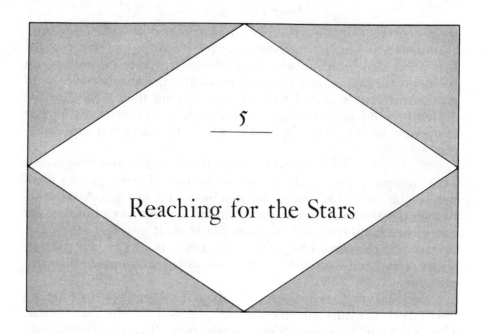

5

Reaching for the Stars

By the time Thalberg started working for him, Mayer was already exhibiting some of the distinctive traits for which he later became noted. When reason or civilized discussion failed to get him what he wanted, he was quite capable of resorting to more dramatic modes of persuasion: he'd shout, cry, cajole, flatter, threaten or utilize any one of a dozen other histrionic tricks. One Hollywood wit remarked that the initials L.B. really stood for Lionel Barrymore. The joke made the rounds and eventually reached Mayer, who accepted it good-naturedly as a kind of compliment. Barrymore was, after all, one of his favorite actors.

Around 1923 Mayer's favorite melodramatic ploy was the fainting spell. Originally these attacks were genuine: Mayer did experience a series of momentary blackouts that caused him to collapse during several embattled conferences. Doctors found nothing seriously wrong, but warned him to stay away from tobacco, alcohol and spicy foods. The spells ended as mysteriously as they began, but Mayer had found them so useful in gaining sympathy or disrupting a losing battle that he started simulating them. Whenever an argument was going the wrong way, he'd suddenly keel over and his secretary would rush in to daub his brow with a wet cloth; then slowly, with a flutter of his eyelids and a few moans, he'd fight his way back to consciousness.

Not many feigned faints were so realistic, not even those played on a stage, but Mayer pulled the stunt so many times that people became suspicious. Still, he went on with it until one day, just as he was enacting the first moments of regained consciousness, screenwriter Bess Meredyth appeared in the doorway with a towel draped over one arm and a basin of water in the other. With the professional heartiness of a ward nurse, she inquired, "And how is our patient doing this afternoon?" Mayer got the point. After that, he banished the swooning shtick from his theatrical repertoire.

Little of this theatricalism, however, was carried into his family life. He had settled happily in Hollywood, but had not—in a recently coined fan-magazine phrase—"gone Hollywood." The Mayers were then still residing on Kenmore Avenue in an unpretentious house in a style that was not very different from the way they had lived in Brookline or Haverhill. The jazz era was in full swing and "flaming youth" was a phrase on the tip of everyone's tongue, but Mayer's family remained faithful to old-fashioned values. There were no flappers in this household. In matters of dress, dating and general decorum, Edie and Irene were subject to constant and rigorous parental supervision.

Since they rarely appeared in public without their mother, Margaret, Irene and Edie were known as the Mayer girls, and Mrs. Mayer was considered the prettiest of the three. Edie, who bore a slight resemblance to her father, was graceful and feminine while Irene, who was closer to her mother in appearance, was serious and strong-minded—Mayer later said she was the only woman who might be capable of running a major studio. Both girls attended the fashionable Hollywood School for Girls where their fellow students included Agnes De Mille (Cecil's niece), a striking platinum blonde named Harlean Carpenter (later known as Jean Harlow) and—among all the young ladies—two somewhat embarrassed male pupils, Joel McCrea and Douglas Fairbanks, Jr.

Mayer usually left for the studio before eight in the morning and was rarely home before eight in the evening. Movies were then made on a six-day schedule, though some studios knocked off at noon on Saturdays. This left little time for entertainment or amusement, and except for the required business dinners and industry banquets, the Mayers preferred to socialize at home. Most of their guests were film people and their families. The conversation was mainly shop talk, but the major attraction was always the food. Mrs. Mayer always hired

a cook with a wide-ranging, home style repertoire that covered everything from Jewish specialties to American apple pie.

Even after his fainting spells had subsided, Mayer continued to
resist the temptation of highly seasoned foods, and became fanatic in
his adherence to a bland, simple diet. But within these limits, he was
something of a gourmet: he provided himself, his family, his guests
and (later) his studio employees with the best foodstuffs that could
be obtained. Kosher chickens were the best chickens, he claimed, and
one bite of fricassee was enough for him to know whether the main
ingredient had come from the poultry shop he recommended. Mayer
also held with the popular notion that corn on the cob must be eaten
not more than an hour after it had been picked. There was a vegetable
stand across from the studio and before leaving his office, he'd call
to say he was on his way. The required number of fresh ears were
always waiting for him, and by speeding to his house, he saw that
they got into a boiling pot and on the table before they lost their
virgin flavor.

Every so often, the Mayer family and a group of friends would
go out for the evening, often driving to one of the restaurants that
were then beginning to pop up along the southern Pacific coastline,
always bypassing the Ship's Café at Venice which was considered
"naughty." Thalberg, who was often a member of the party, would
always ask for a courtesy dance with Irene and Edie, but before the
waltz had ended, Mayer or an appointed surrogate had cut in.

Then as now, Los Angeles was General Motors' dream city.
Driving was necessary for survival—no matter where you were,
there was always a minimum fifteen-minute trip to wherever you
wanted to go, and the same trip by bus or trolley would take three
to four times as long. Mayer retained one Eastern trait: he loved to
walk; but through necessity, he came to rely heavily on a chauffeur-
driven car, though occasionally he elected to drive himself. This was
a decision that created panic among his friends and family. His
grandson Jeffrey remembers that usually he started off at fifty miles
an hour and then accelerated to a cruising speed of ninety. Just before
he left his office, his secretary would alert the studio guards, who
would clear the neighboring streets so that he was assured of a safe
journey for a block or two.

When they first arrived in Hollywood, Mayer and his family
went for Sunday drives, and then he always behaved himself behind
the wheel. Then there wasn't much to see except the Pacific and the
Zoo and Griffith Park and, of course, the studios. Then you could
drive along Santa Monica Boulevard and get a good view of the sets
for the latest Pickford and Fairbanks films, or ride down Vine and

see what was going on at Famous Players–Lasky, or venture farther afield, out to Culver City, and check out the activity at the Goldwyn studio.

One day, around 1920, Mayer stopped outside one of these lots and said, "I'd bet you'd be surprised if I became the head of a place like that."

Heading a major studio was, of course, Mayer's ultimate ambition. He firmly believed in the advantages of bigness. It distressed him to see actors, directors and cameramen sitting idle because he didn't have the scripts or stage facilities to keep them working full-time. He frequently explained to Thalberg the advantages of having fifty stars instead of ten, twenty stages instead of three, thirty directors instead of five, so that the company could turn out a steady supply of pictures, maybe as many as fifty a year. "Think big," he advised his production assistant. "That's the path of the future."

Mayer's opportunity to think and act big finally arrived in the spring of 1924 when he became chief of production at the newly amalgamated Metro and Goldwyn studios. Behind this long-awaited appointment was a series of complicated events which started a year earlier with a slump in the film business.

These recessions occurred periodically, but producers had never learned to take them in stride. The 1923 slump forced Adolph Zukor to call a temporary halt to all Famous–Lasky productions. First National ordered Mayer and its other associated producers to "economize and retrench." And Marcus Loew watched in horror as cracks started to appear in his carefully built empire.

Though Loew had bought out the Metro Company, he had never entirely believed that films would ever amount to much more than "chasers." But by the mid-twenties he was forced to recognize that vaudeville (the cornerstone of his operations) was starting to take second place to moving pictures in terms of audience popularity. There was only one exception to the rule—Metro pictures, which, Loew had to admit, were pretty poor. The studio's only big hit had been *The Four Horsemen of the Apocalypse,* and the cost of that early Valentino extravaganza had strained the company's economic resources while it was in production. Like every other exhibitor/producer, Loew wanted a steady stream of pictures like *Four Horsemen,* but he realized that such a program wasn't possible under the current Metro system. Something had to be done—but what?

Loew found an answer when a friend told him about the Goldwyn Company, which was then wavering on the brink of bankruptcy.

The Goldwyn studios had been formed in 1918 by Samuel Goldfish, former partner of Lasky and De Mille, and stage producer Edgar Selwyn—the *Gold* of Goldfish and the *wyn* of Selwyn had been combined to form Goldwyn, a name Goldfish liked enough to legally adopt as his own. (Hollywood wags later pointed out that with a little juggling of the syllables Goldwyn would have ended up as Selfish.) In 1922, Goldwyn was ousted from the presidency of the financially troubled company, and went into production for himself, releasing his pictures through First National and, later, United Artists. He wanted to remain Sam Goldwyn but his old company obtained an injunction forbidding him to use the name unless it was accompanied by the phrase "not connected with the Goldwyn Pictures Corporation." This disclaimer, which was soon dropped, did not eliminate the confusion; for years, a large section of the public naturally assumed that Goldwyn was one of the leaders of the company that bore his name.

Conditions at the Goldwyn studio had continued to deteriorate during 1922–23, the major problem being a weak and wavering management that seemed incapable of curbing expenses or providing a creative program for the future. Still, many talented people worked there: actors Aileen Pringle, Eleanor Boardman, Mae Busch, William Haines and Lew Cody; directors Erich von Stroheim, Mickey Neilan, and Victor Seastrom (or Sjöström, as he was known in his native Sweden).

Metro, equally mismanaged and extravagant, had just as impressive an array of contract talent, including Jackie Coogan, Mae Murray, Viola Dana, Mae Allison, Laurette Taylor and directors Rex Ingram and Robert Z. Leonard. But few of these people were being used to the full extent of their capabilities. Much to Loew's horror, the studio had just been robbed of the greatest male star of the decade, Rudolph Valentino. After his triumph in *Four Horsemen*, Metro dumped him into productions in which he was either miscast or overshadowed by his leading ladies. Unhappy about his roles and his salary, he accepted a flattering offer from Famous Players–Lasky.

Pulling all this together, Loew came up with the idea of merging Metro and Goldwyn, pooling their talents and placing the combined operations under the supervision of a man with vision and strong executive ability. Loew, who was then sixty-six, was in poor health, so negotiations for the merger were carried out by attorney Bob Rubin and Loew's second-in-command, Nicholas Schenck. The terms of the agreement were fairly simple: Loew would take over the Goldwyn Company through a transferral of stocks—one share of preferred Goldwyn exchanged for one share in the new company,

Metro-Goldwyn, with all common stock controlled by the parent company, Loew's, Inc.

This arrangement was readily accepted by the board of directors and shareholders of the Goldwyn and Metro companies. That left only one outstanding piece of business—the appointment of the man who would take charge of the new conglomerate. Joel Engel, the head of Metro, had been fired a few weeks before the merger took place, and Abraham Lehr of Goldwyn was out of the running because of his past record. Loew was open to suggestions, and once again Rubin recommended his old friend Louis B. Mayer.

A few months before, Loew had paid a visit to his West Coast studio, and while in Los Angeles, he had dropped by the Mayer lot to watch shooting of two future Metro releases, *Thy Name Is Woman* and *Women Who Give*. He had been favorably impressed by what he saw. Mayer's experience in distribution, exhibition and production certainly qualified him as a leading candidate, but Loew wondered whether he was as yet ready to assume the directorship of a major studio. Unwilling to be rushed into a decision, Loew told Rubin he would like to talk to Mayer, but stressed that the nature of the conversations should be left vague.

By this time, the entire industry knew about the upcoming merger, and Mayer could have had few doubts about why he had been invited to Loew's New York office. He was also aware that both Metro and Goldwyn were in deep trouble, and that whoever took control of the new company was sure to face more difficulties than the average studio executive. Just in case he was being considered for the job, he came armed with a list of conditions—these conversations were not going to be entirely one-sided. He also brought along his best asset, Irving Thalberg.

After several days of discussion, on April 10, 1924, a contract was agreed on and signed by Mayer and Loew. Less than a week later, the merger of the Metro and Goldwyn studios was formally announced.

Mayer's agreement with Loew provided that Metro-Goldwyn would purchase outright his studio at $76,000. Besides the physical plant and its equipment, this sale included the contracts of the Mayer personnel, such as directors Fred Niblo, John Stahl and Hobart Henley; actors Huntley Gordon, Norma Shearer, Hedda Hopper and Renée Adorée; and such behind-the-scenes personnel as Thalberg and his recently hired assistant, Harry Rapf.

Mayer was named first vice-president and general manager of Metro-Goldwyn productions at a salary of $1,500 a week; Thalberg was second vice-president and supervisor of production at $650; Robert Rubin became secretary and eastern representative at $600 a week. These three, the so-called Mayer group, were also to receive, after an annual dividend of two dollars a share to common stockholders, 20 percent of Metro-Goldwyn profits. (Ten percent went to Mayer; the remainder was equally divided between Thalberg and Rubin.) All films were to be released under the trademark Metro-Goldwyn or Metro-Goldwyn-Mayer, according to Mayer's discretion, but when the shorter name was used, the films were to bear a title reading "produced or presented by Louis B. Mayer." (This erratic shifting of trademark caused so much confusion that in the fall of 1925 it was decided to use Metro-Goldwyn-Mayer exclusively.)

Once the contracts were signed, Loew had to decide which of the three studios he now owned—Mayer, Metro and Goldwyn—should be headquarters for the new production company. It wasn't a difficult decision—Goldwyn had far and away the best facilities. The studio had once belonged to the Triangle Film Company, whose chief directors were the leading film makers of their day—Thomas Ince, D. W. Griffith and Mack Sennett. When Triangle went into bankruptcy in 1918, the studio was leased to Sam Goldwyn, who later bought it outright and purchased another twenty-six acres of ground to expand its boundaries. After he was ousted as president, Goldwyn sold his interests in his company, property as well as stock, to the shareholders at an estimated (and possibly exaggerated) $1 million.

Whatever its monetary value, the Goldwyn studio could hold its own against any of its Hollywood competitors. There were six well-equipped stages, including one that was reputedly the world's largest; storage quarters, laboratories, dressing rooms, office buildings; lots of land for outdoor sets and plenty of undeveloped acreage adjacent to the studio for future expansion.

Mayer and company moved into the lot just after lunch on Saturday, April 26, 1924. To mark the occasion, a large platform was built on the front lawn. It was draped with the stars and stripes, and in the center was a photograph of Marcus Loew. A navy band supplied music, Fred Niblo acted as master of ceremonies, Mayor Loop of Los Angeles made an opening address, Will Rogers rode his horse up and down and around the grandstand, and the stars in the bleachers cheered as Mayer read congratulatory telegrams from President Calvin Coolidge and Secretary of Commerce Herbert Hoover. At the close of the ceremony, affable Abe Lehr, the former head of the Goldwyn studios, symbolically relinquished his power to Mayer by handing him a huge floral wreath in the shape of a key.

The following Monday, Mayer and Thalberg got down to the most pressing piece of business: producing the supply of pictures that the Loew's theatres would need for the next year. At this time Loew's, Inc. controlled 111 theatres (including the State and the Academy of Music in New York) with an estimated seating capacity of 150,000, and had twelve more houses under construction. As part of the merger, the company had inherited a small chain of theatres owned by Goldwyn, including a half-interest in the New York Capitol, then the largest and grandest of all movie palaces. Within a year or so, it was estimated that total seating capacity of the Loew's theatre chain would be well over 250,000.

And, of course, Loew's primary interest was to see everyone of those seats filled for every performance on every day of the week. In May of 1924, Mayer was quoted by *Motion Picture Weekly* as saying that Metro-Goldwyn was aiming at releasing fifty-two pictures a year —but this was an unrealistic goal. Loew didn't expect quite so much, though he did stipulate that Mayer was to provide his theatres with fifteen pictures in his first year as production chief—otherwise, his contract was subject to cancellation.

Mayer had no difficulty in meeting this obligation; between May 1 and December 31, 1924, Metro-Goldwyn released twenty-eight films. Many of these pictures, however, were completed or already in production at the time of the merger—the carryovers included three productions each from Goldwyn and Metro and two from Mayer. There were also contributions from several independent producers or companies which released through Metro: *Circe, the Enchantress* from Tiffany (Mae Murray–Robert Z. Leonard Productions); *Little Robinson Crusoe* from Jackie Coogan Pictures; and *The Navigator*, a Buster Keaton feature film.

The first Metro-Goldwyn production supervised by Mayer was *Sinners in Silk*, "a picturization of the activities of 'the new generation' whose hymn is jazz, whose slogan is speed." Mayer had chosen the cast and crew for the picture with the utmost diplomacy and impartiality. The director was Hobart Henley, an alumnus of his Mission Road studio; scriptwriter Carey Wilson and the two leads, Eleanor Boardman and Conrad Nagel, had been under contract to Goldwyn; the important supporting roles were mostly filled by former Metro players.

In preparing the year's program, Mayer had the cooperation of nearly all the former Metro and Goldwyn contract people except director Rex Ingram. One out of so many may not seem important, but Ingram's standing in the industry was then so high that his defection cast a considerable shadow over Mayer's leadership. Today he is an obscure figure, but in the 1920s, Ingram (born Reginald

Ingram Hitchcock in Dublin in 1893) was considered worthy of comparison with D. W. Griffith. And while by modern standards even his best films—*Four Horsemen of the Apocalypse, Scaramouche, The Prisoner of Zenda*—are static and dramatically undernourished, they are so visually resplendent that his former reputation is immediately understandable.

He was Metro's most prestigious director, and out of gratitude for his service to the company, Marcus Loew gave Ingram his own unit and allowed him to work in Europe. The first film he had made under this arrangement was *The Arab*, which was to become one of Metro-Goldwyn's initial releases. Ingram had shot it on the Riviera with a foreign cast and crew, the only major exceptions being the leading actors, Ramon Novarro and Alice Terry (Mrs. Rex Ingram). The picture was just this side of a disaster: gorgeous to look at, but boring to sit through, it is a prime example of the kind of 1920s film making which emphasized "pictorial values" above all else.

Returning from Europe, Ingram learned of the merger and told Loew he wanted no part of it. His disapproval had nothing to do with Mayer, whom he had never met, but was an instinctive and self-protective reaction to the trend of consolidation. "My sympathies are all with those directors who stand or fall on their own merits," Ingram told an interviewer. "I have too often seen a good picture, and the career of a promising director, ruined by supervision."

Reading between the lines, one realizes that Ingram is asserting the supremacy of the creative director over money-minded producers who were doing their best to turn picture making into factory work. "I believe that the box office should be the artist's last consideration," he went on to say. "It has been proved over and over again that it is quite impossible to say what the public wants. The public doesn't know. An artist should work to please himself and if he is sincere he is sure to win the appreciation he desires."

Naturally enough, Ingram's ideal director was D. W. Griffith, but the days when Griffith could spend eight months or a year on one film had ended with the financial failure of *Intolerance* in 1916. Four years later, at the opening of *Way Down East*, he had turned to Ingram and said, "We're building on sand, you know," but Ingram didn't *know*—he presumed the cryptic remark referred to the perishability of film stock. Instead, Griffith was thinking of the success of companies like Zukor's Famous Players which had gradually tipped the balance of power away from the director and toward the stars and the producers; he was talking of the studio executives who preferred a series of modestly budgeted, entertaining films that would return a quick profit to one masterpiece that could take months and hundreds of thousands of dollars to shoot, and that might or might not end up in the black.

Ingram wanted no part of the new system. He would not make program pictures, he would not be subjected to a budget and schedule set by a group of front-office executives who knew nothing about the creative side of film making. Loew listened thoughtfully to Ingram and then agreed that he could continue to work in Europe with his own independent production unit.

Mayer was not happy about this arrangement. He argued that there was no efficient way of supervising a director who was working thousands of miles from the home studio. The trade press was also displeased, though for a different reason: Ingram's decision to work in Europe was interpreted as a slur on Hollywood. Loew stood firm, but ultimately Mayer was proved right—Ingram went way over budget on his next film, *Mare Nostrum* (1925), which did, however, return a small profit, as did his following film, *The Magician* (1926). But *The Garden of Allah* (1927), based on an international best seller by Robert Hichens, was so lavishly mounted that it had to attract a large audience to recoup its cost. Despite the fame of Hichens's novel and some very good reviews from the critics, the public showed no great interest in *Allah.* The picture bombed and virtually ended Ingram's career as a director.

There was no way of knowing whether Ingram might have profited from studio supervision. Possibly, like D. W. Griffith (who was to become a Famous Players–Lasky contract director late in his career), he would have had difficulties in finding inspiration and satisfaction in the rigid schedule-and-budget-oriented atmosphere of the centralized, corporate-minded studio. Many directors of equal reputation faced the same problem as they tried to adapt to the new system, which reduced their status from master creator to employee of a massive, assembly-line organization.

So began the great debate about studio versus artist, commercialism versus personal integrity, the desecration of great masterpieces and promising careers through the insensitivity of philistine management. And the storms of protest first gathered around Metro-Goldwyn because Mayer and Thalberg showed from the outset that they were not going to indulge the whims of self-important or temperamental directors. In Mayer's opinion, the director ranked low in the hierarchy of creative personnel behind a film. "If you've got the right script and the right producer and the right star, then practically any director can turn out a good film," he said. In reality, he was not so much anti-director as pro-collaboration, and it was through his leadership of M-G-M that collaborative film making was to become standard practice at all Hollywood studios.

Naturally enough, as soon as he took control of the studio, his power was tested by a few scoffing directors, including Mickey Neilan, Mayer's old nemesis, who was under contract to Goldwyn at the time of merger. Their reunion was an out-and-out fiasco. At the ceremony marking the opening of the new studio, Neilan had pulled himself to his feet and staggered off the grandstand just as one of the honorary guests was describing Mayer as one of "the industry's productive citizens." Hearing these words, Neilan paused and let out a loud, drunken razzberry of disagreement.

Neilan had just then completed a film adaptation of *Tess of the D'Urbervilles* starring his wife, Blanche Sweet. He was proud of the film, which was reasonably faithful to Thomas Hardy's novel—the story had been updated, but most of the key incidents had been retained, including Tess's execution for the murder of the dissolute squire who destroys her reputation. Mayer looked at the film and told Neilan the ending would have to be changed—it was too gloomy to please audiences. Neilan objected, but Mayer insisted he shoot a final scene in which Tess was happily reunited with the man she really loved. Eventually the picture was released in two versions, allowing exhibitors to choose whichever ending they preferred. Most critics, however, were shown the film as Neilan had originally conceived it.

While this compromise might be interpreted as a minor victory for Neilan, it wasn't really. Critics praised the film, but moviegoers weren't impressed—with or without the happy ending, they showed no great enthusiasm for *Tess,* Miss Sweet or Neilan's fidelity to Hardy. There were still two more pictures to go on Neilan's contract with Goldwyn, so in quick succession he made *This Sporting Genius* (with Sweet and Ronald Colman) and *The Great Love* (Viola Dana and Robert Agnew). By assigning him to these routine programmers, Neilan claimed, Mayer was trying to sabotage his career. Actually, he didn't need much help along these lines—his drinking and erratic behavior were enough reason for producers to be wary of hiring him.

Neilan, however, was only a minor irritation compared to Erich von Stroheim, who presented Mayer and Thalberg with one of the biggest problems they had to face during their first year at Metro-Goldwyn. Stroheim had made an adaptation of Frank Norris's novel *McTeague,* which had been financed by the Goldwyn company and was completed before the merger. Its story was harshly realistic; there were no major stars, and in rough cut it ran almost eight hours. Stroheim was convinced this was his masterpiece, and nearly everyone who had seen it agreed, but the question was, what could be done with an eight-hour masterpiece? The most imperious of all "genius" directors, Stroheim considered himself above such bourgeois preoccupations as marketing and exhibition.

An Austrian émigré, Stroheim said his mother had been lady-in-waiting to Empress Elizabeth and that he had once been a member of Franz Joseph's royal dragoons. These claims are of as doubtful authenticity as the "von" of his name—recently discovered documents suggest that his father was a Prussian Jew of humble antecedents—but certainly Stroheim looked the part he had chosen to play: with his bull neck and chest, his shaven head, his monocle and riding crop, he was a walking illustration of Hapsburg militarism.

Arriving in America in 1913 (possibly because of Austrian anti-Semitism), he worked at several menial jobs while learning English, then broke into the movies, first as an actor and later as assistant to D. W. Griffith. In 1918 he persuaded Carl Laemmle to give him the chance to direct a film he had written, *The Pinnacle*—later the title was changed to *Blind Husbands* because (the legend goes) Laemmle felt women wouldn't want to see a movie about a card game. *Husbands* was followed by *The Devil's Passkey* and *Foolish Wives,* all produced by Universal, all successes, all adding to the image of Stroheim (who played leading roles in the first and third of these films) as "The Man You Love to Hate." As publicity tags go, this one was pretty good. As an actor, Stroheim was limited, but his presence was extraordinary—he was the epitome of the glamour of dangerous sex. Ungovernable male lust was a highly marketable quality in the 1920s, but usually it was sold by the likes of Rudolph Valentino, whose rapacious leer suggested nothing more perilous than a game of boudoir let's-pretend. But Stroheim obviously wasn't thinking of Shiek-of-Araby charades when he looked at a woman; the glint in his eyes suggested chains, whips, high heels, silk stockings and other accoutrements of bizarre sexual gamesmanship.

Stroheim was quirky in other ways as well. For *Foolish Wives,* which took place in Monte Carlo, he insisted that an exact duplicate of the resort's major boulevard be built on the Universal lot. When he saw the results, he was displeased: he needed a view of the sea, which the Universal art directors had neglected to include in the design. So, to create atmosphere, he spent several days on the Monterey peninsula photographing gulls flying into the sunset.

"There's a madman in charge," someone reported to Carl Laemmle, who passed along the information to his then new assistant, Irving Thalberg. After looking at the footage, Thalberg marched down to the set and told Stroheim he was calling a halt to the production. The director insisted there were many scenes still to be shot.

Thalberg disagreed—there was more than enough footage to make a perfectly logical, though somewhat overlength, picture.

Inaccurately advertised as the first "million-dollar production," *Foolish Wives* made some money for Universal, and Thalberg, who genuinely admired Stroheim's talent, was in favor of him making another picture for the company. This one was called *Merry-Go-Round*, a drama of marital infidelity set in the twilight years of the Austro-Hungarian empire. It's hard to believe Thalberg would have approved a script that called for 1,500 scenes—two or three times as many as most pictures—several of them promising possible censorship problems, but either he gave approval or (more likely) Stroheim showed him an abbreviated and bowdlerized version of the story. Anyway, Thalberg offered no objections or interference until he learned that Stroheim had spent over $200,000 on shooting less than a quarter of the film.

This time the money had been spent on such sundries as gentlemen's underwear. Stroheim had ordered silk drawers monogrammed with the insignia of the Imperial Austrian Guard for a group of extras who were never to drop their trousers on screen. A bell pull was needed for one scene, and Stroheim insisted it must actually ring, though of course no one would ever hear it since this was a silent film. Worst of all, Stroheim had spent three days teaching some extras how to salute in the correct dragoon manner, and all for a shot that would last no longer than three seconds on screen. This time Thalberg didn't even bother arguing with Stroheim. He simply informed him that he was being replaced by Rupert Julian, the director of *The Hunchback of Notre Dame.*

Leaving Universal, Stroheim approached Goldwyn about filming *McTeague,* Frank Norris's Zolaesque novel of the effects of greed on five people of minimal intelligence. The film, reentitled *Greed,* was to be the fulfillment of one of Stroheim's dreams: he wanted to bring a novel to the screen virtually complete, without any of the telescoping or prettifying of incident that was considered to be the quintessence of the screen adaptor's craft. In short, he planned to start at page one and film every passage of the book until he came to the final paragraph some four hundred pages later.

One of the great mysteries of film history is how Stroheim ever got approval for this insane project. But somehow he managed it, and late in 1922, he began shooting on location in San Francisco and later, for the concluding scenes, in Death Valley, where production conditions were the worst imaginable. When shooting was completed at a cost of $470,000, Stroheim spent many weeks cutting the film down to what he considered the bare minimum, but the Goldwyn Company was not satisfied. There was no feasible way, Stroheim was informed, to release a picture that ran so long.

After the merger, Stroheim immediately approached Loew with the idea of opening a five-hour version of *Greed* in two parts, separated by a dinner intermission. After conferring with Mayer, who predicted the film was bound to be a failure, Loew turned thumbs down—the American distribution system was then too inflexible to handle a film like *Greed*. Occasionally pictures that were considered "special," either because of length or quality, were initially shown in big cities on a two-a-day policy at advanced (legitimate theatre) prices, and then nationally at regular admission prices, and often in abbreviated versions that allowed the exhibitor to stay close to his regular program schedule. *Greed*, however, would need a lot of cutting before it was ready to play the neighborhood houses.

The *Greed* problem was passed along to Thalberg who, with the aid of a studio cutter, managed to get the film down to ten reels or about two hours of screen time. Outraged, Stroheim said his film had been "dismembered" by "a hack with one eye on the clock and his hat." This is not quite fair: the release version of *Greed* is perfectly logical and extraordinarily powerful. Ravaged though it may be, it still stands as Stroheim's one indisputable masterpiece.

But of course it is only the tattered remnant of the picture Stroheim had wanted to make, and purists were quick to accuse Mayer and Thalberg of butchering one of the greatest achievements of film history. Those who defend Mayer and Thalberg argue that they had no choice but to act as they did, and that Stroheim was being self-destructive in deliberately flouting the conventions and realities of 1920s picture making. There is right on both sides, but the debate still goes on whenever and wherever *Greed* is shown, with Mayer and Thalberg invariably ending up as the villains of the melodrama. On one point, however, there can be no argument. As Mayer had predicted, *Greed* was a box office flop—it had no appeal for audiences who went to the movies expecting something more entertaining than an uncompromising portrait of grass-roots capitalism.

"Good people make me look good," Mayer had said. Besides the obvious egocentric meaning of this statement, he was perhaps also implying that "good" people made the studio look good. By kicking up a ruckus about *Greed*, Stroheim had made Metro-Goldwyn look bad, and that was unforgivable. Mayer expected his employees, no matter how talented they might be, to be loyal to him, the studio, Hollywood and the industry. Some part of his argument with star directors (and later with star writers) was their condescension to the system that was feeding them and, in many cases, making them rich. Despite what he said, Mayer would never get on his knees before talent, no matter how outstanding, if that talent lacked loyalty.

An example of the kind of director Mayer liked, one who possessed both loyalty and talent, was Victor Seastrom, a Swede who had been brought to this country by the Goldwyn Company in 1921. Seastrom's first American film, *Name the Man,* was neither a critical nor a popular success, but after the merger, Mayer personally selected Seastrom to supervise one of Metro-Goldwyn's first major productions, an adaptation of Leonid Andreyev's celebrated play *He Who Gets Slapped.* This story of a renowned scientist who becomes a circus clown after being betrayed by his wife was too wordy to be ideal silent-screen material, but by emphasizing the circus background, excising Andreyev's muddled philosophism and building up the importance of the juvenile and ingenue leads, Seastrom and scenarist Carey Wilson turned it into a highly effective film. Mordaunt Hall, the critic for *The New York Times,* wrote, "Seastrom has directed this dramatic story with all the genius of a Lubitsch or a Chaplin," and at the end of the year, placed the film on his ten-best list for 1924.

Before the picture went into release, Mayer called Seastrom into his office and offered to revise the contract the director had signed with the Goldwyn company. The terms of the new pact provided a substantial increase in salary, but included no profit-sharing arrangement as had the former agreement. This, Mayer insisted, was to Seastrom's advantage since it was impossible to predict the returns for any film and therefore the director would be well advised to accept a flat salary. Happy at having a second chance at proving himself in America, Seastrom readily agreed and from then on, he was one of Mayer's most ardent admirers.

Mayer has often been accused of acting deviously with Seastrom, and there can be no doubt that in eliminating the director's percentage, he was hoping to save the studio some money, which was one of the functions of his job. But in the long run, the new contract was to Seastrom's advantage. The best of his subsequent films for Metro-Goldwyn—*Confessions of a Queen, The Scarlet Letter, The Wind*—paid off in prestige, not money.

If Seastrom's reputation never quite equalled that of Chaplin or Lubitsch or Griffith, it was partly because his films were a bit too somber and remote for American taste and partly because he was never really pushed as a "star director." From the outset, the M-G-M press department was geared toward publicizing actors, not directors, a policy that was already evident in the promotional campaign for *He Who Gets Slapped.* In keeping with Mayer's and Thalberg's belief that it was stars who sold box office tickets, the emphasis was placed on the leading players, Lon Chaney, Norma Shearer and John Gilbert. And since Chaney was not as yet under contract to M-G-M, most of the spotlight was centered on Shearer and Gilbert, who were the first actors to be built into stars by the new company.

Norma Shearer was one of the contract people Mayer had brought from his Mission Road studio to M-G-M. A Canadian, she was born in 1900 to a well-to-do family then living in Montreal, but shortly to move to Toronto. Her father, who quickly disappears from all accounts of the family history, was completely overshadowed by his wife, Edith, a glamorous socialite given to wearing costume jewelry, oversized hats, elaborate frocks and too much mascara. (Later her daughter's Hollywood friends referred to her as the Merry Widow.) There were two other children, Douglas and Athole, but when the family savings were wiped out in a 1920 stock market crash, Mrs. Shearer pinned all her hopes on Norma, who had taken top place in several local teen-age beauty pageants.

In a moment of frank self-appraisal, Norma once admitted that she had "bad arms, bad legs and a slight cast in one eye," but she was also vivacious, trim and endowed with a beautiful profile. With time, she learned to make the best of these liabilities. When her mother suggested she try for a career in show business, Norma readily agreed. "I was scared," she later admitted, "but I wanted to help Mother and I figured that if I worked very hard I might make it. Besides, anything was better than being genteel poor in Toronto."

Accompanied by her mother and sister, Norma arrived in New York in the summer of 1920. She tried out for the *Follies*, but after one look at her legs, Flo Ziegfeld advised her to abandon all hope of becoming a Broadway show girl. For several weeks, Norma struggled along until she found work as a bit player in movies—she can be glimpsed briefly in a crowd scene in Griffith's *Way Down East*—and as a model for magazine illustrators. Her first break came when she pushed her head and one shoulder through a tire and posed as "Miss Lotta Miles," a trademark beauty who graced the advertisements of the Kelly-Springfield Tire Company.

Norma did in fact get a lot of mileage out of Lotta Miles. With her picture in every paper and magazine and on the back of every playbill, she quickly progressed from bits to leading roles in feature films made by some lesser independent producers. Her second break came when Mayer wired an East Coast friend saying he was looking for "a sedate and attractive" actress for an upcoming picture. Mayer's friend recommended Shearer, and Thalberg supported the nomination: he too had been impressed by Lotta Miles.

On arrival at the Union Pacific station in Los Angeles, Norma and her mother were met by Irving Thalberg, whom they mistook for an officeboy or secretary. Feeling slighted by this paltry welcome, Norma pulled herself up to full grandeur and haughtily announced that she had accepted Mayer's offer—$150 a week—though it was less flattering than other proposals she had received. Hal Roach had promised her more, but on the condition that she change her name, which she wasn't willing to do, and after that Universal had tried to lure her to the West Coast with a contract starting at $200 a week.

Thalberg listened attentively, nodded his head a few times, but was forced to contradict Norma on one point: Universal had indeed been interested in giving her a contract, but certainly not at $200 a week—he knew because he had then been Carl Laemmle's assistant. Realizing that she had been caught in a foolish lie, Shearer had the good sense to drop her airs and keep her mouth shut until they arrived at the studio.

Later she made no protest when director John Stahl decided she wasn't attractive enough for the part she had been brought from New York to play. Docilely, she accepted a much smaller role in that film and was properly grateful when Mayer and Thalberg rewarded her good sportsmanship with the ingenue lead in another picture, *Pleasure Mad.* This was the story of a middle-aged man who abandons his wife and children for a younger woman, only to discover that he had been temporarily driven mad "by the modern Baal, the false god of those who place pleasure above all else." Norma played the pleasure-seeker's daughter, who is nearly led astray by his superficial values. It was a nice part, with a couple of meaty scenes, but Shearer attacked them in a ladylike manner, seemingly unaware that she was constantly being upstaged by veteran character actress, Mary Alden, who was playing her mother. Director Reginald Barker couldn't flatter, threaten or goose her into showing more emotion, so he spoke to Mayer, who invited Norma to his office for a little chat.

"Things aren't going well," he said, "what's the problem?" In the politest terms possible, she explained that she had difficulties in communicating with Barker, that she admired Miss Alden and wouldn't dream of doing anything to upset her, that she had a migraine one week and a bad stomach the next. The list of rationalizations went on and on until Mayer suddenly jumped to his feet. "You know what's wrong with you?" he shouted. Norma shrunk back into her seat. His face was red and he was waving a finger at her as though it were a bayonet. "The trouble with you is you're yellow!"

This was one of the first performances of a show that, with continual refinements and a constant change of cast, would run for years. It was called Louis B. Mayer's Pep Talk. Sometimes the show was staged for a group, sometimes for a single individual, but no matter what the size of the audience, the performance was pretty much the same. So was the response—no one ever came away unimpressed by Lionel Barrymore Mayer's flair for the dramatic.

The reaction Mayer hoped for, however, was the one Norma Shearer gave him. Contritely, she confessed that she agreed with his estimate of her work, and promised that in the future she would do better. "Please give me another chance—please, I can do it," she begged. This was all Mayer wanted to hear. Norma did shape up and though her performance in *Pleasure Mad* went unnoticed, Mayer was ready to stand behind her.

During her first year and a half with the Mayer company, Shearer made seven pictures, half of them on loan-outs to other studios, but the first time she really registered with the public was as Consuelo, the bareback rider, in Metro-Goldwyn's *He Who Gets Slapped*. (She wears a tutu throughout much of the movie, and her figure looks just fine—so much for "bad arms and bad legs"—but that "cast in one eye" is really a problem.) A short while later, she had another personal success in *The Snob*, the story of a New York socialite working incognito as a schoolteacher in a Pennsylvania Mennonite community.

In both films she appeared with John Gilbert, who was already on the brink of stardom when he came to M-G-M. Entering film in 1916, he had gone from extra work to a leading role in one of Mary Pickford's lesser efforts, *Heart o' the Hills*, to a wide variety of parts in Fox pictures. It wasn't until he came to M-G-M in 1924 that a Gilbert screen personality was finally established. In the three films he made that year—two with Shearer and, most importantly, *His Hour*, an Elinor Glyn concoction in which he played a Romanov roué named Price Gritzko—he emerged as one of the silent screen's great lovers.

Though equally comfortable in costume and modern roles, Gilbert was the epitome of a certain kind of 1920s male glamour: sleek, slender, delicately boned, he had the expensive look of an elegantly kept gigolo. There was something weak, a touch of the effete, about his features, but this was offset by his poise and sexual assurance. The intensity he brought to his love scenes was virile and yet so extravagant that it suggested an earlier and more romantic age when heroes were reputed to die of wounded hearts and thwarted passion.

Offscreen he was carefree, reckless, party-loving, slightly mad in the legendary silent screen manner. That at least is the portrait etched by his friends. His enemies (who are of equal number) claim he was conceited, childish, rebellious and generally impossible. He boozed heavily, though apparently drink was not a serious problem until the very end of his career. There were lots of wives and many gaudy romances, but the untidiness of his love life was not entirely of his own making. One of his wives, actress Leatrice Joy, recently commented, "Every day there were propositioning letters and telephone calls at all hours. Jack was innocent, but I just wasn't able to get used to it."

At M-G-M, Gilbert found a true friend in Thalberg, but his relations with Mayer were not so pleasant. The source of contention was Gilbert's irreverence toward women, particularly his own mother, a stock company actress who went by the stage name of Ada Adaire. As a child, Jack had occasionally acted with his mother and once, when she was playing Empress Josephine, he was cast as a page who carried her train. Before the opening performance, Ada downed a few stiff drinks, and by curtain time she was noticeably unsteady on her feet. Staggering out from the wings, she managed to reach stage center where she tripped and fell on her face. Her train flew up, revealing that she had neglected to put on her bloomers. "And that," Gilbert said, "was the first and last time I saw my mother's bare ass."

Mayer was not amused. He told Thalberg that he wanted no part of anyone who showed so little respect for his mother. Later, when his anger had subsided, he agreed that it would be foolish to dismiss Gilbert on such slender grounds, but within a few weeks the actor dropped another remark that rubbed Mayer the wrong way. In the middle of a story conference, Gilbert casually mentioned that he doubted whether his mother knew who his father had been—she was a whore and he probably was a bastard.

Enraged, Mayer jumped to his feet and threatened to apply a knife to a vital part of the actor's anatomy. As he fled toward the door, Gilbert shot back, "Go ahead. I'll still be more of a man than you!"

Once again Thalberg waded in and calmed the troubled waters. Gilbert could be trying, he admitted, but he was also earning a lot of money for the studio. And what more could anyone reasonably expect? It was unrealistic, he continued, for Mayer to expect to like or be liked by everybody who worked for him. Logically Mayer knew this was true, but emotionally it was hard for him to accept. It ran counter to all his ideas of how a studio should be run.

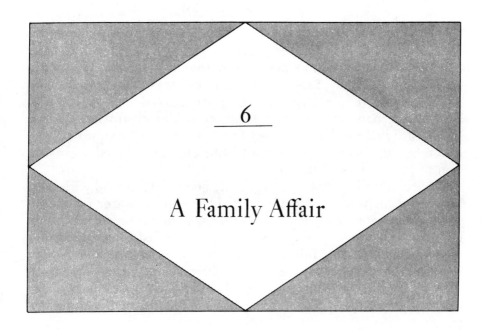

6

A Family Affair

"Think big," Mayer had told Thalberg, and now M-G-M showed signs of becoming bigger than anything either had ever imagined. But despite its size, Mayer wanted the studio to have an esprit, a team or family feeling that didn't exist at other film companies. According to his blueprint, M-G-M was to be one large happy household, built on loyalty and mutual respect, with everyone finding satisfaction and fulfillment in working toward the common goal of making the best pictures possible.

By 1925, with Thalberg's aid, Mayer had already started to assemble his family of workers, many of whom would stay at M-G-M until they died or reached the age of retirement. One of the first of this faithful band was Harry Rapf, who had worked at the Mission Road studio as Thalberg's assistant. A former vaudevillian, with a huge nose and a knack for fractured English ("This is the best pie I ever ate in my whole mouth"), Rapf was ebullient and lovable, closer to Mayer than to Thalberg in taste and temperament. After the move to Culver City, he was given the same title as Thalberg—assistant to the vice-president in charge of production (Mayer)—but his duties remained essentially the same. He was still Thalberg's assistant, though he was given almost total control over the company's lesser, grade B productions.

Though the workload was awesome, Thalberg was reluctant to increase his staff until Mayer promised him that no one would ever be allowed to challenge or usurp his authority. With this assurance, he began building up a small cadre of associates to help him develop and supervise the year's output of pictures. His first recruit was Bernard Hyman, who had met Thalberg at Universal where he had been a story editor; later he tried free-lancing as a director and producer, but with such little success that he eagerly accepted the invitation to join Thalberg at M-G-M.

Next came Hunt Stromberg, a tall, good-looking man with wiry hair and a slight nervous tic, who had been sports editor for the St. Louis *Times* before entering film in 1918 as publicist for the Goldwyn company. Since then, he had written and directed films for various studios, and had also independently produced several low-budget pictures of various types, including three Harry Carey Westerns. "I've got very broad interests," he told an interviewer at the time he joined Metro in 1925. "I kind of pride myself on the way I can change pace."

Perhaps the most difficult position for Thalberg to fill was that of literary adviser, someone who could sift through vast amounts of printed matter—everything from newspapers and magazines to the latest novels and plays—and come up with two or three stories that might be suitable for filming. Thalberg had arrived at some very definite ideas about what kind of material was appropriate for picture adaptation. For instance, he didn't put much faith in spectacles or any other type of story in which the scenery took precedence over the characters. Audiences wanted to connect with the people on the screen, which meant that the people on the screen had to reflect the values and aspirations of the audience. Moviegoers wanted to cheer the hero, hiss the villain and suffer along with the heroine. They wanted to be reassured; they didn't want to leave the theatre feeling confused or angry or threatened.

It was an extremely simple and straightforward approach to film making, one that emphasized narrative and character values above all else. Thalberg's only problem was in finding someone who could spot exactly what he was looking for in a story or script. His search finally ended when Hunt Stromberg suggested Kate Corbaley, a former librarian and creative-writing teacher who had headed the story department of the Ince studio when Stromberg was working there. Mrs. Corbaley had all the qualifications for the job—knowledge, experience, compulsive reading habits. Every night she'd go home with a stack of books under her arm and return the next morning with a detailed appraisal of the screen potential of every-thing she had read.

Thalberg came to rely on her heavily, as did Mayer and the other studio executives, many of whom had neither the time nor the incli-nation to scan the synopses and scripts that had been earmarked as production possibilities. Therefore Mrs. Corbaley was often called in to provide a verbal summation. Since she was an inspired storyteller, her version was usually better than the original: she would embellish her narration to point up the cinematic potentialities of the material under consideration while playing down those elements which might give offense. Mayer was so mesmerized by her talents that she became known as his private Scheherazade. He never bothered to read a script when Mrs. Corbaley was around to tell it to him.

The word spread throughout Hollywood that a hiring spree was in progress at M-G-M, but of course not all Mayer and Thalberg's key personnel were recruited from outside: some members were acquired through the merger. Cedric Gibbons, for example, had been art director for the Goldwyn company, and Mayer and Thalberg agreed that they could find no one more qualified to fill this post for M-G-M.

Born in Brooklyn in 1893, Gibbons came from a family of ar-chitects, and was being schooled to follow in his father's and grandfa-ther's footsteps when he flunked mathematics. Showing an aptitude for painting and sculpture, he enrolled at the Art Students League in New York, and on graduation, served an apprenticeship with muralist and portrait painter Hugo Ballin, who occasionally moon-lighted as a designer of stage and film sets. In 1914, when he became art director for Thomas Edison's studio in Bedford, New York, Bal-lin took along Gibbons as his assistant. The two artists were shocked to discover that the studio still depended heavily on painted scenery —if an actor was required to place his glove on a windowsill, he had to pin it to a canvas flat. Gibbons built a real windowsill, the first of many innovations that quickly earned him a promotion to full-fledged art director.

After two years with Edison, Gibbons went to work for the Goldwyn company, first at its Fort Lee, New Jersey, studio, later at Culver City. His contract stipulated that he receive credit for art direction on every picture the company filmed in whole or in part in the United States. This clause was retained when he signed a new contract with M-G-M.

Handsome and urbane, Gibbons was also somewhat aloof; around the lot he was known as Gibby, but few dared to use the nickname in his presence. A connoisseur of elegance in all forms, from expensive cars to beautiful women, he set high standards for himself and his staff. All his designs were drawn in accordance with what he called his philosophy of the uncluttered—they were clean, functional and often highly stylized, a look that was to cause a major revolution in movie decor.

Another Goldwyn employee who was retained by M-G-M was J. J. ("Joe") Cohn, a tough and wiry individual who had started as a bookeeper at the Goldwyn studio in Fort Lee. Moving west, he swiftly worked his way up to the position of production manager. His major responsibilities were the budgeting and scheduling of every production, two chores he carried out with one motto in mind: "Do everything as inexpensively as possible." He figured that one of the primary functions of his job was to save money for the studio, and if that meant stepping on a few toes, he was prepared to take that step.

From the outset, Cohn's job had its nightmarish moments. At any given time, there could be as many as ten to twenty pictures in various stages of production, all of them requiring daily attention. But near the beginning of 1925, his work load became even more awesome as one of the biggest pictures of the silent era began shooting on the Culver City lot.

Ben Hur started out as a Goldwyn production, one of the company's final efforts to salvage its waning prestige. But from the start, the project was so badly mismanaged that it seemed doomed for failure. The film rights to General Lew Wallace's celebrated novel—the first work of fiction to be blessed by a pope—had been acquired from a syndicate headed by theatrical producer Abe Erlanger (whose father had produced a stage version of Wallace's Roman epic) on a profit-sharing arrangement that guaranteed Erlanger and his partners 50 percent of all *gross* receipts. They were also granted final approval of director, scriptwriter and the casting of the leading roles.

June Mathis, who was then Hollywood's most acclaimed scenarist—she had written the adaptation of Blasco-Ibáñez's novel *The Four Horsemen of the Apocalypse* and was otherwise instrumental in establishing Valentino as a top star—won the assignment of adapting Wallace's novel for the screen. In fact, *Ben Hur* became her baby—she was responsible for selecting Charles Brabin as director, George Walsh for the title role and Francis X. Bushman for the part of Hur's rival, Messala.

All in all, these were very peculiar choices—Brabin had never directed anything nearly as monumental as *Ben Hur*; Walsh was a colorless leading man of the second rank; Bushman (the star of

Mayer's 1915 serial, *The Great Secret*) had seen better days, in terms of his career and his physical appearance. But the Goldwyn executives and the Erlanger syndicate had faith in Mathis and went along with most of her ideas.

There were, however, some murmurs of protest when she decided the film had to be made on location in Rome. Since none of Ben Hur's Rome then existed except in ruins, it's difficult to understand why she thought this was so essential; but she did, and to humor her, the Goldwyn company agreed to send a committee of two over to Italy to investigate the picture-making climate. One of the scouts was Joe Cohn, who was not impressed by the lax habits and unprofessional conditions that prevailed throughout the Italian film industry. But his opinion was challenged by his teammate, Goldwyn vice-president Major Edward Bowes (later to become famous as the host of the famous radio Amateur Hour). Intoxicated by the glory and splendor, the wine and *belle ragazze* of Rome, Major Bowes was expansive and persuasive in his arguments for shooting the film abroad.

At the time of the merger, *Ben Hur* was already in production in Italy. But as far as Marcus Loew could ascertain, not much had been accomplished. There was very little footage to show for all the time and money that had been spent, and none of it was of very promising quality. "The rushes looked like a bad delicatessen sandwich," an industry insider told a fan magazine reporter. "The sets are cheesy, the wigs look like shredded lettuce, the makeup is a mixture of mayonnaise and Russian dressing and the acting is stale ham."

At this point, the picture was entirely Loew's problem. Because of the percentage deal with the Erlanger syndicate, he had not wanted to give Mayer and Thalberg a cut of the profits, and their contracts with Loew's, Inc. specified that *Ben Hur* lay outside their province of interest and control. But as the weeks passed with no noticeable improvement in the footage shipped from Italy, Loew reconsidered and asked Mayer to take charge.

Fully informed about the *Ben Hur* debacle, Mayer immediately suggested that Mathis, Brabin and Walsh be replaced. Loew had already been thinking along similar lines—in fact, he had as much as promised Brabin's job to Rex Ingram. Mayer, however, didn't want Ingram, who couldn't be trusted to stick to a shooting schedule. Instead he suggested one of his Mission Road directors, Fred Niblo, who had staged a couple of the Fairbanks swashbucklers and therefore had some experience in handling the spectacle type of film. And as screenwriter, Mayer wanted another of his Mission Road favorites, Bess Meredyth. Loew accepted these suggestions; he even agreed to replacing Walsh, who had appeared in only a few brief scenes. But he warned Mayer that these changes had to be kept quiet until the Erlanger syndicate had approved them.

Originally Thalberg wasn't much interested in *Ben Hur*—it wasn't his kind of film—but eventually he got caught up in the excitement of trying to rescue this floundering whale of a production. At the very last minute, it was he who came up with the idea of substituting Ramon Novarro for George Walsh as Ben Hur, and of asking Carey Wilson (one of his favorite screenwriters) to help Bess Meredyth in the task of bringing order to June Mathis's jumbled screenplay.

Once the Erlanger group had approved the changes, Niblo, Novarro, Meredyth, Wilson and Robert Rubin (acting as Loew's representative) sailed for Italy. Before leaving, they were asked to tell reporters that they were going abroad for a vacation. The reason for this subterfuge was that the staff working in Rome had not as yet been informed of the shake-up. On learning they were being replaced, Mathis and Walsh accepted the news stoically, but Brabin was outraged. He promptly sued M-G-M for $575,000, claiming his reputation had been irreparably damaged. (The suit was dropped a few weeks later when Brabin was hired as director of *So Big*, an adaptation of Edna Ferber's best-selling novel, starring Colleen Moore.)

All work on *Ben Hur* stopped for two months while Meredyth and Wilson put together a new script. Then they returned to Hollywood and Niblo began shooting in Italy. The problems he faced were horrendous. Few crew members spoke English, and those who did pretended they couldn't whenever it was to their advantage. There were several labor disputes which halted production, and in general the Italians did everything in slow motion because, as a workman told Francis X. Bushman, "When this film is finished, we'll be out of a job for many months."

One of the first sequences Niblo supervised was the sea battle, shot on location at Livorno. For this crucial scene, several sturdy, seaworthy Roman galleys had been constructed and, at a climactic moment, one was to be set afire. The extras had been told precisely what they should do, and they seemed to understand, but once the galley started to burn, they panicked and jumped into the sea. That night several bit players failed to show up at the wardrobe department to exchange their costumes for street clothes. Whether anyone actually drowned has never been determined, but it is now Hollywood legend that many unknown sailors lost their lives in the filming of the *Ben Hur* sea chase.

With negative reports still coming in daily from Rome, Loew asked Mayer to go abroad and find out what was happening. In August 1924, accompanied by his wife, his daughters, Carey Wilson and Bess Meredyth, he sailed on the S.S. *Leviathan.* The party stopped briefly in Paris for some sightseeing and then moved on to Rome, where Mayer was distressed by the morale of the company. Niblo, usually calm and charming, had become slightly unhinged by all the pressure. He flew into a rage when Mayer questioned him about why so little had been accomplished. A bitter quarrel followed —Niblo threatened to resign, Mayer told him he was fired—but eventually things were patched up through the diplomacy of the company's unofficial mediator, Niblo's wife, actress Enid Bennett.

Mayer also laced into Francis X. Bushman for continually up-staging Ramon Novarro. Ben Hur isn't much of a part, and any decent Messala can steal scenes without really trying, but Bushman was definitely going all out to overshadow Novarro—this was his big chance for a comeback. Oblivious to the unflattering reality that he was less important to M-G-M than Novarro (a contract player), Bush-man couldn't understand why Mayer was upset. So he pulled in his stomach and continued to ham his way through the film.

After a few weeks in Rome, Mayer moved on to Berlin to check out what was happening in the German film industry, and then he and his party returned to Hollywood. In the meantime, another mishap had occurred on the *Ben Hur* set. Niblo had started to shoot the film's showpiece, the chariot race in the Circus Maximus, but everything had gone wrong—horses were killed, Novarro couldn't control his chariot, cameras were misplaced—and none of the footage was usable.

From the beginning, Thalberg and Cohn had urged that the production be transferred to the M-G-M lot, but Mayer had wanted to avoid the expense such a move would entail. Now, however, he admitted defeat and agreed that *Ben Hur* should be completed on the Culver City lot. At the end of January 1925, Niblo and company arrived at the M-G-M studio where the rest of the picture was shot —with the exception of a few potentially hazardous animal se-quences filmed in Mexico to escape the supervision of the American Society for the Prevention of Cruelty to Animals.

Cedric Gibbons and his assistant, Arnold "Buddy" Gillespie, had designed new sets in keeping with the style of those created by Camillo Mastrocinque, the film's original art director. Gibbons's $30,000 replica of the Circus Maximus was so huge that it had to be built on a vacant lot near the studio, and through an oversight, no one bothered to check clearance in using the property. One morning, when the set was about half completed, studio employees were dumbfounded to see a bulldozer appear out of nowhere and start ripping it apart. The driver explained that the city of Los Angeles was laying a new sewage system along an underground route that ran just beneath the M-G-M Circus Maximus. Fortunately, not much damage had been done, and the company was able to persuade municipal officials to postpone the excavation work for a few weeks.

Once this near disaster was averted, the production of *Ben Hur* rolled ahead smoothly. The big event was, of course, the shooting of the chariot race, a moment of Hollywood history that attracted a large crowd of celebrity onlookers including Mary Pickford, Douglas Fairbanks, Lillian Gish, John Gilbert, Harold Lloyd, Colleen Moore and Marion Davies. Mayer, Thalberg and Joe Cohn had decided to shoot as much of the sequence in one day as possible. Forty-two cameras were strategically placed around the set. They were hidden behind shields and statues, buried in sandpits, placed on cars and on pillars, strung aloft, positioned among the throngs filling the coliseum.

Standing in the middle of the arena, dwarfed by one of the huge statues that had been designed to give proportion to the set, Thalberg surveyed the crowd. "How many people do you have up there, Joe?" he asked Cohn.

"Thirty-nine hundred," Cohn answered.

"We need more," Thalberg said. Cohn asked where was he to find more extras at eight o'clock on a Saturday morning. "Pull them in off the street, if necessary," Thalberg replied.

That was precisely what Cohn did. From diners, buses, trolleys, restaurants, all-night movies and markets, he and his assistants corralled another four hundred people, got them dressed in togas, and had them seated in the grandstand and ready for shooting when a thick fog rolled in from the Pacific at about 10 A.M. There was nothing to do but wait until it burned off.

Two hours later, the cameras began to turn. Cohn approached Thalberg and told him it soon would be time for a lunch break and there were only 3,900 box lunches for the 4,300 extras. Thalberg said not to worry—they wouldn't break for lunch, they'd shoot straight through the afternoon.

"But those people are hungry," Cohn protested. "They may riot . . ."

"Fine," Thalberg said. "That'll add some realism to the scene."

Ben Hur opened in New York on December 30, 1925, to enthusiastic press and public response. It eventually grossed over $9 million, but because of the huge production cost and the percentage deal with the Erlanger syndicate, it never returned a profit to M-G-M. But in this case, money wasn't everything. *Ben Hur* brought enormous prestige to the studio, especially to Mayer and Thalberg who had taken a film that was destined for failure and turned it into a critical and popular success.

M-G-M publicized the film with a torso shot of Ramon Novarro stripped to within an inch of his pubic hairs. He looked smashing, but the campaign to promote him as Valentino's peer never quite worked. He was to have a substantial, but not dazzling, career in the silent era.

Francis X. Bushman was less fortunate. *Ben Hur* virtually ended his reign as an important star, a turn of events that he accused Mayer of arranging. Mayer, he claimed, disliked him, not only because of what had happened in Rome, but also because of an earlier incident that occurred when he was appearing in a play called *Midsummer Masquerade* in Los Angeles. Mayer and his wife had then gone backstage to pay a courtesy visit, but because of an oversight on the part of his valet, Bushman was never informed they were waiting to see him. This unintentional snub, the actor insisted, was the reason that Mayer later had him "blacklisted" in the industry.

While it is true that Mayer had no great affection for Bushman, no one—except Bushman sympathizers and mogul-haters—placed much credence in this tale of revenge. Even if he had tried to destroy Bushman, Mayer probably wouldn't have gotten very far, since rarely has anyone in the industry, no matter how much power he might wield, been able to blacklist an actor the public wants to see. Behind Bushman's decline, there was nothing more sinister than the fact that at age forty-four, he was no longer the broth of a boy he once had been.

Ben Hur was not the only troublesome picture on M-G-M's 1925 agenda. Mayer also had to contend with another headache called *The Merry Widow,* an adaptation of Franz Lehar's famed operetta which Erich von Stroheim was filming to finish his contract with the Goldwyn company. Erich the Terrible and Lehar the Lighthearted made strange bedfellows, and indeed Stroheim was interested in the operetta only as a framework for an exposé of Austro-Hungarian depravity. "My intention," he said, "is to show the degeneracy lurking behind Lehar's Belle Epoque waltzes."

There was no question that something had to be done about the plot of *The Merry Widow,* which was weak even by libretto standards, but Stroheim's approach was about as exhilarating as exposing the artifice of a Fabergé egg by plastering it with straw and chicken droppings. Worse yet, Stroheim obviously thought of the production as another Stroheim masterpiece while M-G-M clearly intended it as a vehicle for John Gilbert (Danilo) and Mae Murray (Sonya, or as she is renamed in the film, Sally O'Hara). Someone had made a major miscalculation in putting together the talent for this picture. Gilbert perhaps could have adapted to Stroheim's scheme, but Mae Murray, a diminutive blonde celebrated for her "bee-stung" lips, was offended by "pornographic" liberties he took with Lehar's "frothy divertissement." In a moment of unbridled disgust, she called Stroheim "a dirty Hun."

From then on, Stroheim tried his best to shoot the picture with as few close-ups of Murray as possible, and once, as she started to embrace John Gilbert, he made chuck-up sounds and turned his back. "Tell me when it's over," he said. He also insulted her in three languages, and once when she protested that she was, after all, a highly regarded actress, he replied, *"Actrice? Non, vous faites le tapin"* (which translates politely as "your true profession is streetwalking").

Finally Murray complained to Mayer, who was already concerned over rumors of the amount of time Stroheim was spending over shots of elderly gentlemen fondling high-heeled slippers—apparently all Austro-Hungarian aristocrats were shoe fetishists—as well as reports from Joe Cohn that the director was paying no attention to his schedule or budget. He decided it was time to have a chat with Stroheim.

Mayer asked the director to justify his treatment of Miss Murray. Stroheim thought for a moment and then posed a question of his own: had Mayer read the screenplay? Mayer admitted he hadn't. "Sally O'Hara [the heroine] is a whore," Stroheim commented.

"We don't make pictures about whores at this studio," Mayer said.

Stroheim shrugged. "All women are whores," he replied matter-of-factly.

Mayer grabbed the director by the collar and literally kicked him out of the office.

The next day Stroheim was replaced on the set by Monta Bell, a director noted for his sophisticated, light comedies. The crew, however, refused to work with Bell, and a full-scale mutiny was about to erupt when Mayer arrived to give one of his pep talks. There are conflicting reports about what he said and how he said it, but the upshot was that he gained a little and lost a little. He restored morale, but only by rehiring Stroheim, who promised to apologize to Mae Murray after she apologized to him.

Once these courtesies had been exchanged, Stroheim returned to work and turned in a picture that was several thousand feet over length. Mayer told Thalberg to tell Stroheim it would have to be cut. Stroheim said he couldn't do it. "All right," Thalberg replied, "I'll do it for you." Surprisingly, Stroheim didn't protest.

With the aid of editor Margaret Booth, Thalberg got the picture down to regulation length by eliminating most of Stroheim's Krafft-Ebing commentary on the original libretto. The bowdlerized *Merry Widow* is often handsome to look at, a little heavy-handed perhaps, but fun in a mindless way. Gilbert is properly dashing (and occasionally slightly lewd) as Danilo, and Mae Murray is everything any Mae Murray fan might have hoped for. (Stroheim admirers claim this is the one effective performance of her career, but actually, it's not much better or worse than several others.) A hit with both critics and public, *The Merry Widow* was one of the top-grossing pictures of 1925, but Stroheim was never again to work as a director at M-G-M.

While Stroheim was reviving the decadence of Austro-Hungary and Niblo was reconstructing the splendors of Rome, elsewhere on the M-G-M lot King Vidor was preparing a restaging of the Great War for a picture that started small and then grew into *The Big Parade*. And everyone involved in the production grew with it—Mayer, Thalberg, the actors and most of all director King Vidor, who had been working at Metro at the time of the merger. For that company he supervised such fine, though now nearly forgotten, films as *Wine of Youth* (starring his actress-wife Eleanor Boardman) and two charming Laurette Taylor vehicles, *Peg o' My Heart* and *Happiness*. Thalberg recognized Vidor's ability and queried him about his ambitions as a director. "What kind of material appeals to you," he asked. "Tell me the subjects that interest you."

Without hesitation, Vidor answered, "Wheat, steel and war." These three topics reflect Vidor's social and humanitarian interests —he often thought of the heroes of his films as "Mr. Anybody"—and the first two were to provide the foundation for much of his later work. But it was war that intrigued Thalberg. There hadn't been a really powerful movie drama about the war with the arguable exception of D. W. Griffith's *Hearts of the World*, and that had been made seven years before.

With Vidor in mind, Thalberg traveled to New York to see Broadway's latest smash hit, Maxwell Anderson and Laurence Stallings's *What Price Glory?*, a war comedy noted for its raw dialogue and pacifist sentiments. He tried to buy the film rights, but was outbid by the Fox Corporation. So he did the next best thing by hiring one of the *Glory* collaborators, ex-marine Laurence Stallings, to write an original screenplay. Traveling west together on the train, they worked out the outline of a story which Stallings named *The Big Parade*.

Thalberg approved this epic-sounding title, though originally the film was planned as a John Gilbert vehicle and was budgeted accordingly at about $200,000. This meant that Gilbert, not Vidor, was the center of the film, but Vidor, who wasn't afflicted with a Stroheim-sized ego, made no objection. He was happy to have the opportunity to make a film on a subject that truly concerned him and to discover that within certain limitations, he was free to adapt Stallings's sketchy script to his own purposes.

Vidor strengthened and humanized the script's stereotyped characters through improvisations, including the greatly admired scene in which doughboy Jimmy Apperson (Gilbert) introduces Mélisande (Renée Adorée), a French milkmaid, to the joys of American chewing gum. As Thalberg watched the daily rushes, he realized the picture had the potential of being something more important than a Gilbert vehicle. After he had seen the last reel, he told Mayer, "The picture's great, but it isn't finished yet."

After looking at a rough cut, Mayer agreed that *The Big Parade* should have the epic sweep its title promised, but that meant going back into production and shooting new footage that would give the film added dimension of importance. But no money could be spent on revising *The Big Parade* without the approval of Marcus Loew and his associates. And winning their support could be difficult. The picture, as it existed, was already a better-than-average John Gilbert feature, so why spend more cash on trying to improve it?

Feeling certain he could answer this question, Mayer rushed to New York to confer with the Loew's, Inc. executives. At the first meeting, he described and acted out the thrilling scenes that would be added to the picture with such enthusiasm and conviction that he got exactly what Thalberg and Vidor needed—$75,000.

A few weeks later, *The Big Parade* went back into production for the filming of additional battle scenes, including the famous sequence in which a troop of American infantrymen march as methodically as wind-up toy soldiers through a sun-drenched forest to almost certain death. Two other scenes—one involving a cigarette, the other a flower—were equally memorable and both have been endlessly copied in later war films, including the much overrated *All Quiet on the Western Front*.

The Big Parade opened at New York's Astor Theatre as a road show (advanced-priced, two shows a day) engagement in November 1925, to glowing reviews, especially for Vidor and John Gilbert, who for the first (and virtually last) time of his career, received serious critical attention. Costing about $380,000, it grossed almost $3 million, a record-breaking figure for the silent era.

All in all, 1925 was a very good year for Mayer, Thalberg and M-G-M. The studio turned out forty-six films, and while only a handful lived up to the M-G-M motto, *Ars Gratia Artis* ("Art for Art's Sake"), the vast majority were well above average in quality. They were also above average in box office returns. For the fiscal year ending August 31, 1925, the studio showed a net profit of over $4.7 million, and early reports indicated a much greater profit for 1926.

On the strength of this record, Mayer asked Loew's, Inc. to revise the contracts for the so-called Mayer Group, which included Thalberg and Bob Rubin. After lengthy negotiations, Mayer's salary was raised from $1,500 to $2,000 a week; Thalberg's jumped from $650 to $2,000, and Rubin's from $600 to $1,000. Additionally, they were guaranteed that their collective share of M-G-M profits would never fall below $500,000 a year.

The disproportionate increase awarded to Thalberg—bringing him to the same salary level as Mayer himself—was, of course, a reflection of his contribution to the success of the company. His importance had been dramatically illustrated a few months earlier when he collapsed during the shooting of *Ben Hur.* On arrival at the hospital he was given no more than a fifty-fifty chance of surviving. A pall fell over the studio. Workers spoke in hushed tones while a red-eyed and ashen Mayer stayed alone in his office, vigilantly awaiting a message from the hospital.

Good news arrived two days later. Thalberg had passed the crisis and would recover. But, the doctors cautioned, he would need bed rest for a long period. They had not, however, taken into account their patient's determination and ambition. Even before he was able to sit up in bed, he was watching the rushes of *Ben Hur* as they were projected on the ceiling of his room, and once he could be propped up, he read late into the night, taking notes on script problems and story ideas for the forthcoming year. In less than a month, he was on his feet, and two weeks later, defying his mother and doctors, he returned to work.

It was just after this that he demanded a raise that forced Mayer to open new contract negotiations with Loew. There had been little doubt that he would get what he wanted—everyone (including, perhaps, Thalberg) thought Thalberg was indispensable to the continued growth and success of the company. Of course, no one had failed to consider what might happen if someday—and possibly not so very distant a someday—M-G-M had to get along without its production genius. Mayer had given the problem a lot of thought, but encouraged by Thalberg's amazing recuperative powers, he was able to put it out of his mind. Things would stay the way they were.

For the time being.

two

The Thalberg Years

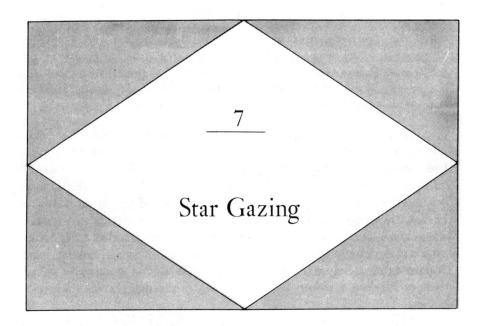

7

Star Gazing

At the start of the fiscal year 1926–27, Metro-Goldwyn-Mayer published a lavishly illustrated promotional brochure listing its solid gold assets. The first page read:

GREAT THEATRES
Loew's State   The Capitol
New York's Home for M-G-M Pictures

THE GREAT TRIUMVIRATE
Marcus Loew   Nicholas Schenck   Louis B. Mayer

GREAT PRODUCERS
Harry Rapf, Irving Thalberg, Hunt Stromberg, Eddie Mannix,
Bernard Hyman

A GALAXY OF GREAT STARS
Marion Davies, Ramon Novarro, John Gilbert, Norma Shearer, Buster Keaton, Lon Chaney, Mae Murray, Eleanor Boardman, Lionel Barrymore, Renée Adorée, Lew Cody, Greta Garbo, William Haines, Owen Moore, Conrad Nagel, Sally O'Neil, Charles Ray, Pauline Starke, Claire Windsor, Joan Crawford, Mae Busch, Roy D'Arcy

FEATURED PLAYERS
Carmel Myers, Aileen Pringle, George K. Arthur, Karl Dane, Lars Hanson, Antonio Moreno, Alice Terry

OUTSTANDING DIRECTORS

Rex Ingram, King Vidor, Fred Niblo, Tod Browning, John Stahl, John S. Robertson, Victor Seastrom, Reginald Barker, Robert Z. Leonard, Hobart Henley, Edmund Goulding, William Nigh, Mauritz Stiller, Monta Bell, Sam Taylor, Christy Cabanne, Benjamin Christensen, Edward Sedgwick, Jack Conway, George Hill, Clarence Brown, Maurice Tourneur

The prospectus then goes on to describe M-G-M's "Top Box-Office Attractions for the next twelve months." Among the sixty titles listed are six or seven well-known films, but the majority would stump even the trivia experts. *Frisco Sally Levy? Tin Hats? Blarney?* Yes, Metro really did produce these and most of the other films on the list, though some of them didn't turn up in theatres until a few years later—for instance, *Naughty Marietta,* announced as a 1927 Marion Davies vehicle, wasn't put into production until Jeanette MacDonald came along in 1934. And *Polly of the Circus,* originally scheduled for Norma Shearer, languished until Marion Davies took it on in 1932.

There were a small number of films that got lost along the way —things called *Three Twins, Ordeal* and *I Can Do It,* which might have added up to a tantalizing triple bill, at least on the marquee. And there were others that should have been lost. "I went to Mayer to complain about a film," says Bessie Love, "but there was no good talking him out of it. 'Look,' he said, 'we've got these lemons from New York and we have to use them. So we have to fill them up with people who are known to the public.' "

That left a bulk of forty-odd films, all of them forgotten today, but money-winners at the time. Twelve months later, the studio announced a net profit of $6,388,200, which was about $150,000 more than any other studio had cleared during the same period. Metro-Goldwyn-Mayer, formed out of desperation and never given much of a chance by industry soothsayers, had become in three years Hollywood's leading studio.

What was the secret of its success? Industry insiders gave most of the credit to Thalberg. His formula for picture making—entertaining, literate stories with meaty roles for star personalities—was as foolproof as any popular dramatic formula could be. There wasn't anything novel about the idea—Scribe, Sardou and other French playwrights of the nineteenth century had plowed the same ground in creating the well-made play, but Thalberg was one of the first to translate this stage idiom into film terms. M-G-M's great star vehicles for Norma Shearer, Joan Crawford and Greta Garbo are all indebted to Sardou, Dumas, Bernhardt, *La Tosca, La Dame aux Camélias* and the tradition of a kind of theatre that was already obsolete as Thalberg adapted it to the exigencies of M-G-M film-making policy: polish, a well-structured dramatic plot, the semblance of literacy and (above all else) a star.

There's barely a film in the 1926–27 prospectus that isn't intended as a star vehicle or as a vehicle that might push a featured player into the star category. There was nothing novel in this, either. All the studios were traveling the same route, but now that they had plenty of money to play around with, Thalberg and Mayer were determined that M-G-M would have the biggest and best star roster in Hollywood.

In its prospectus, M-G-M boasted many new stars, the most renowned being Lillian Gish, who through her work with D. W. Griffith was widely acclaimed as the screen's foremost actress. Early in 1923, Gish had started free-lancing, but like many former Griffith players who found it hard going when they left the master, Gish's career went into a slight decline: her post-Griffith pictures got good reviews, but financially were only modest successes. So when Mayer made her a very flattering offer—"around $1,000,000 for five or six pictures," she recalls in her autobiography, *The Movies, Mr. Griffith and Me*—she accepted without hesitation.

A banner reading LILLIAN GISH IS NOW A METRO-GOLDWYN-MAYER STAR greeted her as she walked through the gates of the Culver City lot. It was a warm reception, but relations cooled as soon as Gish realized this was the only preparation M-G-M had made for her arrival: there was no property lined up for her first Metro production.

She quickly suggested one of her pet projects, *La Bohème*, which for copyright reasons, was based less on Puccini than on Puccini's source material, Murger's novel *Scènes de la Vie de Bohème*. Thalberg gave his approval and left the choice of director to Gish who, after looking at footage of *The Big Parade*, selected King Vidor. John Gilbert was cast as Rodolph, Renée Adorée as Musette, and the art director was the noted fashion illustrator and *Folies Bergères* couturier, Erté, who was then working at M-G-M on a short-term contract.

The studio's first intimation that Gish was an actress with a strong will—she was, in fact, the original "iron butterfly"—came as she looked over Erté's sketches for Mimi's and Musette's costumes. The sketches (which have survived) were exquisite, but Gish didn't like them. They were, she said, too elegant and expensive-looking for a simple seamstress. Erté explained that they would be made of wool, but Gish insisted the dress should be made of "old silk" for authenticity. (Erté later said Gish wanted silk because she wouldn't wear scratchy fabrics.) She won this round: Adorée wore Erté's gowns, while Lilliań appears in designs close to those she rejected, redone in fabrics she chose.

Next she was extremely upset about the rehearsal procedure at the studio. Working with Mr. Griffith, she had become accustomed to rehearsing a film thoroughly prior to production, but at M-G-M, there were only a few perfunctory run-throughs before a scene went before the camera. Gish did the best she could within the time allotted, and her supporting company was amazed or amused by the concentration and absorption she spent on these preliminaries.

Finally, there was the question: to kiss or not to kiss? Gish maintained that the eroticism of the plot would be built up if Mimi and Rodolph never embraced, and Vidor tended to agree. Mayer and Thalberg disagreed. *La Bohème* was also a John Gilbert vehicle, and Gilbert fans didn't expect their hero to be content with a few soulful glances. Gish was ordered (at the very least) to peck at Gilbert, and she did so with all the enthusiasm of a Vestal Virgin.

Gish's Mimi is chaster than Puccini's Mimi who is chaster than Murger's Mimi—the authenticity of her portrayal lies in its fidelity to her own screen image. Within these limitations, her performance is touching, and the film, beautifully directed by Vidor, was both a critical and financial success, possibly because Gilbert, not Gish, lured the public to the box office.

During the next three years Gish made two other noteworthy films at M-G-M, *The Scarlet Letter* (1926) and *The Wind* (1928), both directed by Victor Seastrom, both box office flops. Her Hester Prynne is not precisely Hawthorne's Hester Prynne, but it is one of the great performances of the silent screen, and her work in *The Wind* is almost as good. Still, for jazz-age audiences, she was too austere, too staunchly entrenched in maidenly virtue, to be an attractive figure. One critic noted that "her Hester Prynne is so decorous that some picture fans may wonder whether her scarlet letter stands for anything more daring than 'A is for Apple.' "

By this time, even Mary Pickford had gone coquettish in a couple of films, but Lillian marched to her own drummer: she was content to remain the last of Hollywood's Victorian maidens. Mayer appreciated her delicacy and demure femininity, but his acumen as a businessman here took precedence over personal taste. M-G-M was paying Gish a hefty salary, and to earn it she—like Mayer—had to adapt to popular taste, however displeasing the compromise might be. But Gish wasn't ready to sacrifice her integrity as an artist. One day, she writes, Thalberg suggested that M-G-M "arrange" some sort of "scandal" that would "knock her off her pedestal." She was "startled" by Thalberg's suggestion, but promised to think it over. No, she finally decided, definitely not; her name must remain "clean."

To question the veracity of Miss Gish's report may seem discourteous, but nonetheless it seems wildly out of character for either Thalberg or Mayer to suggest such a ploy. The great Hollywood scandals of the early 1920s had wrecked the careers of many—Fatty Arbuckle, Mabel Norman, Wallace Reid—and had led to the appointment of Will Hays, former postmaster general under the Harding administration, as head of the Motion Picture Producers and Distributors Association of America, whose goal was to maintain "the highest possible moral and artistic standards in motion picture production." M-G-M and Mayer were zealous in their support of Hays and the list of eleven "don'ts" and twenty-seven "be carefuls" he issued to the studios in 1927.

Like the other studios, M-G-M never promoted scandal; it tried to prevent or suppress it. And if Thalberg and Mayer had wanted to knock Gish off her pedestal, certainly they would have tried to do so through her films, not her private life. After *The Wind*, Thalberg did suggest *Anna Karenina*, but nothing came of it. Instead she was cast as Pauli, the tainted Viennese heroine of *The Enemy*, a slick melodrama that had been a big hit for Fay Bainter on the Broadway stage. But as played by Gish, Pauli goes astray with rosary beads in her hand—the World War is on, her husband is fighting in the trenches and there are *kinder* to be fed. Gish's performance was highly praised, the film got good reviews, but again the public wasn't interested.

The Enemy was Lillian Gish's final star production for M-G-M and her last major picture as a leading lady.

After Gish, Metro's most prestigious star in 1926 was Lon Chaney, who, after a period of moving from one studio to the next, settled down on the Culver City lot and was to remain there until his death in 1930. Several other established players joined M-G-M around this time, but in the long run, the studio was to benefit most from developing its own stars. The success of Shearer and Gilbert had shown the practicality of this policy, and in 1926–27, Metro had two new actresses, both signed as unknowns, who were on the brink of legendary careers. One often referred to herself as the Queen of M-G-M; the other was, by general consensus, the first lady of the American cinema between 1927 and 1940.

The Queen was born Lucille Le Sueur in San Antonio, Texas, sometime between 1904 and 1908. Growing up was tough for Lucille, but after a tawdry and transient childhood and adolescence in the

Midwest, she ran off to New York, and after a while got a job in the chorus line of a Broadway show and managed to pick up extra cash as a dancer in an after-hours club. One night in December 1924, one of Harry Rapf's cronies spotted her and decided she belonged in Hollywood. Rapf became her protector and arranged a screen test at the studio. She received a contract at a starting pay of seventy dollars a week.

Arriving at the studio, Lucille was cast in small roles in a couple of minor films, posed for lots of "cheesecake" stills and, as "Miss M-G-M of 1925," introduced clips from the company's forthcoming productions in a promotional trailer shown at conventions for regional distributors. Then she caught the attention of director Edmund Goulding, a cosmopolitan and high-living Englishman who was in the final stages of casting his first Metro production, an adaptation of a hit Broadway musical, *Sally, Irene and Mary.* Goulding, who had a reputation as a ladies' man and was to become one of Hollywood's leading "woman's directors," immediately chose Lucille for one of the three title roles.

Sally, Irene and Mary, as revamped for the screen, was the story of three show girls sharing quarters in a Times Square tenement. (If the plot sounds familiar, it may be because M-G-M remade it unofficially many years later as *Ziegfeld Girl.*) Sally (Constance Bennett) is a gold digger, Irene (Sally O'Neil) is a down-to-earth and practical colleen, and Mary is the innocent who is led astray and winds up in a coffin. Lucille played Mary, with such vitality that though billed under Bennett and O'Neil, she got most of the notices when the film opened in the fall of 1925.

By then, Le Sueur had been rebaptized Joan Crawford. She had also captured the attention of Louis Mayer, who ordered she be given the full star treatment. There was a lot of work to be done. She had superb bone structure, huge eyes and a sensuous mouth, but she was overweight and her teeth were undersized and unevenly spaced. So the M-G-M experts started to overhaul her from scratch.

For the next year and a half, Crawford was spotlighted in a series of programmers, sometimes appearing with up-and-coming leading men (James Murray in *Rose Marie,* William Haines in *Spring Fever*), sometimes with established stars (Lon Chaney in *The Unknown,* Novarro in *Across to Singapore,* Gilbert in *Twelve Miles Out* and *Four Walls*). Along the way, she lost weight, lightened her hair and adopted a makeup that dramatically emphasized her large eyes and mouth. "Everything about Crawford was exaggerated," M-G-M costume designer Adrian once said. "Her bones, her eyes, her mouth, her clothes. Her figure wasn't right for conventional clothes—she had broad shoulders, a long waist and short legs. So her dresses had to be outré, somewhat bigger than life."

Her big break came in the 1928 *Our Dancing Daughters,* in which she did for the Charleston what John Travolta was to do for the Hustle in *Saturday Night Fever.* As Dangerous Diana, a loose-talking and free-loving debutante, Crawford was the dancing personification of jazz-age hedonism. Dressed in a half-slip and a fringed blouse, she launches into a Charleston (as film historian Stephen Harvey has written) "with the abandoned intensity of a pent-up animal who has tasted freedom for the first time." Largely due to Crawford's self-exhilaration, *Our Dancing Daughters* made a deep impression on audiences who identified with, and sometimes applauded, Diana as she lifted her arm and said (via printed titles), "I want to hold out my hand and catch life—like the sunlight."

Diana's rapacious clutching of the joy of life did not sit well with Mayer—God forbid one of his own daughters should start shimmying and stretching her wings! But as a businessman he knew he had to keep up with the times, and while he wasn't about to go full gallop ahead, he wasn't about to be caught lagging way behind, either. The M-G-M films, like the Mission Row films that preceded them, often presented an intoxicating portrait of "the new morality," only to wind up with the sobering message that loose living doesn't bring happiness. And so it is in *Dancing Daughters.* Just before the end, Diana repents and marries the man she has always loved. Next stop —an apron, three squalling kids and a gold star from L. B. Mayer.

But since the message was always tagged on in the last minutes of the final reel, those movie patrons who wanted to reject it had no trouble in doing so. The penitent Diana was an impostor; the real Diana was Crawford, tousling her hair, reaching toward the sun, slapping her flanks in an abandoned Black Bottom.

Dancing Daughters was such a success that it led to a series of "our" pictures *(Our Modern Maidens, Our Blushing Brides)* in which Crawford steers a reckless course as she stretches out to grasp life and live it breathlessly, desperately, dangerously. Her dancing-daughter image was, however, to have a short life-span—the jazz age was soon to crash along with the stock market—but for a time it sustained Crawford's career, and when it was over, she was flexible enough to adapt. Flexibility was, in fact, to become one of Crawford's chief characteristics as an actress, but she never totally discarded anything that had worked in one of her previous incarnations, and for decades to come, echoes of unbridled, pleasure-mad Diana would reverberate through all Crawford films.

At about the time Crawford was playing Dancing Diana, another M-G-M actress was playing Diana Merrick in *A Woman of Affairs*, a loose and silly adaptation of Michael Arlen's infamous and silly novel, *The Green Hat*. The two Dianas had more than name in common—both challenged contemporary mores and each was played by an actress who exemplified the modern feminine mystique, though in sharply contrasting ways. Crawford is jazzy and slightly lewd, while Greta Garbo, the Diana of *Woman of Affairs*, is stark and spiritual. When Crawford launches into a big scene, she comes at you in italics: *"Acting? You want Acting? Okay, watch this, fellas!"* whereas Garbo will arch an eyebrow, curl a lip, shrug a shoulder or twitch a muscle, thereby implying a complexity of character that often transcends the limitations of the role she is playing.

Mayer first met Garbo during his European trip in 1925. After leaving Italy and the *Ben Hur* set, he had traveled to Berlin to check out what was happening in the German film industry. Someone advised him to take a look at *The Story of Gösta Berling*, a Swedish film that had been a huge hit throughout Europe. Mayer arranged for a screening and was enormously impressed by the work of director Mauritz Stiller and the picture's three stars, Lars Hanson, Gerda Lundqvist and Stiller's protégé, Greta Garbo. He had discovered her a year or so before when she was still at Stockholm's Royal Dramatic Academy. Stiller had groomed her for the role in *Gösta Berling*, had changed her name (originally she was Greta Gustafsson), and now they were virtually inseparable.

As Stiller happened to be in Berlin at this time, Mayer asked him to drop by his suite in the Adlon Hotel. Before the meeting, Mayer had run a full check on Stiller, so he could not have been surprised when the director arrived with Garbo on his arm. It was no secret that there was an intense Pygmalion-Galatea bond between the two, though whether the relationship was physical as well as spiritual was doubtful: Stiller admired beautiful and talented women, but his admiration had rarely led him beyond the bedroom door. Garbo, however, may have been the one exception.

By the middle of their Adlon meeting, Mayer and Stiller had reached a tentative agreement—the director would spend three years at M-G-M at $1,500 a week—when Stiller asked, "What about Garbo?" Mayer was prepared for the question, and contrary to legend, not displeased by it. He was interested in Garbo, but since Stiller had already driven a hard bargain, he was determined to sign on the actress for as little as possible. He looked blankly at Stiller, then gazed unenthusiastically at Garbo. After some haggling, he agreed to take her along at $350 a week.

As they were leaving his suite, Mayer turned to Stiller and said, "Tell her in America we don't like fat women." That at least is part of the Garbo myth, and though its authenticity has been questioned, it may be true. Mrs. Selznick says her father would have been remiss if he had failed to mention the actress's excess weight.

By the time she arrived at M-G-M in late 1925, Garbo had shed several pounds, but there was still work to be done. Her teeth were bad, and her figure could best be described as athletic: a flat chest, no waist, broad shoulders, straight hips and big feet. Thalberg thought she was hopeless, but hearing good reports about her performance in *Gösta Berling*, he decided to give her a screen test. The result confirmed his impression that she was impossible, but at Mayer's insistence he requested a second test, this one to be shot under Stiller's supervision, and this time he saw a glimmer of hope.

With Mayer's approval, Thalberg decided to cast her as the female lead in *The Torrent*, a Ricardo Cortez vehicle. The script, based on a Blasco-Ibáñez novel about a famous opera singer and her desperate love for a childhood sweetheart, was not to Garbo's liking, nor was she pleased when she learned the picture would be directed by Monta Bell, not Stiller. Stiller was also disappointed, but he ordered her to cooperate with the studio; through private coaching, he would guide her through the picture just as though he were her director.

Garbo hated *The Torrent*, hated making it, and came away with only one good memory of the production: her first encounter with cinematographer William Daniels. After a few days' work, Daniels was ecstatic about the actress's face, which he claimed had "no bad sides and needed no special lighting" to enhance its natural beauty. (Her figure, however, was still on the chunky side and her teeth were in immediate need of attention from M-G-M's dentist.) Daniels also realized that Garbo was inhibited by the peering eyes of the crew and other on-set bystanders, so he set up a barricade of black screens that created an illusion of intimacy. As a result of this thoughtfulness, Daniels became her favorite cameraman, and was to photograph all but five of her twenty-four American films.

Watching the daily rushes of *The Torrent*, Mayer and Thalberg became increasingly excited about Garbo's performance, and once the film went into release, their enthusiasm was more than justified. Critics had nothing very good to say about the picture or Cortez, but Garbo was hailed, in the words of *Variety*, as "the find of the year." Metro rushed her into an adaptation of another trash Blasco-Ibáñez novel, *The Temptress;* this time she plays a high-born vixen who lures a troop of slobbering he-men to their destruction. Once again she was billed beneath a second-rank leading man, Antonio Moreno, but this time she went into the production in a good frame of mind because Stiller was set as director.

Neither liked the script very much, but Stiller thought he could overcome its many imbecilities, so they set out with high hopes. But after only a few days of shooting, they ran into trouble. Moreno complained that Stiller ignored him and favored Garbo; Mayer became concerned when the production fell behind schedule. Three weeks after the start of shooting, Thalberg called Stiller to his office, and after a protracted and painful conversation, informed him that he was being replaced by Fred Niblo.

This was disastrous news for both Stiller and Garbo. He knew that his chances for a career at M-G-M, and possibly at any other Hollywood studio, were all but finished. She realized that for the duration of her contract she would be deprived of her mentor's guidance. But she went on with *The Temptress*, and when the picture went into release, none of the critics seemed to notice the absence of the Stiller touch. They were too busy mooning over Garbo. Robert E. Sherwood, then the film critic for *Life* magazine, hailed her as his "official Dream Princess."

Garbo looks better and acts better in *The Temptress* than she did *The Torrent*, but it wasn't until her third M-G-M movie, *Flesh and the Devil*, that the Garbo magic began to emerge. In this film, as in those preceding it, she was cast as a seductress, and Stiller warned her that if she continued playing ladies of easy virtue, she would soon be incapable of playing anything else. So she staged a minor rebellion, but after an hour-long pep talk from Mayer, who told her the studio knew best, she reluctantly accepted the assignment.

Just before production started, director Clarence Brown introduced Garbo to her new leading man, John Gilbert. "It was," Brown recently recalled, "a case of passion at first sight. I've never seen such a physical reaction between two people." Later Garbo told a friend she loved "Yackie" for exactly five days, but their relationship endured far beyond that. She moved into Gilbert's home on Tower Road in Beverly Hills, and for a while, the fan magazines predicted that they would soon marry. Gilbert was all for the idea, but "Flecka" (his pet name for Garbo) kept disappointing "Yackie"—always at the last minute, she got cold feet. Gilbert blamed Stiller, and he may have been right. But it's also possible that Garbo couldn't see Gilbert as a husband or herself as a wife, and decided that for them love without marriage was the only practical arrangement.

Whatever her offscreen feelings for Gilbert may have been, Garbo adored him as a leading man, and the four films they were to make together are just about the only four in which Garbo does not emasculate or erase from the screen her co-star.

Gilbert was her favorite leading man, and as a double blessing, on *Flesh and the Devil,* she met her favorite director, Clarence Brown, who admits he was initially perplexed by Garbo's idiosyncrasies. "She never seemed to be doing anything, and when I'd ask for a bit more, she wasn't terribly responsive," Brown recalled recently. "Well, I thought, we've blown it, but then I'd see the rushes, and it was all there. She had this remarkable ability to register thought and emotion without doing much of anything. You couldn't see it on the floor, but on screen it came across. I can't explain it—it just happened. That's the Garbo mystery."

When Mayer saw *Flesh and the Devil,* he loathed it. Brown and Daniels had indulged in a lot of fancy photographic effects—shadows, chiaroscuro lighting and all the other distorted mannerisms that characterize the then-fashionable school of expressionistic film making. Mayer despised this kind of arty stylization. He believed people went to the movies not for silhouettes or landscapes or pretty pictures, but to watch the actors, and that therefore the leading man and woman should be well lit and at the center of the frame whenever possible.

Critics, however, overpraised *Flesh and the Devil* precisely for the reasons Mayer hated it—its cinematic pretensions. The public knew better—they flocked to see the film because Gilbert and Garbo's love scenes were, as described by *Variety,* "a big kick." Today that means they're a real turn-on, and even judged by current permissive standards, that's exactly what they are. "They're the best love scenes I ever shot," says Clarence Brown. "Maybe they're the best love scenes *ever* shot, but I can't take the credit. I was working with raw material."

Flesh and the Devil was a runaway hit, and the studio tried to rush Garbo into another vamp vehicle, *Women Love Diamonds,* which was no better, no worse than her previous M-G-M films. Garbo said she'd rather not—and this time she meant it. She wanted better roles and a better salary. Thalberg talked to her several times, but Garbo just shook her head mournfully. So Mayer invited her to his office for a friendly chat.

Mayer was stunned when she calmly asked for a salary of five thousand dollars a week. With all the equanimity he could muster, he explained that the studio had spent a tidy fortune on promoting her as a star, and that it was unprecedented for an actress of such limited experience to receive such a huge salary. Garbo was unruffled. Tentatively Mayer suggested that a raise could be arranged, though certainly only a fraction of what she had requested, provided she started work on *Women Love Diamonds.*

Garbo shook her head. "No more bad women," she moaned. M-G-M didn't make pictures about bad women, Mayer protested. *Women Love Diamonds* was the story of New York socialite Mavis Ray who, on the eve of her wedding, discovers she is really in love with her chauffeur, Patrick Reagan . . .

Mayer soon became so engrossed in the story that he started acting the entire plot until he reached its shattering climax: "Patrick, now a taxi driver, rushes a hit-and-run victim to the hospital where he is reunited with Mavis, working as a volunteer nurse . . ."

Mayer mopped his brow and looked at Garbo. She was impassive. "Well," he asked, "are you ready to play Mavis?" She gazed into space for a moment and then replied, "Maybe yes, maybe no. But I t'ink I go home."

In years to come, Mayer was often to tell this story and laugh, but in 1927, it wasn't terribly funny. No one at M-G-M imagined Garbo was bluffing—there was every reason to believe she was ready to pack up and go home. Stiller had already done so. Leaving M-G-M after the *Temptress* fiasco, he had gone to Paramount and made a modestly successful Pola Negri vehicle, *Hotel Imperial,* but he became so disillusioned by the American process of film making that he had returned to Sweden long before the picture went into release.

Mayer wasn't sorry to see him leave; he hoped that Garbo would become tractable once her mentor was gone. But in the meantime, she had employed Harry Edington as her manager, and Edington was a tough customer. Starting out as an M-G-M accountant, he had eased his way upward to become John Gilbert's manager, and from Gilbert to Garbo was a simple step. As he forged ahead, Edington collected a corps of faithful enemies, including Mayer, who prophesied that percentage-hungry agents and managers would be the death of the Hollywood system.

Possibly Garbo went home because Edington urged her to do so until they got the salary they (he) wanted; possibly she went home because she needed a vacation from Gilbert. For whatever reason, she did return to Sweden and stayed there for six months. M-G-M placed her on suspension, and put *Women Love Diamonds* in production with two so-called stars, Pauline Starke and Owen Moore. It did all right, but certainly it would have done better with Garbo, so the studio stepped up its campaign to bring her back to Hollywood. She, however, was content to stay in Sweden until she got exactly what she wanted—five thousand dollars a week plus the promise of more dignified film projects in the future.

The first picture of her new contract was an adaptation of Tolstoy's *Anna Karenina*, which sounds pretty impressive, except that it was completely overhauled by the M-G-M production staff. The title was changed to *Heat*, Gilbert was cast as Vronsky, no one was cast as Levin and Kitty because there were no Kitty or Levin in the script, and the setting was updated to the present. Altogether, it had little to do with Tolstoy.

Production was a series of problems. Gilbert was edgy and, at his insistence, Dmitri Buchowetzky, a "renowned" Russian stage director, was replaced by the affable Edmund Goulding; the title was changed to *Love* because it was feared that marquees advertising GARBO and GILBERT in HEAT would alienate the matinée trade; and, at Mayer's insistence, two endings were shot—one showing Karenina throwing herself under a train, the other closing as she is happily reunited with Vronsky. Exhibitors were allowed to choose whichever they thought their audiences would prefer.

Love gets under way with Garbo, covered to her eyes in sable and fox, racing across the snowy steppes in a sleigh, a pack of ravenous wolves snapping at her behind. Gilbert rescues her at the last moment and takes her to a quaint Russian inn, where they snuggle down beside a fireplace, but it's *heat*, not kindling, that keeps them warm.

The love scenes, however, are tamer than those in *Flesh and the Devil*, which also boasted a better script and sharper direction, but for the first time Garbo impressed critics as an actress of ability and singularity, a woman who stood apart from the other love goddesses of the screen. Karenina took her out of the vamp category and gave her a character that allowed her to express some of her individuality. From here on she would usually play women who have strayed from the moral standard, but who are nonetheless more sinned against than sinning, who suffer more than they provoke suffering. In *Love*, the characterization is still hazy, but it can be glimpsed, and in the next two years Garbo and the M-G-M production staff were to bring it into sharp focus.

Garbo's development as an actress is only one side of the Garbo myth, the other (equally important) side being the creation of her offscreen persona as the Swedish Sphinx, the shy and reclusive star who wanted to be alone. This image was forged out of necessity and therefore was not a total fabrication, but it took several months before the M-G-M publicists realized they should promote, not minimize, Garbo's diffidence.

When she arrived at M-G-M, Garbo swiftly became "the pet of the publicity department." Despite what biographer John Bainbridge once called her Swedish reserve, she obliged studio photographers by doing all the things she didn't do in real life: she's seen strumming a mandolin outside the Miramar hotel, toeing the starting line for a track race, cuddling up to Leo, M-G-M's mascot lion. There are also shots of her petting a pet monkey, modeling tank-style swimsuits and trying to look glamorous in a leather coat lined with marmoset. Crawford went through the same rigamarole with aplomb, but Garbo was out of her element—she's obviously trying to be a good sport, but all too often she looks as though she's suffering from a virulent case of morning sickness.

Photographs were fine, but Garbo was uneasy about interviews. Stiller had always done all the talking. "Shut up," he'd say, "don't say anything," and, acutely aware of her lack of formal education, she readily obeyed. In Hollywood, there was another problem—her grasp of English was limited to heavily accented Berlitz phraseology. Still, when pressed for interviews, she did her best to cooperate. Her best, however, was not good enough for reporters. All personal questions were met with silence; everything else was answered monosyllabically or evasively. Asked how she liked Hollywood, she said she was enjoying the climate. (Perhaps Stiller had prepped her for that question, she was rarely so witty.) For a time, an M-G-M publicity representative accompanied her to all interviews (a routine that would soon become studio policy), but this did not improve matters. Asked to describe Stiller, Garbo replied, "He is a great director." (Maybe Stiller prepped her on that one, too.) In desperation, a fan-magazine reporter titled his noninterview with Garbo "The Mysterious Stranger," and the image of the Swedish Sphinx was born.

From then on, all M-G-M publicity about Garbo emphasized her dignity as a serious actress and her aloofness as a woman. It was meant as a protective image, and if it didn't work out that way—if some reporters tried to solve the riddle by writing off Garbo either as a certifiable looney or as a sharpie who recognized the best way to gain publicity was to run the other way—no one is to blame, certainly not M-G-M.

In handling Garbo, the studio publicity department learned a valuable lesson. All contract players required a custom-tailored campaign, one based on careful examination of their capability to deal with stardom and with their screen image. In time, anyone who signed on with the studio was assured the most proficient and intelligent buildup in Hollywood. In keeping with Mayer's concept of M-G-M as a family unit, the studio took care of its own through thick or thin.

Mayer placed the creation of an efficient publicity department high on his list of priorities when he took control of the new company. The merger had left him with three publicity directors—Joe Jackson at Goldwyn, Charlie Condon at the Mayer Mission Road studio and Howard Strickling at Metro. Strickling eliminated himself by accepting a post with Rex Ingram, Condon was small fry for such a big job, so by default, the position went to Jackson, who lasted only a few weeks. Jackson was competent, but he played favorites, promoting those stars he liked the best, particularly Carmel Myers, about whom he was slightly dotty. Mayer had nothing against Miss Myers—she was a family friend—but her status didn't warrant the kind of coverage Jackson was lavishing on her. So he started looking around for a less romantically inclined publicity chief.

His advisers informed him that the best press man in the industry was a keen-witted, prickly natured individual named Pete Smith, who ran his own agency with such prominent clients as Colleen Moore, Corinne Griffith, Mickey Neilan and child star Wesley Barry. Smith was tops, but as Mayer was warned, he would come expensive, if he were available at all. Smith did agree to talk to Mayer, and as predicted, he asked $1,500 a week or about five times what the average publicist then earned.

Mayer was astounded, but not put off. "Typically he tried every angle," recalls one long-time M-G-M employee. "If Mayer couldn't get in the front door, he tried the back; if he couldn't get in the back, he'd try the chimney; if he couldn't get in the chimney, he'd try to blow the house down." This time, however, he was up against a brick wall. Smith was not about to dismantle his highly profitable stable of stars for less money than he had originally specified. Mayer called him into his office and said, "Okay, great publicity man, they tell me you're the best and we want the best and we're ready to pay for it."

In the first months of Smith's regime, M-G-M publicity was standard Hollywood nonsense—Leo the Lion was flown across country in a much publicized flight that ended abruptly when the plane made a forced landing west of Colorado—and was to remain standard until Garbo came to town and caused a small upheaval.

By that time Smith had acquired an assistant, the same Howard Strickling who had left Metro at the time of the merger—he was afraid "heads would roll" once Mayer took charge of the studio. Smith was convinced Strickling would be a valuable asset to the company, and before Mayer went off on his *Ben Hur* European tour of 1925, he asked him to look up the young publicist, who was then working with Rex Ingram in Paris.

They met in a hotel just off the Champs Elysées. Mayer opened the conversation by asking Strickling why he had left Metro. "I told him I left because I found him intimidating," Strickling recalls. "He looked very surprised, and went out of his way to win my confidence. When I left the meeting, I still wasn't sure what I should do, but after talking it over with Ingram and his wife, Alice Terry, I decided to join Mr. Mayer."

A year or so later, Smith became seriously ill, and Strickling took over temporarily as head of the publicity department, a position he would officially assume in the 1930s when Smith was promoted to producer of a series of well-remembered comedy shorts *(Pete Smith's Specialties)*. By then, and mainly through Strickling's and Smith's efforts, the publicist was becoming an important and respected member of the film industry. "When I entered the business," Strickling says, "publicists were a joke. They were flunkies, with a flask in one pocket and a list of girls in the other. They got drunk and screwed around, and when they got down to business, they sold a product they knew nothing about—and couldn't have cared less."

M-G-M changed all this. The studio publicists started with a film when it was no more than an idea being thrashed out on a typewriter and followed it through all subsequent stages of development. This engendered a sense of involvement which is the keynote of Strickling's philosophy of publicity. "Early on I learned that people need help, and the secret of my job was learning how to help them. Help them and they help you. That's what M-G-M was all about, and it was particularly true for the actors—most of them were insecure and overly sensitive and self-centered, so you had to convince them you had their best interests at heart."

Strickling credits Margaret Mayer with helping him reach a deeper understanding of his boss. "She anticipated his every wish and had a knack for putting people at their ease when they were around him," he recalls. "She showed me that there were many ways I could help him." Strickling quickly gained entry into Mayer's inner circle and became (in his words) "a company man." His terse memos, typed on pink paper, sent the fear of God coursing through the blood of his staff. "I don't care what you do after 5 P.M., but for the rest of the day, you belong to M-G-M," he'd say, or around lunchtime, "Think less about your stomachs and more about your pencils."

Strickling's company loyalty makes it difficult for him to speak harshly of any M-G-M employee, but he does admit to having differences with Wallace Beery, who refused to cooperate with, and made fun of, the studio publicists. Nearly every other department had complaints about Beery, who was on the best of days about as sunny as W. C. Fields without a pitcher of martinis by his side.

Eventually Strickling felt obliged to go to Mayer about the complaints he had heard. "Beery is stealing the props off the set, and he won't . . ." The list of affronts went on and on until Mayer broke in to say, "Yes, Howard, Beery's a son-of-a-bitch . . . but he's *our* son-of-a-bitch."

Strickling got the point. A family has to be tolerant of its black sheep, particularly if, like Beery, they brought a lot of money into the family fold.

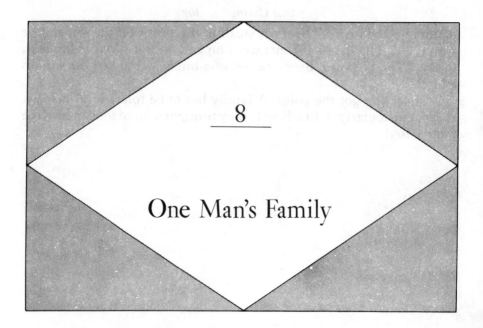

8

One Man's Family

Shortly after taking control of M-G-M, Mayer dropped by the studio commissary for lunch. As he walked in the door, he noticed that the room was half-empty and that the only people he recognized were the group of executives he had brought with him. Two bites of the blue plate special, and he knew why: the food was slop. Like most movie commissaries of the period, the one at M-G-M was run by a concessionaire whose institutional meals drove most of the stars and top-salary personnel outside M-G-M at lunchtime or sent them in search of the studio bootlegger who provided liquid refreshment that was consumed in dressing rooms. The rate of afternoon absenteeism kept rising so alarmingly that Mayer decided positive action had to be taken. Believing that the family who ate together stayed together, he ordered an overhaul of the M-G-M commissary.

He fired the concessionaire, hired a chef and sent him to spend a day with his own cook, Matilda. She taught him to make chicken soup—boil kosher chickens, remove them from the broth, skin them, strip them of their meat, place equal amounts of broth, shredded meat and matzoh balls in a bowl and serve piping hot at thirty-five cents a bowl. Matilda also passed along the secret for several other specialties with such success that the M-G-M commissary soon earned the reputation of serving the best and cheapest home-style meals in Los Angeles. The studio chef also catered to the culinary preferences of the stars, supplying a particular brand of bacon for Wallace Beery, Dijon mustard for Joan Crawford and finnan haddie on hand—it was one of Mayer's favorite dishes. There was always to be a clique of holdouts who preferred eating out (particularly after the repeal of prohibition), but the Metro restaurant became, in art director Bob Hoag's words, "a wonderful, convivial place, a kind of clubhouse where you met friends, made friends, and caught up on what was going on, who was doing what with whom."

Mayer's private life was run along similar lines—it was a cozy, clubby, family-style kind of existence. Around this time, he moved into a white stucco house at 625 Ocean Front (today the Pacific Coast Highway) in Santa Monica; with four master bedrooms and a patio facing the Pacific, it was frequently described as a mansion, though it was modest compared to some of the neighboring villas. An eighth of a mile up the beach, Ocean House, Marion Davies's $7 million "bungalow," was nearing completion, and a few hundred yards in the opposite direction, Irving Thalberg would later build a French provincial house that was an architectural absurdity along this stretch of the Pacific coastline.

The Mayer household had expanded a bit over the past two years. Jacob Mayer, now a dignified and mellow old man, had come to live with his famous son, and while there was no deep affection between the two, Mayer amazed his friends by the courtesy and deference he showed his father, always giving him the place of honor at the dinner table. Mrs. Mayer planned two menus each day, one for family and guests, one for her father-in-law, who observed the Jewish dietary laws. Contrary to legend, Mrs. Mayer wasn't much of a cook and ever since the days in Haverhill, she had household help to do the cleaning. Now her staff included Matilda, a handyman named Morris Zink, a butler, a gardener and two maids.

Entertainment at 625 Ocean Front was ordinarily limited to Sunday buffet for family and business acquaintances: there were no gaudy parties to attract the attention of the gossip and society columnists. As Pete Smith soon realized, Mayer liked to see his name in the papers, but not for anything as frivolous as hosting a poolside masquerade or post-match supper for Will Rogers and his team of Hollywood polo men. Mayer was looking for a more dignified kind of publicity; one that emphasized his patriotism, his civic-mindedness and his work for the political party of his choice, the G.O.P.

The image that Mayer wanted to project was that of an Important American Personage—this is the way he saw himself and this is the way he insisted he be presented to the public. A few years later (in the early 1930s), when playwright S. N. Behrman was employed at M-G-M, Mayer asked him to ghostwrite a speech he was scheduled to deliver at a Saint Patrick's Day celebration in San Francisco. Behrman was not thrilled by the assignment, but he decided that since it had to be done, he would do it with as light a touch as possible —epigrammatic wit was, after all, what he, the author of *The Second Man* and *Biography*, was noted for. But Behrman had miscalculated. Mayer rejected the rough draft, saying, "This is not what they expect of me." He suggested by his tone of voice that what was expected was something "solemn and lofty."

Behrman's assessment—it appears as an anecdote in his memoir, *People in a Diary*—is not far off the mark. Mayer wanted to break with the flamboyant, jodphur and riding crop, sin and scandal stereotype of the Hollywood bigwig, and chose instead the image of the powerful, corporate American entrepreneur. He dressed that way, in the custom-tailored, conservative suits; he thought that way; he voted that way. It may seem strange that an immigrant boy who struggled up from ghetto poverty should wind up as a Republican, but Mayer —like many Hollywood bosses of this period—was concerned less with alleviating the social injustices that had victimized him in the past than with establishing himself as a member of the American elite.

Mayer's active participation in politics began with the 1924 presidential election when he campaigned extensively for Calvin Coolidge. This led to a large number of speaking engagements at various organizations in which he promoted America, the film industry and his political beliefs, not necessarily all together and not always in that order. His speeches were often ghostwritten, either by one of the M-G-M scenarists or by a member of the studio's publicity department—his grasp of English grammar, as well as English spelling and punctuation, was never to be strong. Contrary to all reports, he never received elocutionary lessons from Conrad Nagel or any other actor. He was an excellent speaker, his only failing being that he would go on talking long after he had reached a climax and made his point.

Those who disliked Mayer and his politics claim his entrance into the arena of public affairs was motivated solely by vanity and an ever-increasing appetite for power. The accusation can't be entirely refuted, but requires modification. Yes, he was vain; yes, he wanted power; but no, ambition and glory were not his only motives. By getting his own name out of the entertainment section and into the front pages, he also planned to increase the prestige of M-G-M specifically and the film industry in general.

Mary Pickford and Douglas Fairbanks had brought an aura of respectability to Hollywood by entertaining minor potentates and titled or newsworthy personages at Pickfair, their home in Beverly Hills. Consequently, they (Mary in particular) often referred to themselves as Hollywood's ambassadors to the world—not unjustifiably so, though their good-neighbor policy was largely a by-product of their (particularly Fairbanks's) social climbing. Mayer was to pick up where they left off. He recognized the value that could come from the reflected glory of linking the film industry with the world of international affairs, and like Mary and Doug, he built a bond between the rich and powerful, the famous and fashionable, and M-G-M.

Leafing through the press clippings of the late twenties and early thirties, one immediately recognizes the precise moment when Mayer and M-G-M took over the lead from Mary and Doug. It occurred at the 1932 Olympic Games in Los Angeles. At that time, the Fairbankses were discreetly estranged, but Mary, who knew Doug would come home for the games, refurbished Pickfair in anticipation of the event. Doug did return, and there were lots of parties at the spruced-up Pickfair, but most of the press coverage at the opening ceremony went to Mayer, looking spiffy (and just a trifle ill at ease) in a top hat and English-cut morning suit.

Even before this, M-G-M had managed to steal some of the spotlight from Pickfair. Just before he announced that he chose not to run for another term, Coolidge paid a brief visit to California. Mary and Doug asked him to use their home as the summer White House; he declined, but on arrival in Los Angeles, he was officially welcomed by Mary and other selected members of the Hollywood elite, who took him off on a tour of the leading studios. Coolidge looked grim and said little as the group motored from lot to lot, and judging by photographs, by the time they reached Metro, everyone was as sober-faced as the President, especially Mary, who seemed to have aged twenty years during the ordeal.

At M-G-M, Coolidge and company visited the set of *The Road to Romance,* a Ramon Novarro programmer. On the set were Novarro, Marceline Day and a trained bear, which went on a rampage as soon as the camera started turning. Bruno's trainer screamed that everyone should relax and stay calm, but naturally there was a flurry of activity as the Secret Service agents tried to get Coolidge off the set. He refused to budge, his hatchet face crinkled into a grin, then broke out into a full smile, and finally he was nearly doubled up with laughter. He didn't leave until the bear was under control, and later he told the press that his visit to M-G-M was the highlight of his Hollywood trip.

Starting in the late 1920s, there was a steady flow of important personages visiting M-G-M—presidents, congressmen, English MP's, Japanese admirals, ambassadors and such literary lions as H. G. Wells, Hugh Walpole and George Bernard Shaw. Often they were entertained at lavish banquets held on one of the studio stages which had been specially decorated by Cedric Gibbons and the art department. The settings for these occasions were just as spectacular as anything created for a Metro superproduction—one luncheon featured a waterfall that was "second only to Niagara in width."

M-G-M was fortunate in having its own resident VIP, newspaper tycoon William Randolph Hearst, who had entered the film business in 1917. Hearst had founded and funded Cosmopolitan Pictures primarily as a showcase for his lady friend, Marion Davies, whom he had met when she was appearing as "The Girl on the Magazine Cover" in Irving Berlin's 1915 revue, *Stop! Look! Listen!*. Cosmopolitan was releasing its films through Goldwyn at the time of the merger, and Hearst agreed to stay on with the new corporation under the following conditions: Davies would receive a salary of ten thousand dollars a week; Metro-Goldwyn would foot the costs of her productions, but would split the profits equally with Hearst/Cosmopolitan.

This arrangement—particularly Davies's salary—lifted a lot of Hollywood eyebrows. Only stars of Chaplin and Pickford caliber earned that kind of money, and Davies wasn't in their class. Only a few of her movies had ever returned a profit. The disappointing box office returns couldn't be attributed to incompetence—she was extraordinarily pretty and a better-than-average actress with an instinctive flair for comedy; she wasn't Pickford or Connie Talmadge, perhaps, but she was as good (and not nearly as affected) as Gloria Swanson or Norma Shearer. Critics were not blind to her talents. She got consistently good reviews, and not only from the Hearst reviewers. Her performance in James M. Barrie's *Quality Street* is the main reason that film was the only M-G-M release to make the *New York Times* ten-best list in 1927. Her performance is in fact far more pleasing and far less mannered than Katharine Hepburn's in the 1937 remake of Barrie's play.

There are any number of explanations for Marion's troubles at the box office. She was a victim of her relationship with Hearst—a small portion of the public was offended by the unorthodox nature of the liaison—and she was also a victim of publicity overkill. Rarely a day went by without the Hearst papers mentioning her, usually with superlatives, and Davies served up daily with breakfast toast and coffee was too rich a diet for the average citizen. But the biggest problem was her early Cosmopolitan vehicles. For the most part, they were either stilted historical pageants or soupy romances, so overproduced that Davies was nearly suffocated by the elaborate pictorial values. And it didn't help that she was being forced to ape Mary Pickford, whom she resembled in face but not in figure or spirit. Not surprisingly, her best pictures are such modest productions as *Zander the Great, The Patsy* and *Show People,* all produced by M-G-M, all allowing Marion ample opportunity to show her individuality as a light comedienne.

Davies's dressing room at M-G-M was a fourteen-room "bungalow," built on the lot and costing about $75,000. (Hearst paid the bills.) It was furnished with antiques from the Hearst collection, and was often borrowed by the studio for intimate parties for its most illustrious visitors. When Bernard Shaw lunched there in 1933, Marion played hostess—she was seated on a throne chair with Shaw on her right and Mayer on her left, all three looking stiff and uncomfortable in photographs commemorating the event.

Marion's bungalow was the Versailles of studio dressing rooms, and the press sometimes referred to her as the Queen of M-G-M, but around the lot she was known as the Fairy Godmother. She never forgot birthdays or Christmas, and anyone who paid her a passing kindness was amply rewarded over and over again. There are lots of stories about her drinking, her amours, her rowdiness and her unbecoming behavior at the time of Hearst's death, but Marion was much loved in Hollywood. She lacked dignity, but she was genuine; she was a good sport. She enjoyed the wealth, the beach house, her stardom and the "perks" that went with it, and yet never forgot that she had been born Marion Douras in Brooklyn, sometime around 1897. Like many stars she grew younger as she got older—late in life, she had subtracted so many years from her birthdate that she would have been (by her calculation) not quite ten when she met Hearst.

Like everyone else at M-G-M, Mayer adored Marion, and became enraged whenever anyone asked him why he continued to keep her on the studio roster of stars. "Why does our company continue to release those Davies clinkers?" asked a Loew's exhibitor at a sales conference. Though caught off guard, Mayer immediately launched into a pep talk, rambling on about Marion's beauty and Hearst's contribution to American society. By the time he was finished, no one dared raise an objection, and it wasn't until much later that anyone realized that he hadn't really answered the question.

He could have quoted facts and figures. By the late 1920s, the

Hearst publishing empire owned or controlled twenty-two daily papers with a circulation of 3,028,437, fifteen Sunday papers with a circulation of 3,587,871, and seven American and two British magazines with a circulation of 2,773,784. That added up to over 9 million readers who would (by tacit agreement) see a lot about M-G-M, its stars and future productions while flipping through the pages of their favorite Hearst periodical.

Hearst had also agreed to present certain important M-G-M pictures as Cosmopolitan productions, with the understanding that he would be the judge of which films should be so sanctioned. Among those he chose were Garbo's *Temptress* and Crawford's *Dancing Daughters,* both of which were sent off with fireworks from the Hearst press. As a bonus, the Hearst publishing empire syndicated the column of Hollywood's leading tattletale, Louella Parsons. She called herself "the gay illiterate," and who would argue? She was daffy and ungrammatical and prejudiced, but she was also (according to her partisans) loyal to the business. "Louella was a fan, she was enthusiastic, unlike so many of the Hollywood reporters," says Howard Strickling. "There were about one hundred and fifty of them by the early 1930's—and they'd say 'Norma Shearer? Who wants to hear about Shearer, who cares?' They wanted to be superior to what they were covering. Louella, on the other hand, really wanted to know what was going on. She did her homework. When the studio bought a book, she read it and called up to find out who was going to play which part."

But the greatest benefit was neither Parsons nor the 9 million readers, it was Hearst himself—at least for Mayer, who respected the publisher and took enormous pride in his friendship. (He was the last of the older, prominent men with whom Mayer formed close, substitute father-son relationships, a pattern that started with George Elliott and Charles Poore in Haverhill.) Hearst responded in kind—Mayer was one of the few members of the film community to be invited to his private hideaway, Wyntoon, an imitation Bavarian estate on the McClous River in Northern California. Davies hated the place—she called it Spittoon—which may explain why so few movie people were invited there. Marion's friends preferred San Simeon, Hearst's fabled castle (he called it a ranch) near San Luis Obispo.

Though they had grown up on opposite sides of the track, the two men had much in common. That was one of the wonderful things about America, Mayer thought; one man was born with a silver spoon in his mouth, another was lucky if he got enough mother's milk, but they could still end up scratching each other's backs. Hearst doted on his mother, Phoebe, just as Mayer worshipped Sarah; they were both incurable romantics; they had similar views about the tastes of the American public. In one of his first editorials, Hearst had justified the policy of his papers by writing, "The public is even more fond of entertainment than it is of information," a remark Mayer could have used to answer charges that M-G-M was Hollywood's foremost dream factory. Both condemned any form of salaciousness, though neither was against the presentation of what Mayer (in an interview with a Hearst reporter) termed "normal, real, beautiful sex. A man and a woman are in love with one another. That's sex and it is beautiful, in the movies and in life."

Neither liked kitchen-sink realism, neither had much time for arty theatre and film making; both preferred the lighter forms of entertainment—musicals, bright comedies, sentimental dramas, anything with uplift and a wholesome view of American life and love. Director Clarence Brown (who was a close friend of both Mayer and Hearst) points out that the two tycoons operated in a similar fashion. "When Hearst got his first newspapers, he wasn't an editor or a reporter, and he didn't know shit about the newspaper business," Brown said recently. "But he had ideas and this inborn sense of what the American public wanted to read. He was also smart enough to know that there were some things he didn't know, so he hired the best newspaper corps in America, stole them away from other papers. Mayer did exactly the same thing. Of course he wasn't exactly green when he took over at M-G-M, but still he had his weak spots, and he got the right people to fill them in. Like Hearst and Henry Ford, he was an executive genius."

Hearst and Mayer did not always see eye to eye, and as time went by, they had more and more differences, particularly on political issues. Both were staunch Republicans, but often did not agree on party matters, and during the 1928 presidential convention, they found themselves supporting different candidates. Hearst was behind Andrew Mellon, secretary of the treasury under the Harding and Coolidge administrations, while Mayer backed Herbert Hoover, the secretary of commerce. At the party convention in Kansas City, Mayer (a Republican state committeeman) worked hard to get Hearst on the Hoover bandwagon, but Hearst was reluctant to abandon Mellon, who was in favor of abolishing or reducing the income tax. He stood firm until it became apparent that the seventy-two-year-old Mellon didn't stand a chance; then, urged on by Mayer, he joined the winning team and helped Hoover win the nomination on the first ballot.

As a reward for his part in the Republican victory that year,

Mayer was invited to the Inauguration, and later was the first visitor officially entertained by the Hoovers once they took possession of the White House. Rumors spread that Mayer might be offered an ambassadorship, possibly to Turkey, and while some cynics have suggested that the rumors originated in the M-G-M publicity department, they were creditable enough to be reported by *The New York Times.* The offer never materialized, but Mayer wasn't overly disappointed: privately he indicated he would never abandon the movies, certainly not for an ambassadorship to anti-Semitic Turkey. He was already amply rewarded: in terms of publicity and prestige, the gossip about the possibility of a presidential appointment was nearly as prestigious as the real thing.

Unlike Mayer, Thalberg stayed clear of politics, and unlike Mayer, he sought no public recognition for his contribution to the M-G-M success story. He refused to accept any screen credit for work, claiming that "the credit you give yourself is worth absolutely nothing." And he abided by this rule, except on three occasions—he did take supervisory credit on Stroheim's *Merry-Go-Round* (produced at Universal) and on *The Great Divide* and the original release prints of *Ben Hur* (both produced by Metro in 1925). It was not until eleven years later that his name would appear on a screen, and then it was in the form of a posthumous tribute.

This don't-blow-your-own-horn attitude won many friends and admirers, especially among those people who were offended by the super self-importance that surrounded every Hollywood celebrity. It can also be seen as the reverse side of the same coin—false modesty as a cover for a heightened sense of superiority. Whatever the interpretation, Thalberg was consistent in his behavior. He shied away from interviewers, disliked everything that was written about him and tried to discourage anyone from writing anything more about him. He was the Greta Garbo of M-G-M's front office.

Thalberg's private life-style also differed widely from Mayer's. Befitting his status as a bachelor still in his twenties, he enjoyed the pleasures offered by the fun-loving Hollywood scene, though he always took pleasure in moderation. He was chummy with several high-living playboys including John Gilbert, director Jack Conway, and Howard Hawks, and Hawks's brother, Kenneth. They and his other friends came from the studio world that was the center of his existence. Many of them were members of his production staff, which now included such newcomers as Lawrence Weingarten (soon to marry his sister, Sylvia, then working as an M-G-M scenarist); Albert Lewin, a former college professor, who first came to M-G-M as an assistant to Kate Corbaley; and Paul Bern, a German-born director and screenwriter, who met Thalberg while squiring Barbara La Marr, an actress who appeared in several of Mayer's Mission Road productions.

Though forbidden strenuous sports, Thalberg dabbled at swimming and liked to be photographed holding a tennis racket. He loved to gamble, and he was something of a shark at bridge and poker, which he played for very high stakes. He also liked to live dangerously with women, once taking on Peggy Hopkins Joyce, the quintessential gold digger, a Ziegfeld show girl with a talent for catching wealthy husbands and lovers. His romance with Rosabelle Laemmle had stopped and started several times since he had left Universal, but finally came to an end when Rosabelle wanted him to pay more attention to her and less to his work. Then came a brief attachment with Constance Talmadge—a serious one for Thalberg, a lighthearted one for Connie, who was, as Thalberg's mother pointed out, too frivolous and flighty to make a suitable wife.

Standing on the sidelines was Norma Shearer, who called herself (referring to her career as Lotta Miles) "Irving's spare tire." Whenever he needed a pretty girl for a premiere or social event, Thalberg called Norma, and however last-minute the invitation, she was always available. Her patience and good sportsmanship was rewarded when, one night on the dance floor of the Coconut Grove, Thalberg suddenly said, "Hey, why don't we get married?" Norma smiled and answered, "I can't think of any reason why we shouldn't" —or so she later told a magazine reporter.

After a honeymoon at Del Monte on the Monterey peninsula, the Thalbergs settled down in Beverly Hills and became one of the film industry's most elegant and taste-setting couples. Norma was a fresh, outdoors type—she was good at tennis and she was a wonderful swimmer and skier—but as Mrs. Irving Thalberg, she started to play the role of society hostess, and for a while, went around tossing off quips like the Mayfair ladies in a Frederick Lonsdale play.

Norma's life could not have been easy at first. She was the wife of an industry leader, a man who was in poor health and who had never untied the apron strings. Ever since Henrietta and William had arrived in California, they had lived with Irving, and Henrietta was not yet ready to give up the keys of her kingdom. So for a couple of years it was Henrietta who ran the household and played the hostess at dinner parties. Norma accepted the situation graciously—graciousness was, after all, one of her outstanding characteristics as an actress. Going into the marriage, she was fully aware that it would take time and tact to wean Henrietta from her son, and since she had her own career to look after, she was willing to let her mother-in-law play chatelaine for a while longer. Cooperation, she realized, was the surest way of winning Henrietta's respect, the only way of convincing Henrietta that she, too, believed Irving was a national treasure.

The Shearer-Thalberg wedding in September 1927 was a high point in the history of M-G-M unity. All the top studio executives were present, not only as a matter of protocol, but because they were part of one big happy family. Of course, as in most happy families, there were occasional hostilities and ruptures, but none was so grievous that it couldn't be put aside for a glass of good bootleg champagne —or permanently settled by one of Mayer's pep talks.

This solidarity was to last for another year or so, but in the weeks preceding the wedding there had been a series of events that were eventually to lead the studio into a prolonged siege of divisiveness. For several years, Marcus Loew had been in failing health, and in the late fall of 1926, he contracted pneumonia. He made a partial recovery, but in late August of 1927, he again became ill, and on September 6, at the age of fifty-seven, he died at Pembroke, his estate on Long Island.

Since he had been widely respected throughout the industry, and since he was the first of the great pioneers of the film business to die, Loew was given a tribute that has subsequently been awarded only for the deaths of presidents and other national leaders: on the day of his funeral, all movie theatres closed their doors at two P.M., and kept them shut until the following day.

The list of honorary pallbearers reads like a who's who of the film industry. It begins with Adolph Zukor, a lifelong friend whose daughter, Mildred, was married to Loew's son, Arthur. Then come William Randolph Hearst; Nicholas Schenck, Loew's second-in-command; his brother, Joseph; Mayer; Thalberg; J. Robert Rubin; Carl Laemmle; William Fox; Cecil De Mille; and D. W. Griffith.

Loew's will left a third of the company' stock, a total of 400,000 shares, to his family. This bequest guaranteed them control of Loew's empire, including the M-G-M studio, and put them in a position to name Loew's successor. Acting in accordance with his wishes, on September 30, Nicholas Schenck took over as president of Loew's, Inc. The appointment was expected but unsettling news for Mayer and his staff at M-G-M. Schenck had caused problems in the past and there was no reason to believe he would become more amenable in the future.

Relations between him and Mayer had been cool ever since 1926, when Metro-Goldwyn had been expanded to Metro-Goldwyn-

Mayer. Schenck was one of the few Loew's executives who objected to the new logo, possibly because (as his foes claimed) he would have preferred to see it changed to Metro-Goldwyn-Schenck.

Mayer and Schenck had much in common—in fact, if similar backgrounds make for good relations, they should have been the best of friends. Like Mayer, Schenck was born in a small town in Russia, probably in 1881. Neither Nick nor his older brother, Joseph, was certain of the year of his birth, though Joe was sure he was born on a Christmas day—a date not easily forgotten when your relatives are the only Jews in town. Around 1885, they emigrated with their parents, and on arrival in New York, Joe was immediately sent out to work in a factory. After school, Nick collected pennies as a paperboy, but it was Joe who kept the family eating and provided his brother with a rudimentary education. In time, Joe got a job in a drugstore and ingratiated himself enough with his employer to get Nick hired as his replacement when he went off duty to attend night-school courses.

By 1901, the brothers had managed to scrape up enough money to buy a drugstore in lower Manhattan, on the outskirts of Chinatown. Within two years they were able to buy another shop, this one on Third Avenue and 110th Street.

They were still dreaming of building their own drugstore empire when one Sunday they visited Fort George, a quiet community on the New York side of the Hudson River. City slickers sneeringly referred to the area as South Albany, but the Schencks saw it as an excursion center for working families who wanted to escape the city on hot weekend afternoons. For eight hundred dollars, they bought a decrepit dance hall, refurbished it and launched it successfully in the summer of 1908. A year later, they acquired an adjacent piece of property, built a ferris wheel, then a scenic railway and other amusement rides. They called it Paradise Park.

By 1910, Paradise Park had become such a major attraction that Marcus Loew approached the Schencks about showing films on the premises. Nick and Joe liked the idea; an agreement was reached, and so began a long and mutually rewarding relationship. With Loew as a silent backer, the Schencks acquired a piece of land in Fort Lee, a community on the New Jersey side of the Hudson, and opened the Palisades Amusement Park. In its range and variety of amusement rides and entertainment, Palisades surpassed Paradise, and pretty soon it surpassed it in revenue too. By the early 1920s, on a sunny Saturday or Sunday, the ticket gate was often $100,000.

By then, the Schencks had handed over the management of the parks to outsiders, though they continued to hold an interest in

Palisades until the mid-1930s. Around 1912, both brothers joined
Loew's staff, Nick quickly working his way up to the position of
secretary in charge of theatre development, while Joe oversaw the
management of the company's booking offices. Two years later, Joe
resigned (but remained a Loew stockholder) and went into independent production, met and married Norma Talmadge, who was then
second only to Mary Pickford in the fan magazine popularity polls,
and set her up in her own production company, of which he was
president, vice-president, secretary, treasurer and business supervisor. By 1920, he had made similar arrangements with Constance
Talmadge (Norma's sister), Fatty Arbuckle and Buster Keaton (who
later married the youngest of the Talmadge girls, Natalie).

Nick, in the meantime, stayed on at Loew's, rising from secretary to vice-president, showing an astuteness for assessing real estate
values.

Nick was steady, Joe was flamboyant. According to one business
associate, "Joe Schenck was one of the ugliest men that ever lived.
But after you met him, if anybody asked you to describe him you
would have said he was one of the most attractive, charming people you'd ever met." He was also, according to various sources,
"shrewd," "a ruthless individual," "a lone wolf who refused to run
with the rest of the pack," "a perpetual traveler" who moved restlessly from Europe to New York, from New York to California and
from studio to studio—Select, Paramount, Metro-Goldwyn, United
Artists, Twentieth Century. He had a hand in all of them. A lot of
wheeling and dealing went on, some of it just beneath the margin of
legality, and eventually, Joe was to spend several months in prison
for federal offenses.

So, in any comparison of the Schenck brothers, those who prefer
the straight and narrow are sure to choose Nick over Joe. Nick was
steady, responsible and reliable—qualities that endeared him to
Loew and his other business associates.

Steady, responsible and reliable are not, however, the warmest of
positive adjectives, and so there are those who insist that Nick faded
into insignificance as he plodded along in his brother's shadow. Nick
knew what people said, and was determined to prove them wrong.
That at least is the premise behind one theory of the animosity
between Mayer and Schenck, between M-G-M and the East Coast
offices of Loew's, Inc.

The theory goes something like this: Joe had style; Nick was
drab. Joe flitted around the artistic perimeter of film making; Nick
stayed in New York, plugging away in the business end of the industry. Joe married a glamorous movie star; Nick lived with the wife of

a Brooklyn cop, whom he later married; his second wife, Pansy Wilcox, was part of a vaudeville act that never got beyond the provincial circuits. Pansy was as pert as her name, everybody liked her and agreed she was the perfect wife for Nick, but nobody ever mistook her for Norma Talmadge.

Therefore, when Nick became President of Loew's, Inc., he felt he had finally found the opportunity to prove himself his brother's equal. But blocking his path were Mayer and Thalberg, whose success in running the Metro studio tended to overshadow Nick's considerable achievements in managing Loew's, Inc. This was the start of a prickly situation that would get more so as the years passed: Mayer and Thalberg were Loew's employees, Schenck was their boss, but in terms of public attention and prestige, he was ignored and they got all the glory.

One of the first disagreements between Mayer and Schenck had occurred over this specific issue—which came first, the interests of Loew's, Inc. or the interests of M-G-M? The battle started in 1925 when Schenck was virtually in charge of the company because of Loew's poor health. Mayer suspected that Schenck had approved a plan to rent M-G-M films to Loew theatres at prices substantially lower than those available on the open market. This meant less money would be returned to the distributor (also Loew's, Inc.) and, in turn, less money for the studio and those executives (the "Mayer Group") whose contracts guaranteed them a share of Loew profits.

Mayer realized that the prime value of the studio to Loew's, Inc. was to provide its theatre chain with new pictures, and had no argument with the policy of giving "the family" first choice of the studio product. But to carry this favoritism further, to extend it to cut-rate rental fees, was sacrificing one child to feed another. Furthermore, through their expansion and consolidation, the M-G-M studios were producing more and better films, and at cheaper prices than Metro had in the past. This, to Mayer's mind, was a sufficient lagniappe for Loew's theatre owners and leasees.

Schenck vehemently denied Mayer's allegations of favoritism, but Mayer ordered his New York "people," headed by Robert Rubin, to keep a careful eye on the Loew's books. In retaliation, Schenck dispatched one of *his* "people," Eddie Mannix, to Culver City to act as watchdog over studio operations. The stratagem did not, however, work out as Schenck had planned. Once in California, Mannix became a loyal admirer of Mayer, and without losing the respect of Schenck, he would for the next twenty years act as a moderating force in all battles between the East and West coasts.

Mannix had first encountered the Schenck brothers while employed as a bouncer at Palisades Park. They brought him into the Loew's organization and later Joe hired him as manager of the Norma and Constance Talmadge picture units. Known around the M-G-M lot as either the Irishman (because of his heritage) or the Chinaman (because of his slanting eyes), he looked "like a boxer, with a cauliflower ear for a face," seemed "to have no nerves in his body" and "always played his cards face up on the table." Tough, masculine, but sympathetic, he was universally respected and trusted by even the most temperamental actors and directors at M-G-M.

Possibly because of Mannix's presence as a stabilizing influence, the mutual distrust between Mayer and Schenck didn't surface immediately. The time wasn't right for power plays or internecine warfare; it was one for union and fortification. Little more than a month after Schenck's appointment, a film opened in New York that would cause a revolution in picture making and severely challenge the resources of every Hollywood studio. It was called *The Jazz Singer*.

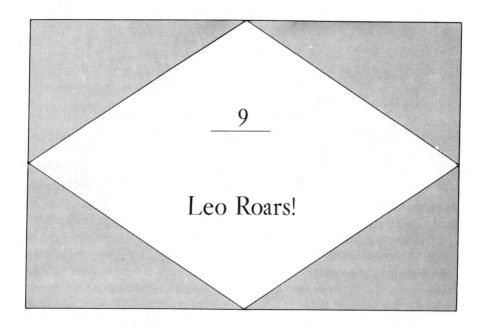

9

Leo Roars!

On September 24, 1926, American theatre owners reported a 50 percent decline in ticket sales for the previous evening. Most people, it seemed, had stayed home that night to listen to the broadcast of the Jack Dempsey–Gene Tunney fight from Philadelphia. But the decline turned out not to be a one-night phenomenon. Business remained spotty for the rest of the year, and by early 1927, it was evident that the industry had once again slipped into a period of recession.

Some industry analysts blamed this turn of events on radio, others offered different explanations, but no one came up with a solution, and by mid-1927, nearly all the studios were stocking up on red ink. Hardest hit of all was Warner Bros., and fighting for its life, this half-caste studio (not quite first-class, not exactly poverty row) would lead its betters out of the slump.

The four Warner brothers—Harry, Albert, Sam and Jack—had formed their own production and distribution company in 1918. For the next few years, they remained solvent through the incongruous assets of Rin-Tin-Tin and John Barrymore, but by 1926, not even these magnificent beasts could keep the creditors from the door. By then, Sam Warner was already interested in the possibilities of the sound film, and as a trial run, had added music and sound effects to *Don Juan,* a Barrymore vehicle released in August 1926. Except for the delicacy and beauty of Mary Astor, there was nothing much to recommend the film, but audiences loved all of it, including the pseudosymphonic musical score.

Encouraged by the reaction, the Warners went ahead with what is now regarded as the first talking picture, *The Jazz Singer,* though in fact, the talk is limited to just a few words—the rest is background music and Al Jolson singing a few songs. Grossing over $3 million, the picture was a sensation, and pushed all the studios into sound production. None of them was enthusiastic—the transition from silent to sound production was obviously going to be an expensive, time-consuming and messy business; new stages would have to be built; theatres would need new equipment; actors, writers and directors would have to master an entirely new form of movie storytelling. And virtually no one in Hollywood knew anything about sound recording, not even which of the two imperfectly developed methods of recording was preferable: the Warner Vitaphone method, which recorded sound on discs, or the Movietone process being developed at the Fox studios, in which a sound track was printed on the same strip of film as the photographic image. (The Fox process, being the more practical, quickly won out.)

M-G-M was the last of the major studios to enter the sound era, and for a very good reason. Mayer and company had coasted through the 1926–27 recession, had in fact shown a gross profit that was about $200,000 above the previous year's record. Such a piffling advance was no reason for celebration, but compared to the financial statements of the other studios, it was no occasion for panic, either. Furthermore, neither Mayer nor Thalberg had much faith in the artistic or economic future of the sound film. It was a fad, they believed, that would wear itself out in a few months or however long it took the public to realize that the addition of dialogue would turn the motion picture into a slavish and inferior copy of the legitimate theatre.

So for almost a year they resisted the trend toward talking pictures, with encouraging results. In 1927–28, M-G-M turned out some of its finest films—Clarence Brown's epic Western *The Trail of '98,* King Vidor's moving tribute to "Mr. Anyman," *The Crowd,* the Gish-Seastrom *The Wind*—along with a number of its greatest crowd-pleasers—Garbo in *Woman of Affairs* and *Wild Orchids,* Crawford in *Our Dancing Daughters,* Davies in *The Patsy* and *Show People,* Lon Chaney in *Mr. Wu* and *The Unknown* and *London After Midnight.* By the end of the fiscal year, the company's profits had risen to $8.5 million, a jump of nearly $2 million over the previous year.

Just then, in July 1928, Warners released its first all-talking picture, a prohibition melodrama called *The Lights of New York*. It is a front-runner for any list of the ten worst films ever, but the public flocked to see it, and within a few months, it had grossed over $2 million.

Money talks and the talkies made money—it was as simple as that. Up to this time Nick Schenck had also been convinced that talking pictures were a fad, but now he decided that M-G-M would be foolish not to cash in on the novelty while it lasted. Mayer and Thalberg reluctantly agreed.

The studio had no sound stages, but there was no problem about renting one while M-G-M built its own. The pressing problem was finding someone to develop and oversee a sound department. Eddie Mannix was the only one who could come up with a candidate. "We've got a fellow in the special effects department who does camera work and trick stuff," he reported to Mayer. "Doug Shearer—Norma's brother. Why not throw the sound problem in his lap?"

"So overnight I became the one-man sound department," Douglas Shearer recalled. "They ordered me to do the job, they didn't just give it to me. And probably they wouldn't have given it to me except that they were desperate."

Shearer had come to Hollywood in the mid-1920s to visit his sister, and stayed on when he got a job in the Warner Bros.' prop department. His main chore, he later recalled, was cleaning up after the livestock in the pictures starring Rin-Tin-Tin, the first canine superstar of the American cinema. Later Shearer moved to M-G-M as a member of the special effects department, where he showed an aptitude for trick photography, engineering and electronics. "But what I knew about sound you could have put in a nutshell," he later said. "So I went off to the Bell Lab to see what I could learn. I also picked up a sound crew, which I stole from every which where— from Bell, from colleges, from other studios."

M-G-M moved into sound production by experimenting with sound effects and musical tracks rather than jumping directly into dialogue. With Douglas Shearer in charge, the first films were scored and recorded at the Victor Phonograph Company in Camden, New Jersey, and in August 1928, audiences first heard Leo, the M-G-M trademark lion, roar from the screen. The film was *White Shadows in the South Seas*, a semidocumentary by W. S. Van Dyke and Robert Flaherty which was more notable for its location photography than for its story or musical score.

For its first experiment with dialogue, the studio decided to reshoot the final reel of an already completed silent film, *Alias Jimmy Valentine*, starring William Haines, Leila Hyams and Lionel Barrymore. The new scenes were filmed at Paramount since M-G-M's sound stages were still under construction. On completion in the fall of 1928, they were to be used in eight-hour shifts around the clock as the studio hastened to catch up with its sound competitors.

The new stages were, according to an M-G-M press release of the period, "the largest to be found at any studio. . . . Each stage is 100 by 125 feet, surrounded by eight-inch concrete walls. When the two-ton doors of the stages are closed by machinery, the interiors are hermetically sealed, ventilation being supplied through sound filters. . . . Each stage contains six sound-proof camera booths, housing, in addition to the camera equipment, motors synchronized with the recording instruments in the two-story building abutting on the tall windowless stages."

The first sound film shot on the M-G-M lot was *The Broadway Melody*, the original "100% All Talking! All Singing! All Dancing!" Hollywood extravaganza. It was entirely appropriate that M-G-M's first major sound production be a musical. Mayer was known to be a sucker for a pretty tune, and in the past, had been largely responsible for the studio's filming silent versions of *The Student Prince, Rose Marie, The Red Mill* and *Sally, Irene and Mary*, though inevitably the scores of these shows were reduced to orchestral or piano accompaniment. Now the songs could pour from the screen as they were intended to be heard, and this, for Mayer, was the principal blessing of the advent of sound.

Broadway Melody was the backstage story of a sister act (Bessie Love, Anita Page) broken up by an amorous songwriter (Charles King, a recent import from the New York stage). The original script had been intended as a silent production, so Broadway playwright and comic James Gleason was called in to write dialogue; Gleason was noted for his snappy, slangy repartee—one of his biggest hits was called *Is Zat So?* Billy Rose was approached about writing the songs, but Mayer and Thalberg eventually chose a little-known composer and lyricist team, Arthur Freed (words) and Nacio Herb Brown (music). It turned out to be a happy choice—the score for the picture included three hits: the title song, "You Were Meant for Me" and "The Wedding of the Painted Doll."

The production supervisors were Harry Rapf and Lawrence Weingarten, but as usual they were closely supervised by Thalberg. After seeing the early footage, he decided the picture, originally planned as a part-sound film, was so promising that it should be expanded to become M-G-M's first all-sound venture. That meant added pressure for director Harry Beaumont, his cast and crew, nearly all of whom were plodding ahead by trial and error, but they kept at it despite some very thorny problems.

One was the lack of a permanent staff of musicians. The studio had no orchestra, and for every musical sequence, was obliged to hire outside players at great expense and with no guarantee of continuity —a violinist who worked on Tuesday would be booked for another engagement on the following Thursday. After a series of needless and costly delays, Douglas Shearer complained to Thalberg, "Look, we've got no carry-over, no system here."

"Well, what should we do?" Thalberg asked.

Shearer suggested telephoning Major Edward Bowes, manager of the Loew's Capitol in New York, and asking him to dispatch the theatre's music library to the studio, along with its arranger, music librarian and conductor. Thalberg agreed, and after checking with Mayer, placed a call to Bowes in New York. This was the beginning of the M-G-M music department which was, like the studio's sound department, to become the most distinguished in all of Hollywood.

Once the film was finished, Thalberg looked at it and was pleased except for one production number, shot in a crude version of Technicolor, "The Wedding of the Painted Doll." Too static, he decided, and ordered the sequence to be refilmed with added zest. That meant added expense for a picture that was already over budget, so Douglas Shearer suggested that since there was nothing wrong with the music already recorded, it could be played through loud-speakers as the actors mimed the number for the cameras; then the film could be joined to the prerecording in the labs.

"Can that be done?" Thalberg asked.

"Well, it *should* work," Shearer replied.

It did work, and from then on, for better or worse, prerecording became standard procedure on all Hollywood musicals.

Today *The Broadway Melody* looks pretty tacky—the story is simple-minded, the acting is stilted, the chorus girls are dumpy, the dialogue is a stream of colloquial clinkers—but when it opened in February 1929, critics and public concurred in proclaiming it a nearly perfect entertainment. Costing about $280,000, it was to gross over $4 million by the end of the year. Selected by *The New York Times* for its ten-best list, *Broadway Melody* was also the first M-G-M production to win the best picture award from the Academy of Motion Picture Arts and Sciences, founded two years previously.

The studio's first all-dialogue picture, *The Trial of Mary Dugan*, was not so well received by the critics. An adaptation of the hit

Broadway play by Bayard Veiller, it was dismissed as "canned theatre," an accurate description of a film whose action was restricted to one main set (a New York courtroom) and whose center of gravity was the actors' performances and their scrupulous enunciation of Veiller's lengthy and less than immortal dialogue. But the literalness of the transcription didn't bother the audiences, who flocked to see it and came away enormously impressed by Norma Shearer's portrayal of the title role.

Shearer was the first of the important M-G-M stars to risk the transition to sound, and a good deal of thought and care went into the choice of an appropriate vehicle for her debut. The courtroom story of *Mary Dugan* keeps the heroine listening tensely to testimony for most of the picture, then lets her loose on a big emotional scene: it was a risky, but highly dramatic way for Shearer to take the plunge into sound, and her daring was amply rewarded with praise for her "modulated voice," her "excellent diction" and "unbridled emotional power." (She had been coached by the eminent Broadway comedienne, Mrs. Leslie Carter.) Her performance hasn't stood the test of time very well—film historian John Kobal recently suggested the film should be titled "Mary Dugan, You're a Trial to Me"—but then, few Shearer sound performances have aged well. Nonetheless, at the time, *Mary Dugan* added luster to Shearer's reputation, and shortly she was being called the First Lady of American movies, even by people who should have known better.

Norma Shearer's success in *Mary Dugan,* following fast on the success of *Broadway Melody,* convinced Mayer and Thalberg that the sound film was more than a passing fad. Throughout 1929 the studio ground out talkies on the two stages at Culver City and at a third on 127th Street and Second Avenue in New York. (The East Coast facilities were being used mainly for the production of Metro Movietone musical shorts, produced "under the supervision of Major Edward Bowes.") There were a lot of flops along the way, as well as some expensive decisions—because of a monumental number of out-of-sync foul-ups, the studio soon abandoned Vitaphone sound-on-disc for Movietone sound-on-film recording—but by the end of 1929 the balance sheet was resoundingly in favor of the sound film. M-G-M–Loew's profit for the year was a record-breaking $12,107,026.

"When sound came in, everything was new all over again," David O. Selznick once said. "It was the first Western with sound, the first war picture with sound, the first swashbuckler with sound." The stars also had to start all over again, too, proving that they spoke just as gracefully as they had once moved across the dream surface of the silent screen. In the long run, the established genres proved to be more adaptable than the established stars, many of whom suddenly became self-conscious about such formerly picayune blemishes as a Brooklyn accent or an inability to speak English. The lispers, the stammerers, the foreigners, the peacock-voiced he-men, the femmes fatales with bourbon baritones, anyone with a trace of a regional accent, anyone without a certificate from an elocution teacher—they all woke up one morning and saw their careers in jeopardy.

Once again, as in 1916 when Zukor, Triangle and Lasky launched the feature film with stage stars, screen actors were faced with the competition of their Broadway brethren: the studios fell over each other as they rushed to sign up New York actors, even those whose stage experience amounted to nothing more than saying "Yes, M'Lord" in an overnight Broadway flop. M-G-M was no exception. In the souvenir program for *The Broadway Melody,* a company spokesman announced that the studio had already signed such "noted stage players" as Elliott Nugent, Charles Bickford, Kay Johnson, Lowell Sherman, Louise Groody, Ruth Chatterton, Raymond Hackett, Mary Eaton and Oscar Shaw for forthcoming sound productions. But, the anonymous writer hastened to assure the fans, "every star and virtually every featured player on the Culver City lot has already demonstrated an ability to meet vocal requirements for talking films, many of the players amazing the producers by the recording quality of their supposedly 'untrained' voices."

M-G-M eased most of its major players into sound production with *The Hollywood Revue of 1929,* a plotless mishmash conceived as the cinematic equivalent of the George White–Florenz Ziegfeld–Earl Carroll Broadway revue entertainment. It was shot on the "graveyard shift" (midnight to 7 A.M.) since most members of the all-star cast were working elsewhere on the lot during the day. Conrad Nagel, a former stage actor with impeccable diction, acted as master of ceremonies; Joan Crawford, perched on a piano à la Helen Morgan (but dressed like Baby Peggy), sang "I've Got a Feeling for You" and then pranced around while a quintet of top-hatted gents hummed and strummed a ukelele accompaniment; Marion Davies sang a solo and tapped out a mating call on a King-Kong-sized drum; Bessie Love emerged from Jack Benny's pocket to pout-sing "You Can't Do That to Me"; Norma Shearer and John Gilbert appeared in a technicolor *Romeo and Juliet* balcony scene, updated with flapper language.

Most of the stars came across with flying colors. Marion Davies's stammer disappeared when she was singing or speaking from memory, and Joan Crawford's low, husky voice suited her tough, sexy appearance. The only major problem was Gilbert. At a preview, the audience broke up every time he opened his mouth. His lines were meant to be funny, but people were laughing at him and not at what he said. The trouble was his light, thin voice which recorded "white" —high-pitched and effeminate.

When a second preview audience also scoffed and jeered at Gilbert, Thalberg decided the *Romeo and Juliet* sequence should be cut from the picture. But the M-G-M sales department protested and Nick Schenck also argued that the deletion would weaken the all-star appeal of the film. So the sequence went back in, much to the detriment of Gilbert's subsequent career.

At this time, Mayer was negotiating a new contract with Gilbert's manager, Harry Edington, who was asking for the moon and the stars and anything else he could get as a bonus. When discussions reached a deadlock, Schenck offered to handle the matter himself. Edington went to New York and returned with nearly everything he wanted: M-G-M would pay Gilbert $250,000 every three months —in other words, a guarantee of $1 million a year. The contract was for five years.

Mayer and Thalberg were appalled, but there was nothing they could do except find a flattering vehicle for Gilbert that would cancel out his poor showing in *Hollywood Revue*. They chose *Redemption*, the Broadway version of Tolstoy's play *The Living Corpse*. The result was such a disaster that it was shelved for later release while Gilbert was rushed into another production, Ferenc Molnar's *Olympia*. By the time of its release the picture had been renamed *His Glorious Night*, a title that suggests the silent screen at its most rococo. In keeping with the title, Gilbert's performance is in the plummy, overexaggerated style of the silent-screen Lothario. As he murmured, "I love you, *I love you*, I LOVE YOU," while nibbling Catherine Dale Owen's arm from fingertip to shoulder, audiences giggled, then hooted with derision.

His Glorious Night was a flop; so was *Redemption* when it was finally released a few months later. Mayer called Gilbert to his office and offered to buy up the remainder of his contract. Many sound-embarrassed stars took this route—Corinne Griffith, the Vitagraph "Orchid Lady," was one—and some received such handsome settlements that they were able to live comfortably for the rest of their lives. (A few, like the Talmadge Sisters, withdrew voluntarily. Said Connie: "Leave them while you're still looking good and thank God for the trust funds Mama set up.") But Gilbert needed stardom more than he needed money: he insisted M-G-M fulfill the contract to the letter.

So the comedy—or tragedy—was played to the bitter end. In

1931, the studio hired Mervyn LeRoy, Warners' hotshot director of *Little Caesar* fame, to direct Gilbert in an underworld drama, *Gentleman's Fate*. By this time, the sound technicians had Gilbert's voice under control, and he gives a perfectly adequate performance in a modestly entertaining film. He can't really be faulted, he isn't as ludicrous as in some of the earlier talkies, but he's lackluster; he could be replaced by ten or twenty other leading men without harming the impact of the film. The magnetism, the individuality, the grace of his silent performance are sadly missing.

Gilbert complained that the studio was straddling him with weak material, so Thalberg told him to make his own selection. He wrote an original story, *Downstairs*, which became the best of his sound films, but it too failed to intrigue the public. When his contract expired at the end of 1932, Gilbert's career and self-confidence had been shattered and he was already off and running on a course of self-destruction that led to his death, at age thirty-eight in 1936. "In my opinion, John Gilbert died of a broken heart," says Howard Strickling.

In his final years, Gilbert often accused Mayer of deliberately destroying his career because of an incident that happened in 1926. Gilbert was set to marry Greta Garbo in a double wedding ceremony with Eleanor Boardman and King Vidor, but only one half of the match came off—Garbo failed to make an appearance. Distraught, Gilbert had rushed to the men's room where he met Mayer who advised him, "Forget about marriage, just sleep with her." Gilbert hauled off and punched L.B., causing him to topple over and strike his head on the tile floor. This blow, Gilbert later reckoned, had made his decline at M-G-M a foregone conclusion. This story, says Mrs. Selznick, a guest at the ceremony is "whole cloth." The only foul-up at the wedding was an incident concerning Vidor's shoes. He was wearing brown oxfords, and Boardman refused to be married until he found a suitable black pair.

Certainly there was no love lost between Gilbert and Mayer, but there is no concrete evidence that anyone at M-G-M ever tried to sabotage the actor's career. For all his final films, he was given good writers, good directors and good supporting casts, and by and large his screenplays were no weaker than those assigned him in the silent era. Certainly Gilbert's vocal problems could have been remedied by a higher level of sound technology than existed at the time, but even if it had, there is no assurance of his successful transition from silence to sound: his voice, even after the pitch had been corrected, was the least expressive, least dynamic component of his equipment as an actor. And the sound era demanded voices as well as faces and physiques.

Buster Keaton, the great stone face of silent screen comedy, was Metro's only other major casualty to sound. All the films he made between 1924 and 1926 were released by M-G-M, but when Joe Schenck, his mentor, became president of United Artists at the end of 1926, he went along with his boss. Two years later Schenck informed him that he was disbanding the Keaton production unit, but had arranged ,for Buster to work at M-G-M as a contract player. Keaton was stunned, but accustomed to following Joe's advice, he did as he was told.

Buster was warmly welcomed to M-G-M by Thalberg, who admired Keaton just as Keaton admired Thalberg. And the comic's first film as contract player, *The Cameraman* (his last silent), was topnotch, as good as anything he had done in the past. But things went downhill after that. Thalberg assigned his brother-in-law, Larry Weingarten, to supervise the Keaton productions, and while Keaton liked Weingarten, he wasn't accustomed to having a supervisor. Joe Schenck had always allowed him to choose his own staff of writers and directors, and had given him the final say on all artistic decisions.

Keaton's relations with M-G-M took a turn for the worse when, in the early thirties, he was cast opposite Jimmy Durante in a couple of vaudeville pastiches, *The Passionate Plumber* and *What, No Beer?* Lovable and talented as he was, Durante wasn't really in Keaton's class, but Buster suspected that the Schnozzola was being groomed to replace him as M-G-M's top banana.

Finally, in 1932, Mayer and Keaton locked horns over what was essentially a trivial matter. As part of its public relations campaign, M-G-M frequently provided guided tours of the studio facilities for groups of important out-of-towners. These visits usually concluded with a couple of M-G-M stars playing a short scene before an unloaded camera; it was fake, but the actors usually managed to create the illusion of actual shooting conditions. This charade had been performed by everyone from Shearer to Garbo. Now it was Buster's turn. On the following Saturday he and Durante were to run through a comedy sketch for a group of Illinois schoolteachers.

Keaton was ready to perform until he remembered that Saturday was the date of the UCLA–St. Mary's football match at which he was scheduled to appear as "mascot" for St. Mary's.

"Sorry," he told Mayer, "I'll have to take a rain check."

Mayer repeated the request. Then, losing patience, he ordered Keaton to be on the lot that Saturday.

"I can't," Buster said, and walked out of the office.

St. Mary's lost that Saturday and on the following Monday,

Keaton lost too. Shortly after he arrived at the studio, a messenger presented him with a note, signed by Mayer, which read, "As of this date, Buster Keaton's services are no longer required at Metro-Gold-wyn-Mayer."

For Keaton and his fans, this incident was a prime example of Mayer's petty vindictiveness, but what they fail to mention is that there was more than a football game behind Keaton's dismissal. Relations between the comedian and the studio had been strained for some time. Keaton's years as an independent agent made it difficult for him to adapt to the M-G-M production system, and he became progressively more querulous and temperamental as the reviews and returns of his films declined. Perhaps, as Buster contended, the studio should have let him do things his way, for when he did, he turned in his best work—namely, *Doughboys* (1930), the most successful of his sound films. But M-G-M was interested in utilizing Keaton as a performer, not as a producer, for the simple reason that in the time it took to develop a project, he could have appeared in two or three pictures set up by the studio's production staff.

There was a second problem. Around the time he came to M-G-M, Keaton began drinking heavily, partly because of professional problems, partly because of difficulties with his wife, Natalie Talmadge. Eventually Buster moved out of the gaudy Beverly Hills villa he had built for Natalie and took up residence in his trailer–dressing room on Metro's back lot. There he entertained his cronies and their girl friends at what studio gossips termed "orgies." According to one story, the "debauchery" was reported to Mayer, who decided to visit Keaton's dressing room unannounced. He wasn't pleased by what he saw. Buster told him to mind his own business and then ordered him to leave the trailer. Mayer obeyed, but his face was red with rage as he left.

"For the most part, Mr. Mayer and Buster had a good relationship," Howard Strickling insists. "The only problem was that Buster worked hard at being comic both off and on the screen. He was a practical joker and prankster, particularly when he wasn't busy making one of his pictures. His antics sometimes interfered with the production activities of others, so occasionally Mayer had to call him on the carpet and lay down some rules."

Keaton's dismissal brought protests from Eddie Mannix and Thalberg, who prevailed upon Mayer to rehire the comedian. But Buster couldn't forget the insult to his pride. Instead of returning to M-G-M, he went off on a binge, and by the time he had pulled himself together, he was considered unemployable by all the major studios.

By the end of 1929, all but two members of the M-G-M stock company had made their talking debuts. One of the holdouts was Lon Chaney, who had a stage background and possessed a resonant voice, but was reluctant to abandon the visual art of silent picture panto-mime. Eventually Irving Thalberg argued him into remaking one of his earlier triumphs, *The Unholy Three*, a story that would utilize his gift for vocal impersonation as well as his talent for outré disguises. The picture turned out to be an unqualified success, many critics and a large portion of the public preferring it to the 1925 silent version.

Unfortunately it was not a success that M-G-M or Chaney could build on. During the production of the picture, the actor was discom-forted by a throat irritation, and once shooting was completed, he underwent an operation for a tumor that proved to be malignant. As his condition worsened, he lost the ability to speak, and he was forced to communicate through mime and sign language which he had learned as a child from his deaf-mute parents. Soon he slipped into a coma, and in August 1930, two months after the release of *The Unholy Three*, he died.

Metro's other sound delinquent was Garbo, whose English was understandable, but heavily accented. As late as 1928, according to director Clarence Brown, her struggles with the language were a constant source of mirth on the Beverly Hills party circuit. People would crack dumb double-entendre jokes for her benefit, and if she laughed (and she was known to laugh at anything), she would be asked to explain what she found so funny. Gamely, she tried to paraphrase the intricacies of risqué American humor, winding up in a morass of triple entendres that convulsed everyone, including the actress.

Garbo's last silent picture, *The Kiss* (1929), was also M-G-M's last major silent production, and certainly it was made only because the studio was trying to protect the actress's reputation. It's middling Garbo—stylishly directed by Jacques Feyder, but undernourished in plot and characterization. Still, worse Garbo pictures had made lots of money in the past, so the disappointing box office returns for *The Kiss* made it clear that the actress had either to speak or to pack her bags and go home to Sweden.

Everyone agreed that Garbo's first sound picture should be something special, ideally an adaptation of a distinguished literary property. Thalberg saw her as Shaw's *Saint Joan*, but Shaw didn't. He refused to sell M-G-M the film rights. Thalberg then approached Danish director Carl Dreyer about remaking his great silent picture, *The Passion of Joan of Arc*, but Dreyer declined. He was not interested in working for a Hollywood studio. Next Thalberg hit on the idea of casting Garbo as the Swedish-American heroine of Eugene O'Neill's Pulitzer Prize melodrama, *Anna Christie*, and set about obtaining the screen rights from First National which had produced a silent version of the play in 1923. Everything went smoothly until Garbo decided O'Neill's play was denigrating to Swedes. She thought she'd rather not play the role. Both Thalberg and Mayer gave her pep talks, but the actress couldn't make up her mind. One day it was yes; the next day, no.

Blanche Sweet (an effective Anna in the otherwise overrated silent version) insists that at one point M-G-M approached her about taking over for Garbo, and that when she mentioned this during the course of a dinner-party conversation, Garbo stared incredulously. The next morning, she called Thalberg and agreed to go ahead with the project. According to another report, Garbo's manager, Harry Edington, told Mayer that *Anna Christie* was out of the question, and Mayer told Edington that Garbo would cooperate—or else. Since the actress was then financially strapped—this was shortly after the stock market crash—she decided cooperation was the best policy.

M-G-M promoted *Anna Christie* with the slogan "Garbo Speaks!" and the critics and public were enthralled by every syllable she uttered. Only Garbo was disappointed. "Look at that!" she muttered while watching herself on the screen of a Beverly Hills theatre. "Isn't that terrible? Who ever saw Swedes act that way?"

She was much happier with a German-language version of *Anna Christie* produced by M-G-M for foreign release. Directed by Jacques Feyder (a Belgian who was trilingual) and featuring Garbo's good friend, Salka Viertel, in the Marie Dressler role, this production is superior to the Clarence Brown original, partly because O'Neill's dialogue always sounds better in a foreign language and partly because Feyder gives the film a visual elegance missing from the English version. Garbo reportedly regards the German *Anna Christie* as one of her finest films.

During the first three years of sound production, the major studios often made foreign-language versions of their important pictures for the French, German and Spanish markets. Those stars who were bilingual (Garbo, Edward G. Robinson, Jeanette MacDonald) or those who could memorize their lines phonetically (Buster Keaton) would appear in one or more of the foreign versions; those who could not would be replaced by actors who were popular in their native country—Charles Boyer's first "American" film was the 1930 French-language version of M-G-M's *The Big House*.

In some instances these foreign counterparts were better than the original stars, but audiences abroad rejected them as imposters.

"The films shot in foreign languages just didn't work," remembers Robert Vogel, a member of Loew's International Department. "A lot of them used stage people and audiences weren't interested. They wanted to see Garbo and not Signora Delores Martinez or whoever —so after a couple of years, we dropped these productions. The Latin countries preferred synchronized dialogue [dubbing]; the others went for subtitling. So we prepared versions to accommodate both tastes."

The foreign market was important for the American studios, and the prospects of losing it had been one of the prime reasons why so many producers and executives had decried the coming of sound; they were sure the talkies would halt the flow of foreign currency into their bank accounts. These fears, however, proved to be groundless. Once the technicalities of dubbing and subtitling had been worked out, it became evident that the francs and pesos would keep rolling in. The American movie was still king in Europe.

Having made the transition to sound with a minimum of upheaval, M-G-M should have been in the peachiest of corporate conditions. And outwardly things did look fine—M-G-M-Loew's profits rose to $14 million in 1929–30, not quite so good as Warners, but better than the other Hollywood companies. Internally, however, there were problems. For some time a rivalry between the East and West coast arms of the studio had been developing, and during this period of transition, it nearly turned into out-and-out warfare. It was the beginning of Schenck versus Mayer, a battle that was to go on for twenty years.

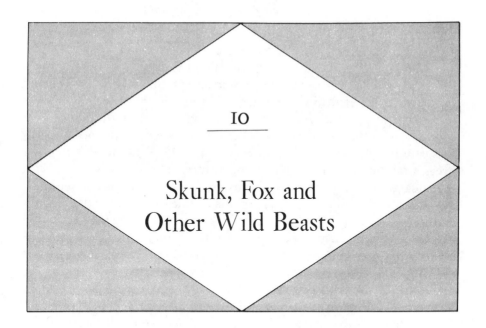

10

Skunk, Fox and
Other Wild Beasts

People were always mispronouncing Nicholas Schenck's name. "Skenk," Mayer would say, "Nick *Skenk.*" But once, in 1929, when someone mentioned Mr. "Shenk," he replied, "Skunk. You mean Mr. *Skunk.*"

Schenck became Skunk because of an incident that occurred in the fall of 1928. Mayer was walking to his car one night when he was approached by a suspicious-looking character who claimed he worked for the Fox studios. He went on to explain that he had been entrusted with finding out whether Mayer could be interested in a deal to amalgamate the Fox and Loew corporations. Mayer brushed him aside, climbed into the back seat and slammed the door.

That was the end of that, he thought, but in the weeks that followed, he started hearing rumors that Fox was planning to take over M-G-M and Loew's. He checked with Robert Rubin, his agent in Schenck's New York office, but Rubin reported that he had heard nothing. So Mayer forgot the whole thing and set his mind to solving pressing studio problems—this was the period when Metro was switching to sound production, and there was a new crisis every day. He was struggling with one of them when an associate burst into his office and reported that Winfield Sheehan, Fox's production manager, was snooping around the lot, checking out the facilities just as a prospective tenant checks out the closets in a new apartment.

Mayer dropped everything and called Rubin. Yes, he said, there were rumors, but no, as far as he could ascertain, there was no reason for alarm. That Rubin was unaware of the gravity of the situation is testimony to the skill and secrecy with which the skullduggery was carried out. Despite all the gossip, nearly everyone in the industry was caught off guard when, on March 5, 1929, William Fox told the press that he was buying out the interests of Loew's, Inc. Nick Schenck was sitting next to him as he made the announcement.

The news broke while Mayer was in Washington for the Hoover inauguration. He rushed to New York, where he was met by Rubin and by Thalberg, who had hopped on the Super Chief as soon as he heard what was going on. Schenck talked to them several times, but nothing was resolved, not even Schenck's purpose in hitching up with Fox. If the transaction went through, Fox would be president of the new company and Schenck would probably be out of a job.

Within a few days, Mayer had discovered the reason for Schenck's deviousness. He had agreed to sell his Loew's stock to Fox and had persuaded Loew's widow and children to do the same. In short, Schenck was going to make a handsome profit from the transferral, close to $8 million, which was ample compensation for stepping down from the Loew's presidency. There was also speculation that he would probably get a bonus by being appointed to a high position in the new company.

Fox invited Mayer to his office for an informal chat. They had met before, of course, and had gotten along pretty well, though they were never close friends. They came from similar backgrounds—Fox had been born in Hungary, had worked as a tailor in New York, had opened a nickelodeon and by 1912, owned one of America's major theatre chains. Then he moved into production. The Fox Corporation was one of the oldest of Hollywood's six major studios, and though its product was never much more than average, it got through the 1920s handsomely, and with the coming of sound, it had a number of bright stars, especially pert and petite Janet Gaynor, who was the leading heiress apparent to Pickford's title of America's Sweetheart.

Fox's trump card, however, was his possession of the rights for the sound-on-film (Movietone) recording process, which by 1929 had been adopted by most studios rather than the Warner Bros. sound-on-disc system. Everything was going Fox's way, except that he needed more stars and more theatres if he were to become kingpin of the industry. Taking over Loew's and M-G-M would guarantee him front position.

Mayer's meeting with Fox in 1929 got off to a bad start.

"Call me Bill," Fox said.

"Yes, Mr. Fox," Mayer replied.

Fox then tried to break the ice by assuring Mayer that the deal would not jeopardize his position as head of M-G-M production. Of course, there had been some mistakes in M-G-M policy, he added. "What mistakes?" Mayer asked sharply. Fox cited the recently signed $1 million contract for John Gilbert. Mayer pointed out that Schenck had arranged the Gilbert deal and Fox, smiling, said, "Well, if you want to get rid of Gilbert, I'll tell you how to do it. Give him a couple of bad parts. That'll ruin him and you can buy up his contract."

Fox had never forgotten that Gilbert had left his company for Metro where virtually overnight he was to emerge as a star. It was, in fact, a sore point with him that his company had failed with Gilbert while Metro had succeeded, and now he seemed to be seeking some kind of perverse revenge by suggesting that Metro could and should destroy Gilbert. His stratagem was based on the knowledge that there was no love lost between Gilbert and Mayer.

Mayer, however, did not rise to the bait. "I don't want to break contracts," he said, "and I don't like anyone who does."

Then he questioned the legality of a merger of the Loew and Fox enterprises. For the past few years, the Federal Trade Commission and the Justice Department had taken a lively interest in the monopolistic trend of the film industry. In 1923 the Trade Commission had, in fact, gone as far as filing suit against Adolph Zukor and Famous Players–Lasky when Zukor started buying up First National stock. That deal had been aborted by government intervention, and so it seemed only logical that the same thing would happen now that Fox was trying to buy out Loew's, Inc.

"Don't worry," Fox said, "I've got a friend who's got Hoover in his back pocket."

This slur on one of his heroes was too much for Mayer. Seething with anger, he marched out of Fox's office and called one of *his* friends in the Hoover administration, and was assured the government would look into the matter immediately. Returning to Hollywood, Mayer told the M-G-M front office not to worry, that Fox and Skunk would get their comeuppance, and that the Skunk would have to pay for his Machiavellian machinations.

The Fox-Loew merger did fall through, though not precisely as Mayer had foreseen. On July 17, 1929, before the details of the consolidation had been worked out, Fox was seriously injured in a car accident while en route to play golf on Long Island with Nick Schenck. Doctors predicted a hospital stay of at least three months. His associates advised him to sell the Loew stock he had accumulated, as the market had gone sky-high and he could turn in an enormous profit.

"Goddamit," he shouted, "my bones were broken, but my brain's whole. I can manage the deal even if I am stuck in this goddamn bed."

Three months later—October 29, 1929—Fox had reason to regret this decision. The stock market crash didn't wipe him out, but the damage was considerable. Fox had financed his Movietone interests by obtaining loans, amounting to about $300,000, from the Bell Telephone Company and his bankers. These obligations were in the form of "short-time paper," maturing in the winter of 1929–30. To get control of the Loew's stock, he had taken out additional bank loans and bought shares on margin. Now, it seemed unlikely that he could meet all the financial deadlines.

The final blow fell in November 1929, when the Justice Department fulfilled Mayer's expectations and filed suit against Fox. A month later, he was compelled by court order to relinquish control of his company to a board of trustees headed by his largest creditors. That put an end to the Fox–M-G-M consolidation and eliminated Fox from the front rank of Hollywood moguls.

As Mayer had forecast, Schenck had to pay heavily for the affront to his colleagues. He tried to conciliate Mayer, Thalberg and Rubin with an indemnity of $750,000. Thalberg took his share and considered it paltry. He wanted more, thought he deserved more, knew he needed more.

A few months before, he had received a letter from the Internal Revenue Service saying his tax returns had been checked and found fraudulent—he had taken deductions to which he was not entitled. His explanation that the deductions had been recommended by his tax adviser did not impress the IRS. He was informed that if found guilty of fraud, he might face a jail sentence.

Thalberg wrote an emotional letter of appeal, trying to justify a transferral of stock to his mother as a common practice and pointing out his contribution to American society. The IRS agreed to reconsider its threat of criminal action, but refused to drop the case or to accept his offer to pay whatever assessment was demanded of him. He was still under suspicion, still liable for monetary penalties.

Then came the stock market crash. All the M-G-M executives suffered from the crash—Mayer came off the best since most of his investments were in real estate—but Thalberg, who had invested heavily in stocks and bonds, was nearly wiped out. Then Norma became pregnant—Irving, Jr., was born in August 1930—and the need for money became more pressing. Thalberg's health had been good, better than the doctors had predicted, but still he had to think about the future.

Schenck's conscience money provided some relief, but it wasn't enough. Thalberg went to see Mayer, and Mayer said he would do what he could. Through his friends in Washington, he got some of the pressure taken off Thalberg, but that wasn't enough for Irving. Thalberg was then earning four thousand dollars a week at a time when banks were closing and Loew's stock was plummeting on the Wall Street board. Mayer couldn't ask Schenck to raise Thalberg's salary, but he could ask a more generous percentage deal for Thalberg, even if it meant a personal sacrifice—which it did. In December 1929, Mayer consented to give him 10 percent more of the "Mayer's Group" benefits, the 10 percent coming out of his own pocket. This brought Thalberg's share up to 30 percent and reduced Mayer's to 43. Rubin's share remained steady at 27 percent.

And so the trouble began: Mayer was making sacrifices for Thalberg which Thalberg accepted as his due. There were other problems as well. Increasingly, Thalberg was being given entire credit for the success of the M-G-M product while Mayer, who oversaw contracts, swung deals and waged war with the Loew's hierarchy, was regarded as a figurehead, a mere businessman who made noise while Thalberg made the artistic decisions and did the hard work. Mayer knew of these reports and resented them—with good reason. Without his support and full cooperation, Thalberg would never have been able to do half the things he did.

No executive ever had a more worshipping staff than Thalberg, and as soon as they realized a rift was developing between Mayer and their boss, they rallied around him, arguing that he was overworked and underappreciated. Mayer also had his supporters, but his position was weakened by his low visibility—at this time he was often away from the studio as he drummed up prestige for Metro in Washington and across the country.

So gradually a second schism started destroying company unity —now it was not only Schenck versus Mayer but also Mayer versus Thalberg. And one animosity fed the other, since it was not long before Schenck realized that he could strengthen his own position by pitting Thalberg against Mayer.

The period between 1929 and 1936 was one of strife for M-G-M, but it was also a time of expansion and maturation. The studio grew

and changed and streamlined its operations until it became techno-
logically the most sophisticated of all Hollywood dream factories.

In 1929, the main entrance was on Washington Boulevard, and
from the outside, the most imposing structure was the "Front
Office," a three-storied building that dated back to the Ince days. It
was a nondescript, cream-colored structure given an air of importance by a portico of ten (plaster) Corinthian pillars. Inside, Mayer,
Thalberg and the other top executives had their offices. Mayer was
on the first floor, Thalberg on the second. Each of their suites con-
sisted of a private room, a waiting room for visitors and a room for
their secretaries. Mayer's quarters were slightly larger than Thalberg's, and they were decorated in different styles. Mayer was surrounded by beautiful mahogany paneling and traditional furniture,
while Thalberg favored fashion and Art Deco.

The studio was divided into two general areas—lots 1 and 2. The
Front Office was on Lot 1. Behind it were the sound stages—there
were twenty-two by 1935—the laboratories, the trade shops, storage
areas, makeup and costume departments, a hospital, the commissary
and several rehearsal halls.

Adjacent to the Front Office was a low, two-story building that
was home for directors and writers, who dubbed it the Triangle
Shirtwaist Factory—it was crawling with insects and rodents. Behind it were dressing rooms and offices for the studio's contract
writers. A few yards away was Lot 2, a kind of early Disneyland, a
conglomerate of permanent sets including a waterfront, a village,
several squares and many city streets. The landscape was crazy—
Fifth Avenue led into Copperfield Street which crossed Christiana
Plaza.

Lot 2 was called Cohn Park in honor of its chief architect,
Joe Cohn, the company's general manager. Back in the *Ben Hur* days,
Cohn had taken a negative position toward location shooting, and his
attitude had never changed.

"There was the case of *Trader Horn* in 1929," he recalls. "It was
an important production, and the front office wanted to shoot in
Africa, so we never even tried to work out a budget—who knows
what's going to happen when you're shooting in Africa?"

In the case of *Trader Horn*, the worst that could happen did
happen. Edwina Booth, the leading lady, contracted a rare tropical
disease (from which she never fully recovered), director W. S. Van
Dyke and his crew kept guzzling gin, and the footage brought back
to the M-G-M laboratories was visually stunning but dramatically
incoherent. Following Cohn's suggestion, Thalberg had much of the

film reshot on Lot 2—there were a few side trips to Mexico—and in 1931 it was finally released and became a resounding financial success. Neither the critics nor the public seemed to care that some scenes looked more authentic than others.

"There was never any hard and fast rule about location work," Cohn says. "Sometimes it was called for, sometimes it was merely an extravagance. Even in the 1920s, if you took a company to Sherwood Forest [an area north of Los Angeles] you'd spend $1,800 before you got outside the studio gates. And if there was bad weather that day was lost. But at the studio, if you had bad weather—and a day's shooting often represented an outlay of $25,000 in the 1930s—you could move into a stage and save some of the money.

"When I suggested building a park on the lot, people told me I was crazy. But I went ahead—Cedric Gibbons laid it out and it cost about $8,000, as I remember. No one used it for a while, except for some of the extras who did their 'courting' there, but eventually a director decided to shoot at the 'park' instead of spending three days in Pasadena, and what he saved by working on the lot made a big impression.

"When we made *David Copperfield*, we built a bit of old England down near the beach. When it was over, we took those buildings and brought them back to the lot and that—with some changes—became our New England street, the Andy Hardy town."

"Cohn's Park" would grow until M-G-M had six lots, covering an area of 180 acres. (Lots 2 and 3 housed permanent sets; 4, 5 and 6 were used for temporary constructions.) And by 1935 the studio employed close to four thousand workers—waitresses, stenographers, craftsmen, technicians, executives, stars, artisans.

"Once I figured out that there were more than 150 crafts and professions involved in film making," says Howard Strickling. Each of those crafts and professions was represented on the M-G-M lot. Metro-Goldwyn-Mayer was, in fact, a total city, and with the addition of a cabbage patch, some livestock and legalized gambling, it might have qualified as totally self-sufficient.

Self-sufficiency is the first step toward economy, and as Cohn points out, M-G-M was the most economical of studios. "Everyone thought we were extravagant, but we weren't—the pictures look that way but we cut lots of corners. I know for a fact that when other studios learned what our budgets were, they were astonished."

Not all M-G-M directors were thrilled by the way Cohn grasped the studio purse strings. "Metro was a studio of departments," recalls Clarence Brown. "Every department wanted to impress Cohn or

Mayer with how goddamned much money they were saving, so every time I wanted another light or some minor adjustment, I'd get an argument. It got to be a real pain in the ass sometimes."

"There was no such thing as a 'typical budget' at M-G-M," Cohn said. "I separated my duties as a general manager very sharply. If Mayer and Thalberg wanted to pay a star $400,000 for a picture, that was their business. That had nothing at all to do with how the picture was going to be made, which was always as cheaply as possible. Usually a film was budgeted after the script was finished. I'd read it, and talk to Thalberg, and ask how is it to be treated. He'd say, 'It's an important production,' or, 'It's not so important,' and I'd know how far I could go. And in scheduling the films, I had to make another adjustment: we knew that George Cukor and Woody [W.S.] Van Dyke and Clarence [Brown] didn't work at the same speed, or bring the same values to the films—we knew it took George a lot longer to make a film than Woody. So we scheduled it accordingly, and with no regrets because they brought different values to their productions.

"If there was any argument about budget, Mayer was the arbitrator. On the first *Tarzan* film, I went to Thalberg and showed him a budget that he thought was too high—*Tarzan the Ape Man* was originally intended as a programmer. I argued that some special effects might help the film, though they would add maybe $100,000 to the budget. Thalberg sent me to Mayer. He said, 'Do what you can,' which meant, I deciphered, 'Do it right *but* do it as cheaply as possible.' The picture cost about $450,000, a considerable amount for that time, but it grossed about $2 million, and I doubt that it would ever have made that much had it been produced on the cheap."

Once a film had been completed, it was taken to a theatre in the Los Angeles suburbs for a "sneak preview." This procedure became a ritual. In late afternoon on the day of the preview, a Pacific Electric railway car would arrive outside the studio—tracks had been laid especially for this purpose. The car was then stocked with soft drinks, cards and several picnic hampers provided by the studio commissary. At about six P.M., Thalberg and his staff would get aboard; then came Mayer and his guests for the evening. As the train chugged along to its destination, the passengers ate a little, drank a little, and played a lot of pinochle or bridge at high stakes. Sometimes Mayer sat in for a hand or two—he was not much of a gambler, and whenever he picked up the cards, it was understood that the game was strictly penny ante.

Arriving at Glendale or San Bernardino, they rushed into the theatre, watched the audience watching the film, and then rushed back to the railway car. The next morning there would be a meeting of the studio's "College of Cardinals," during which Mayer, Thalberg and the other executives would hash over the strengths and weaknesses of the film they had viewed the night before.

If reaction or the comment cards handed out at the end of the preview had been negative, and if one of the cardinals had spotted the source of the trouble and had devised a practical way of correcting it, the film was put back into production for reshooting; sometimes the changes were so extensive that by the time of its release a picture would bear only the faintest resemblance to the version shown at the preview. M-G-M second-guessed so many films in this way that it was called "Retake Valley," and one of its films, *I Take This Wife,* was revised so many times that it became known around the lot as *I Retake This Wife.*

This method of picture making was not unlike the Broadway tryout system, and M-G-M "saved" films after disastrous previews just as certain plays have been "saved" after out-of-town fiascos. But it was expensive, and M-G-M was frequently accused of extravagance in utilizing it. The policy is, in fact, unthinkable except under the studio system which kept actors and technicians under contract and thus on daily call for whatever services might be required of them. Even in the thirties at M-G-M, there were problems—sometimes a set had been struck and had to be rebuilt for the reshooting; sometimes the original director was working on a new production and couldn't be spared for retakes (a circumstance that accounts for the multiple, largely uncredited, directorial work on many M-G-M films).

Therefore Thalberg never made a criticism, never ripped apart a script, never sent a picture back for reshooting unless he had a constructive plan for improvement. He tried not to throw good money after bad. Once, when one of his associates suggested a cosmetic change for a film that needed major plastic surgery, Thalberg said, "Why spend cash and time transforming a lemon into a lime?" Effort was expended only on those pictures which could be moved from the good to the excellent category, in terms of both quality and gross receipts.

One of Thalberg's greatest coups was the overhaul of *The Big House* (1930), one of Metro's few gangster films, a genre that neither Mayer nor Thalberg liked very much. Nonetheless, *Big House* was treated as an important production and there was every indication that it would be one of the smash hits of 1930. But something went wrong: the first preview was a disappointment; so was the second. The college of cardinals was at a loss to explain the apathetic audience reaction. Thalberg listened attentively to a couple of half-hearted suggestions, shook his head and said, "I think I know what's wrong. When Chester Morris gets out of prison, he goes to see Bob Montgomery's wife and gets into a romance with her. Women don't like that. So suppose we make the girl [Leila Hyams] Montgomery's sister instead . . ."

The necessary changes were made, and at a third preview, the audience was enthusiastic. The retakes added about $25,000 to the film's total cost of $410,000; without them, *The Big House* might have ended up in the red; with them, it returned a profit of $460,000.

The screenplay for *The Big House* was written by Frances Marion, a veteran scenarist whose career dated back to 1916 and Mary Pickford's *The Poor Little Rich Girl*. After preparing many of Little Mary's best films, Marion went on to work for Hearst-Cosmopolitan and later for M-G-M, and by the end of the silent era, she was one of Hollywood's highest paid and most sought-after screenwriters. She made the transition to sound with flying colors—first *Anna Christie*, then *Big House*, then *Min and Bill*, the film that established Marie Dressler and Wallace Beery as major stars. A year later, she came up with the idea for a film pitting curmudgeonly Beery against waifish, ten-year-old Jackie Cooper; it was called *The Champ*, one of the teariest and best loved of all M-G-M films.

Marion's forte as a screenwriter, according to her own estimation, was original story ideas and continuity, not dialogue. Other screenwriters moving successfully from the silent to the sound era might (had they been honest) have admitted to the same weakness. The actors in the first sound films often seem to be speaking titles written for a silent picture, and what was acceptable in print sounded pretty dreadful when spoken. So Hollywood studios started looking toward Broadway and Publisher's Row for its new scenarists.

So began the influx of the literati to The Garden of Allah—Beverly Hills and environs. M-G-M had more than its share of the famous names—*Fortune* magazine once said the studio employed "more scribes than it took to produce the King James version of the Bible." Quite a few of them failed to master the craft of screenwriting, however, and soon their high-bracket salaries were considered an unnecessary expenditure by several studio executives. "They didn't do much to merit the kind of money they got," says one of Mayer's associates. "But I guess you could say they earned their keep as window dressing—their names looked impressive in the lists of film credits."

The "New York writers"—Ben Hecht, Donald Ogden Stewart, S. N. Behrman, Anita Loos, among many others—made sport of Mayer, and their open disdain caused them to be disliked in certain studio quarters. "Mayer was always a sitting target because of his open defiance in standing up for what he thought and stood for," recalls Howard Strickling. "He was considered 'corny' for advocating happy endings, for believing every film needed a hero and heroine, for protecting star properties, for sponsoring *The Champ*, the Andy Hardy films, the Beery-Dressler vehicles. "

Thalberg, on the other hand, was adored by the New York writers, who became almost lyrical in their descriptions of his "story sense" and intuitive genius. One of his greatest fans was Anita Loos, a veteran screenwriter who left Hollywood in the early 1920s, went on to write the fabulously successful *Gentlemen Prefer Blondes* and several Broadway comedies, only to return to Hollywood in the first years of sound production. "I wasn't keen on going back," she recalls, "but at the time I needed the money, and so off I went. But with regrets and reservations. Thalberg changed that—he was brilliant and I loved working with him; he made it fun and he taught me a lot."

Besides investing heavily in eminent authors, M-G-M also bought up a number of Broadway plays (some of which it silently backed) and put under contract many Broadway actors. All the studios were pursuing this policy, but M-G-M had more success than the others. It got most of the big hits and a good percentage of the top Broadway actors and actresses.

One of the first imports was Helen Hayes, who initially played hard-to-get. She had already turned down several picture deals when Robert Rubin, acting on behalf of Thalberg, tried to entice her with an M-G-M contract. Hayes said she really didn't think she had the face or personality for pictures, and besides, what Metro was paying was only about half of what she earned on stage. Rubin came back with a better offer and, since her husband, playwright Charles MacArthur, was already working in the M-G-M scenario department, Hayes thought she might as well accept.

The MacArthurs and the Thalbergs quickly became close friends, so MacArthur was enraged when he read the script Thalberg had chosen for Hayes's first film. "Goddamit," he shouted, waving a script in Thalberg's face, "do you know what this chestnut is? It's *The Lullaby!* Jesus, that was rancid back in 1924 when Florence Reed played it on Broadway—and you want Helen to play it *now*—would you ask Norma to wade through that crap?" "You don't like it?"

Thalberg said quietly. "You're a writer, you fix it." MacArthur tried valiantly, but it wasn't his kind of material. The first preview was a dismal failure, and Mayer advised Thalberg to shelve the film and send Hayes back to New York.

A few days later, Thalberg came up with a less drastic solution. "Look," he told MacArthur, "there's nothing wrong with Helen's performance and there's two-thirds of a picture there; I think with some rewriting and reshooting we can supply the missing third."

Mayer argued that good money was being thrown after bad, but eventually he gave in and sent the film into production. Under the title *The Sin of Madelon Claudet,* the revised picture was to become a big money-maker for M-G-M, and brought Hayes the "best actress" Oscar for 1931–32.

Hayes's career at M-G-M went on for another five years, but never again was she to match the success of *Madelon Claudet.* The camera emphasized her weaknesses as a stage actress—a tendency toward coyness and calculation—and failed to pick up her strengths —charm and affability. In 1935, she announced that she would not extend her M-G-M contract. "I am leaving the screen because I don't think I am very good in pictures," she told the press, "and because I have a beautiful dream that I'm elegant on stage."

Next came Alfred Lunt and Lynn Fontanne, both of whom had appeared in a few silent films before they became famous as the Lunts, the most celebrated stage couple since Mr. and Mrs. Kendal were the toast of London in the 1880s. Like Hayes, the Lunts had rejected several film offers, but Thalberg was sure he could persuade them to change their minds.

He and his wife stopped to see them on their way east for a European vacation—the Lunts were then playing the Chicago area in a touring edition of Maxwell Anderson's *Elizabeth the Queen.* Fontanne was unnerved by Shearer's worshipful glances, but otherwise the meeting went beautifully. A few days later, it was announced that the Lunts had made a one-picture deal with M-G-M to appear in a film version of Ferenc Molnar's *The Guardsman.*

This wispy comedy—the plot concerns a jealous actor who tests the fidelity of his actress wife by attempting to seduce her while disguised as an Austro-Hungarian dragoon—had been one of the Lunts' first stage triumphs. Which is precisely why Thalberg had selected it as their talking picture debut—they had played the roles many times, were comfortable in them, and any staginess that might creep into their screen performances was entirely in keeping with the theatricality of Molnar's setting and characters.

Production of *The Guardsman* went smoothly, but from their first day at M-G-M, the Lunts had misgivings. After watching some of the daily rushes, Fontanne reported to her husband, "It was awful . . . you were charming and you looked handsome and your voice was wonderful. You'll have to do something about your makeup because you don't seem to have any lips. But me—it's hopeless. I look too fat and my voice is raucous and my eyes are too small and I'm hopeless, hopeless!"

Lunt gazed into space for a moment and then said, "No lips, you say?"

The Guardsman bombed out at its first previews, and as Thalberg read aloud the audience comments, Fontanne became indignant and argued that the picture was too sophisticated for San Bernardino and Bakersfield.

She was right—the picture got great reviews, did good business in the big cities and then died in the provinces. *The Guardsman* lost almost $100,000, but Thalberg wasn't discouraged—flop or not, it was the kind of prestige picture he believed M-G-M had to produce now and again if it were to retain its position as the leading Hollywood studio. He got permission to sign the Lunts to a new multipicture contract. Two properties were already earmarked for them—Maxwell Anderson's *Elizabeth the Queen* (a scene of which serves as a prologue to *The Guardsman*) and Robert Sherwood's *Reunion in Vienna,* another of their recent stage successes. The pay was attractive, but the Lunts ultimately rejected the contract because it did not give them final approval of script, cast and director for future projects. Nor did it give them time off each year so that they could return to the stage.

Mayer and Thalberg were not prepared to grant final approval about anything to anyone nor were they in favor of actors dividing their time between Hollywood and Broadway. Two years earlier, when Edward G. Robinson asked for a six-month contract, Thalberg responded, "We don't work that way at M-G-M. If we're going to build you into a star, we want to enjoy the cumulative benefits." Robinson wasn't interested in a long-term deal—like the Lunts, he considered himself to be basically a stage actor and felt uncertain about his future in film. But many others were happy to play it the Mayer and Thalberg way, including Robert Montgomery, who became one of M-G-M's top leading men in the early thirties.

Montgomery hadn't done much on the stage when he came to M-G-M—at least, he hadn't made much of a name for himself as a stage actor. The same was true of Rosalind Russell (another M-G-M Broadway import in the 1930s) and of James Cagney, Bette Davis,

Sylvia Sidney, Miriam Hopkins, Katharine Hepburn, Spencer Tracy, Henry Fonda, Margaret Sullavan and many others who came to film after one or two noteworthy performances on Broadway. Being young and only tentatively established, these actors were willing to take on five- or seven-year pacts (though some demanded contractual clauses that allowed them to return to the stage every so often) and, unlike veteran stage players who were set in their ways, they had no trouble in adapting themselves to the special demands of screen acting.

Of course, not all the new stars of the sound era came from the Broadway stage. Quite a number were found on the back lots of Hollywood where they had been working in small roles or second leads, waiting impatiently for their big break. And in this area, M-G-M had an unusual degree of luck—three of its biggest stars of the 1930s were plucked from the ranks of the kids who had never quite made it.

"I can't prove this," Clarence Brown says, "but I think Mayer had set up a spy system—certain employees at other studios were paid to tell him when an actor was being dropped. And if he was interested, he'd get in there and start negotiations before even the agent knew his client was about to be out of a job."

One of the first players Mayer rescued from anonymity was Myrna Loy. By the time she came to M-G-M in 1931, Loy had appeared in almost seventy films, often as an oriental (her eyes were naturally slanted) or as the bad-girl second lead. The studio experts soon streamlined her image and made her high-fashion: elegantly gowned and coiffured, she was every bit as smart as the ladies in the illustrations of *Vogue* and *Vanity Fair*. But there was nothing stiff or artificial about Loy; she viewed herself and the world around her with great good humor. Her most individual trait was her voice—so satiny, and yet with a touch of grit to it—and her strongest asset as an actress was the lift she brought to even the most banal dialogue.

If Myrna Loy was the chic socialite, Jean Harlow was M-G-M's resident floosie. With her Art Deco eyebrows, her staccato, honky-tonk voice and a mop of hair that looked as though it had been marinated in peroxide, Harlow was always on the alert for the next rough-and-ready rider. In her own way, she was as frank about sex as Mae West (her closest counterpart in the 1930s), but with one significant difference: with Mae, it was all fun and games, while for Harlow, it was first and foremost a cash arrangement. When Franchot Tone looks adoringly at her in *Bombshell* (1933) and says, "I'd like to walk barefoot through your hair," one somehow expects Jean to snap back, "That'll cost another five smackers, ya creep!"

Unlike Loy, Harlow had had a taste of stardom before she checked in at M-G-M. She had become an overnight sensation when in *Hell's Angels* (1930) she told her leading man, "Wait until I slip into something more comfortable." Since she wasn't wearing much to begin with, audiences gasped either in anticipation or with disapproval. From then on, there was never much between Harlow and her leading men except some flimsy, silky garment barely concealing her bosom and always outlining her nipples (which seemed to be in a perpetual state of excitement). Howard Hughes, producer and director of *Hell's Angels*, kept her under personal contract for the next two years, lending her out to various studios (including Metro) with mixed results. She made a couple of decent pictures—*Public Enemy, Platinum Blonde*—and a lot of instantly forgettable, grade B productions. By 1932 her career was on the decline and most industry insiders were saying her performance in *Hell's Angels* was just flash-in-the-pan stuff.

Mayer disagreed. He liked Harlow's performances in the two quickies she had made for M-G-M, and decided to buy her out of the Hughes contract (at a cost of $60,000) and bring her to Culver City.

At first Thalberg had no interest in Harlow—the way she came across on screen was too obvious for his taste; he preferred actresses with refinement. But Paul Bern, who was closer to Thalberg than any other member of the M-G-M production staff, had taken a shine to Harlow and kept promoting her for the lead in *Redheaded Woman*, a picture that was giving Thalberg a lot of problems.

Based on a *Saturday Evening Post* serialized novel by Katharine Bush, *Redheaded Woman* was the story of a tenement girl who whores her way to the top of the social ladder. It was standard sleaze, but nothing to get riled up about, except that Hollywood had now entered its twin-bed, one-foot-on-the-floor-at-all-times era, inaugurated when the studios had adopted the Motion Picture Code in March 1930. Mayer and Thalberg were both in support of the code, though Thalberg became irritated as more and more taboos were added to the list of restrictions. Still, he believed that sex could be presented on screen "without offense"—whatever that may mean. What it didn't mean was a line like "Meet me at the pawnshop and I'll kiss you under the balls," which was excised from a Mae West script at the request of the Production Code administrators. But apparently it did sanction *Redheaded Woman* (at least, the *Saturday Evening Post* version) which was prurient without being witty or tongue-in-cheek raunchy.

Once Thalberg had bought the serial, he didn't know what to do with it. So he assigned it to F. Scott Fitzgerald, hoping he'd give it a touch of class, but Fitzgerald's treatment was as pedestrian and pointless as the original story. Anita Loos took over the job, and came up with a script that was perky and a little naughty—much too naughty for Jack Conway, who was to direct the picture.

"You can't make jokes about a girl who deliberately sets out to wreck a family," he complained.

"Why not?" asked Loos. "Look at that family. They deserve to be broken up!"

Thalberg agreed with Loos, and her screenplay was used as the basis for the shooting script. Meanwhile, a search for the actress to play redheaded Lil Andrews was going on. Nearly every leading lady on the lot had been tested, including (as a joke) Marie Dressler. Joan Crawford was the top contender, but Thalberg wasn't satisfied; he kept looking around, even testing a few outsiders for the part. Finally, though not with much conviction, he went along with Paul Bern and gave the part to Harlow.

The picture bombed out at its first previews. "People don't know whether they're supposed to laugh or not," Thalberg told Loos. "We need an opening scene that will set the mood." Loos wrote a prologue that introduces Harlow/Lil Andrews as she appraises her new hairdo in a hand mirror. After admiring herself for a moment, she turns to the camera, winks and says, "Gentlemen prefer blondes??—Sez who!!!"

Then there's a quick wipe to a shot of Harlow leaving a department-store fitting room. "Is this dress too tight?" she asks a salesgirl.

"It certainly is!" exclaims the clerk disapprovingly.

"Good!" says Harlow as she shimmies out the door, her breasts bouncing with joyful, bra-less abandon.

Audiences got the point—they were supposed to laugh at this gold-digging tramp who was *shtupping* her way to riches. Critics laughed, too, and many were amazed by Harlow's hitherto untapped gift for comedy. "She will amaze you," wrote the New York *Daily Mirror.* "Her emoting has immeasurably improved," said the *Daily News,* while Lucius Beebe in the *Herald Tribune* singled out her "satirical characterization."

Another reviewer, punning on the title, called the picture red-hot; indeed, for the do-good segment of the American filmgoing public it was definitely too hot for clean-living citizens. The problem was not that Harlow lifted her skirts for any guy with a six-figure bank account, but that she got away with it—at the end of the movie, after attempting to kill her husband (Chester Morris), whom she has abandoned for an aging multimillionaire (Henry Stephenson), she is seen at a race track in France with a new aging multimillionaire and with the same lover-boy chauffeur (Charles Boyer) who had comforted her in the past. There is no explanation of how she beat the murder rap; no explanation (though none is really needed) of why Boyer is still in the driver's seat.

Mayer disapproved of this ending, as did bluenose movie fans across the country—*Redheaded Woman* served to intensify the hue and cry for censorship. Women particularly disapproved of Harlow's tramp characterization, and eventually the studio revamped her image along softer, more sentimental lines. But fortunately, not before her next M-G-M picture, *Red Dust*. In this, one of the most enjoyable of all 1930s M-G-M films, she plays Vantine, a lady of easy virtue who is given twenty-four hours to get out of Saigon. She leaves with barely a stitch on her back, and ends up on a rubber plantation in remote Indochina, where she vies with ice-hot Mary Astor for the attentions of an unshaven, perpetually perspiring stud played by Clark Gable.

In the picture's most provocative sequence, Harlow takes a bath in a rain barrel as Gable watches on with that characteristic glint in his eyes. It's tame stuff, really, except for Gable's leer, which is none too subtle. Marriages may be made in heaven, but teamwork like this was the special province of Hollywood. Gable and Harlow were perfectly matched—she was no lady and he was definitely not a gentleman. Gable was, in fact, a new hero for a new era; not suave and sophisticated like Gilbert, but tough and straight-shooting; a guy who had come up from nowhere, who had picked up everything he knew on the sidewalks of some city slum; who was street smart, who lusted after life and women, who had no time for phonies or utopian dreamers who promised a world with a chicken in every pot. Anything he wanted, he could get, thank you very much, for himself—all it took was brains, charm and guts, so why should he look for outside help?

At the time of *Red Dust*, Gable had been with M-G-M for little more than a year, and yet he had already established himself as one of the studio's most valuable players. Fan magazines called him an overnight sensation, but as one Loew's executive was fond of saying, "It takes ten years to make a star overnight."

It took Gable only about seven years. He had arrived in Hollywood in the mid-1920s and found some work as an extra or a bit player—he can be spotted in the background of Stroheim's *Merry Widow*—but when nothing more lucrative was forthcoming, he moved to New York and tried for a stage career. In 1928 he got good notices for his performance in a pseudo-expressionist drama called *Machinal,* and these reviews led to a leading role in the West Coast company of *The Last Mile,* a play that had starred Spencer Tracy on Broadway.

Several film producers saw the play when it opened in Los Angeles. There was a flurry of interest in Gable, who was screen-tested by a couple of studios, including Warner Bros. Darryl Zanuck, then production chief at Warners, wasn't impressed, but Gable did get a part in a grade-zero Pathé Western, *Painted Desert.* He also played a major role opposite Barbara Stanwyck in one of Warner's B productions, *Night Nurse,* and almost got the Douglas Fairbanks part in *Little Caesar.* Disgusted by the snail's progress of his career, he was about to return to New York, when he got offers from RKO and Metro. He chose M-G-M.

Thalberg had seen one of Gable's tests, and like Zanuck, he found it hard to imagine film fans accepting a leading man with bad teeth and jug ears. But Eddie Mannix and Bennie Thau (the head of M-G-M's talent department) both felt the actor had a certain "something" that might be developed, so Thalberg eventually agreed to give Gable a one-year contract at $650 a week.

That "something" came to the fore in Gable's first appearance in a posh M-G-M production, *A Free Soul,* based on a semiautobiographical novel by Adela Rogers St. Johns, which had been successfully adapted to the stage a few years before. The film version centers on the relationship between Jan Ashe (Norma Shearer), a silk-and-ermine-draped debutante, and her father (Lionel Barrymore), a big-time attorney with a hard-drinking problem. Intertwined with this story is a subplot involving Jan's well-born and sensitive fiancé (Leslie Howard) and gangster Ace Wilfong (Gable), who takes Jan as his mistress and is later shot by her fiancé.

The seamy liaison between Jan and Ace was pretty daring for the times in that it presented the woman as the aggressor. In one torrid scene, Shearer clutches at Gable's arms and pleads, "Come on, come on, put 'em around me," and later, as they fall onto a couch, she sighs, "A new man! A new life!"

Shearer got good reviews, Barrymore won an Academy Award, but Gable was the real sensation of the picture. Shearer was one of the first to spot his potential—and to try to douse it. According to director Clarence Brown, after watching the first rough cut, she suggested a few alterations, most of them involving the elimination of Gable's best scenes. Brown conferred with Mayer, who ordered the film released as it stood.

Mayer had been away from the studio when Gable arrived, but even before *Free Soul,* he had recognized the actor's appeal and ordered the red carpet treatment for him. Gable was promptly fitted with dentures, which he hated—once after one of several disagreements with L.B. over casting, he was heard to say, "Jesus, I can't wait for the day when I can throw these clackers through L.B.'s window" —and put under the supervision of Howard Strickling, whom he adored. Strickling urged him to get out of his New York dandy duds and into more casual wear, part of a program to promote Gable as an outdoor, sporty type who was always ready to bag any kind of game. Gable liked the image and began to live it.

Meanwhile the star system was building up Gable in other ways. Between *A Free Soul* (1931) and *Red Dust* (1932), he made seven films, appearing opposite most of the studio's reigning queens, including Garbo *(Susan Lenox—Her Fall and Rise)*, Crawford *(Possessed)*, Davies *(Polly of the Circus)* and Shearer *(Strange Interlude)*. None of them made film history and two *(Susan Lenox* and *Strange Interlude)* were perfectly dreadful, but—with the possible exception of *Interlude*— none of them dampened the public's mounting enthusiasm for Gable. He was already well on his way to becoming the King of the Metro lot, a position he would hold virtually unchallenged for the next two decades.

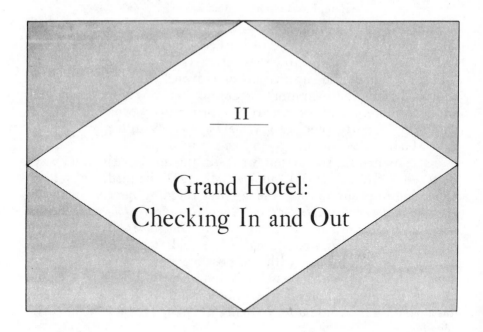

II

Grand Hotel: Checking In and Out

If one picture can be selected as typifying the M-G-M style of the early 1930s, that picture would be *Grand Hotel*. This adaptation of a popular novel and play by Vicki Baum is the progenitor of those movies in which a group of characters (carefully chosen to represent a cross-section of humanity) come together in some out-of-the-ordinary locale (an ocean liner, a lifeboat, a stagecoach, a sky clipper, a hospital), brush shoulders for a brief while and then go back to their everyday existences. In the interim, their lives have been dramatically altered, for better or worse.

Nearly all these pictures are salted with a liberal dash of silliness, and *Grand Hotel* is no exception. But as a movie experience, it's totally satisfying in ways its later counterparts are not. Partly this is because of the production values which, while hermetic and heavily literal (like so much M-G-M art design), are also as deluxe and dreamy as the photographic fantasies of an overpriced fashion magazine. But the real magic is Garbo and Crawford, the Barrymore brothers, Wallace Beery and Lewis Stone. In the genre of the I-never-saw-you-before- and- never- will- again- but- this- meeting- is- going- to- change-my-life movie, every scene is an excuse for a star turn, so there had better be stars around to flesh out the cardboard characters. And

M-G-M, which was now advertising its product with the slogan "More Stars Than There Are In Heaven," shot the works on *Grand Hotel*.

Irving Thalberg first became interested in *Grand Hotel* when he read a studio-prepared synopsis of the German play script in 1930. But the film rights were not as readily available as he had hoped. The play was then scheduled to be staged in New York by neophyte Broadway producer, Harry Moses, a former hosiery manufacturer from Chicago. Moses was prepared to put up most of the production money himself, but he was looking around for a silent partner who would chip in about $15,000. The script looked promising, but there was one hitch: Moses insisted the part of Grusinskaya be played by his wife, a woman of high ambition and small professional experience. Somehow investors couldn't picture a marquee reading "Elsa Moses in *Grand Hotel*," and no one was willing to gamble on the chance of her becoming an overnight sensation. This was, after all, theatre, not a Busby Berkeley musical.

Learning of Thalberg's interest in the play, Moses came up with a proposition: M-G-M could have the film rights in exchange for a $15,000 investment in the stage production. After conferring with Mayer, Thalberg accepted the deal. In doing so, he was taking only a minimal risk. If the play bombed—which seemed likely with Mrs. Moses in the lead—M-G-M would then probably be able to get the rights for a lot less, but $15,000 wasn't a lavish expenditure for a property that was ideal film material.

As it turned out, the investment paid off better than anyone had hoped. Moses eventually took a back seat to an experienced producer-director, Herman Shumlin, and after a few days of rehearsal Elsa Moses voluntarily withdrew in favor of Eugenie Leontovich, a Russian actress of considerable allure and technique. The play was a huge hit, running for over two years in New York and on the road.

Thalberg had originally earmarked the play as a John Gilbert vehicle, but by the time of production, Gilbert's days at M-G-M were coming to an end, and John Barrymore was assigned the role of Baron von Gaigern. This was smart casting, and Garbo was an obvious choice for Grusinskaya. (Some years earlier, Stiller had considered buying the rights to Baum's story as a vehicle for his protégée.) But Thalberg didn't stop with Garbo and Barrymore—he kept adding star name after star name to the cast, and by the time the final lineup had been announced, the industry was sure Thalberg had gone berserk. Why put all those stars in one picture when two or, at most, three would have nearly the same box office draw?

But Thalberg knew exactly what he was doing. The all-star

Grand Hotel type of film was financially a sound proposition under the studio star system. All of the leading players were under contract to Metro, and since most appeared in just a few scenes, only a handful of which required ensemble playing, they would be employed only for a couple of weeks, and then would be available for another film; if necessary, their schedules could be arranged so that they could shoot *Grand Hotel* in tandem with another production: Garbo could be doing scenes while Crawford was working elsewhere, and so forth and so on.

Grand Hotel cost $700,000, which is less than the combined salaries of Jane Fonda and Michael Caine for the latest of *Grand Hotel*'s stepchildren, Neil Simon's *California Suite*. Even in 1932, $700,000 wasn't that much—M-G-M had spent over $1 million on an historical romance, *Rasputin and the Empress*, which was a fiasco.

Grand Hotel returned a clear profit of $950,000 and won the best-picture Oscar for 1931–32. This was reason enough for Thalberg to celebrate, and there were other reasons as well: he was the father of a healthy child and his wife's career was blooming—Norma had won an Academy Award a year earlier for *The Divorcée* under his direction as production supervisor. M-G-M was winning awards and citations and applause from all directions. But instead of finding pride and satisfaction in his achievements, Thalberg was despondent and irritable.

Thalberg's siege of depression sprang from multiple sources. He had been greatly upset by the suicide of his friend and associate Paul Bern and by the squalid aftermath of that event, which cast a shadow of scandal over M-G-M and Jean Harlow (who was married to Bern at the time of his death). In the past few months Thalberg had made two bad mistakes in judgment, one resulting in a libel suit over a Crawford film, *Letty Lynton*, the other involving the studio in a lengthy and very costly plagiarism case concerning *Rasputin and the Empress*. Most of all, he was overworked, exhausted, underpaid and underappreciated—or so he felt.

"Why should I be working my butt off so Mayer and Schenck can get rich and sassy?" Thalberg muttered to an associate.

The root of the problem, as was so often the case with Thalberg, was money. He was still having financial problems, and as part of an economy drive inaugurated by the studio after the Depression, he had taken a temporary cut in salary. Bern's death, though by suicide, served as a reminder of his limited life expectancy, and now that he was a father, he felt the need to build for the future. Within the industry his position was strong enough for him to set his own terms, but first he would have to get out of M-G-M, where he believed he was being taken for granted.

Thalberg spent many weeks brooding before he went to Mayer with his decision. He was sick and wanted to be relieved of his position as head of production.

Whether Thalberg really wanted to resign or whether he was taking a calculated risk can't be determined—quite possibly he didn't know himself. But if it was a calculated risk, then it worked out the way he had planned. Mayer and the Loew's hierarchy were thrown into turmoil. If Thalberg were to defect to a rival company, M-G-M would suffer a damaging blow, both in prestige and organization: the studio had no contingent plan that would permit operations to proceed smoothly without Thalberg. Mayer argued and argued, but Thalberg wouldn't budge: he wanted out. As a last resort, Mayer called Schenck and asked him to come to the West Coast as arbitrator.

Five days later, Schenck and Bob Rubin met with Thalberg and Mayer in a suite at the Beverly Hills Hotel, and the conferences were, according to Mayer, "hellish." Schenck threatened Thalberg with a lawsuit for breach of contract, at which Thalberg laughed. It was a cold, aggressive laugh that implied the joke was at Schenck's expense, not his.

Eventually Schenck made an offer that Thalberg found acceptable. He would stay on at M-G-M at his current salary, but would be allowed to purchase over a period of years 100,000 shares of Loew's stock at a cost far below the market price. With a nod in the other direction, he promised Mayer the opportunity to buy 80,000 shares under the same terms. Mayer did not accept the offer.

Thalberg was content with the arrangement; Mayer was not. For the first time in his dealings with Loew's, he had drawn lesser terms than his protégé, and that was something he couldn't forget or forgive. Intentionally, Schenck had finally succeeded in creating an impassable gulf between Mayer and Thalberg. The studio divided into enemy camps supporting one or the other of these two opponents who were once united in pursuit of a mutual goal: M-G-M, the paragon of Hollywood studios.

The animosity spread outward, touching everyone who was close to Thalberg and Mayer, even those who didn't want to take sides.

"My father couldn't have done it without Thalberg and Thalberg couldn't have done it without my father," says Irene Selznick. "The trouble between them was so terrible because my father never loved anyone the way he loved Irving."

Howard Strickling, who retained equal respect for both men, tried to act as mediator, but with little success. "I'd go to Irving with a routine question and he'd say 'Did Louie tell you to say this?' I'd say no, and at first he didn't believe me, but after a while, both he and Mr. Mayer came to respect me and anyone else who wasn't carrying tales back and forth."

In the fall of 1932, Thalberg contracted influenza, and for several days his condition was listed as serious. When he recovered, he went off to New York for a short vacation, though his health was still precarious. After checking in at the Waldorf Towers, he held a press conference to refute reports that he was leaving M-G-M. *The New York Times* carried his statement, but then went on to say: "That Thalberg may have to retire from all activity for a time remains the current rumor . . . his condition has been so precarious for several days that even the slightest movement of his arms might precipitate an attack of the heart ailment which is the main cause for alarm."

But Thalberg fooled everyone. Within a few days he was back at his desk, working as hard as he ever had. Then on December 24 the studio shut down early for the annual Christmas party. Thalberg was in particularly high spirits—he drank more than his usual allotment of one weak Scotch and soda, and embraced more than his share of pretty M-G-M employees. And he stayed around the studio until all the revelers had vanished.

Later that night he had a heart attack. It was serious, so serious that the doctors told Norma that he was to have no visitors. When Mayer came to call, she told him politely but firmly that he could not see Irving until his condition improved.

After the New Year, Thalberg was still seriously ill, and Mayer was forced to assume control over production. He was also forced to consider the future of M-G-M without Thalberg as his right-hand man. He decided that it was time to pump some fresh blood into the studio. First he thought of Darryl Zanuck, whose record as chief of production at Warners was first-rate, but for various reasons, discarded the idea, and turned to his son-in-law, David O. Selznick.

Both the Mayer girls had taken husbands in the spring of 1930. On March 19, Edie had wed William Goetz, an assistant supervisor at Fox, and six weeks later, Irene married Selznick. About Edie's choice, Mayer had made no objection, but when Irene started seeing Selznick, he was initially displeased. David was the son of Lewis J. Selznick, with whom Mayer had formed a brief and unhappy business alliance back in his pre-Hollywood days. That episode had left him with a distaste for anyone and anything that bore the name Selznick.

"No Selznick will ever work at M-G-M!" Mayer had shouted when in 1926 Harry Rapf reported that he had just added David to his staff as a reader. Rapf was surprised by Mayer's reaction—he liked Selznick and had lured him at coolie wages, seventy-five dollars a week—but Mayer's word was law to Rapf, and he dutifully notified Selznick that his employment was terminated.

Selznick went straight to Nick Schenck, who was in Hollywood on one of his frequent visits to the studio. "Look," he said, "all I'm asking is for you to take a $150 gamble. Hire me for a two-week probationary period and if I don't work out, then fire me." This sounded reasonable to Schenck and he told Mayer to rehire Selznick. Mayer complied, but Schenck's intervention only served to stoke his distaste for the Selznicks.

Selznick passed his probationary period with high marks, and in record time, he was promoted from a reader to manager of the M-G-M script department, to head of the script department, to associate story editor, to "stooge for Harry Rapf" (Selznick's words), to assistant supervisor and then to full-fledged supervisor of Tim McCoy Westerns. All the McCoy Westerns, he realized, fit a pattern, and it would be just as easy—and far less expensive—to make two of them at the same time. So he sent out one director with two scripts and two leading ladies, and made two films simultaneously for just a fraction above the cost of one. It was not a new idea—the same thing had been done in the very early days of Hollywood history— but it saved money, and economy was an important credential for any up-and-coming producer's portfolio.

At this point (1928), Selznick was given the chance to be assistant to Hunt Stromberg, who had become one of the studio's top supervisors. Their first project together was *White Shadows in the South Seas,* based on Frederick O'Brien's book on the decimation of the Polynesian culture by the white man. Selznick had fallen "madly in love" with the book, and he wanted as director, W.S. (Woody) Van Dyke, whose only major credits were several of the better McCoy Westerns. Stromberg, however, wanted Robert Flaherty, a renowned director whose "true life" dramas, *Nanook of the North* and *Moana,* had established the documentary as a feasible form of commercial film making. Eventually it was decreed that both directors would work on the film, much to Selznick's disapproval: knowing both men, he realized they were not ideally cast as collaborators.

Later Selznick was astounded when Stromberg admitted that for him *White Shadows* was nothing more than a "tit and sand epic"—the picture's ethnic authenticity was just an excuse for showing a lot of ladies baring their bosoms. Probably Stromberg was being facetious when he made the remark—it's typical show biz deprecation—but Selznick ("still a very idealistic young man," as he says in his autobiographical notes) chose to take it seriously. Stromberg, in turn, took exception to Selznick's indignation, making it clear that he was the supervisor of the picture while Selznick was just an assistant.

Selznick took his grievances to Thalberg and Thalberg sided with Stromberg. "I was fired," Selznick later remembered. "[Thalberg] gave me the chance to apologize for not having agreed with him [Stromberg], which I refused to do, and I was out of a job."

On leaving M-G-M, Selznick moved to Paramount as assistant to B. P. Schulberg, the studio's production chief. By then he had already met Irene Mayer at a New Year's Eve party.

According to Hollywood legend, the three-year courtship that ensued was stormy, thanks to L. B. Mayer, who disapproved of his daughter's suitor. *"That's not true!!"* Mrs. Selznick insists. Both girls were carefully guarded, and if Mayer had truly disapproved of Selznick, Irene never would have been allowed to see him. The relationship between Selznick and Mayer was warm, if not intimate. Though they were frequently to disagree, each maintained a healthy respect for the other's opinion.

Mayer and Selznick had different ideas about film making, which came to the fore in 1931 when Selznick left Paramount to set up an independent production company with director Lewis Milestone as co-partner. To get the project off the ground, Selznick needed a guarantee that one of the major studios would take on his films as part of their yearly program—otherwise, he would have no access to the distribution and exhibition outlets he needed to make his company a financially viable proposition. That guarantee was not forthcoming because, as Selznick later learned, Mayer had called a meeting of the heads of all the leading studios and warned them against setting a dangerous precedent. If Selznick succeeded, soon all producers and directors would start setting up their own independent units and the Hollywood studios would end, like the walls of Jericho, as a pile of rubble.

Stated bluntly, what Mayer was saying was support the system and not my maverick son-in-law. It was a slap in the face, of course, but David was philosophical enough to accept it as a professional, not personal, insult. Placing his dream of independence on the back burner, Selznick took charge of production at RKO, a stumbling, borderline major studio that had been founded a few years before by RCA. Within a few months, Selznick had raised the status of the company by several notches. He functioned at RKO much as Thalberg did at M-G-M—he kept tabs on all films produced by the studio, reserving a few top-budgeted films for "personal supervision." Among them were the first Katharine Hepburn picture, *Bill of Divorcement* (also the first major film for director George Cukor); *Bird of Paradise* with Dolores Del Rio; and the best version of *Topaze*, starring John Barrymore, and (on loan from Metro) Myrna Loy.

Selznick's stay at RKO won him a reputation as a second Irving Thalberg, but when his contract came up for renewal, the RKO money men weren't prepared to meet his terms. He wanted, and was refused, total say over what RKO produced. So, at the time Mayer approached him about joining the M-G-M production staff, he was in the right frame of mind to listen.

Nonetheless Selznick's initial reaction was to reject the offer. It smacked of nepotism, and Selznick didn't want anyone to imagine he was getting ahead through the influence of Big Daddy-in-Law. And despite repeated assurances that he would operate as a free agent, he wondered how free he would be once he was working for Mayer. But the offer was too tantalizing to be dismissed without careful consideration: a two-year contract at four thousand dollars a week, with a guarantee that he could have his pick of stories, stars and studio personnel.

Just at this time, his father became fatally ill. Lewis Selznick and Louis Mayer had patched up their quarrel at the time of their children's marriage, and they had become even closer when Irene presented them with a grandson, Jeffrey. That, at least, is the way the story is usually told, though Irene Selznick says the two men never liked each other very much. Still, when David asked his father whether he should accept Mayer's offer, Lewis Selznick advised him to do so.

Then Lewis Selznick died and David O. Selznick checked in at Metro-Goldwyn-Mayer.

He was not, it must be emphasized, hired as Thalberg's replacement, though there is good reason to believe Mayer was thinking of grooming him for that position when and if Thalberg retired. For the time being, he was placed in charge of his own independent unit, meaning that he was answerable only to the Front Office and was not subject to Thalberg's supervision, when and if Thalberg returned to the job.

Only once since the merger had M-G-M made such an arrangement with a producer or director. Late in 1928, under terms roughly similar to those of Selznick's contract, Cecil B. De Mille had signed a three-picture deal with Metro and Thalberg had accepted the arrangement without any fuss. De Mille made the kind of spectacle picture that held little interest for him. And as it turned out, De

Mille's career at M-G-M was short and not very happy. *Dynamite,* his first production, made a little money, but the two that followed, *Madam Satan* and *The Squaw Man,* each ended up well over $300,000 in the red.

The De Mille alliance wasn't much of a precedent, but possibly, Mayer had it in mind when he went to tell Thalberg about hiring Selznick; he hoped Irving would act as he had previously, that he would make no fuss. But this time Thalberg wasn't so congenial— he flew into a towering rage. He had nothing against Selznick—they were good friends and he had no objections to his working at M-G-M. What infuriated Thalberg was that he had not been consulted about the plan, that everything had been done behind his back. Mayer tried to explain that no one was allowed to see Thalberg for several weeks, but Thalberg was in no mood to make allowances. He refused to be placated, and the meeting ended on a note of seemingly irrevocable bitterness.

A few days later—February 2, 1933—Loew's, Inc. formally announced that Selznick had "signed a contract with Metro-Goldwyn-Mayer as an executive producer." Since "executive producer" was a title coined by Selznick to cover his duties at RKO and since these duties were substantially the same as Thalberg's at M-G-M, the press release immediately raised speculation as to how Thalberg would fit into studio operations: rumors started circulating that he was on his way out. "Preposterous," retorted Thalberg and Schenck, but there were no indications that Thalberg was planning to resume his post at M-G-M. Instead, two weeks later *The New York Times* reported, "Irving Thalberg . . . seriously ill for many weeks now, was able to take a brief auto ride last Sunday. Present plans are for him to go to Europe, probably Bad Neuheim, for at least four months' rest as soon as he can travel. . . ."

The article implied that Thalberg was still grievously ill, but in fact he had once again confounded his doctors by making an astonishing recovery. Mayer began to suspect that the cause for Thalberg's prolonged absence from the studio was petulance, not ill health, and undoubtedly he was at least partly correct. But a week before Irving's departure for Europe, he tried to patch things up with a conciliatory letter. In it, he expressed regret that their last meeting (about Selznick) had ended "in a loss of temper"; then he went on to say that he had only been trying to carry on in Thalberg's absence, that he felt the young man's absence keenly, that he blamed "so-called friends" for clouding their good relationship and that he prayed for Irving's speedy recovery and return to M-G-M.

He closed by saying, "I assure you I will go on loving you to the end."

Thalberg's answer was frigidly correct. He too regretted "any words that I may have used that aroused bitterness"; he too deplored the false friends who had brought about dissension, but went on to say that he had "sustained a deep hurt" because the principles on which M-G-M had been founded were no longer defended by his three closest friends. (The principles and the friends go unnamed, but presumably the latter were Mayer, Rubin and Schenck.) He closed by offering his "sympathy, understanding and good wishes in the task you are undertaking; no one more than myself would enjoy your success, for your own sake even more than for the sake of the company."

On February 28, Thalberg, Norma and Irving, Jr., sailed to New York from San Pedro Harbor on the S. S. *California* with Charles MacArthur, Helen Hayes and their daughter Mary as traveling companions. Three weeks later, after a stopover in New York, the party boarded a ship for France. After two weeks in Paris, the Thalbergs went off alone to Bad Neuheim in Germany, where Irving was to visit a cardiac specialist recommended by W. R. Hearst and also undergo a tonsillectomy—inflamed tonsils were thought to have contributed to his recent illness. Their stay, however, was briefer than originally planned; witnessing several incidents of anti-Semitism, Thalberg decided to get out of Germany as soon as he had recuperated from the operation.

Three weeks later, they rejoined the MacArthurs on the French Riviera. It was while staying at a hotel in Eden Roc that Thalberg received a decisive cablegram from Mayer. He had been relieved of his duties as head of M-G-M production.

"I am doing this for you," Mayer said.

Mayer was also doing it for the good of the studio.

Thalberg's illness, his European jaunt, the indefinite reports about when he would return and what his status would be if he did, all had led to an uncertainty and unease that infiltrated every department of the studio: from top to bottom, no one seemed to know what was going on or what changes might be lurking around the corner, or when the ax might fall, the pink slips might start appearing, the studio might go up in smoke.

This siege of anxiety was not, of course, totally caused by Thalberg's absence; chiefly it was the result of the menacing presence of the Depression. Suddenly everything seemed to be built on toothpicks, even the great Hollywood studios. At first, the stock market crash hadn't hurt box office grosses, but by the spring of 1932, sales were beginning to drop off drastically, theatre owners were offering a free dish with every ticket and, as a last resort, started accepting canned goods in place of ready cash. M-G-M had suffered less than the other studios—its net revenue had declined in the past two years, but not devastatingly so. There seemed to be no real cause for concern.

But then, on March 5, 1933, President Franklin D. Roosevelt proclaimed a bank holiday. This was real reason for panic. On that gloomy day, M-G-M had enough funds on hand to pay their employees in cash, but the other studios were not so fortunate. Universal immediately suspended all contracts on the basis of a national emergency. Fox informed its staff that it could not pay salaries. Two or three other companies threatened to close their doors for the duration.

Immediate and decisive action was needed to forestall the collapse of the entire industry. But what could be done? Mayer, who had recently been elected to the presidency of the Motion Picture Producers Association, hadn't a glimmer of an idea; neither did any of the other studio bosses. Out of desperation and as a last resort, they turned to the board of directors of the Academy of Motion Picture Arts and Sciences.

This organization, of which Mayer was one of the founding fathers, had been formed in 1927 as an alliance of the creative elite of Hollywood—its initial membership included actors, directors, producers, cameramen and a sprinkling of other technicians. Its original purpose had nothing to do with the doling out of bronze statuettes for artistic excellence—the Oscar was an afterthought, a way of calling attention to the goals of the Academy—it was designed to provide a forum for the exchange and development of artistic and technical views, to create a bureau of standards for the industry and, should the occasion ever arise, to act as a mediator in disputes among the various artists, technicians and craftsmen involved in picture production.

The last of these three aims was the most controversial. For Hollywood liberals and left-wingers, it suggested that Mayer and his cohorts had mainly their own interests in mind when forming the Academy: they were desperately trying to forestall the unionization of studio employees.

The charge was not entirely unfounded.

Faced with the 1933 crisis, the Academy's board of directors* came up with a startling proposal, one that was regarded by the

*In 1933 the Academy Board Members included Conrad Nagel (president), John Cromwell (vice-president), Fred Niblo (secretary), Frank Lloyd (treasurer) and Frank Capra, Donald Crisp, Louis B. Mayer, B. P. Schulberg, Karl Struss, Carey Wilson and Darryl F. Zanuck.

enemy camp as either unduly alarmist or unduly slanted in favor of the studio bosses. The Academy recommended that all employees, top to bottom, accept a salary reduction of 50 percent for eight weeks. This sacrifice had to be made by everyone at every studio, regardless of contracts or guarantees; otherwise, the Academy directorate prophesied it would be curtains for the silver screen.

The plan, which had been formulated in great haste, had two weak spots. What was a genuine sacrifice for some people was merely a momentary tighten-the-belt irritation for others. What did it matter to a contract actor earning $1,000 a week if he took a pay cut for two months? And what did it matter to Mayer, who had earned, in salary and dividends, about $400,000 the previous year? On the other hand, what a serious matter it was for the clerk-typists and minor technicians and gatekeepers who took home fifty dollars a week or less.

Furthermore, not all the studios were in equally dire financial trouble. M-G-M's profits had dropped during the early Depression, but the studio was making a profit, and Loew's, Inc. was reported to have cash reserves of $5 million. Human nature being what it is, why should the M-G-M employees be expected to make a sacrifice to bail out a couple of sinking sister studios?

A cool, level-headed account of why unilateral action was necessary might have sufficed, but at the meeting of star and top-echelon M-G-M personnel, Mayer presented the Academy's proposal with fire-and-brimstone emotionality. There was some heckling at first—people had come forewarned of what they were going to hear—but Mayer pulled out the stops and silenced the cynics.

He claimed that every studio gate in Hollywood would soon be closed if the cut were not accepted. He envisioned a world without M-G-M, Warners, Fox, Paramount, RKO: without Garbo, Crawford, Beery or Dressler. He choked up as he told of the thousands of extras and technicians and maids and valets and stenographers who would be thrown out of work if every member of the industry failed to support the Academy's program. Then he wept openly and unashamedly.

An actor's agent, who had crept into the meeting unnoticed, commented in a whisper, "That performance should get the [Oscar] for the best acting of 1933." The rest of the audience was not so hard-boiled: they cheered Mayer to let him know they were staunchly behind the Academy's plan.

But Mayer's triumph was short-lived. Three days later, the electricians and carpenters refused to take a cut—these craftsmen were already unionized—and they were quickly followed by the cameramen, who also vetoed a reduction in wages. With the plan in jeopardy, the Academy board of directors reconvened and proposed an amendment to their original proposal: anyone earning less than fifty dollars a week would not take a cut; those earning more than fifty would waive a percentage of their salaries, on a sliding scale, up to 50 percent.

This formula worked, but it was later to cause a good deal of discontent, and served only to further the demands for the unionization of Hollywood craftsmen. Once the crisis had ended, it became apparent that some studios had cried wolf long before the wolf was anywhere near the door. M-G-M was one of them. At the end of the fiscal year, Loew's, Inc., paid a dividend. It was smaller than usual, but a dividend nonetheless. The estimated savings of $800,000, achieved mainly through the salary cut at the studio, had not been used for overhead, or even interests on bonds. It went into the coffers of Loew's, Inc., and became part of the 1933 profits. Many people maintained, not unreasonably, that at least a part of the dividend should have been distributed, on a reverse sliding scale, to those employees who had taken pay cuts during the crisis. Instead, the only M-G-M workers who shared in the dividend were those who held Loew's stock: Mayer and Thalberg and Rubin.

Thalberg, who learned of the wage reduction while in New York on his way to Europe, was fiercely opposed to it. He told reporters that "such desperate measures" would surely lower morale at the studio. He was right, of course, but when he received his share of the 1933 profits, he didn't dole them out as a morale-boosting gesture. Thalberg had a way of sounding more liberal and humanitarian than he actually was, and in opposing the 1933 wage reduction, he was thinking as much of his own paycheck as of those of the little people at M-G-M.

Once the bank-holiday crisis had been averted, Mayer sat down and took a long look at the Thalberg problem. How was the studio to get along without Irving as production chief? Some industry commentators assumed that Selznick was about to take over the job, but Selznick wasn't interested: he looked on his stay at M-G-M as a stopgap engagement while he was waiting for an opportunity to step up into independent production. Three months after he came to M-G-M, Selznick pleaded with his father-in-law to release him from his contract; Mayer refused, but he realized he couldn't count on Selznick as a replacement for Thalberg.

There were also predictions that Mayer was about to take the reins of production into his own hands. Not so, says Howard Strickling. "Mr. Mayer never thought of himself as a 'picture man.' That was one of his great strengths and one of the things that separated him from Zanuck and other studio heads who have nursed a secret ambition to be producers."

Mayer and Schenck fooled all the industry Cassandras by coming up with a plan that eliminated Thalberg's post and established an entirely new form of production procedure. This program they presented to Thalberg's staff of assistant supervisors in the spring of 1933.

"We don't know when or if Irving is going to return," Schenck said. "But should he come back, then Louie and I want to protect his health by relieving him of the terrible duty of running all of M-G-M production. So what we want to do is break up the studio into separate units, and we'd like each of you to head one of these units."

"You'll all be promoted to full-fledged producers, and you'll get screen credit," Mayer added. "And when Irving returns, we want him to have his own unit, too."

Mayer and Schenck were afraid that affection for Thalberg would prove a deterrent to the acceptance of this plan, but their fears were groundless. The enticement of promotion and public recognition (plus the possibility of a salary increase) was irresistible, and without much soul-searching, nearly every member of the production staff endorsed Mayer and Schenck's plan enthusiastically.

The new program was already in operation when Thalberg returned to New York in July 1933. Disembarking from the S.S. *Majestic,* he looked older and heavier, but also rested and remarkably fit. During a dockside press conference, he smiled continually and fielded reporters' questions with charm and diplomacy. What were his future plans? He was thinking of setting up an independent production company and had already lined up several projects for Norma—*La Tendresse,* a French play by Henri Bernstein; Charles Morgan's best-selling novel *The Fountain; Marie Antoinette, The Portrait of an Average Woman* by Stefan Zweig.

Would he be affiliated with M-G-M in the future? Thalberg was evasive: his plans were still indefinite. What was the nature of his problems with M-G-M? Thalberg answered, as he had on his departure for Europe, that it was mainly a question of money.

The Thalbergs then checked in at the Waldorf Towers for an "indefinite stay." The next day Nick Schenck called and invited them to spend the weekend at his Long Island estate.

The weekend went just the way such weekends were supposed to go according to the precepts of teacup dramaturgy. Good manners, laughter, chitchat and then, once the children were in bed and the ladies had retired after dinner, Schenck and Thalberg got down to brandy, cigars and business.

Shortly thereafter Thalberg announced, as he boarded a train for Los Angeles, "I shall organize [at M-G-M] a production unit that will make as many pictures as I am capable of making. These pictures will be of the quality and type I have endeavored to make in the last fourteen years. I have found the public more discriminating than ever in their desire for fine product."

Four days later, arriving in Pasadena, he said much the same thing, but in a more emphatic way. "Quality pictures pay. We're in this business to make money, naturally, but the quality production which is more often than not the expensive production is the one that pays big returns."

After a nine-month absence, Thalberg returned to the M-G-M studio in mid-August 1933. He posed with Norma and Mayer for the studio photographer—they all grinned like Cheshire cats—and then went to inspect his new office. He had been assigned to the bungalow once occupied by Cecil B. De Mille, but redecorated by Cedric Gibbons according to Thalberg's taste. But Thalberg felt uncomfortable—the only homey touch was the presence of Albert Lewin, the sole assistant supervisor who decided to stay with Thalberg rather than become a screen-credited producer.

Out of gratitude, Thalberg promised to bill Lewin as associate producer on all future films. And then together they got down to the business of making quality pictures—a chore which, Thalberg had implied in his recent statements to the press, had been sadly neglected since his departure from Hollywood and Metro-Goldwyn-Mayer.

Irving Thalberg, Louis Mayer and Harry Rapf show censorship czar Will Hays (wearing topcoat) around the M-G-M lot. To the left of Thalberg are Edith Mayer and actress Eleanor Boardman; at the extreme right, Conrad Nagel, one of M-G-M's busiest actors. During the first eighteen months of the studio's existence, Nagel made thirteen films.

In 1925 the main entrance to the studio was on Washington Boulevard. The Corinthian pillars added a touch of class to an otherwise mundane stretch of landscape.

Shooting the sea battle at Livorno for *Ben Hur*.

The M-G-M Commissary in the early 1930s.

Erich von Stroheim and John Gilbert share a joke on the set of *The Merry Widow*. The source of their amusement may well have been Gilbert's co-star, Mae Murray.

Louis B. Mayer's "prize-lily," Anita Stewart.

"Le mani...al caldo...e dormire": Mimi (Lillian Gish) dies in Rodolphe's (John Gilbert's) arms in the 1926 *La Boheme*.

Jeanette MacDonald entertaining a rival songbird, Lily Pons, on the M-G-M lot.

Louis Mayer, Marion Davies, Norma Shearer and Irving Thalberg on their way to a Hollywood function, c. 1928.

Joan Crawford wearing a dress featuring a modified version of "the Letty Lynton sleeve." M-G-M costume designer Gilbert Adrian decided Crawford needed a puffy, frilly look to soften the contours of her shoulders, and his designs for *Letty Lynton* created a new fashion.

Garbo looking sultry? angry? troubled? Take your pick.

Greta Garbo and John Gilbert on the set of *Love*. One assumes Garbo's inhaler contains perfume.

Greta Garbo as Marguerite Gautier in *Camille*, her greatest performance.

Edith, Margaret, Irene and Louis B. Mayer at a film premiere in the late 1920s. The woman standing behind Irene is Mrs. Robert Rubin.

All Singing! All Dancing! All Talking!: A production number from *The Broadway Melody*, M-G-M's first all-sound film.

The Irving Thalberg Building at M-G-M, also known as "The Iron Lung."

Members of a chorus line in a more innocent age: Bessie Love and Anita Page in *The Broadway Melody*.

Thalberg's Folly: The duel scene from *Romeo and Juliet*, with Leslie Howard and Basil Rathbone. Howard didn't want the part of Romeo; Rathbone had already played the role in the 1934 Katharine Cornell stage production which inspired Thalberg to make the picture.

Thalberg brings Broadway to Hollywood: Lynn Fontanne and her husband, Alfred Lunt, made only one major sound film together, *The Guardsman* for M-G-M in 1931. The Lunts weren't happy with the results; neither was the public. Here Miss Fontanne consults with director Sidney Franklin.

Here William Powell and Jean Harlow seem not to have eyes for each other, but at the time this picture was taken, only a few weeks before Harlow's death, it was rumored that they would soon be married.

Clark Gable and Tully Marshall watch as Harlow rids herself of uninvited bed vermin. The film is *Red Dust*, and it's as much fun today as when it was first released in 1932.

An M-G-M publicity coup: Jean Harlow shows fan magazine readers how to apply the eyebrow pencil.

(*Above*) David O. Selznick, Eddie Mannix, Al Lichtman (an M-G-M executive) and Clark Gable watch as Mayer examines Gable's contract for *Gone With the Wind*.

(*Below left*) The M-G-M war effort: Robert Montgomery, Clark Gable and Robert Taylor in uniform.

(*Below right*) The King and The Princess: Gable and Margaret O'Brien.

"Gable's Back and Garson's Got Him in *Adventure*": Gable wasn't fond of his co-star, wasn't mad about the picture, loathed the slogan. But he did like Victor Fleming, who directed several of his best pictures, including *Red Dust* and *Gone With the Wind*.

Director Edmund Goulding watches Wallace Beery and Joan Crawford rehearsing a scene for *Grand Hotel*. Goulding had chosen Crawford for her first important role in *Sally, Irene and Mary* (1925).

(*Above left*) Thalberg and Shearer on board the S.S. *California*, sailing from San Pedro to New York, the first leg of their 1933 European vacation. While abroad, Thalberg was to be relieved of his post as M-G-M production supervisor.

(*Above right*) The Married Mogul's friend: Jean Howard.

(*Below*) The inevitable still: Groucho Marx and Margaret Dumont in *A Night at the Opera*.

Another premiere, a little richer, a little less friendly this time: Shearer wears chinchilla, Thalberg and Mayer smile politely while she poses. Maybe something has gone wrong with their relationship?

(Below left) Mayer dancing with his thoroughbred star, Greer Garson.

(Below right) Judy Garland and Mickey Rooney on a promotion tour for an M-G-M film.

Mr. and Mrs. Vincente Minnelli (Judy Garland) with Mayer at a Hollywood nightclub.

Tracy and Hepburn in a typical scene from one of their co-starring vehicles: here they are in the first of the lot, *Woman of the Year* (1940).

Helen Hayes, another of Thalberg's Broadway imports, poses here with two extras costumed for the carnival sequence in *The White Sister* (1933), Hayes's third film for M-G-M.

Lana Turner on the set of *Two Girls on Broadway* (1940), one of several films she made while being groomed for stardom.

A bird's-eye view of the major section of the M-G-M studio in its great days, 1930–1950.

Battleground, Dore Schary's first production on returning to M-G-M in 1948. Actors *(left to right)* Van Johnson, John Hodiak (with book), Jerome Courtland, unidentified, Ricardo Montalban, Don Taylor, George Murphy. The old regime at Metro expected the film to be a flop; it wasn't but it wasn't *The Big Parade*, either.

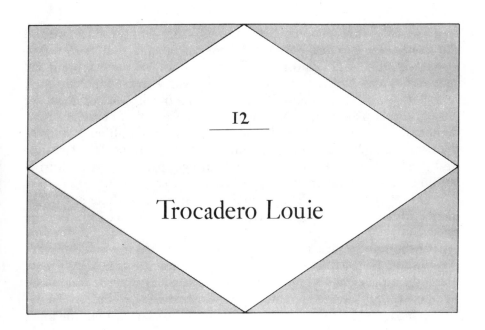

12

Trocadero Louie

Thalberg returned just in time for the studio's annual Labor Day picnic at director Clarence Brown's ranch in the San Fernando Valley. These picnics, which were dedicated to the proposition that M-G-M was one big happy family, were old-fashioned affairs with chilled watermelon, roasted weenies, hamburgers, high spirits and lots of all-American games. There was a traditional bout of tug-of-war, with Mayer and Thalberg captaining opposite ends of the rope, and there were always a few innings of softball. Discarding his straw hat, jacket and tie, Mayer would straddle home plate and swat lustily at the ball. More often than not he managed to make at least a base hit, and more often than not there was a studio photographer close by to record the event for posterity.

This holiday-spirited Mayer was a far cry from the workaday Mayer who strode around the M-G-M lot with an air of conservatively tailored authority. That Mayer was an imposing, at times intimidating, figure. "When Mr. Mayer walked into the studio," recalls Myron Fox, Mayer's financial adviser, "the ground shook, the buildings shook and the elevator went twice as fast as it did for anyone else."

Though he rarely visited the sound stages unless he was forced to do so as an intermediary, Mayer was a familiar presence around the studio. He enjoyed playing the role of official greeter to politicians and other VIP visitors, and as he conducted them around the sets and stages, he introduced them to nearly everyone they met, whether it was Clark Gable or Norman Nebbish, the gofer on the latest Shearer production. No one could accuse him of being less than democratic about his introductions—the studio publicity department briefed him on the backgrounds of the visiting celebrities, but he boned up himself on the names and occupations of the myriad studio employees he encountered every day.

On other occasions he marched along sternly, without a smile or glance in any direction, inspiring dread in the hearts of those he passed.

"I thought he was terrifying," remembers Maureen O'Sullivan, who joined M-G-M in 1932 and was to become the company's most pleasing and versatile ingenue. "We were all in awe of him as he strode through the lot in company with the other producers. To me he was a paternal figure. I suppose the myth was larger than the man, and I never dared to look beneath the façade. He would have been a great actor—his emotional speeches were something to remember!"

Mayer, the might-have-been-great-actor, made a specialty of playing the father figure, alternately severe and loving, admonishing and forgiving, and he had mastered the role (if it was a role) so well that others, far more knowing and experienced than the young Maureen O'Sullivan, were overwhelmed by his manipulative expertise.

Joan Crawford, for example, was also awed by Mayer's patriarchal persuasiveness. By the mid-1930s Crawford had grown tired of the dancing daughters and shopgirls she had been playing for the last seven years, so she went to Mayer and begged for better roles in better pictures. Norma Shearer had Thalberg to look after her, Marion Davies had Hearst, but Crawford, like Myrna Loy and Jean Harlow, was forced to fight for herself; for a long time she accepted without complaint roles cast off by Davies, Shearer and Garbo, but the time had come when she had to speak up. "Give me a chance to show I'm a real actress," she pleaded. Mayer listened attentively, assured her that he had never underestimated her talent, but went on to remind her that she had been unknown before M-G-M put her under contract, that the studio had made her a star and would continue to do right by her in the future. In other words, M-G-M and Mayer knew best.

Crawford never understood how it happened, but she always left these conferences feeling "guilty and disloyal." Which, of course, was precisely the way Mayer wanted her to feel. He was a virtuoso at improvising variations on the loyalty theme; if sympathy and flattery didn't work, he'd drop a dark hint as to what could happen if a studio decided to let an uncooperative contractee go. "We made you," he would snarl, "and we can always break you."

Not all the stars were so easily intimidated. Garbo, for instance, would sit silently through Mayer's harangues, and then announce haltingly that maybe . . . after all . . . it would be best for her . . . to go home. She wasn't bluffing—when her contract expired in 1934, she returned to Sweden, and it took M-G-M over a year to get her back to the studio.

Myrna Loy took the same route when in 1936 she went on strike, claiming justifiably that she was overworked—in three years, she had made twenty films. Metro threatened legal action, but Loy thumbed her nose at the threat and got on a boat for England, where she was to stay until M-G-M promised her a new contract with more money for less work.

Garbo and Loy were stars, so they had some leverage when it came to contract or working disputes. Supporting players on the way to becoming stars were in a more vulnerable position. There was, for example, the case of Charles Bickford. He was Garbo's leading man in *Anna Christie,* and he might have found a permanent place in the M-G-M galaxy had he not become known as "the friend of the extras," meaning he was pro-union, anti-studio.

One day at shut-off time, with about twenty minutes of filming to be completed on a scene that called for two hundred extras, Bickford refused to work overtime. "Damned if I'll do it!" he shouted as he walked off the set. By leaving, he was guaranteeing the extras another day of work.

Mayer was called to the set, but Bickford repeated what he had said before, only in more vivid terms. By this time, Mayer was close to fifty; he had grown a double chin and the beginnings of a potbelly, but in spirit he was as muscular as when he was overseeing the salvage crews in Saint John, New Brunswick; if Bickford wanted a fight, he was ready to oblige. "It never went that far," recalls Howard Strickling. "We got them separated before that, but Bickford didn't work much at M-G-M afterwards."

One area of friction between Mayer and the M-G-M players was his eagle-eyed supervision of their private lives. "He insisted on strict morality, and any scandal was severely frowned on," recalls Maureen O'Sullivan. To encourage his actors to walk the straight-and-narrow, he was lavish with his advice on love, marriage, family planning and divorce, the gist of the advice being: (1) think before you leap into bed; (2) remember that there is a time and place for everything; (3)

what is good for the heart and the loins is not necessarily good for the career.

Pretty good advice, particularly in the early 1930s when the fan magazines were brewing up a scandal about the large number of unwed "Hollywood couples." But a good number of the M-G-M actors didn't want Mayer as their Papa, and resented living by Production Code morality off the set as well as on. Moreover, many felt Mayer was hypocritical, that he used his Big Daddy image manipulatively, even tyrannically, and that he cared not a whit about actors as people; to him, they were chattels that could be discarded as soon as they became outmoded.

A popular saying that made the rounds of the studio at this time seems to support this view: "Film making is the only business in which the assets go home at five o'clock." The unspoken conclusion of this witticism is, of course, "And God knows what they'll do overnight to become liabilities." And from here, it's only a short step to another prevalent 1930s Hollywood concept: nearly all actors are emotionally, intellectually and professionally ill-equipped to handle the sudden fame and money that stardom brought them.

It would be naïve to believe that Mayer did not at times regard his players as high-risk commodities, but on the other hand, it would be unduly cynical to believe that his fatherly concern was nothing more than a pretense. Once Myron Fox made some slighting remark about actors, and Mayer cut him off: "Don't ever say anything bad about actors," he said sharply. "If it weren't for actors, I wouldn't be where I am."

This too could be taken as a confession of self-interest, but there's no reason to believe Mayer was less than sincere in concern for his "children." Of course, he had his favorites, and of course, most of them were staunchly loyal to M-G-M.

"He could be very considerate," recalls Bessie Love. "Once he called me into his office and told me regretfully and as gently as possible that my contract wasn't being renewed. I don't think any other studio boss would have taken on that unpleasant duty, at least no studio boss I had ever met."

Marie Dressler was another of Mayer's pets. By 1933, she had become one of Metro's most valuable players through her work in such films as *Min and Bill, Tugboat Annie,* and *Dinner at Eight.* Her vehicles cost between $400,000 and $600,000 and several returned a clear profit of over $1 million, and her broad comedy style, laced as it generally was with a generous dollop of sentimentality, suited Mayer's taste to perfection. He adored her offscreen as well, and was deeply saddened when in late 1933 he learned she was dying of cancer.

The news came just as Dressler was about to go east for a charity benefit in New York. Her doctors didn't want her to go but Dressler was looking forward to the trip, and unaware of her terminal illness, refused to give it up. "So, some mornings I don't feel so good," she argued. "But that's never stopped me before and it's not going to stop me now."

Mayer stepped in and, playing the villain, told her she couldn't make the trip—M-G-M needed her. "For what?" Dressler asked. Mayer told Strickling to keep planting items in the columns about future projects for Dressler, but she knew they weren't true, and soon she had her first real argument with Mayer. "Look, Marie, I need you at M-G-M right now," was all he would say.

Soon enough she realized she was terminally ill and expressed appreciation for Mayer's concern, though at times his attention became almost smothering. "You are trying to run my life," she told him at one of their final meetings. Mayer took it the way it was meant. As Dressler had once told an interviewer, "I've been known to grand-dame it, at times."

Another of Mayer's favorites was Lionel Barrymore, who started at M-G-M in 1924 and was to remain there until his death thirty years later. The hammiest member of the hammy Barrymore clan, he was a valuable addition to the M-G-M star system, as a leading man, character actor and director. For Mayer, he was "the best," and he supported Barrymore through a very difficult period. For many years Barrymore had suffered from arthritis, and in his attempt to find relief, he had become addicted to opium, as had his actress-wife, Irene Fenwick. To support his habit, Barrymore often had to ask Mayer for an advance on his salary, and Mayer always came through with the money.

But the money was always doled out with a lecture, and in time Barrymore resolved to try to kick his habit. "It was painful to watch," remembers Howard Strickling. "He sat there in a chair in the sanitarium, his fingers and knuckles white from gripping the armrests, gasping 'I'm going to do it! I'm determined to do it!' He succeeded, and Mr. Mayer was very proud of him."

During his first decade at M-G-M, Mayer had changed only superficially—he had become stouter, grayer, more assured, smoother and more sophisticated in outward appearance, possibly a bit more vain and forthright in exercising his rights of domain. But the pattern of his life had altered hardly at all. "For the first ten years, he was M-G-M twenty-four hours a day," says Myron Fox. "The studio was his entire life." He got up early, ate breakfast, went to the studio and returned home for a quiet dinner with the family. Social engagements were also strictly business—industry affairs that had to be attended, studio executives and employees that had to be entertained.

Then around 1933 the pattern suddenly became more intricate, less insular, and of endless fascination for the Hollywood gossips and fabulists. It was the beginning of the "Trocadero Louie" era of Mayer's life.

By then his daughters were married and starting their own families with husbands who were rising swiftly in the industry. Bill Goetz, with a financial boost from Mayer, became a major stockholder in the newly formed Twentieth Century company, headed by Joe Schenck and Darryl Zanuck, and joined the staff as Zanuck's executive assistant. (Mayer also made a hefty investment in Twentieth Century, and helped it get on its feet by lending it the services of such top Metro stars as Gable, Loy and Wallace Beery; this policy continued even after Twentieth Century merged with Fox to become one of Hollywood's major studios.)

In the six-week interval between Edie's and Irene's marriages in 1930, Jacob Mayer had died, making L.B. the official head of the Mayer clan, a role he had played unofficially for many years. Nearly all his brothers and sisters had migrated to California, and he had made certain that they were well provided for: brother Jerry worked at the studio as did Ida's son, Jack Cummings (who was to become one of M-G-M's lesser producers, his most notable achievement being the best of the Esther Williams swimmusicals). Rudy, the black sheep brother, was a constant source of anxiety. Rudy's devilish, get-rich-quick ways appalled Mayer, but family was family, and L.B. was always ready for a handout, provided Rudy stayed clear of the law and brought no shame to the family name—Mayer as in Metro-Goldwyn. (The studio was family, too.) Rudy did his best to oblige.

In both the professional and the private spheres of his life, Mayer had achieved the status of patriarch, a position he had always aspired to but one he was not able to enjoy once it had been achieved. Around this time, Margaret had a hysterectomy, and then, as has been known to happen after such operations, she was afflicted with a severe form of melancholia. From then on, Mayer was to return every night to an invalid wife, not his beloved Margaret who had supported him and shared so much of life.

Friends, relations and associates kept urging Mayer to find some hobby or activity that would allow him to unwind after the pressures of a day at M-G-M. But for a man who had channeled all his energy into becoming a success, this was a tall order. He enjoyed an occasional hand of pinochle or bridge, but he played so emotionally and for such low stakes that he wasn't welcome in card-shark circles. He liked to walk, and like Harry Truman, sometimes took an early morning constitutional before beginning his workday, and was famous for striding through the studio lots, accompanied by associates who would have preferred to cover the distance by car. For lunch appointments, he would start out early on foot, arriving at the restaurant just as his guests were getting out of their chauffeured cars.

Around this time, one of his doctors suggested he take up golf for exercise and as a release from business tensions. Mayer had always enjoyed golf; had in fact worked up a speedy variation of the game. He teed off not once but five times, and had at least three caddies out spotting or scouting the location of his drives; as soon as they were found, he whammed away again, and as soon as he hit the green, it was time to tee up for a new hole. Speed, not accuracy, counted, and when he got to the locker room of the Hillcrest Country Club, he would interrupt the other golfers' discussion of score and par to ask, "I did nine holes in sixty minutes! What was your time?"

Later Mayer slowed down and played golf as golf was intended to be played and became pretty good at it, but at this time, he was looking for a more stimulating form of amusement. Occasionally he spent a night on the town with the boys, and then started stopping by some of Hollywood's top-echelon stag parties. Some of the festivities got pretty raunchy—the host usually provided a bevy of aspiring "starlets" as party favors—but Mayer walked the straight and narrow; he wasn't interested in "bums," his private name for the ladies who had decided that prone was the best position for a girl who wanted to get ahead.

One of these parties provided Mayer with an introduction to a man who was to become one of his closest companions in the next decade, and who was also to cast a shadow of disrepute over Mayer's career.

"Frank Orsatti was bad news," says Mayer's grandson Jeffrey Selznick. "Looking back on it now, I get the impression that my mother carefully monitored my visits to Grandpa. Partly I think this was because she didn't want us infected with 'mogulism,' but mainly because she didn't want us around when Grandpa was entertaining people like Orsatti."

And Myron Fox once asked Mayer why Orsatti was always hanging around. "Look," Mayer answered, "I've got certain things that have to be done and there are things I can't ask people like you to do."

Frank Orsatti came from a respectable San Francisco family consisting of an archetypal Italian mama, a successful but mild-mannered father who acted as the West Coast representative for an international steamship company, and three younger brothers, Vic, Al and Ernie (who, for a time, was outfielder for the St. Louis Cardinals). But Frank had strayed into a life of demicrime—he operated a couple of popular Frisco speakeasies and used his sailing boat to run liquor into the United States from Mexico. Though he rarely took part in these smuggling expeditions, he walked with a rolling sailor's gait, an affectation that was meant to suggest piracy and romance on the high seas.

Eventually Orsatti ran afoul of the law. When his speakeasies were boarded up by the San Francisco authorities, he fled to Los Angeles and ran his bootlegging activities from a top-floor suite at the Roosevelt Hotel on Hollywood Boulevard. Always fascinated with show business, he managed to ingratiate himself with the wealthy Hollywood high-steppers, and pretty soon he was supplying their liquor (Mayer was one of his customers) and ringmastering their revels. He was blessed with personality and irresistible charm—even the people who didn't entirely approve of Frank had to admit that he was fun to have around.

Mayer took to him immediately. He was impressed by Orsatti's devotion to his family, and used his political pull to keep him out of jail. He encouraged Frank to go straight and helped him establish a talent agency with his three brothers as assistants. The Orsatti agency had no trouble getting off the ground, as it soon became known that Mayer was partial to its clients. In later years, this favoritism was to cause hard feeling in Hollywood since rival agents who placed clients at M-G-M were often expected to share their percentage with Orsatti, though it is untrue (as reported by Bosley Crowther in *Hollywood Rajah*) that he requested—or got—50 percent of the fee.

Mayer started traveling with Orsatti—once he took him to visit President Hoover at the White House; they played golf together, saw each other nearly every day. "Mr. Mayer came to rely heavily on Frank," remembers Howard Strickling. "He'd say, 'So-and-so is playing the Trocadero or the Mocambo; go and see if they're for M-G-M.' So Frank would check it out, and if he liked what he saw, he'd find out if the talent involved was committed elsewhere, and if not, how much it might cost M-G-M to negotiate a contract." In exchange for his gratis talent-scouting, Orsatti would, of course, often get a new client and the standard agent's fee once the pact was signed and sealed.

Orsatti moved into a beach house between Santa Monica and Malibu, where he lived on a very grand and loose scale, frequently entertaining his cronies at playboy parties overflowing with booze and floosies. Mayer was often the guest of honor. He had become an enthusiastic practitioner of ballroom dancing, particularly when there was a Latin beat to the music—the rhumba was to be his specialty—and Orsatti always saw to it that he got the prettiest girl as his partner for whatever he might want to do, either on or off the dance floor.

Mayer was not immune to the allure and availability of the ladies Orsatti shoved in his direction. In fact, for the first time since his marriage in 1904, he was susceptible to the temptations of playing around.

Doctors had warned Mayer that it was no longer wise for him to have sexual relations with his wife. Margaret was in fact living for most of the year in a sanitarium in Massachusetts, returning to California for occasional visits on an irregular basis. During her stays, she would go out once or twice a week with Mayer, and occasionally she was well enough to travel with him. But she was always to be an invalid.

Suddenly Mayer found himself with neither a wife nor a home. And the lack of companionship was highly distressing. "I'm just as virile now as I was when my mother told me I should make love only to have babies," he reportedly remarked to one M-G-M associate. And Howard Strickling, with a gesture toward his crotch, recalls, "Mayer thought that was for making babies or going to the bathroom. It wasn't until after he was fifty that he realized it was for fun, too."

But, Strickling went on to emphasize, as a Casanova, Mayer was something of a washout. The flesh was ready and able, but the spirit wasn't. The straitlaced values Mama Sarah had implanted back in Saint John proved stronger than any momentary sexual itch, and so Mayer was the leading member of a small California cult, the Jewish Puritans. Well-intentioned cronies kept telling him that he should learn to relax and enjoy it, no one would blame him if he did; Orsatti kept egging him on, "Come on, boss, I'll fix ya up." Mayer flirted with the party girls, danced with them, showered them with courtly attentions, but rarely, if ever, bedded them. His scorecard was so low it became a joke: "L. B. Mayer couldn't catch a piece of tail in a cathouse."

"I can't make love to a girl I don't really care for," Mayer explained. That was the problem—Orsatti's girls weren't the kind you cared about for much longer than the proverbial seven minutes. But inevitably, he found the kind of girl he was looking for, even though much of what he saw in her was the product of his imagination.

Jean Howard, a blonde beauty with an air of inbred refinement, was in her mid-twenties when Mayer met her at the beginning of 1933. A few years earlier she had left her native Texas and gone to New York to break into show business, eventually wangling a job as a show girl in the 1931 edition of *The Ziegfeld Follies*. This engagement did not bring any bigger stage assignments, but it did lead to a close friendship with another member of the *Follies* cast, Ethel Borden Harriman, the dilettante daughter of a wealthy and socially prominent East Coast financier. (To protect her old-guard relatives, Miss Borden abandoned the Harriman name when she embarked on her theatrical career.) Through her friend, Jean began to move in elite and café society circles, and from the outset, she acted as though she were to the manor born. "There was nothing of the show girl about her," recalls one acquaintance. "She was bright, graceful, beautifully groomed, well mannered and thoroughly housebroken—you could take her anywhere."

Bert Taylor, the president of the New York Stock Exchange, introduced her to Bob Rubin and urged Rubin to give her a screen test for an M-G-M contract. The results of the test were inconclusive—yes, she was stunning, but no, she wasn't going to win any awards for her acting—still, with some polishing and coaching, she might make the grade. She got a contract and left for M-G-M, where in 1933 she was to play small parts in two minor productions, *From Broadway to Hollywood* and *The Prizefighter and the Lady*.

Arriving at the studio, Howard went through the routine procedure of introductory interviews prescribed for all new contractees. She sat for the photographers, talked to the publicity department, met with producers who might find a part for her in their next picture. Then she was summoned to Mayer's office. He had been briefed on her background, including her illustrious social connections, and was immensely impressed by her natural refinement and wellborn manners. Here was a real lady, not one of Orsatti's "bums," and by the time Miss Howard walked out of his office, Mayer was ready to take a personal interest in her career.

Within a few weeks, Mayer's interest in Miss Howard had gone beyond being merely professional. He showered her with attentions and small favors, not the least of which was his sponsorship of Howard's bosom buddy, Ethel Borden. The two women had come to

Hollywood together, and Jean took the first opportunity to introduce Ethel to Mayer. Her friend, she explained, was a gifted playwright who had turned out several stylish comedies, and if they hadn't as yet been produced, it was because New York producers were too dense to realize that Ethel was the Noel Coward of America. Mayer swallowed the bait, and Borden was soon a member of the M-G-M writers department at a salary of three hundred dollars a week.

Though the friendship caused a good deal of speculation, Mayer paid it no attention. Indeed, Borden became an important ally in his courtship of Howard; from all reports, she was in favor of the romance, which was sure to prove beneficial to both her and Jean's careers. Also she was a convenient "cover" or chaperon for those infrequent evenings when Mayer and Howard went out on the town.

In his dual biography, *Mayer and Thalberg*, Samuel Marx quotes Miss Howard as saying that her "romance" with Mayer was entirely a public affair. They were never intimate, she insists, never crossed the boundary between the platonic and the passionate, though, she admits, had he asked, she might have been willing. Given Mayer's puritanism, her account sounds plausible, but many of those close to Mayer find it somewhat hard to swallow.

The romance reached its unhappy conclusion in the spring of 1934. By then Mayer's wife was an invalid; the best specialists had prescribed the most fashionable treatments—everything except hormones—but nothing had worked. Deciding Maggie might benefit from a change of scene, Mayer worked out a plan for a European excursion that would be part pleasure, part business, part rest cure. The pleasure was to be provided by Miss Howard, who was to join Mayer in Paris a week or so after he had settled his wife and himself in a suite at the Hotel George V. Ethel Borden was to accompany Jean as her "traveling companion."

The trip turned out a nightmare for all concerned. Only a few hours after arriving in Paris, Mrs. Mayer was rushed to the American Hospital with a severe case of pneumonia and was to remain there for several weeks, watched over by an around-the-clock corps of prominent European doctors, including an Englishman who was the house physician at Buckingham Palace. Then Mayer got another piece of bad news. He had hired a private detective to tail Miss Howard, not a gentlemanly thing to do perhaps, but partly justified by the fact that Miss Howard was not acting precisely the way a lady should. As the detective reported to Mayer, she had been carrying on a torrid affair with an up-and-coming agent named Charles K. Feldman.

"Charlie didn't have much of a backbone," says one business

associate. "But he was very bright, nice, easygoing, a good dancer and very handsome—he was sometimes called the Jewish Clark Gable." His meeting with Jean Howard was a case of lust at first sight. "We couldn't keep our hands off each other," she told Sam Marx many years later.

She told Mayer the same thing when he confronted her with the detective's report in Paris. She was amazed at the intensity of his feeling—none of the other rich men who had taken a shine to her had ever carried on in this way. Mayer told Howard that since she couldn't keep her hands off Feldman, she should return to the States and marry him—after all, they were both unattached and over twenty-one. And, a few months later, that's precisely what they did.

After the marriage, Howard worked sporadically in pictures until the mid-forties, piling up a list of trivia ("Was *she* in *that?*") credits. She fared better as a café society celebrity, living in high style in all the right places with all the right people, even occasionally with husband Charlie, who was doing very well. Shortly after the wedding he broke up his agency partnership with Ad Schulberg (wife of former Paramount president B.P., mother of novelist Budd) and formed his own organization, which was backed by a lawyer named Ralph Blum, who was married to Carmel Myers, who happened to be one of Mayer's earliest Hollywood friends. A persistent, unsubstantiated and seemingly incredible rumor has it that the money Blum gave Feldman to build up his agency actually came out of Mayer's pocket—his wedding present to Jean Howard.

But if Mayer set up Feldman's business, why did he go to such lengths to blackball Feldman not only at M-G-M but throughout the industry, as, according to Hollywood legend, he tried to do? Strickling and Myron Fox say the legend is pure fabrication. "It would have been out of character for Mr. Mayer to do that," says Howard Strickling. "Mr. Mayer always wanted the best for M-G-M, and if Feldman had the best, then he'd approve the deal, though he would never arrange it for himself."

This was not uncharacteristic of Mayer, who had a very practical approach to dealing with his enemies. "Keep that bastard off the lot," he'd yell, "until I tell you I need him."

Though his pride and heart had been wounded, Mayer was too preoccupied to brood over the Howard affair. He was deeply distressed about his wife's health, and though her condition proved not to be as serious as was at first feared, he refused to leave Paris until she was able to travel with him. He detested being trapped in the suite at the George V, remembers Howard Strickling (who was traveling with the Mayers on the trip). "Mr. Mayer was like a caged lion. He had two or three telephone conversations all going at once, and he'd jump back and forth between one phone and the next, champing at the bit because everything had to be done at long distance."

When Mrs. Mayer was well enough to travel, it was decided she should return to California. Mayer, of course, returned with her. Never at ease with his indiscretion, he became deeply repentant when confronted with his wife's illness. Margaret soon returned to the Massachusetts sanitarium and for a while Mayer stayed clear of the spotlight of Hollywood nightlife. But there was no possibility of a permanent happy relationship unless Mrs. Mayer recovered— which was highly unlikely. So the era of Trocadero Louie hadn't really ended; in fact, it was just getting up steam.

On his return to Hollywood in the fall of 1934, however, Mayer was to find little time for the rhumba or for courting a replacement for Jean Howard. He was faced with a multitude of problems, some petty, some grievous, some related specifically to the studio, some with wider ramifications. Foremost among the latter was Upton Sinclair, the socialist muckraker, who was then campaigning for the governorship of California.

Two years earlier, M-G-M had produced a film adaptation of Sinclair's *The Wet Parade*, a study of prohibition and alcoholism. It's one of the weakest of Sinclair's novels, but Thalberg thought it would make a good movie and got the studio to buy the film rights over Mayer's opposition. Mayer didn't know much about socialism, didn't care to know much since it was clearly anti-capitalism and thereby, anti-Hollywood and anti-American, but he told Thalberg it was okay if Sinclair worked on the lot—as long as he never set eyes on "the bum."

By the time *The Wet Parade* got to the screen, it wasn't about much—the controversial political sting had been taken out of it—and it's memorable only because Myrna Loy, blondined and shimmering in a silver paillette gown, comes across for the first time as a major movie personality. Sinclair hated the film and had no affection for Mayer, whom he cast in an unflattering light in his biography of William Fox (*Upton Sinclair Presents William Fox*, published in 1933).

Sinclair entered the California gubernatorial campaign as a token candidate—he never expected to win, probably never wanted to win and certainly wasn't prepared to win: he had no political experience to qualify him for the job.

But he came up with a potent campaign slogan—EPIC, an

acronym for End Poverty in California. It also suggests, of course, a Cecil De Mille spectacle. Did Sinclair have that in mind when he invented the slogan? Maybe not, but the twelve-point EPIC platform certainly starts off with a typically De Mille-esque rumble of celestial displeasure over the ways of the world:

> God created the natural wealth of the earth for use of all men, not the few.

As the platform proceeds from Point 1 to Point 12, it becomes obvious that God was a socialist whose vision has been corrupted by capitalist entrepreneurs (i.e., the ungodly) who allowed "some men [to] live without working [while] other men are working without living" (Point 5). The remedy (Point 11) was to give workers "access to the means of production," which could be brought about by "an action of a majority," which (Point 12) was "the American Way."

So the Sinclair brand of socialism was both godly and all-American, apple pie with a hot-cross-bun topping. It was sloganistic, emotional, vague and impractically utopian, but still it attracted many thousands of Depression-ridden Californians who had given up on the professional politicians who talked facts, figures and surefire remedies, but did nothing to relieve the misery.

By the time Mayer returned from Europe, Sinclair's candidacy for the governorship had to be taken seriously. A few months before, he had quietly changed his registration from Socialist to Democrat, and in the 1934 Democratic primary he outran his eight rivals by an impressive margin. People who had once joked about Sinclair as "the red menace of Sacramento" listened apprehensively as he stripped away the utopian vapors from the EPIC program and developed a list of unmistakably left-wing specifics. He proposed a sales tax; he advocated a graduated income tax, starting at $5,000 and increasing to a point where all incomes over $50,000 would be taxed at 50 percent; he wanted additional inheritance taxes, a gift tax and graduated corporate income taxation. Worst of all, he wanted a special tax levied against film studios.

Speaking for all movie bosses, Mayer issued a statement warning Sinclair that if a tax were imposed against the studios, the studios would pull up stakes and move to Florida.

"That's a piece of bunk," Sinclair retorted. "They couldn't move out if they wanted to. It would cost them too much. . . . Besides, think of what those big Florida mosquitoes would do to some of our film sirens. Why, one bite on the nose could bring a $50,000 production loss." Sinclair was right—the moguls were threatening idly when they talked of moving to Florida. But they were desperate, and not only because of Sinclair's proposed picture tax.

In 1934, there were 300,000 unemployed in Los Angeles, and every day more Depression drifters entered the state, drawn there by the area's reputation for sunshine, easy living and ample job opportunities. This influx of indigents came at a time when property value was rising steadily and real estate speculation was (and had been since the twenties) one of the favored sports of the film rich. Sinclair's EPIC program was viewed as an open-doored invitation for tramps to set up Hoover towns in Southern California, thereby obscuring the palm trees and plummeting real estate prices toward zero.

The enemy camp struck back with a new interpretation of the EPIC acronym: it meant, said Sinclair's detractors, Empty Promises In California. It was argued that Sinclair would never be able to turn his program into working law, and if he did, his reforms would lead to crippling strikes throughout the state. Not without reason, Sinclair was portrayed as a political naïf, though this bothered Sinclair and his partisans not a whit—after all, it was the experienced politicians who had gotten the country into this god-awful mess. Just look, for example, at Frank Merriam, who was running for reelection on the Republican ticket. What had he done to relieve his people of their burden?

Merriam was an unimaginative man with an unimpressive record as governor. No one expected him to do very much to help California through the Depression, but the oil companies, the banks, the railroads and the public utilities all jumped on his bandwagon, working fervidly and spending lavishly in the hope of defeating Sinclair. They were, in effect, campaigning *against* Sinclair rather than *for* Merriam.

According to the press, the opposition was directed by Hollywood, with Mayer invariably being singled out as the mastermind behind the many dirty tricks pulled on Sinclair. *The New York Times*, for instance, carried a story reporting that all M-G-M employees making over a hundred dollars a week were forced to contribute part of their salary to the campaign to reelect Frank Merriam. "Many employees were given blank checks made out to Louis B. Mayer," said an anonymous interviewee (identified only as "a screenwriter"). The article went on to say that M-G-M was not the only studio enforcing this policy, but Mayer, alone among the studio bosses, was mentioned by name. Possibly this is because Sinclair was firmly convinced that Mayer was the Antichrist of Hollywood bossism, which could be taken as a sort of backhanded compliment to Mayer and the power he wielded over the film industry in the 1930s.

The dirtiest of the dirty tricks played against Sinclair was a series of fake newsreels distributed free of charge to California theatres in which a series of neatly groomed, clean-cut, all-American ladies and gentlemen spoke favorably of Merriam while scrofulous bums with foreign accents pledged allegiance and votes to Sinclair. Another edition of this newsreel (called *The Inquiring Reporter*) showed trainloads of hoboes and Joads on their way to California to enjoy the largesse promised by Sinclair's EPIC program.

As soon as these newsreels hit the screen, Sinclair exposed them for what they were—propaganda practiced at the most reprehensible level. The footage was not actual but staged, and most of the people who appeared in it were bit actors from Central Casting, not passersby who had been haphazardly caught as a cross-current of public opinion.

It was rumored (correctly) that the films had been made under M-G-M supervision, and (incorrectly) that Mayer had ordered them into production. Nearly everyone believed Mayer was responsible, until one night at a party Thalberg told Fredric March (a liberal who was shocked by what he heard), "I had those shorts made. Nothing is unfair in politics. I used to be a boy orator for the Socialist party on the East Side in New York. Do you think Tammany ever gave me a chance to be heard?"

There is no way of gauging the effectiveness of these newsreels in pulling votes away from Sinclair, but most of the credit for his defeat should probably go to the smear campaign conducted by the California papers, particularly those owned by Hearst. Merriam won the election with 1,138,620 votes; Sinclair got 879,537, and the other progressive candidate, Raymond Haight, received 302,519, which suggests that had Sinclair and Haight consolidated their power (as they were urged to do), one or the other might have defeated Merriam by a slim margin.

Much later, Sinclair said that he didn't really lose the election. In less than a year, Roosevelt was to send to Congress a tax program designed to redistribute wealth and power in America along the same lines Sinclair had proposed in his EPIC plan—increased inheritance taxes, a gift tax, graduated corporate and individual income taxes. And no sooner was Merriam reelected than he too adopted part of Sinclair's program, much to the outrage of his supporters. An editorial in the San Francisco *Argonaut,* one of the most virulent of the anti-Sinclair newspapers, commented, "Would Sinclair have done worse . . . ? He might even have done better for he had an atom or two of genius in his composition while all one can discern in Merriam is cobwebs from an empty skull."

Merriam also toyed with the idea of levying a special tax against the film studios, and once again Mayer, as spokesman for the industry, threatened a move to Florida. But nothing ever came of Merriam's threat, which was lucky for Mayer. None of the studios was prepared for a major move, and Mayer had enough headaches without crating and hauling M-G-M to Miami.

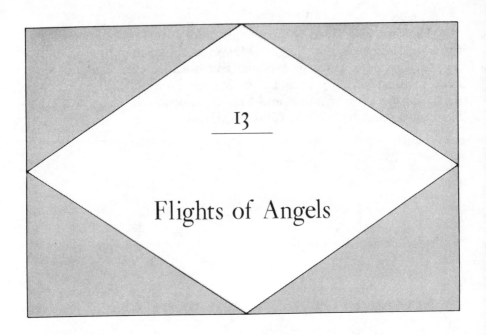

13

Flights of Angels

First and foremost there was the Thalberg problem.

After his return to M-G-M, Thalberg and Mayer acted outwardly as though they had patched up their differences. But Howard
Strickling admits that "they were never to be as close as before." The
distance between them was more of Thalberg's making than Mayer's:
Thalberg kept on nursing his grievances, remained suspicious of
Mayer, often spoke disparagingly of his abilities. When young and
progressive-thinking Walter Wanger joined the M-G-M stable of producers, he asked Thalberg how he should handle Mayer. "Don't even
try," Thalberg answered. "Just ignore him."

For his first production at M-G-M since his illness, Thalberg
chose to remake *The Green Hat,* Michael Arlen's purple-prosed account of Belgravian promiscuity, originally filmed with Garbo as
Woman of Affairs. Naturally, it was to star Norma Shearer, who had
been off the screen for over a year, and the script was to be written
by Charles MacArthur. But MacArthur couldn't carve a presentable
screenplay out of Arlen's story, so writer/director Edmund Goulding was assigned to the project, and he came up with something
that was less an adaptation than a script in the style of *The Green Hat.*
It was called *Riptide.*

Playing opposite Norma were Robert Montgomery and a distinguished supporting cast headed by C. Aubrey Smith and Mrs. Patrick Campbell, the illustrious English actress who created the role of Eliza Doolittle in *Pygmalion*. (As famous for her wit and erratic behavior as for her talent, Stella Campbell once turned to Thalberg and said, "Your wife, my dear, has the most beautiful *tiny* eyes." Thalberg was not amused.) *Riptide* had everything going for it that money could buy, but its first preview was a disaster. Audience dissatisfaction became vocal when Aubrey Smith rolled off the following line as though it were prime Shakespeare: "Ah, this sweet air of England! Presently I shall hear the nightingale." What was heard in the theatre was neither the nightingale nor the lark, but a rousing Bronx cheer.

Critics went easy on *Riptide*, and it returned a small profit, mainly because Shearer fans were hungry for any Shearer film, no matter how bad. But the fact remained—and the industry took careful note of it—that Thalberg had stubbed his toe on his first personal production. He was to stub it again on his next picture.

Once more, he chose to make a new version of one of M-G-M's past hits, *The Merry Widow*. This time, however, there was some logic behind his choice: the first M-G-M *Merry Widow* had been silent; this one would feature Lehar's melodies, brought up to date by Lorenz Hart and Richard Rodgers, Broadway's leading composer-lyricist team; they would be sung by Maurice Chevalier and Jeanette MacDonald. And as director, Thalberg hired Ernst Lubitsch, the German-born director noted for his impudence and visual wit.

At Paramount, Lubitsch had made such stylish operettas as *The Love Parade, Monte Carlo* and *The Smiling Lieutenant*—but this time, he couldn't get the magic going. *The Merry Widow* isn't bad, but it's overproduced and far too conscious of its own cleverness (a frequent failing of Lubitsch films). And the teamwork of MacDonald and Chevalier is off by several beats—he overdoes the ooh-la-la; she's aggressively coy in one scene, insufferably hoity-toity in the next. Critics liked the picture, but the public didn't—costing over $1 million, it lost almost $115,000.

With one near and one outright flop behind him, Thalberg found himself in an awkward position at the start of 1934. People whispered that he had lost his touch, that his first two pictures showed he had lost contact with Depression audiences. To make matters worse, his run of bad luck was inevitably compared to David Selznick's great success at M-G-M. Starting in 1933 with the dazzling *Dinner at Eight* (one of the few film adaptations of a Broadway hit that is far superior to the original), Selznick had produced a string of critical and/or popular successes, including *Night Flight* (with Gable, Loy, Helen Hayes and the Barrymore brothers), the Eisensteinesque *Viva Villa!* (Wallace Beery as the Mexican bandit) and *Dancing Lady* (Crawford, Gable and, in their film debuts, Fred Astaire and Nelson Eddy).

There was an attempt on the part of the press and certain studio employees to set up a rivalry between Thalberg and Selznick, but neither man nibbled at the bait. They had always been and always were to be good friends. Whatever hostility or frustration Thalberg felt was directed toward the studio and Mayer. He claimed he wasn't given the director he wanted for *Riptide* or the writers he needed for *Merry Widow* and consequently the pictures hadn't worked out as planned. In other words, Mayer and the studio were trying to sabotage his operations by denying him the first-class personnel he required and deserved.

The truth was that Thalberg was often unreasonable in his demands—he wanted all the best actors, the best writers, the best directors—and while Mayer bent sideways to oblige, he had other producers to consider. "Mayer did everything he could to accommodate Thalberg," Joe Cohn recalls. "Schedules were rearranged, shooting dates were delayed or set ahead, all to give Thalberg whatever he wanted. But some times it just wasn't possible. After all, Mayer was running a studio, not a one-man Thalberg operation."

There are any number of incidents that illustrate Mayer's favoritism toward Thalberg, but the most dramatic of all concerns the film adaptation of Rudolph Besier's *The Barretts of Wimpole Street*.

Shortly after the Barretts became the smash hit of the 1930–31 Broadway season, M-G-M bought it as a possible Norma Shearer vehicle, but Shearer wasn't keen on portraying Elizabeth Barrett, a role Katharine Cornell had made virtually her own as far as stage audiences and critics were concerned. So the play was shelved until after *Riptide* when Thalberg convinced Norma that she could survive the inevitable comparisons with Cornell.

Meanwhile, W. R. Hearst had decided Elizabeth Barrett was the perfect role for Marion Davies. He told Mayer he must have the property for Marion. Poor Mayer. Refereeing between actresses fighting for the same part was not a new experience, but this occasion was unique nonetheless. This time he had to choose between Hearst and Thalberg as well as between Davies and Shearer, and no matter how he chose, he was sure to lose as much as he won.

As far as the industry was concerned, there was only one logical choice. Shearer might not be Katharine Cornell, but she was miles ahead of Davies in the *Barretts* sweepstakes—who could imagine

Marion as an English poetess so sickly she had to versify the ways in which she loved instead of demonstrating them in a more forthright fashion? To prove Davies could handle the part Hearst forced the actress to make a test, which was directed by Clarence Brown. "Marion was damned good," Brown remembers, but Mayer wasn't convinced audiences would accept her in the role. Between 1931 and 1933, Davies had made seven films, only three of which made any money. The other four cost M-G-M about $980,000. The M-G-M exhibitors were beginning to complain about the losses they suffered on the Davies films, and Mayer found it increasingly more difficult to justify them as first-rank Metro productions.

In addition, Mayer and Hearst's close-knit relationship had started to unravel a few years before. It began when Hearst supported Roosevelt rather than Hoover in the 1932 presidential election. Feelings became more strained when Hearst's Cosmopolitan Company got behind an M-G-M release, *Gabriel Over the White House,* a political fantasy which Mayer regarded as a veiled libel on Harding and other recent Republican presidents.

There were, however, many times when Mayer and Hearst were on the same side of an issue. They were together on the Upton Sinclair campaign, and in 1933, when Mayer became concerned about Nazi anti-Semitism, he wired Hearst (who was vacationing in Germany) and urged him to request an interview with Hitler. Hearst did manage a brief audience, during which Hitler assured him the Jewish persecution was a temporary measure. This information was relayed to Mayer, who found it somewhat less reassuring than did Hearst.

There was one final factor that had to weigh in the balance between Norma and Marion. The Hearst papers gave M-G-M lots of favorable coverage, and it was within the realm of possibility that if Davies lost the role, that coverage might come to a halt. But Mayer was ready to gamble on the durability of his long-standing friendship with Hearst. He gave the *Barretts* to Shearer and Thalberg.

The Hearst papers carried no publicity about *The Barretts* during its production, but Hearst himself maintained cordial, if somewhat reserved, relations with Mayer while Marion was working on *Operator 13,* a Civil War melodrama in which Davies plays a Yankee spy who masquerades as a mulatto laundress to uncover confederate secrets. "Do you think the South will like it?" Mayer anxiously asked an Alabama-born screenwriter. "No," the writer answered, "and the North won't either." The picture lost about $225,000.

Hearst insisted Davies's waning career was the result of weak roles, and in an attempt to pull her out of the slump, he was once again to come in conflict with the Thalbergs. Late in 1933, at Thalberg's behest, M-G-M had bought the rights to Stefan Zweig's popular biography of Marie Antoinette for Shearer and Charles Laughton (as Louis XVI). The picture had been announced as one of Thalberg's first productions on his return to the studio, but was repeatedly postponed "because of script problems." There was still nothing resembling a shooting script at the beginning of 1935 when Hearst informed Mayer that he wanted the Zweig novel for Marion.

It wasn't a bad idea—after all, Marie Antoinette wasn't one of the virgin queens, and Davies was at least as well suited to the role as Shearer. But the picture was going to cost a lot of money. Versailles would have to be constructed on one of the back lots—and Mayer had good reason to believe Davies was a poor risk as the main support of such a giant undertaking. He was in a very ticklish position. After the *Barretts* incident, he couldn't reject Marion as *Marie Antoinette* without incurring a direct confrontation with Hearst. Thalberg and Norma knew Davies wanted the role—Marion had told Norma so during a party at San Simeon—and they were prepared to give it to her. They were beginning to lose interest in the picture. Mayer, however, was convinced that Marion was primarily a comedienne and wouldn't be able to handle the heavy dramatics that were an essential part of the story.

He came up with a cagey solution to the problem. He told Hearst that though he couldn't see Marion as Marie Antoinette, she could of course have the role, as long as Hearst financed the production with his own money. Hearst refused, certainly not because he couldn't afford to foot the bills (though the Depression and San Simeon had put a considerable pinch in his fortune), but because he felt the offer was an insult to Marion. What Mayer may not have expected (though he must have considered the possibility) was that Hearst would immediately break off his relationship with M-G-M. Within weeks he had arranged to move Marion, her elaborate bungalow and the Cosmopolitan productions to the Warner Brothers lot in Burbank.

On the day the Davies bungalow was carted off the lot, Mayer stood and watched as a caravan of ten flatbed trucks passed through the front gate. Marion came up to him and said goodbye.

"The queen is leaving the lot," he murmured tearfully.

"Not the queen," Marion replied softly, "the *king.*"

Later that year Mayer lost another valued and valuable associate. Son-in-law David O. Selznick had decided the time had come to move into independent production. Backed primarily by John Hay

("Jock") Whitney, he left Metro when his contract expired in 1935 and formed Selznick-International, which was to release its productions through United Artists, a company formed in the early 1920s by Pickford, Fairbanks and Chaplin as an alternative to the studio system. Mayer, Schenck and Thalberg all urged Selznick to stay at M-G-M, but Selznick insisted that he had to fulfill his ambition of having his own company, of having total authority over his own productions. Thalberg and Shearer eventually made a $200,000 investment in the company, but Mayer offered no financial support. He was convinced that Selznick was making a grave mistake in going against the studio setup.

"The problem with David is he has no flywheel," Mayer told one of his cardinals. "He won't listen to reason. He'll have to learn the hard way."

The trade papers also took a skeptical view of Selznick's chances for success outside the Metro fold, many of them quoting a headline from *The Hollywood Reporter* account of his arrival at the studio, "The Son-in-Law Also Rises." Which was clever, but grossly unfair to Selznick who had more than proved his executive capabilities at M-G-M. In 1935, his last year at Metro, he was responsible for three of the studio's most prestigious hits—*David Copperfield, Anna Karenina* and *Tale of Two Cities,* tasteful and reasonably faithful literary adaptations which were the precursors of the PBS *Masterpiece Theatre* series.

During the same period Thalberg also had a string of hits, although of a somewhat less elevated nature. After *The Barretts,* he produced *China Seas,* a deluxe retread of *Red Dust* starring Gable and Harlow, as "China Doll, the swellest gal on the Archipelago." Then came *A Night at the Opera,* which rescued the flagging career of the Marx Brothers, who a year earlier, after a series of critically acclaimed but financially unsuccessful films at Paramount, were all but washed up in Hollywood. Thalberg had never shown much interest in slapstick but he had a theory about the Marx Brothers. The trouble with their earlier films had been a lack of coherent structure: what was needed, he believed, was a tight story line, embellished with music and love interest, and with the three brothers restraining themselves long enough to establish the semblance of consistent characterization.

It has frequently been argued that only someone who didn't understand (or like) the Marx Brothers could come up with such a wrongheaded proposition, and that Thalberg "stunted their growth" by "forcing them" into "an artistic straitjacket." But *Opera,* their first M-G-M film and one that followed the Thalberg blueprint, was to become their most popular.

For his third production in 1935, Thalberg chose a classier sort of project, one that would bring him again into conflict with Mayer. L.B. had been told the story of *Mutiny on the Bounty,* the best-selling account of the English mutineers who settled on Pitcairn Island, and didn't much care for it: he couldn't see a mutineer as a hero, particularly not the hero of a big-budget film. He tried to talk Thalberg out of it, but to no avail.

One of the reasons Thalberg was attracted to *Mutiny* was that the role of Captain Bligh was perfect for Charles Laughton, who had been so splendid as Papa Barrett. As for the obstacle of presenting a mutineer as hero, that could be overcome, Thalberg insisted, by casting a sympathetic and magnetic actor in the role of Fletcher Christian. Robert Montgomery was up for the role for a while, but Montgomery, polished and professional though he was, didn't really grab the audience at the vital spots. What was needed was someone like Clark Gable—in fact, why not Clark Gable?

Mayer thought this was a terrible idea, and so did Gable. He was a modern American type; how could he carry off a pigtail, white knickers and a British accent? What would his fans think if he appeared as an early nineteenth-century fop who may or may not have harbored a latent sexual itch for the villainous Bligh?

Thalberg and Eddie Mannix told Gable he could handle the role, and eventually he allowed himself to be talked into playing Christian. Thalberg was right—Gable had no trouble handling the part. He looks great, not a bit silly or effeminate in his dandy outfits (though he looks a bit tubby in the Tahitian sequences when he's bare-chested and wearing what looks like an oversized Pamper). And as for the accent, no problem; his Gable-ese is as authentic as anything spoken by 90 percent of the cast. Gable played Fletcher Christian as Gable, and that's just fine—Gable as Gable was enough reason for anyone to go to the movies: the man had real magic in those days.

Mutiny got spectacular reviews and great word-of-mouth. It won Oscar nominations for Gable, Laughton, Frank Lloyd, its scenarists and editor. The Academy voted it best picture of 1935. People who saw it on release remember it as a grand show and TV late-movie addicts keep on promoting it as one of Hollywood's all-time greats.

The picture went a long way toward cementing any remaining chinks in Thalberg's reputation—once again he was talked about as Hollywood's leading producer. And his next major production was one befitting his reputation, an extravagantly mounted *Romeo and Juliet* with—who else?—Norma Shearer in the leading role.

Mayer was aghast. Hollywood's past excursions into Shakespeare had been box office disasters, he reminded Thalberg. Pickford and Fairbanks had lost money on their *Taming of the Shrew,* and the Warner brothers could have financed six or seven gangster films on what they spent on Max Reinhardt's star-studded "cinemazation" of *Midsummer Night's Dream.* Thalberg argued that the Reinhardt *Dream* and the Pickfair *Shrew* had failed because they were bad films, not because they were Shakespeare. Mayer wasn't buying that, but when Schenck and the New York office okayed the production, he grudgingly bowed before the inevitable.

Thalberg's first chore was finding a Romeo. There were rumors that Gable was under consideration, but that was pure gossip-columnist fantasy. Fredric March, who was offered the role, turned it down without a thank-you. Leslie Howard, Thalberg's second choice, wasn't enthusiastic either: at forty-two, he was too old to play a moony adolescent, and he didn't care much for the role to begin with. But then, for reasons he never divulged, Howard did an about-face and decided to take on the part.

Under the supervision of Professor William Strunk, a noted scholar who had worked on Katharine Cornell's much-admired stage production of *Romeo,* a script was prepared which expunged most of Shakespeare's bawdyisms but otherwise provided an acceptable acting version of the original. Agnes De Mille came from New York to choreograph the dances. English designer Oliver Messel was signed to help Cedric Gibbons and the M-G-M art department with sets and costumes. Two voice coaches were hired to help the principals with the iambic pentameter. English actress Constance Collier (later to work with Katharine Hepburn on her Shakespearean roles) tutored Norma, while the celebrated Margaret Carrington, who had coached John Barrymore for *Hamlet* and *Richard III,* once again tried to get the actor into condition for the role of Mercutio.

George Cukor (who had come from RKO to M-G-M with David Selznick) was slated as director: this was his first Thalberg production, and undoubtedly he was chosen because he had a solid stage background. Cukor decided that for the benefit of the actors it would be best to shoot the picture in very long takes and as much in sequence as possible. Thalberg agreed, though this plan meant an expensive and very lengthy shooting schedule for a picture that was already costing enough to send Mayer, Schenck and the New York executives into mass cardiac arrest.

The long shooting schedule kept getting longer every time Barrymore stepped before the cameras. Cukor had worked with Barrymore on *Bill of Divorcement* and *Dinner at Eight;* there had been no problems then, he expected none now. But three years had passed, hundreds of gallons of liquor had been consumed, and Barrymore now looked like a final sketch for the portrait of Dorian Gray. He was also beginning to have trouble memorizing lines, and take after take was ruined as he lost his way through the maze of Shakespearean verse. He agreed to stay in a sanitarium while the film was in production, but once or twice he outwitted his nurses and went off on a binge, and the shooting schedule had to be hastily rearranged while he sobered up. Eventually Cukor asked to have Barrymore replaced and Thalberg talked to William Powell, who adamantly refused out of loyalty—Barrymore had been responsible for Powell's first film role (*Sherlock Holmes,* 1922)—and because the part was well outside his range as an actor.

So for better or worse, Thalberg and Cukor were stuck with Barrymore, who plays Mercutio as a flaming queen. By all conventional standards, he's perfectly awful, and yet he's rather wonderful too. The sheer perversity of his performance is galvanizing, and the film needs all the energy it can get. Howard walks through Romeo as though he were auditioning for Ashley Wilkes, and Shearer is all stardust, moonbeams and girlish mannerisms.

Mayer, however, was mightily impressed by the performances and the opulence of the production, and swept away by his enthusiasm, he predicted *Romeo* would be a huge success. It wasn't. Despite generally favorable reviews and a generous share of Oscar nominations, it was a box office bomb. Costing in excess of $2 million, it lost almost $925,000. Thalberg was unperturbed. The picture, he insisted, had been made for prestige, not money.

Meanwhile, relations between Mayer and Thalberg had not improved. If anything, they continued to deteriorate. Dissatisfied with his position in the company, Thalberg started making plans for the formation of his own company, the I. G. Thalberg Corporation, which would release its films through Loew's but would be an autonomous organization, free of any supervision from Mayer or M-G-M. Thalberg wanted exclusive control over Shearer, the Marx Brothers and any other talent, including directors and writers, he had developed during his years at M-G-M.

Nick Schenck was agreeable, but Mayer bitterly opposed Thalberg's plan (which was similar to Selznick's arrangement with United Artists). Not only did it encroach on his power, it also set a dangerous precedent for the other M-G-M producers, who might decide they too deserved independent units. He reminded Thalberg that his present contract did not expire until the end of 1938, but Thalberg brushed that aside. He knew what he wanted and was determined to get it. He wouldn't budge and neither would Mayer.

Eventually, friends and associates intervened on Thalberg's behalf, and Mayer, persuaded that Thalberg was under enormous strain, backed off. An agreement was reached whereby Thalberg would stay at the studio until the expiration of his contract. Then he would be allowed to set up his own company, which would be financed by and release through Loew's. He would also be allowed to sign on any five or six M-G-M stars of his choosing, with the exception of Gable and Garbo. He would no longer share in Loew's profits, but would receive a healthy percentage of the profits of his own films, as well as $2,000-a-week salary.

With this guarantee, Thalberg plunged into his work for the next three years. In 1936 he had one film in production, an adaptation of Pearl S. Buck's *The Good Earth*, which had been in the planning stages for over two years. Two other films were about ready for production—*Camille*, directed by George Cukor and starring Garbo, and *Maytime*, a MacDonald-Eddy operetta. In various stages of preparation were a number of other projects, including *Marie Antoinette;* a new Marx Brothers picture; *Pride and Prejudice* (with Shearer and Gable pencilled in for the leading roles); and adaptations of two best sellers, Franz Werfel's *The Forty Days of Musa Dagh* and James Hilton's *Goodbye, Mr. Chips.*

It was a formidable lineup, far too strenuous for someone of Thalberg's precarious health, but he refused to slow down, much to the distress of friends who sometimes suspected he was deliberately overtaxing himself. They urged him to take a long vacation with his wife and children (Norma gave birth to a daughter, Katharine, in June 1935), and Thalberg often talked of going east for a couple of months, visiting Charles MacArthur and Helen Hayes or maybe renting a house on the New England seacoast. But the plans never materialized. Norma, who had made only two movies in three years, devoted much of her time to conserving her husband's strength, a losing battle since Irving insisted they continue to play an active part in Hollywood social life.

On Wednesday, September 2, 1936, they attended a benefit for the Actors' Fund at the Hollywood Bowl. Thalberg looked deceptively fit and relaxed as he chatted with Douglas Fairbanks, Sr., and his new wife, Sylvia Ashley, and with Gilbert Roland, Constance Bennett, Myrna Loy, Margaret Sullavan and her husband, William Wyler. Two days later, at the start of the Labor Day weekend, he and Norma checked in at the Del Monte Club on the Monterey peninsula. Nine years before they had spent their honeymoon there, and they had returned frequently ever since. The place was filled with pleasant memories and just far enough away from Los Angeles to serve as an ideal weekend retreat.

On this trip they were joined by a group of friends, including Mr. and Mrs. Mervyn LeRoy, Mr. and Mrs. Sam Wood, Jack Conway and Harpo Marx. Business was to be mixed with pleasure—Thalberg wanted to talk to Harpo and Sam Wood about the next Marx Brothers movie (A Day at the Races) and he also wanted to play bridge, a game which Harpo and several other members of the entourage played at Culberston level.

Every evening they sat down for a couple of rubbers on the veranda of the Del Monte Club. The night air was brisk, unseasonably cool, and Norma kept urging Thalberg to put on a jacket or sweater, but he refused to be coddled in front of his friends.

He returned to the studio on Tuesday, September 8, with a bad head cold. But he worked all day, then drove over to the Hollywood Bowl for a dress rehearsal of a Max Reinhardt superspectacle, Everyman. Again the weather was damp and chilly, but as a sponsor for an event which provided funds for Jewish charities, Thalberg felt obligated to sit out the evening and offer his suggestions and congratulations to Reinhardt and the cast.

Two nights later, at the premiere of Everyman, Thalberg was again on hand to take a bow for his patronage of the evening's entertainment. The weather on September 10 was cool and overcast.

The next morning Thalberg was too ill to report for work. Norma summoned his regular physician, who confined him to bed and confirmed what Norma suspected—Irving's condition was serious. Norma suggested sending for the specialist who had treated him at Bad Neuheim, now a refugee from Nazi Germany and practicing in New York, and within hours, Dr. Franz Groedel was on his way to California. There was also talk of rushing Thalberg to the Mayo Clinic in Rochester, Minnesota, but before the travel arrangements could be worked out, it was decided he was too ill to be moved.

On Sunday, September 13, Thalberg developed pneumonia. It was the day of the annual M-G-M picnic, and Thalberg (more likely Norma, acting for her husband) telegraphed his regrets: "Only illness keeps me from being with you." The message was read aloud over a loudspeaker, and for a while the holiday mood evaporated, but soon the guests shook off the gloom and got into beer, tug-of-war and baseball, with Mayer, as usual, leading off as star batter.

Only a few M-G-M executives were aware of the seriousness of Thalberg's condition. Mayer, of course, was fully informed. On the day after the picnic, September 14, he stayed cloistered in his office with a group of close studio friends, waiting for a phone call. Early that morning, the news had been promising—Thalberg's breathing had become easier and it looked as though he was pulling through the crisis—but his condition was still grave.

Shortly before eleven A.M., the phone rang. Mayer picked it up and listened, then hung up without saying a word.

As he strode out the door, he confirmed what the men gathered in his office had already guessed. Thalberg was dead at age thirty-seven.

His last words, spoken to Norma, were, "Don't let the children forget me." The cause of death was lobar pneumonia; ironically, his heart had suffered no further damage during this final illness.

Mayer rushed to the Thalberg home at 707 Ocean Front in Santa Monica to offer sympathy and assistance to Norma. All day there was a steady flow of visitors, calling cards, notes of sympathy and tele-grams, and by the end of the afternoon, papers were carrying front-page obituaries and editorial tributes.

The funeral services were held two days later at Temple B'nai B'rith in Los Angeles. At Norma's request there were no pallbearers. The ushers included Joe Cohn, Cedric Gibbons, Moss Hart, Douglas Fairbanks, Clark Gable, Fredric March, and M-G-M directors Robert Z. Leonard, Sam Wood, Sidney Franklin and W. S. Van Dyke. Cards of admission were issued to 1,500 persons, including all the M-G-M stars and producers—Freddie Bartholomew, who had just made *Little Lord Fauntleroy* for David O. Selznick, wore one of the little lord's velvet-and-doily suits. Grace Moore (once under contract to M-G-M) opened the services by alternately singing and sobbing the Twenty-third Psalm. Rabbi Edgar Magnin recited the Hebrew ritual for the dead, read letters of condolence (including one from President Roose-velt) and ended with a personal recollection of Thalberg which com-pared his love for Norma to that depicted "in the greatest motion picture I have ever seen—*Romeo and Juliet.*"

Mayer was visibly distraught as he rushed in and out of his limousine, shoving aside the reporters and photographers who at-tempted to block his path. This was a private moment, not to be shared with the press or the public.

While the service was in progress, every studio in Hollywood closed down for five minutes, and M-G-M shuttered for the entire day.

After Rabbi Magnin had concluded the ceremony, close friends and special guests filled twelve limousines which escorted the gar-denia-blanketed copper casket to its final resting place in Forest Lawn Memorial Park. According to one (possibly fictitious) report, Wallace Beery flew a plane over the burial site and pelleted rosebuds on the mourners beneath. Norma, shielded by her brother Douglas, Bernie Hyman and a squadron of M-G-M policemen as she made her way to the mausoleum, was steady throughout, but Henrietta, Irving's mother, gave way and had to be physically supported, half-carried through the ceremonies.

So with showmanship and sincere sorrow, Thalberg was put to rest, but the aftermath was not precisely silence. There were the usual laudatory, well-intentioned and solemn assessments of Thalberg's career, led off by *The New York Times* which proclaimed, "He helped, perhaps more than any other man in Hollywood, to make the motion picture a medium of adult entertainment. . . ."

The industry paid its respects by speculating whether M-G-M would continue to produce high-quality films without Thalberg as a watchdog over the studio's product. Mayer-haters contended that Thalberg had been totally responsible for the Metro productions with character and class, and now that he was gone, they foresaw a period of retrogression in which Mayer and the New York money men would increasingly concentrate on grinding out routine pictures of minimal interest and artistry.

Mayer was well aware of what was being said, and there's every reason to believe he welcomed the opportunity to disprove them. Since the inception of M-G-M, he had taken a back seat to Thalberg —"He was," as one observer noted, "sometimes blamed for things Irving was responsible for while Irving often got the credit for things Mayer had done"—but from now on, there could be no confusion about the leadership of M-G-M.

This does not mean that Mayer found secret pleasure in Thalberg's death, as hostile commentators continue to maintain. He regretted that they had been unable to settle the differences that had separated them for over four years. These unresolved difficulties were to haunt Mayer until Norma told him that a few weeks before his death, Irving said he had come to regard Mayer as a true friend and sincerely regretted the circumstances that had pulled them apart.

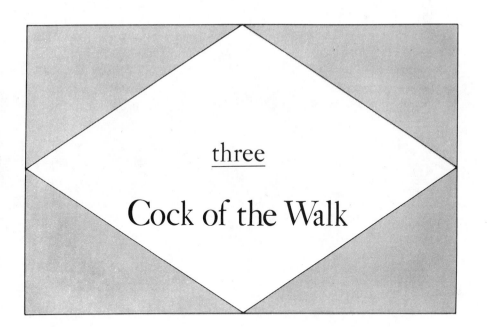

three

Cock of the Walk

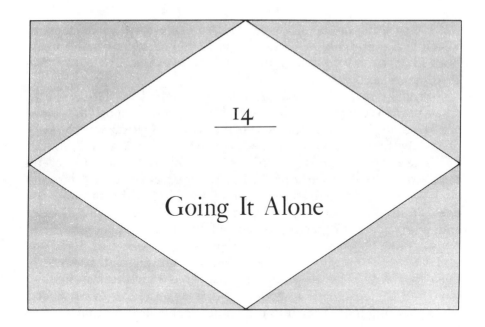

Going It Alone

14

What would happen to Metro-Goldwyn-Mayer now that Thalberg was gone?

In some quarters, there were high hopes that Mayer would finally show his true colors and sweep all the Thalbergites out of the studio. But that was not to happen; Mayer was not to live up to his reputation for vindictiveness. A few people left M-G-M on their own volition, a few more failed to have their contracts renewed when the time came due, and that was that. There was no pogrom, no dramatic upheaval. In a feature story about "the turmoil" created at M-G-M by Thalberg's death, *The New York Times* could cite only one direct clash between Mayer and a Thalberg partisan.

Thalberg left behind some unfinished business. At the time of his death, he had four films in various stages of preparation. Two, *The Good Earth* and *Camille,* were finished and waiting for release; the third, *A Day at the Races,* was midway through shooting; and the fourth, *Maytime,* was just about to go into production.

Mayer assigned *Camille* and *Good Earth* to Bernie Hyman, the first of Thalberg's production assistants, giving him a free hand to do whatever was necessary to make them a fitting tribute to Thalberg. *The Good Earth* was too close to its release date to be tinkered with, but Hyman did shoot some additional footage for *Camille*, most of which was eventually discarded as superfluous to the central story. Both films went into distribution very much in accord with Thalberg's original design.

Production on *A Day at the Races* was halted for a week or so. Then Larry Weingarten, Thalberg's brother-in-law, took charge and worked along the lines Thalberg had devised. *Maytime* was the only one of the films that was completely overhauled at Mayer's request.

The original libretto of this 1917 Sigmund Romberg operetta centered on two sweethearts who, though separated by circumstances and forced to marry elsewhere, remain faithful to their vow of everlasting love—fifty years later, they are still staring into space and singing the umpteenth reprise of "Will You Remember?" In revising the libretto for 1930s audiences, Thalberg had asked the screenwriters to retain only the skeleton of the original story, fleshing it out with new and more sophisticated characterizations and incidents, including a few sequences that suggested the sweethearts had something more carnal to remember than a fleeting touch of the lips.

Mayer had never approved of these alterations. Suggestiveness, however muted or tasteful, had no place in a big, expensive picture intended as family entertainment, particularly when the picture was a showcase for Jeanette MacDonald, one of Mayer's personal pets. She was, in his eyes, a patrician beauty who possessed, according to his ears, an entrancing, silvery voice of operatic caliber. At the start of the sound period, Mayer had tried to promote Grace Moore as M-G-M's leading songbird, but Moore couldn't stay on a diet, and while she was a lightweight by Met standards, on screen she made Mae West look like Olive Oyl. So MacDonald came to M-G-M as Moore's replacement, and at the outset, it seemed as though Mayer had made another miscalculation—MacDonald's first Metro films, *The Cat and the Fiddle* and the Thalberg-Lubitsch *Merry Widow* (both released in 1934), were bombs. But Mayer didn't lose faith; he called Jeanette in for a little chat.

He began by buttering her up. She was beautiful, she was blessed with a heaven-sent voice. She was a good actress. But something was missing, as her track record showed. She had made some successful films with Ernst Lubitsch at Paramount, but they hadn't established her as a star, and neither had her M-G-M pictures, though the studio had surrounded her with the best of everything and everyone.

Something was definitely lacking and he thought he knew what it was. Heart, emotion—call it what you would—she wasn't getting that across to the audience: she was remote, removed; she wasn't quite real. What she needed was warmth, a sense of involvement as she hit those high C's and E's. And to demonstrate what he meant, Mayer launched into "Eli, Eli," the traditional ballad of Jewish lamentation.

As the performance ended, MacDonald wiped away her tears and promised to do better. Her next picture, *Naughty Marietta* (1935), was a huge hit, but it's difficult to determine whether Mayer's lecture played any part in its success: there's not much difference between MacDonald's pre- and post-"Eli, Eli" performances, except that the latter become progressively more coy and cloying. M-G-M attributed some of the success to the co-starring presence of Nelson Eddy (a new contract player), but Eddy, who sang and moved as though he were Pinocchio's big brother, was never much of an asset, as Metro was to learn when he was cast in films without MacDonald. The success was probably due to a witty script, a fine ensemble of supporting players and a production that toyed with, but never violated (except by its overripe orchestration of Herbert's melodies), the conventions or spirit of traditional operetta.

Naughty Marietta was followed by *Rose Marie*, another Mac-Donald-Eddy bonanza for M-G-M, most memorable for a penultimate sequence in which MacDonald has a nervous breakdown while performing the last scene of *Tosca:* She's singing "Mario! Mario!" while in her inner ear she keeps hearing Eddy crooning "When I'm calling you-oo-oo-oo." Metro then separated the team and pitted MacDonald against Gable and Spencer Tracy in the lavish, foolish and irresistible *San Francisco,* one of Mayer's favorite films and M-G-M's top box office grosser for 1936. Even before *San Francisco* was released, the word was out that it was a winner and would establish "brave Jeanette" as a major star.

Thalberg, who liked to have the pick of the M-G-M crop, had heard the reports and had decided to take on the next MacDonald-Eddy operetta, *Maytime.* He had wanted to go back to the Lubitschesque MacDonald, resophisticate her and make the movie as naughty as operetta often was in its Viennese heyday.

But Mayer saw it differently. After Thalberg's death, he ordered a fast rewrite of the script to eliminate any hint of immorality. He scrapped the idea of making *Maytime* M-G-M's first all-Technicolor sound production, recast several roles (John Barrymore replaced Paul Lukas), removed Edmund Goulding as director in favor of W. S. Van Dyke and assigned the production to Hunt Stromberg. There's an easily perceived logic behind all these decisions. Technicolor was a costly process, still not beyond a rudimentary stage of development, which M-G-M was to use only sparingly in the next decade. Van Dyke, called One-Take Woody because of the speed with which he completed a film, had become one of M-G-M's most trusted house directors, while Goulding had the reputation of being an unreliable perfectionist. Stromberg (with Van Dyke as director) had turned out the first two MacDonald-Eddy operettas, as well as such other top-grossing Metro pictures as *The Thin Man, Red Dust* and *Wife vs. Secretary.*

But Albert Lewin, assistant producer on all of Thalberg's personal productions, chose not to see the practicality of Mayer's decisions. When *Maytime* was revamped, he left the studio (according to *The New York Times*) because he felt "incompetent to carry out at least a portion of Thalberg's program as designed," and because in not assigning him as supervisor of *Maytime,* the studio left him no choice but to believe that it was trying to relegate him to "a minor position." His statement carried the implication that he was not the only victim, that in fact the studio was downgrading everyone in the Thalberg camp.

But this simply was not true. Business, production, went on as usual, just as Mayer and Schenck had planned when they introduced the producer system in 1934 as a safeguard against Thalberg's early demise. And the system worked. Metro turned out a number of top money-makers in 1937, though in terms of prestige and awards the studio product was dominated by Thalberg's last two productions, *Camille* and *The Good Earth.*

Camille is almost a great film. It has its weaknesses—there is a lot of vulgarity, particularly on the part of the supporting players (Lionel Barrymore and Lenore Ulrich are the prime culprits) and the Gibbons art department. But there are also a strong script and a genuine respect and understanding (on director George Cukor's side) of the theatrical tradition that had spawned *Camille,* and there is Garbo, giving the greatest performance of her career.

The Good Earth is not in the same league. It's long, solemn and stuffed with more pretensions and good intentions than any single film can handle. It's also technically weak—the locust sequence is justly celebrated, but the editing in general is below Metro standards. But the critics went all out for it—even Otis Ferguson, normally so hostile to Culver City fireside-classic film making, heaped praise on it—just as literary critics had gone all out for Pearl Buck's novel when it first appeared. Book buyers had made the novel a best seller, but the film public wasn't so gullible, so susceptible to overpraise. *The Good Earth* was in release for many moons before it returned a penny of profit to M-G-M.

At Oscar time, *The Good Earth* received five nominations. It lost the big one to *The Life of Emile Zola* (a Warner Bros. production that would start a vogue for film biographies), but won in two other categories. Karl Freund, who deserved the award for *Camille* (which he had also photographed), won instead for his cinematography for *Good Earth.* And Luise Rainer, as the long-suffering O-lan, won in the best-actress category over such worthier nominees as Garbo *(Camille)* and Barbara Stanwyck *(Stella Dallas).*

Rainer's victory was one of those instances that allow fans and journalists to bemoan the role industry politics play in the doling out of the Oscars. Rainer's Oscar was seen as compensation for *The Good Earth*'s not taking top honors as best picture, a way for the Academy to show they had not forgotten Thalberg's past achievements. Of course, granting the award to Garbo would have carried the same message—*Camille* was also a posthumously released Thalberg production—but M-G-M had singled out *The Good Earth* with an opening dedication that rang down the curtain on Thalberg's career as decisively as R.I.P. on a tombstone. *The Good Earth,* not at all inappropriately, had been chosen as Thalberg's monument.

The Academy paid its final respects to Thalberg in another, more memorable way. At Mayer's suggestion, the board of directors established the Irving G. Thalberg Memorial Award, which (according to the original pronouncement) was to be "given each year for the most consistent high level of production achievement by an individual producer, based on pictures he has personally produced during the preceding year." The first recipient of the award was Darryl F. Zanuck; two years later it went to David Selznick.

Metro paid one final tribute to its former chief of production by naming its new administration quarters (completed in 1937) the Irving Thalberg Memorial Building. Around the studio, it was known as the Iron Lung, which was a good description of the imposing structure—stark, monumental, institutional. The building offered a spectacular view of a mortuary establishment—the studio had been unable to buy out the undertaker, so it built around him—and that house of death was, for Metro detractors, a fitting emblem of the studio in the post-Thalberg era.

The third floor of the Thalberg Building was the most exclusive since it was there that Mayer and his college of cardinals held court. The holy of holies was, of course, Mayer's office, and the altar was a huge, horseshoe-shaped desk, situated at the far end of a large room with white leather walls. Behind it sat L.B. on a chair constructed to make him look taller than he actually was. The grandiosity of the setup intimidated some of Mayer's visitors. "You need an automobile to reach your desk," snapped Sam Goldwyn (whose own office was nearly as imposing as Mayer's). "Some people found it very intimidating," a studio aide says. "Others took it in stride. Your reaction depended a lot on where you came from."

But beyond any reasonable doubt, the room was definitely designed to impress the impressionable. Behind Mayer's desk was a wide window covered by a shade with slats that could be arranged to blind or otherwise discomfit the supplicant. Adjoining the main room of the office was a small parlor with a private elevator leading to a rear exit of the building. A legend was to grow that it was used secretly by starlets who visited Mayer's office every afternoon for very personal services, but actually it served no more devious purpose than allowing him to avoid anyone he wasn't prepared to see. (Unlike Thalberg, Mayer never used the psychological ploy of keeping people waiting for hours at a time; generally he was very prompt about his appointments.)

Running alongside Mayer's office were the offices of his secretaries and his secretaries' secretaries. And nearby were suites for his private flock of executives, each containing a main room, a conference room and a private bathroom. (A few also included kitchen facilities.) The fourth floor of the Thalberg Building housed a gymnasium and an executive dining room where lunch meetings for the inner circle were held on special occasions. But four days out of five, at noon, Mayer left his office, walked to the commissary and moved through the tables, greeting everyone no matter how minor their position, before entering the commissary's private dining room (the "Lion's Den") where most of his cardinals were waiting to greet him.

The foremost member of that select group who lunched with L.B. or had offices adjacent to his was Bennie Thau. With the decline of his relationship with Thalberg, Mayer had begun to rely heavily on Thau, and after Thalberg's death, he was (in Howard Strickling's words) "the first person Mr. Mayer called in the morning, the last person Mr. Mayer called in the evening." Nominally in charge of talent—he personally negotiated or oversaw all Metro contracts—Thau wielded power far beyond these immediate duties; he was eventually to become a studio vice-president. A diminutive, dapper man who spoke so softly his listeners often had to lean forward or cup their ears to understand him, Thau was universally respected by the M-G-M staff, especially the actors, all of whom remember him with genuine warmth.

Then there was Eddie Mannix, who had replaced Joe Cohn as general manager of the studio. (Cohn had gone on to head the first of M-G-M's "B" production units.) Mannix hadn't changed much since his first days at M-G-M—clear-eyed, down-to-earth, sardonic, he was an easygoing mediator between all the warring parties in all the innumerable intermural battles.

But M-G-M stars with a real problem or gripe had discovered that their best access to Mayer's office was through Ida Koverman, who was, the rumor went, the open sesame to Mayer's heart. A native Californian of Scottish descent, Koverman had studied to be a concert pianist, but recognizing that she lacked the talent for that career, she worked her way up through a variety of jobs until she became Herbert Hoover's private secretary at a time when Hoover was still primarily known as a rich California engineer. She and Mayer met in 1924 as co-workers in the campaign to keep Coolidge in the White House, and Mayer, impressed by her aristocratic bearing and keen mind, soon lured her to M-G-M as his executive secretary. Ida (or "Kay" as she was sometimes called) spent very little time typing, transcribing or supervising Mayer's pool of underling secretaries. Her intelligence, intuition, discrimination and unwavering loyalty quickly brought her a promotion to assistant (and unofficial gatekeeper) to Louis B. Mayer. "She was everyone's aunt," remembers one Metro executive, "and she knew everyone's troubles."

Along with Howard Strickling, these were the people Mayer relied on as he forged ahead in the post-Thalberg era. The last few years had made little change in his working habits or professional style, though he was now required to spend most of his time at the studio and cut down on the political and other outside activities that during the early 1930s had earned him the derogatory and unwarranted epithet of "absentee landlord of M-G-M." Now, nearly every day, he arrived at the studio early and left late.

He also started allowing himself a little more leeway in enjoying the power and panoply that came with being the top boss of the top Hollywood studio. Never noted for having a tight grip on his temper, he now soared into Olympian rages which subsided almost as suddenly as they had arisen. He fired people only to rehire them a day or so later. "Christ," said Billy Grady, one of Metro's talent executives, "Mr. Mayer's fired me six or seven times, but this time I think he means it." But of course he didn't, and Grady was soon back at work.

Mayer's philosophy of film making was refined, but not radically altered, during this period. As he later told Alan Jay Lerner, he believed the three most important ingredients for a successful film were "a good story, the right star and a smart producer." When the combination worked out, "then any director with a brain and two months' experience could shoot the blasted thing." This didn't mean, God forbid, that he dismissed directors as nonentities, not at all: M-G-M had under contract King Vidor, George Cukor, Clarence Brown, Woody Van Dyke (who was a lot better than his One-Take Woody nickname suggests), Jack Conway and Robert Z. Leonard, all gifted men—and talent of any form was something L.B. always respected.

But overall the M-G-M system worked in favor of the producer. There were several executive producers, each with his own unit and two or three assistant producers working under him. Each unit specialized in making a certain type of film, though there was often a good deal of overlapping. The studio would acquire a property either because it was suited to a contract star or because a novel, play or a piece in a magazine had caught the fancy of a producer (who more likely than not had discovered it through a synopsis prepared by the story department). Generally the studio wouldn't buy a property for a star unless a producer expressed interest in it, and usually a producer wasn't interested in material that offered no role for a Metro star. Thus the star and producer systems crisscrossed and mutually supported each other, and kept the studio from buying properties that would lie on the shelf for a long time before the right combination of talent came along.

Once a script had been approved and budgeted, Mayer stayed away from the production unless he was called on as arbitrator for some unforeseen problem. He left his producers alone, though of course all the producers were aware of his taste and of what could happen if they transgressed the boundaries of what he thought proper.

This does not mean they were yes-men. Mayer believed that sycophants had been the undoing of his friend, B. P. Schulberg, who had earlier been dethroned from his seat of power at Paramount. Still, there were stories which suggested that L.B. wasn't entirely immune to flattery. One day a Metro screenwriter almost had his foot cut off when the elevator door of the Thalberg building closed with unexpected speed. "Be careful," a companion warned. "Yesterday that door nearly slammed on Mayer's ass." After a pause, the writer said, "Oh, did Mr. X get his tongue cut off?"

There were similar stories about Arthur Freed, who was to become the head of Metro's celebrated musical unit. "Everytime Mayer went to the bathroom, Freed was waiting to hand him the toilet paper." People derided Freed, but Mayer, who was fully aware of Freed's toadying, also recognized he had talents that could be utilized by M-G-M. "Yeah, sure," Mayer would say whenever anyone complained about Freed. "But let's see what happens. I think he can do good work for us."

Mayer also knew that two or three Metro executives hankered after his job and suspected that their ambitions were encouraged by Nick Schenck. But at this time he was secure enough to take an imperial view of the hounds snapping at his behind. Furthermore, he believed a little rivalry was a good thing: competition, he felt, kept people on their toes and working at peak capacity. Occasionally he was guilty of pitting one producer against another, but usually he didn't have to rely on artificial measures. The Metro producers were naturally competitive, each and every one of them keeping tabs on any show of favoritism to the others, whether it was the assignment of a choice property or star, an invitation to lunch with Mayer in his private dining room or the allocation of an extravagantly large budget for a new production.

Then there was always the possibility that Mayer might soon designate one of them as his new Thalberg. Worse still, he might bring in an outsider and grant him Thalbergian power over the entire production staff. Which is exactly what seemed to be happening when Mayer brought Mervyn LeRoy into the company in 1937.

Responsible for such critical and financial successes as *Little Caesar* and *I Was a Fugitive from a Chain Gang,* LeRoy was throughout the 1930s Warner Bros.' resident boy genius. Though best known for his social-conscience dramas, he was equally adept at handling musicals *(Gold Diggers of 1933),* comedy *(Tugboat Annie,* made on loan for M-G-M), slick melodrama *(Three on a Match)* and historical pageantry *(Anthony Adverse).* He and Thalberg were close friends, and on one occasion Thalberg urged him to come over to M-G-M. LeRoy was mildly intrigued, but the matter was still pending at the time of Thalberg's death.

Several months later, Mayer called and asked if he would be interested in taking over the production reins at M-G-M. LeRoy was flabbergasted. First of all, he was a director, not a producer (though he had worked in both capacities on a few films). Second, he wasn't eager to be saddled with the kind of responsibility such a job would entail. And third, he was then married to Harry Warner's daughter, which could make for a very ticklish family situation.

But in the long run Mayer's offer was too tempting to turn down: a guarantee of $300,000, double the salary of the other top M-G-M producers. The terms of the contract, Mayer warned LeRoy, were to remain secret. According to Metro press releases, the director-turned-producer would be paid $150,000 annually, and a dummy contract specifying that salary was drawn up for the studio files. The ploy fooled no one, and other M-G-M producers soon discovered LeRoy's real salary. And the rumbling of discontent might have set off a major earthquake when they learned LeRoy had been assigned an office on the third floor of the Thalberg building, just a few steps away from Mayer's quarters.

But once established there, LeRoy did not immediately start functioning as the new Thalberg, a role not to be his until he had proved that he could handle it. Things got off to a bad start. As his first M-G-M production LeRoy drew *Dramatic School*, ostensibly based on an obscure Hungarian play, but all too conspicuously similar to RKO's *Stage Door* of the previous year. The picture, starring Luise Rainer, was such a dud that LeRoy makes no mention of it in his autobiography, *Take One*. His next M-G-M assignment was *Stand Up and Cheer*, a standard prizefight melodrama which wasn't bad, but hardly lived up to its title. Then came *The Wizard of Oz*, a long, arduous and expensive production which, contrary to popular belief, was a critical and financial flop at the time of its release. Most reviewers felt the fantasy sequences were heavy and overly literal, and the box office take, while substantial, wasn't enough to cover the production, print and advertising costs. (Years later, *Wizard* did return a hefty profit through its TV showings.)

After *At the Circus*, a middling Marx Brothers comedy, LeRoy asked to be relieved of his executive production duties; he wanted to concentrate on direction and was willing to take a pay cut to do so. Mayer readily agreed—he was, after all, not so much losing a producer as gaining a first-rate director. Once he reverted to his former calling, LeRoy's record was estimable; he was to turn out a large number of Metro's most profitable and prestigious pictures of the 1940s.

Once LeRoy demoted himself, Mayer made no further serious attempts at finding a new Thalberg. Quite possibly he had never really intended LeRoy to have that job. The disintegration of the father-son relationship that existed between Mayer and Thalberg in the best of their collaborative years was a painful memory, an experience that Mayer did not want to repeat. Or at least, it had left him in a divided state of mind. Part of him wanted another protégé or son figure; the other part pulled back, reluctant to go through that heartbreak a second time.

Then, too, there was the matter of Mayer's vanity. Undoubtedly he enjoyed holding the reins of production in his own hands, of outwitting the prognosticators who foresaw a decline in the Metro product once Thalberg was no longer in command. Mayer would never again, many people felt, willingly relinquish or share his power with a second force. And why should he, since he was perfectly capable of doing the job himself?

Of course, there was a group of industry-watchers who went on arguing that he was not doing the job capably, that there had been a decline in the quality of Metro pictures, if not in their box office receipts. According to these critics, most of them Thalberg loyalists, M-G-M films were not so richly detailed as before, not so daring in choice of material, not so deft in handling plot and character development. It is quite easy to make a selection of Metro films that will support this contention, but on the whole, it's not true. Between 1936 and 1946, the quality of M-G-M pictures remains pretty consistent.

There was, however, a slight shift, a new facet to the personality of the Metro product. More and more pictures were dedicated to upholding the dignity of motherhood, family life and other sacred values of middle-class American society. Among the most representative were the Andy Hardy comedies, of which Mayer was extremely proud. The series (based on *Skidding,* a 1928 Broadway hit) began with *A Family Affair* (1937), featuring Mickey Rooney and Lionel Barrymore (as Judge Hardy, a role later assumed by Lewis Stone). These modest little pictures immediately earned the scorn of New York and Hollywood sophisticates, and through the years have been so unjustly vilified that a word or two has to be said in their defense. For the most part they are charming and the best of them hold up a lot better than many of M-G-M's more acclaimed productions. Given the choice of another look at *Love Finds Andy Hardy* or *The Good Earth,* only the self-flagellating members of the Late Show sect would choose the Thalberg opus.

Beyond this emphasis on wholesomeness, there was little noticeable change in the M-G-M product: it was, as before, strong on gloss and entertainment, weak on the presentation of challenging or controversial subjects. Any number of Metro pictures start off with a crisp or intriguing idea, only to set it aside and revert to standard operational methods—lots of romantic high jinks, lots of soft-focus close-ups for the leading lady, lots of Adrian dresses and lush Cedric Gibbons settings, lots of predictable melodramatic highs and lows, all leading to the inevitable happy ending. This tendency to turn any story into pulp wasn't, however, something Mayer introduced or forced on his staff or producers; it dated back to Thalberg and beyond (was, in fact, a characteristic of studio film making for as long as there had been studios in Hollywood). The M-G-M style had been set by early 1932, a time when Mayer and Thalberg were still working pretty much in tandem. Yet on tally sheets of M-G-M accomplishments, Thalberg always gets the credit and little blame, while Mayer gets the dirt and little glory. Every good film turned out by the studio was applauded as worthy of the Thalberg heritage; every bad one was denounced as a Mayer aberration.

Mayer knew what was said, even joked about it. It was all part of the game. "M-G-M turns out a winner," he'd say, "and everybody takes some of the credit, everyone's standing in line to take *all* the credit. But when the film's lousy, who gets the blame? I do."

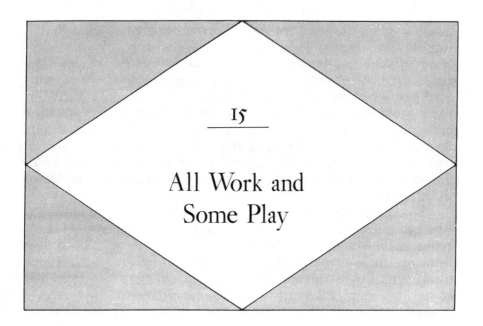

15

All Work and Some Play

It had been a rough year, the twelve months since Thalberg's death, and Mayer felt entitled to a vacation. In the summer of 1937, he decided to take a trip abroad—his first European jaunt since the Jean Howard debacle of 1934. This time he was traveling without a Howard stand-in but his wife went along with a nurse and maid as companions. Other members of the entourage included Howard Strickling, Benny Thau, Joe Schenck (whom Mayer liked almost as much as he disliked brother Nick) and one of Schenck's closest friends, a gambler named Lou Wertheim.

Mrs. Mayer's condition confined her to an early-to-bed schedule, so Mayer had lots of time to play with his cronies, and with Joe Schenck along, it was a foregone conclusion that the night life would be loose and easy. But pleasure was to be combined with business. Mayer's first stop was England, where he was to inspect the new production facilities that Loew's had leased near London, the Denham studios. Also he wanted to look over the local talent (which was very rich—this was one of the great periods of English theatre and film) with an eye to shipping the best of it back to Culver City.

With the threat of massive conflict hanging over Europe, this was not perhaps the best possible moment to open a studio in England, but the rationale behind the move was logical enough. The English film industry had come of age in the early thirties, and the home product had begun to cut into the market for foreign films, particularly American films. Furthermore, American critics and a small portion of the American public scored points against the Hollywood studios by underlining the superiority of English pictures, particularly in the areas of acting, writing and depiction of adult themes. But no one had ever claimed that British pictures were as technically advanced as Hollywood's and no one argued that the British studios had the ability to develop an actor into an international film star.

Therefore Mayer had come up with the idea of combining the strength of English picture making—the wealth of talent, especially acting talent—with the gloss of American expertise. The M-G-M Denham studio would turn out films set in England, cast predominately with English actors, but with a sprinkling of American stars in the important roles and with American directors in charge of production. Also Denham would serve as a hatching ground for new talent—any of the English players who showed promise and clicked with the American public would be rushed to California for the full star treatment.

To get the plan rolling, Mayer had placed Ben Goetz, the brother of his son-in-law, in charge of the Denham facilities and, on the recommendation of friends, Goetz had hired a young Englishman, Michael Balcon, to assist and advise him. The first production, *A Yank at Oxford,* had been cast before Mayer had left Hollywood— the title role was to be filled by Robert Taylor (who was mobbed by fans as he got off the boat train from Southampton); other prominent roles had been assigned to Maureen O'Sullivan and Lionel Barrymore, and as director, the studio was sending over Jack Conway. That left Balcon with the task of overseeing the selection of the supporting cast, the most important part being that of the second leading lady. He picked Vivien Leigh, and had no misgivings about the choice: she was a beauty, an actress of proven ability and a marquee name in England.

But Mayer had never heard of her. (That he hadn't, suggests that the M-G-M talent department was sleeping on the job, since Leigh's spectacular success in a 1935 West End play, *The Mask of Virtue,* had been covered in the theatrical pages of most New York papers.) He immediately laced into Balcon for taking on a nonentity for an important role in what had to be an outstanding production all the way down the line. Everyone, everything, had to be first class if the initial production of the Metro-Denham combine were to receive the appropriate champagne send-off. Neither Leigh nor Balcon was dismissed, but the incident wasn't conducive to improving Anglo-Hollywood relations (which were weak to start with—the English equivalent of Actors' Equity and the London press resented Hollywood's interference in the British film industry). Stories about the misunderstanding were fast in circulating, and newspaper reports of Mayer's conference to announce the opening of the Denham factory were etched in acid.

Mayer paid no attention. Ignoring Balcon (who was to sit out his contract as a figurehead), he collaborated with Goetz on working out plans for Metro's second English production—an adaptation of A. J. Cronin's *The Citadel*, to be directed by King Vidor and to star Rosalind Russell (both from Culver City), co-starring Robert Donat and a stellar English supporting company including Ralph Richardson, Emlyn Williams and Rex Harrison.

With this business behind him, Mayer set out looking for more talent, new properties. One of the biggest hits of the West End season was *Balalaika*, an Anglicized adaptation of a schmaltzy, sub-Strauss German operetta. Mayer adored it and ordered Goetz to start negotiations toward purchasing it for Metro. It would be, he thought, an ideal vehicle for Eddy and MacDonald.

M-G-M's London office had lined up a number of plays for him to see, but one night, with no tickets waiting for him at the box office, he was restlessly holding court in his hotel suite when he noticed a newspaper advertisement for a show called *Old Music*. "Hey, you galoots, why didn't you tell me about this?"

Ben Goetz explained that *Old Music* was a straight play, written by Keith Winter, a popular English dramatist of the period, and while M-G-M had recently purchased an earlier Winter play *(The Shining Hour)*, this one didn't seem so promising. But Mayer brushed this aside. Something called *Old Music* just had to have some old music dancing through it, and Mayer liked the old tunes best of all. With strains of Viennese waltzes lilting in his head, he sent Strickling out to purchase tickets at the St. James Theatre.

But, as Goetz had predicted, there was no music, old or otherwise, in *Old Music*. It was one of those teacup English comedies that are brewed too weak for American taste. Mayer fidgeted in his seat, paying no attention to the action or to the actors (among them several well-known West End players and one up-and-coming star, Celia Johnson) except when a redheaded beauty held center stage. In the play she was Geraldine and, checking the cast list in his program, Mayer saw that Geraldine was Greer Garson. At intermission, he sent an emissary backstage to invite Miss Garson to supper and Miss Garson replied that the honor would be all hers.

American film historians have implied that Garson was a nobody appearing in sleazy vaudeville when Mayer discovered her. Nothing could be further from the truth. She was a well-educated Irishwoman (aged twenty-nine) with substantial professional credits behind her, and was on the brink of a major West End career. Two years before, in *The Golden Arrow* (a play produced by and starring Laurence Olivier), she had made a vivid impression on London critics and audiences, and needed only the right role in the right play to take her across the board. Geraldine in *Old Music* wasn't the part or the play, but it wasn't cheap: it was a legitimate, very tony West End production.

After the final curtain, Garson went home, changed into something chic yet discreet and then, with her mother as chaperon, set off to meet Mayer at the Savoy Grill. Deliberately or not, Garson had stage-managed her entrance to perfection. Mayer liked girls who liked their mothers and who knew the difference between décolletage and indecent exposure. By the end of the evening, he had promised Garson a screen test, and after seeing the results, put her under contract. Once *Old Music* closed—November 1937—she was free to leave for Culver City, but it was to be another year before Mayer found the right role for her screen debut.

From England, Mayer and his companions moved on to Paris and Vienna, acquiring talent in both cities, most notably German-born Rosa Stradner, a promising actress who was to abandon her career when she married M-G-M producer and writer, Joseph Mankiewicz. In Vienna, nearly everyone seemed to know Mayer had a soft spot for Straussian music, and his suite at the Bristol was bombarded by publishers and composers bearing moth-eaten song sheets. "Every time we entered a café," Howard Strickling recalls, "a waiter would come over and implore Mayer to listen to a song he had written the night before." Mayer bought practically everything he heard, with the result that the Metro music department owned the largest collection of waltz music in Hollywood. It was not as foolish an investment as it might sound at first—the songs came cheap and over the years provided a steady income from recording, publishing and performance rights.

After Vienna, Mayer's group took a train to Carlsbad, the elegant Czechoslovakian spa (today known as Karlovy Vary) which had been included on the travel agenda mainly because Joe Schenck wanted to get in a few days of gambling before returning to America.

The baccarat tables held no fascination for Mayer; he looked for diversion elsewhere. One night he went to the opera for a performance of *Aida* and was enchanted by the offstage voice singing the high priestess's aria at the end of the first act. Once again he sent an emissary backstage, and was delighted when the voice returned the message that she would be happy to join him for supper. He was even more delighted when his dinner guest turned out to look every bit as good as she had sounded. She was the Hungarian-born Ilona Hajmassy, a statuesque blonde with a strong voice, albeit one of something less than international operatic caliber.

She was also a superb dancer, as Mayer discovered later that night when they executed an intricate rhumba on the floor of one of Carlsbad's cabarets. For the rest of his stay they went dancing every evening, and when it came time for him to say *auf Wiedersehen*, Ilona Hajmassy had acquired a new surname (Massey) and an M-G-M contract. (She was to replace Jeanette MacDonald in Metro's production of *Balalaika*.)

The European tour ended with a return to London where, just a few days prior to his sailing on the *Normandie*, Mayer encountered Hedy Kiesler, an Austrian film actress who was then in the process of divorcing her husband, Fritz Mandl, one of Europe's leading munition manufacturers. They had met once before—in 1934 the Mandls and Mayer had been house guests at Leopoldskron, Max Reinhardt's baronial estate in Salzburg. Mayer instantly recognized Mrs. Mandl as the star of the scandalous 1933 Czech film *Exstase*, an arty piece of soft porn in which the lovely (but flat-chested) Kiesler had cavorted in a forest stream à la "September Morn" and had been shot in close-up while having sexual relations (feigned for the cameras, of course) with a forester who happens upon her during her open-air ablutions. Mayer had seen *Exstase*, found it disgusting, and told Kiesler that no Hollywood studio would take on an actress who had degraded herself in such a spectacular way. At the time Kiesler couldn't have cared less—she was then quite content being Madame Mandl.

But once the marriage fell apart, she became determined to resume her career, preferably in Hollywood. Her 1937 meeting with Mayer in London was arranged by her agent, who warned her not to expect too much. *Exstase* (or *Ecstasy*) had recently opened in America in a bowdlerized version that left everything to the imagination except the puny expanse of Kiesler's chest; therefore her chances for a contract seemed pretty slim. Mayer started off the interview by repeating what he had said three years before at Leopoldskron: it was, in his opinion, doubtful whether even M-G-M could make a star of an actress who had so openly breached the code of public morality. But after chastising her for a half-hour or so, he did offer her a contract—she was, after all, one of the great beauties of her time— but at only a fraction of the salary she had expected. She walked out without bothering to refuse.

An hour later she had second thoughts. Mayer, however, was leaving the next day, and as there was no opportunity to see him before he sailed, she decided to book passage on the *Normandie*. But that was impossible—the liner was filled, from steerage to first class. As luck would have it, her agent also happened to be sailing on the *Normandie* with his family, and Kiesler wangled her way aboard by posing as governess to his children.

On the day the ship arrived in New York, the Metro press department issued a release announcing that "Miss Hedy Kiesler, Viennese actress and star of the Czechoslovak film *Ecstasy*" had signed a contract with the M-G-M studios. It went on to say Miss Kiesler would be "henceforth known as Miss Hedy Lamarr." (Mrs. Mayer chose the new name as a tribute to Barbara La Marr, a striking beauty who had starred in several of his Mission Road productions and who had died at age twenty-eight in 1925.) From then on, the studio publicists did their best to dissuade the press from mentioning Lamarr in connection with *Ecstasy*, but without much success. References to her youthful indiscretion were nearly as numerous as the coarse-grained frame enlargements of her nude bathing scene, which were high-priced collector items in the early forties.

On his return from Europe, Mayer received the welcome news that his share of the Metro profits, combined with his salary for the 1937 fiscal year, had earned him $1.2 million. That made him—according to a Treasury Department bulletin—the highest-paid executive in the United States.

It so happened that Mayer's contract with Loew's was about to expire. The timing could not have been more propitious—in the year since Thalberg's death, Metro's profits had climbed dramatically compared to the profits of other studios, and Mayer had shown beyond any doubt that he didn't need Thalberg to keep the money coming in. He was in a good bargaining position and he led off with an opening maneuver brilliantly calculated to catch everyone off guard. He let it be known that he was thinking of resigning.

At any other time, such rumors might have been tidings of joy to Nick Schenck, but Schenck was astute enough to realize that Mayer's record at the studio was beyond reproach and that if he were allowed to pull out, there could be hell to pay with the stockholders.

Mayer had restructured the studio production system so that it depended heavily on him: he was the tip of the pyramid; topple him and the whole edifice could come crumbling down. Schenck had been told as much by members of the M-G-M college of cardinals, and had independently decided that the studio wasn't ready for another executive upheaval so soon after Thalberg's death.

Schenck rushed out to California for a conference with Mayer, but Mayer wasn't available—he was under the weather with a particularly virulent strain of flu, possibly (he hinted) something worse. When he regained enough strength to creep to his chauffeured car, he drove to the Beverly Wilshire for a chat with Schenck. Yes, he admitted, he was thinking about resigning; he wasn't in the best of health. But he left open the possibility of being persuaded to stay on. So Schenck started to persuade. And after a suitable lapse of time (spent, Mayer said, consulting with family and friends), he reluctantly agreed to stay on at Metro.

In gratitude, Schenck gave Mayer a new contract at three thousand dollars a week with an annual bonus of 6.77 percent of the profits of Loew's, Inc., after payment of a two-dollar dividend on common stock. For the next eight years, this pact was to make him the highest salaried man in the United States—he earned more than Franklin Roosevelt, more than Nick Schenck, more than Henry Ford.

Mayer had not been fibbing when he told Schenck he was ill. He had been feeling peckish even before his European jaunt, and during the trip, he had been checked out by a noted specialist who spotted a low blood count which might lead to cardiac problems. Though Mayer's heart was strong for a man of his age (he was now in his middle fifties) and arduous business activities. The doctor asked about Mayer's recreation, and Mayer said he occasionally played golf. "Too strenuous," the doctor warned. "Try something more relaxing. An occasional day at the races might be just the thing." Mayer said he'd take it under consideration.

Mayer liked horses. In his early Hollywood years, he and Irene had gone riding before breakfast, and during the season, he'd visit Santa Anita or Caliente. But he got no kick out of playing the ponies and never understood the fascination the sport held for such friends as Joe Schenck and Leon Gordon, an English playwright and bon vivant who worked intermittently at Metro.

Gordon was more than a fan; he owned a horse that had won a couple of small purses and was soon to race at Hollywood Park. Gordon wanted L.B. to be a member of his party on the big day, but Mayer said he'd have to take a rain check, he'd be busy at the studio.

But when Gordon's lady friend got on the phone, Mayer changed his mind. She was one of the few people who came right out and teased Mayer about his foibles, treated him as if he were just one of the guys, and he loved it: she could always wrap him around her little finger. So when she promised to bring along one of her girl friends to keep him company, Mayer fell in with the joke, and said, sure, he'd come along.

Much to everybody's surprise, Gordon's nag won the race that day. Watching his friend in the winner's circle as he received his trophy, as his horse was draped with a blanket of flowers, Mayer felt a surge of envious emotion. This was almost as good as winning an Academy Award. From then on, he was a passionate convert to the favorite pastime of kings and tinhorns.

He started out slowly. At the beginning, he knew, says Clarence Brown, "about as much about horses as a hog knows about Sundays." His first acquisition was a slow-starting, slow-finishing dud stud which he boarded at Brown's ranch. Undeterred by the lack of immediate results, he went on to buy a group of Saratoga yearlings, costing him more than $78,000, including two offspring of Man O' War. This collection also proved to be a disappointment, but served to notify the racing world that Mayer had taken up horse breeding as something more than a hobby; that he was, in fact, ready to pay big money for the right horses. He had picked the best of all possible moments to go into the business. With the war getting under way in Europe, horse prices were declining steadily, and on occasion Mayer was able to buy up stock at bargain prices.

He charged into horse breeding just as he had charged into film making; knowing very little, but with an instinct for hiring the people who were experts in their field. He was very rough—it became a joke in horse circles that "he changed trainers the first and fifteenth of every month"—but he was also very successful, and would eventually be recognized as California's most influential breeder of the 1940s.

At first Mayer's stock was kept at Kingston Farm in Lexington, Kentucky, but he envisioned a ranch which was to be located in the Southern California desert. In 1941 the dream became a reality with the opening of the Mayer Stock Farm, located in Perris, seventy miles south of Los Angeles on the edge of the Mojave Desert, where a strip of almost five hundred arid acres had been turned into an oasis through massive irrigation. The ranch was equipped with several fireproof, ingeniously designed barns which made it, in the words of a specialist magazine, "an efficient and modern farm, worthy of the finest horses in the world."

Shortly after the opening of the ranch, Mayer paid $100,000 for Australia's leading sire, Beau Père. As a racehorse Beau Père had been a consistent also-ran, but several of his offspring had been champions, and as it turned out, for stud purposes, the English-bred stallion was worth every penny of his purchase price. Mayer also made a million-dollar bid for Man O' War, but owner Samuel Riddle refused. "Tell Mr. Mayer that Man O' War is not for sale at any price," Riddle commented. "I don't know what he wants him for, but I think he might want to use him in pictures and I wouldn't want that. He wouldn't know how to treat the old fellow!" Mayer made a similar offer for an English derby winner, Hyperion, and was again refused, but he did manage to buy one of Hyperion's sons, a chestnut colt named Alibhai. The two stallions, Beau Père and Alibhai, were the cornerstones of Mayer's stock farm, and their offspring raised California's status as an important breeding center by several notches.

The role of gentleman rancher appealed so much to Mayer that for a time he thought of branching out into raising other kinds of livestock, starting with chickens. He sent an agent to the East Coast to buy as many prize-winning Rhode Island Reds and Plymouth Rocks as he could find. The scout wired that the mission had been a success and the birds were on their way to California. But through some mix-up they were shipped to the studio, not the Perris ranch.

They arrived on a Saturday afternoon when the studio was virtually shut down for the weekend, but the commissary chief, alerted by the guard at the front gate, said, "Send them over, Mr. Mayer's holding a get-together at his ranch and the chickens are probably intended as part of the picnic." So the prize hens were decapitated, plucked and roasted, then packaged for shipment to Perris. Meanwhile Mayer had been alerted that the Rhode Island Reds were on the way, so he and his guests ran out to watch them being unloaded. There were gasps of horror when the birds came off the van, not in crates, but done to a turn and bedded on watercress.

Mayer the gentleman rancher spent his weekends dressed in riding trousers, open-necked shirts and rakish slouch hats. The rest of the week, as studio boss, he was conservatively groomed in expensive, English-tailored suits, except for the nights when he donned a tux to play the bon vivant at Ciro's or the Mocambo. Mayer was stepping out a lot at night and rarely was the stepping done with his wife.

Mrs. Mayer made no protests about her husband being seen in public with lovely ladies, and Mayer interpreted her silence as acceptance of an awkward situation. Most of Hollywood knew that Margaret was an invalid, so there was no reason for surprise when L.B showed up at a premiere or industry function escorting someone other than his wife. But gossip there was, nonetheless. There was talk of Mayer making crude passes at Myrna Loy and Jean Harlow, of bottoms being pinched, of relay races around his horseshoe desk. The most salacious of the stories concern Jeanette MacDonald, who was noted for sweeping into L.B.'s office unannounced, smiling radiantly as she brushed aside whoever happened to be waiting for the next appointment. Her high-handed manner gave birth to rumors that behind the closed door Mayer and MacDonald were doing something more intimate than discussing Nelson Eddy.

Most of Mayer's friends, however, suggest that there was no foundation for this gossip. Whenever Mayer went out with a woman, he was usually chaperoned by another couple, and the fact that he was being seen in public was in his opinion proof that he wasn't doing anything naughty in private. He couldn't understand how people could suspect he was carrying on with his dance-and-dinner partners. Had he been having an affair he would never have flaunted the relationship by appearing with his mistress in a nightclub. Furthermore, he would never have insulted his wife by flaunting his infidelities in this fashion.

So many former Metro stars have included in their memoirs accounts of Mayer's amatory propensities that it is difficult to dismiss the evidence as so many cheap shots as some Mayer partisans would have us do. They say these ladies mistook genuine gallantry for the tawdry substitute to which they, as actresses, were accustomed, but it's hard to imagine a woman as savvy as Rosalind Russell making such a mistake. Russell sloughed off the incident without much fuss, suggesting that she didn't think Mayer was serious, which he probably wasn't. Sometimes it's easiest to make a pass when you're sure the pass is going to be incomplete.

All this is not meant to suggest Mayer was celibate during this period, but his bed partners, whoever they may have been, did not come from the front rank of Metro contract players. Two of them were nonentities whose names have never been linked with Mayer's. It is also safe to assume that Mayer never at any time used his office as a love-nest or courting ground. That would have seemed as blasphemous to him as bedding down on the couch in the living room of his Ocean Front home.

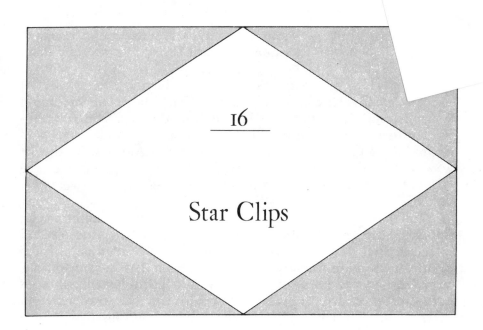

16

Star Clips

"More Stars Than There Are In Heaven" (a slogan created by Howard Dietz, M-G-M's New York publicity chief) was only a slight exaggeration. By the mid-thirties, the studio firmament was the most resplendent in Hollywood. The galaxy was, of course, Mayer's pride and joy. He wanted the best of everything for his pampered darlings —the best designers and hairdressers and makeup artists, the finest cinematographers, the kinds of stories that would present them in the most flattering light. They were groomed and pruned, protected and cossetted, advised and tutored by experts who guided them through such everyday tribulations as knotting a bow tie, choosing the right spoon for the soup course, and changing from the Super Chief to the Twentieth Century on transcontinental trips.

The red carpet treatment kept the M-G-M stars from wandering off to other galaxies, and as a result, an astonishing number of actors spent the major part of their professional lives at Metro. Still, the star roster was always in a state of flux. Each year there were new ascendants to the firmament (Garson and Lamarr, for example) as well as withdrawals, either because the studio failed to pick up an option (rare in the case of the top stars) or because of illness (William Powell, who made few films in the late thirties and early forties, a period when he underwent operations for stomach ulcers and rectal cancer). Then, too, there was attrition by death. First Lon Chaney, then Marie Dressler, and in 1937, Jean Harlow.

A few weeks before her death, Harlow became ill on the set of *Saratoga*, a potboiler comedy co-starring Clark Gable. Her condition demanded hospitalization, but Harlow's mother, a Christian Scientist, withheld permission. Finally Mayer intervened and Harlow was moved to the Good Samaritan Hospital in Los Angeles. By then it was too late. On June 7, 1937, Harlow died of cerebal edema, the result of an unchecked case of uremic poisoning. She was twenty-six years old.

Hollywood's whispering chorus reported that her condition had started with an internal injury inflicted by Paul Bern, or been set off by the massive doses of peroxide applied weekly to her hair, or was the aftermath of an ineptly executed abortion. (At the time of her death, Harlow was having a romance with William Powell, who was in the process of divorcing Carole Lombard, who was involved with Clark Gable.) The truth is that Harlow's death was caused by uremia and her mother's staunch Christian Science beliefs.

Harlow's death left Metro straddled with the problem of the unfinished *Saratoga*. The star's few remaining scenes could be shot with a double, but wasn't there something distasteful, almost ghoulish, about promoting a film featuring a dead actress? Wouldn't Metro be wide open to charges of exploitation? Some studio executives thought so, but Mayer reasoned that it was no more unseemly than publishing a posthumous novel. Within six weeks, *Saratoga* had been completed (with stand-in Mary Dees replacing Harlow) and rushed into distribution. The haste with which all this had been carried out aroused a storm of protest on the part of the press, but Harlow's fans didn't care—they flocked to see the film and made a game out of spotting the scenes in which Dees replaces Harlow. (It's not much of a game—the doubling is badly executed.)

Most of the stars in M-G-M's 1937–41 rosters were genuine stars, but some of them began to slip in this period. One was Norma Shearer, whose relations with the studio and Mayer turned tepid after Thalberg's death. She didn't really want to go on with her career, but had to—the only other alternative was the poorhouse, as she put it.

According to first reports, Thalberg had left Norma comfortably off. She was the principal heir of an estate estimated at $10 million. But within days, the estimate of the estate's value dropped to $7 million, and when the will was finally probated, the actual figure was much lower. As *Variety* reported, "Tax claims since his death have reduced the estate of Irving G. Thalberg from $4,500,000 to about $2,000,000, it was revealed in probate court, where Norma Shearer obtained approval of the payment of U.S. taxes amounting to $754,239 for the years of 1932–36."

Norma announced that her share of the estate would yield an income of less than $15,000 annually. That sum suggested she needed a new investment adviser, but whatever the estate may have yielded, it was certainly less than Shearer needed to support her way of life. After Thalberg's death, she had talked of retiring from the screen, but now she promised that soon she would be returning to work, probably in *Marie Antoinette*. M-G-M and Mayer were eager to get her back on the lot—close to half a million dollars had been spent on the preproduction preparations for *Antoinette*, which originally was to have been a Thalberg film—but the conditions Shearer set for her return gave Mayer heart palpitations. She demanded that Loew's, Inc. continue to honor the profit-sharing terms of Thalberg's contract until its expiration in December 1938.

Mayer liked Shearer, paid tribute to her as an ever-bright star in the M-G-M heavens—but flattery and friendship went only so far. Over the past ten years, Mayer had taken cuts in his own share of the profits so that Thalberg could have a larger portion; now it seemed only equitable that Thalberg's share should be divided between Bob Rubin and him, the surviving members of the original "Mayer group." Shearer, on the other hand, felt her husband's outstanding contribution to the success of M-G-M should now be bountifully repaid to his destitute widow (which is precisely the way she presented herself to interviewers).

The ensuing battle was long and bitter, ending only when Schenck requested Mayer to bring it to a halt; the proceedings, avidly followed by all Hollywood, were beginning to cast a sordid shadow over everyone involved. Furthermore, something had to be done about getting *Antoinette* into production. Shearer refused to compromise, so eventually she got everything she wanted—maybe even a little more. She would continue to receive Thalberg's share of profits until 1938; thereafter, she would get 4 percent of the net profits on every M-G-M production made between April 1924 and December 1938. (As the profit-sharing durability of a film was then considered to be very short, this arrangement seemed to be virtually worthless; it proved, however, to be a windfall once M-G-M began leasing its backlog of films for TV and 16mm distribution in the 1950s.) In exchange, Shearer signed a contract to make *Marie Antoinette* and five other films at a salary of $150,000 each, exactly what she was earning at the time of Thalberg's death. Perhaps she could have held out for more—Sam Goldwyn was reported to have offered her $200,000—but Shearer had never wanted to desert the company that had made her a star.

Still, when it came to casting *Marie Antoinette,* she was not so generous. To play Antoinette's Swedish lover, Count Axel Fersen, Shearer wanted only Tyrone Power, who was then under contract to Twentieth Century–Fox and one of the top box office stars of America. Mayer kept arguing that Robert Taylor or another M-G-M contract player would do as well (Fersen was just another pretty-boy part), but Shearer insisted on Power. Gritting his teeth, Mayer called Darryl Zanuck and worked out a swap, whereby M-G-M got Power in exchange for lending Fox Spencer Tracy (for *Stanley and Livingston*) and Myrna Loy and Clarence Brown (as star and director of *The Rains Came*).

Marie Antoinette, a genuine M-G-M superspectacle, got good reviews and made a tidy profit, though it cost close to $2 million. But Thalberg admirers tore it to shreds. Never, they claimed, would Thalberg have approved of such a shoddy script; never would he have chosen One-Take Van Dyke as director of such a prestigious picture. For this hostile group, *Marie Antoinette* was a prime example of the deterioration in Metro film making since the demise of Thalberg.

But this is nonsense. The script and direction are perfectly adequate; the production values are impressively extravagant; the supporting cast is admirable (especially Robert Morley's Louis XVI). If the movie fails to be as entertaining as it might have been, it is largely because of Shearer, who plays Antoinette in the grand manner, absurdly so. Outside the opera stage, rarely has there been such a display of posturing and semaphoric gesturing. Shearer's performance here is a ripe example of Hollywood acting at its dippiest.

Shearer's popularity had started to decline even before *Antoinette,* and none of the five films she made after it was to help her regain her former position. The final two, *We Were Dancing* and *Her Cardboard Lover* (both 1942), were unmitigated disasters for which she accepts total blame. "On those two," she later commented, "nobody but myself was trying to do me in."

Which implies that she believed someone *was* trying to do her in on earlier pictures. The accusation, if that's what it is, won't hold water. Shearer had more than enough will power to withstand the suggestions of a director who wanted to shape her interpretation in ways she found displeasing. (George Cukor, who directed three of Shearer's films, has been known to clasp his hands and look toward the heavens at the mention of her name.) Mayer allowed her to pick her own vehicles, even though she often chose ineptly—why would anyone want to play Mary, the long-suffering wife in Clare Booth Luce's *The Women* (1939)? Shearer allowed no one, nothing, to curb her insatiable passion for nobility. In these late films, she seems to be functioning less as an actress than as Mrs. Irving Thalberg, the *doyenne* of the American film industry.

Mayer was ready to renew Shearer's contract in 1942, but certainly he wasn't distraught when she decided to leave the screen forever. She did so quietly—there was no formal announcement of her retirement—and slipped easily and happily into her new life as a private person.

Joan Crawford was another Metro star whose career began to slip in the late 1930s. Ever since her glowing reviews for *Grand Hotel*, she had been campaigning for juicier roles, but Mayer kept dumping her in glamor-girl vehicles in which she invariably played either a bored socialite or a shopgirl with upward mobility on her mind. (Endless variations were wrought on the latter role—sometimes Joan was a speakeasy "chantoosie," sometimes a cabaret dancer, other times a very private secretary.) Some of these pictures—*Sadie McKee* and *Forsaking All Others* spring instantly to mind—are enormously entertaining, and were meat-and-potato movies for M-G-M: they didn't cost much to make and returned a substantial profit. But Crawford found them unfulfilling: she hankered after richer stuff.

In 1936 she started crusading for the leading role in *The Gorgeous Hussy*, Samuel Hopkins Adams's best-selling account of the life of Peggy O'Neal Eaton, the mistress of Andrew Jackson. The production was earmarked for the full-scale Metro treatment, and Eaton was the kind of plum role that usually went automatically to Norma Shearer. But Shearer wasn't interested, so the coast was clear for Crawford. Mayer tried to dissuade her—he thought she was too modern for costume parts—but when RKO refused to lend him Katharine Hepburn for this one picture, Mayer bowed before Crawford's persistence. Certainly the studio owed her a favor, and sometimes it was wisest to let a star stub his or her own toe: that way they became more manageable in the future.

As it turned out, Mayer was right about Crawford—she didn't seem at ease in period costumes, and the picture turned out to be a real clinker. Despite the abysmal reviews, *The Gorgeous Hussy* returned a small profit, but the studio mail made it clear that Crawford fans were severely disappointed. So Crawford was sent back to her shopgirls and socialites, but by this time the old formula had lost its magic. In 1937, exhibitor Harry Brandt, president of the Independent Theatre Owners of America, placed her on a list of stars whom his group considered "box office poison." She was in good company —Greta Garbo, Katharine Hepburn, Fred Astaire, Marlene Dietrich and Mae West were also on the Brandt index.

Mayer chose to ignore the "poison" label. Crawford had been loyal to the company and now the company would be loyal to her. When her old contract, at $125,000 a picture, lapsed in 1938, she was offered a new one-year pact at $150,000 per film. Crawford, however, preferred security to money, so Mayer gave her a five-year deal, calling for three pictures annually for a total of $1.5 million. It looked impressive on paper, but boiled down, it meant that she would be making $100,000 a film, or $25,000 less than she had in the past.

M-G-M's subsequent handling of Crawford showed that it had some reservations about her power as a box office draw. One of her first films under the new pact was *The Shining Hour,* in which she took a back seat to Fay Bainter and Margaret Sullavan. Then she was cast in an out-and-out stinker, *Ice Follies of 1939,* in which she was overshadowed by the real stars, the Shipstad and Johnson ice company.

Both pictures were bombs, so once again Crawford started pounding on Mayer's door. This time she had set her sights on the part of Crystal Allen in *The Women.* The role was only a slight variation on the shopgirls Crawford had played in the past, but Crystal, unlike the earlier Crawford heroines, was a conniving bitch, the villainess of the piece. Mayer never liked to see his stars cast in unsympathetic roles, and he warned Crawford that at this point in her career she was taking a grave risk in undertaking such an unflattering part. But Crawford wouldn't be talked out of it, and Mayer eventually gave in, partly because director George Cukor assured him that Crawford could carry it off. Which she did, superbly. It's the first and best of those dragon-lady performances that were to make her the darling of drag queens and female impersonators. There was high praise from the critics for both her and the film, but *The Women* was a box office disappointment, as were Crawford's next two pictures, *Susan and God* (1940) and *A Woman's Face* (1941). Gradually Metro started to ease Crawford back into program productions, and by then, Crawford realized there was nothing to be gained from knocking on Mayer's door once again. She and Metro had reached a stagnation point, and the only thing to do, she decided, was to end the relationship. Late in 1942, she asked to be released from her contract and Mayer, after a suitably protracted period of reluctance, allowed her to depart. Phase One of Crawford's career had ended;

Phase Two was about to begin. Leaving Metro, she signed on with Warners, and a year later started filming *Mildred Pierce.*

As for the M-G-M men, Gable was still the King, but he too went through a bad patch in the mid-1930s. After *Mutiny on the Bounty,* he made a couple of pleasant pictures, including *San Francisco,* a blockbuster success, and *Wife Vs. Secretary* (both made in 1936), but they were fluff, the kind of thing he could play in his sleep, not the sort of distinguished assignment he felt he deserved after his success in *Mutiny.*

So with him in mind, the studio bought *Parnell,* a modestly successful Broadway and West End biographical play about the Irish patriot who had championed home rule in the English Parliament. The purchase of this dubious property could be justified by trendiness—the mid-thirties was an era in which the studios, excited by the success of Paul Muni as Emile Zola and Louis Pasteur, were biography oriented—still, Parnell was a dubious choice: how many Americans had ever heard of him? Furthermore, the play dealt almost exclusively with Parnell's adulterous romance with the wife of a British MP, an affair that was to destroy his political career, and while that provided a topical parallel to Edward VIII and Wallis Simpson, it also ran headlong into the Production Code's anathema against sympathetic presentations of extramarital relationships. Then there was the question of whether Gable was really suited to the role of a nineteenth-century Irish gentleman.

Mayer wasn't sure he was, and was unhappy about the project from the outset. But this was something Gable wanted, and Mayer gave the go-ahead, once again allowing one of his stars to hoist himself on his own petard. (Once the picture was finished, Mayer changed his mind: after the first screening he was convinced *Parnell* was a masterpiece. No one else, however, shared his enthusiasm.)

Gable wanted Crawford as his leading lady, but after the fiasco of *The Gorgeous Hussy,* she wanted nothing to do with another period production, so the part went to Myrna Loy, who was one of the few people on the Metro lot who had any faith in the picture. The predictions of disaster proved to be accurate—*Parnell* lost $637,000 and brought glory to no one except Loy, who looked stunning in Adrian's period costumes. Gable tries to play Parnell as Gable, which would be fine, except that the Production Code-sanitized Parnell doesn't allow him much opportunity to play Gable, which is not so fine.

Parnell was to be a lifelong embarrassment to Gable. Whenever he got on his high horse, which wasn't often, Carole Lombard (whom he married, following a lengthy romance, in 1939) would simply say, "Remember *Parnell,*" and he was out of the saddle, both feet on the ground.

Parnell did no permanent damage to Gable's career, however. He was to remain the undisputed King of M-G-M until the end of World War II, his only real competition coming from Spencer Tracy, who was ironically enough (in *San Francisco, Boom Town,* and *Test Pilot*) the most congenial of Gable's late-thirties co-stars. (They were the Paul Newman and Robert Redford of their time.)

Tracy came to M-G-M in 1935 after a checkered career as a Fox contract player. From the start, he was recognized as a fine, naturalistic actor, but his toby mug of a face made him a doubtful proposition as romantic lead—or so Fox thought. A black Irishman with a sporadic drinking problem, Tracy could be difficult to work with: he was prone to ugly moods and occasionally went off on benders. After one of his sprees, Fox decided he was more trouble than he was worth. He was released from his contract in the spring of 1935.

Thalberg had urged Mayer to bring Tracy to M-G-M, but Mayer had had reservations. "We've already got one galoot," he said. "We don't need another." Probably he was referring to Wallace Beery, but he may also have had in mind Lee Tracy—no relation to Spencer— who nearly caused an international incident when, during the 1934 location shooting of *Viva Villa!* (starring Beery), he walked out on his hotel balcony and urinated on a parade of minor Mexican dignitaries. (He was immediately sent back to the States. Stuart Erwin then took over his role in *Villa!*)

Mayer eventually changed his mind about Spencer Tracy, and only a few days after leaving Fox, the actor moved to Culver City. Metro immediately cast him opposite its most glamorous leading ladies—Harlow, Rainer, Crawford, Loy, MacDonald—thereby disproving the theory that he had no sex appeal. His Oscar-winning performances in *Captains Courageous* (1937) and *Boys Town* (1938) made him a superstar and earned him a reputation as Hollywood's finest actor. He had his share of fiascos, but even the worst of his 1936–41 films are worth watching because of the strength, wit and quiet authority he brings to them.

Mayer came to respect Tracy, but personal relations between them were always on the cool side. Outwardly, of course, there was a strong show of harmony. On the night Tracy won the Oscar for *Captains Courageous,* Mayer told the audience, "I'd like to praise Spencer Tracy's sense of discipline. Tracy is a fine actor, but he is most important because he understands why it is necessary to take orders from the front office . . . because he understands that when the publicity department asks him to cater to certain visitors, it is a necessary inconvenience."

Tracy wasn't at the 1937 awards ceremony—he was recuperating from a hernia operation—but when informed of Mayer's speech, he was nonplussed. "What the hell is that supposed to mean?" he asked. "Is it a compliment or a threat?" All the things Mayer said Tracy understood, he didn't understand, though he had come to accept them grudgingly.

The only direct confrontation between Mayer and Tracy occurred in 1939 when Tracy was working on a film he didn't want to do, *I Take This Woman* (originally *A New York Cinderella*), co-starring Hedy Lamarr. It is an involved story, and to understand what happened, it is necessary to sketch in Lamarr's progress since her arrival in Hollywood in 1937.

Mayer really didn't know what to do with her, so when Walter Wanger (a former Metro producer) called and asked to borrow Lamarr to appear opposite Charles Boyer in *Algiers,* his remake of the famous French film *Pépé Le Moko,* Mayer readily agreed. On its release in 1939, *Algiers* became a sensational hit and made Lamarr an overnight household name. Her part in *Algiers* emphasized her strong point—her incredible beauty—and minimized her noticeable lack of acting ability.

Whatever reservations Mayer had had about Hedy Kiesler now melted away as he envisioned Hedy Lamarr as the next Garbo or Dietrich. He realized that Lamarr couldn't act; but then Dietrich hadn't exactly been the second Sarah Bernhardt either. Thinking about this, Mayer got the idea of hiring Josef von Sternberg, Dietrich's mentor, to guide Lamarr through her first M-G-M film. Charles MacArthur was commissioned to write a screenplay—something about a doctor who sacrifices everything for a frivolous and ungrateful wife—which no one liked very much except Mayer.

Now everything was set except a leading man. Enter Spencer Tracy. He hated the script and wasn't keen on propping up Miss Lamarr, but Mayer managed to convince him that he had to take part in what was going to be a very important picture.

Production began with Mayer taking an unusual amount of interest in its progress—usually he stayed away from the set, but he was forever hovering on the sidelines of *I Take This Woman.* After two weeks, Sternberg quit—for reasons that are unclear. (It has always been assumed that he withdrew because he resented Mayer's interference, but in an unpublished 1965 interview, Sternberg said he never had difficulties with Mayer, about whom he had pleasant, if vague, memories.) Sternberg was replaced by Frank Borzage, but the production continued to be troubled. Smelling disaster, Mayer became excited and started giving helpful hints to everyone, even in a rash moment telling Tracy how he should read a line.

Tracy stared at him in disbelief. He didn't say anything, didn't have to—Mayer got the point. From then on, he went back to standing on the sidelines of the production. A week or so later, *I Take This Woman* was shelved while Tracy and Lamarr went off to make other films. Several months later, production started again with a revised script, a new supporting cast, and a new director (W. S. Van Dyke). Most of the Sternberg-Borzage footage was scrapped, as perhaps the entire film should have been. This was one fiasco that even Tracy couldn't redeem.

Other male members of the M-G-M stock company who approached or achieved stardom in the late thirties and early forties were James Stewart, Walter Pidgeon and Robert Taylor. The first of this trio to be signed by the studio was Stewart. He came to Metro through the recommendation of Hedda Hopper, who had appeared with him in a Broadway flop starring Judith Anderson, *Divided by Three.* Metro had missed out on Henry Fonda, so Stewart was the next best thing. His gangliness, rube charm and halting delivery impressed audiences in *Rose Marie* (1936), in which he played Jeanette MacDonald's outlaw brother. Four films later, all made in 1936, he was elevated to leading man, first in a "B" picture, *Speed,* and then in one of M-G-M's lavish Eleanor Powell productions, *Born to Dance,* in which he self-consciously half-croons Cole Porter's "Easy to Love."

He kept playing important roles in both major and minor Metro productions, never losing ground but never quite making it to the top. The breakthrough came in a series of films he made on loan-out to various studios in 1938–39—*You Can't Take It With You, Vivacious Lady, Mr. Smith Goes to Washington* and *Destry Rides Again.* The latter two films were especially successful in shaping Stewart's screen personality as Mr. American Everyman, with *Smith* bringing him a best-actor citation from the New York Film Critics. M-G-M immediately cast him in important starring roles, and in quick succession he made *The Shop Around the Corner,* one of the best of Ernst Lubitsch's sound comedies, and *The Philadelphia Story,* which brought him an Oscar.

Walter Pidgeon arrived at M-G-M in 1937 after a very up-and-downhill career. He started as a Broadway song-and-dance man, then came to Hollywood during the silent era as a leading player at Paramount, First National and Fox; at the beginning of the sound era, he returned to First National, where he spotlighted as the screen's answer to Lawrence Tibbet in several uninspired operettas. Failing to make any headway, he went back to Broadway, and got fine reviews for his performance in Ayn Rand's *The Night of January 16*. Universal offered him a contract and he accepted, but after another frustrating year of doing nothing much in "B" pictures, Pidgeon wasn't surprised when Universal neglected to pick up his option.

Therefore, he was astonished when Metro offered him a contract. Given his past history and his age (he was forty), it is interesting to speculate on why Mayer decided to take him on. It is possible, as Metro executives later claimed, that Mayer recognized that Pidgeon had potentialities unexplored by other companies. But more likely he was taken on as a cover for William Powell, Robert Montgomery and Melvyn Douglas (who was then under contract to both Metro and Columbia)—in a pinch, Pidgeon could take over the suave, sophisticated roles that were their speciality.

In his first two years at M-G-M, Pidgeon was cast as the second male lead: he lost Jeanette MacDonald to Nelson Eddy in *Girl of the Golden West*, Myrna Loy to Clark Gable in *Too Hot to Handle*, Margaret Sullavan to James Stewart in *Shopworn Angel*. In *Man-Proof* (1938), he does win Myrna Loy from Franchot Tone, but that was no real victory, since Tone was about to be dropped by Metro.

Once again, as was the case with Stewart, the breakthrough came not through an M-G-M production, but from a loan-out assignment to another studio. In 1941, Mayer lent Pidgeon to Fox for Fritz Lang's *Man Hunt* and John Ford's *How Green Was My Valley*, both of which brought Pidgeon excellent reviews. On his return to Metro, Mayer cast Pidgeon opposite Greer Garson in *Blossoms in the Dust*, thereby creating another of those co-starring partnerships for which Metro was becoming famous: Garbo and Gilbert, Harlow and Gable, Loy and Powell, and now Garson and Pidgeon. The sexual spark burned a little lower with each new combination, but no one seemed to mind, least of all Mayer, who disapproved of his stars carrying on torrid romances on screen as well as off.

Pidgeon was one of his favorite stars. They had both grown up in Saint John, New Brunswick, which Mayer never failed to mention whenever Pidgeon asked for a raise. "We come from the same place," Mayer would say, "we understand each other, we can talk sensibly to each other." After the first of these pep talks, Pidgeon said, "Mr. Mayer, I still think I deserve a raise and I'm sure you'll do right by a Saint John's boy. I'll leave it in your hands." Mayer almost doubled his former salary.

Robert Taylor (born Spangler Arlington Brough, renamed by

Ida Koverman) came to M-G-M in 1935, about the same time as James Stewart. Several studios had spotted him during his collegiate years at Claremont College in California, and he tested for a few, but only Metro offered him a contract. He was beautiful, extraordinarily beautiful, and that was about it. Next to Tyrone Power, he was just about the prettiest man in America.

But pretty-boy looks have both their plus and minus sides. They brought Taylor to stardom, first in *Magnificent Obsession* (made on loan-out to Universal) and then in the Garbo-Cukor *Camille;* it also allowed journalists to dust off their powder-puff imagery, laid to rest since Valentino's death and misapplied to Taylor who was not effeminate, except around the eyes—his brows are possibly too sable-like and the lashes a millimeter too long. M-G-M went to great lengths to beef up his image, casting him as prizefighters, soldiers and other muscle-bound heroes, with enormous success. Never more (or less) than a competent actor, never a distinctive personality, Taylor was nonetheless a bona fide star for over two decades, thanks mainly to Metro's faith and skillful management.

Mayer took a paternal interest in Taylor's career, and Taylor repaid this kindness by unbounded loyalty to Mayer and the company. "As I knew him, Mr. Mayer was kind, fatherly, understanding and protective," Taylor told an interviewer in 1964. "He gave me picture assignments up to the level that my abilities could sustain at the time, and was always there when I had problems. . . . My memories of L.B. will always be pleasant, and my days at M-G-M are my happiest period professionally."

Whenever Mayer conducted important visitors around the studio, he would always point out with special pride M-G-M's Little Red Schoolhouse. With its gabled roof, its chimney and quaint front porch, it might have been part of a set for an Andy Hardy picture, but was in fact a real school, run by a real teacher (Mary MacDonald) and supervised by the Los Angeles Board of Education. All Metro moppet players and stars, indeed any actor or actress under the age of eighteen, was obligated by law to spend three hours a day (nine to twelve) five days a week at the schoolhouse, unless their parents preferred to hire private tutors. In the afternoons they would disperse for individual lessons from M-G-M's Special Service Department (a subdivision of Strickling's publicity office) in a wide variety of subjects: dancing, singing, elocution, French, poise, good grooming.

When the child actor was working on a film, lessons were held on the set, either in a dressing room or in a makeshift schoolroom set up in some out-of-the-way spot on the sound stage. By law, in addition to lessons, the child had to be given one hour of recreation in each eight-hour day, and had to be accompanied at all times by either a teacher or a studio publicist. The law was strictly enforced and never abused at Metro.

Metro's first child star, Jackie Cooper, signed on at the studio in 1931, just after his first success in *Skippy,* a Paramount production which brought him an Academy Award nomination. His first M-G-M assignment was playing opposite Wallace Beery in *The Champ,* and the success of that film led the studio to cast Beery and Cooper in two subsequent films, including a first-rate adaptation of *Treasure Island* in 1934. Cooper was to grow up to become a good actor, but as a child he had a bad case of the cutes, and like Shirley Temple (whom he resembled) his performances are endearing chiefly to people who are what the Germans call *kindernarr,* "child crazy."

Cooper was Mayer's first choice for the title role in David Selznick's M-G-M production of *David Copperfield,* but Selznick didn't want an American boy. He was pushing for Freddie Bartholomew, an English lad discovered by George Cukor at Italia Conti's renowned school for young actors and actresses in London. After seeing a screen test, Mayer was won over and Bartholomew became Metro's second child star.

But his career was to be brief. Though effective in *Copperfield,* as Garbo's son in *Anna Karenina* and opposite Spencer Tracy in *Captains Courageous,* Bartholomew exuded a prissy precocity that did not sit well with the American public. He always seemed stuck-up or stuck on himself. Soon he was being overshadowed by one of *Courageous* and *Fauntleroy* fellow actors, Mickey Rooney, the boy wonder who could act, sing, dance, play the clown or wring the heart. He could do just about anything but curb his inclination toward mugging and scene-stealing.

Brought to M-G-M by Selznick to play Clark Gable as a boy in *Manhattan Melodrama* (1934), Rooney was put under contract and given showy supporting roles in the Bartholomew pictures, in Clarence Brown's superb adaptation of Eugene O'Neill's *Ah, Wilderness!* (1935) and as Puck in the Reinhardt–Warner Bros. *Midsummer Night's Dream.* Then came the Andy Hardy pictures, in which he played Mayer's ideal representation of modern youth, a boy who was as American as the Fourth of July.

The Fourth was, of course, the birthday Mayer had chosen for himself, and the Hardy pictures were not so distant from the Horatio Alger romances Mayer is said to have admired so much in his youthful years. Was there, then, some kind of identification on Mayer's

240 / COCK OF THE WALK

part between Andy/Rooney and himself? Maybe—if Mayer could have had any childhood he wanted, probably he would have chosen one something like Andy Hardy's. Possibly that's why the Andy Hardy movies meant so much to him—vicariously, they allowed him to experience the childhood he had never known.

Certainly Rooney (whose background was as alien to Andy Hardy's as was his own) was one of Mayer's favorites, another of those M-G-M stars in whom he took a paternal interest. And for a long while Rooney honored him with filial respect, but when he became a teen-ager, problems started to arise.

At the time when Andy Hardy was discovering love, Rooney was a teen-aged man-about-town, into (Howard Strickling's words) "gambling and hookers." Sometimes he went after higher-class women. Clarence Brown (who directed Rooney in three films) recalls going with Mickey to a dance performance featuring one of America's leading ballerinas. As she was executing a dazzling series of fouettés, Rooney nudged Brown and whispered a smutty remark. Brown was shocked, not because of Rooney's playboy proclivities, but because he could see nothing more in the ballerina's performance than the occasion for an off-color comment.

Rooney's mother became so disturbed by her son's behavior that she spoke to Mayer, and Mayer spoke to Mickey, who took the dressing down badly. After all, he was a man biologically, if not legally; he earned a man's salary (plus some) and he worked a man's hours. So why should he allow Mayer to dictate to him? Mayer failed to prevent him from taking on a manager who encouraged Rooney's drive for independence—with disastrous results, according to Howard Strickling.

Rooney's rebellion wasn't an isolated incident in M-G-M history. Other child stars came to resent Mayer and what they came to consider studio exploitation of their vulnerability. They were treated as commodities, trotted out for L.B.'s Fourth of July birthday party, asked to blow out the candles, ordered to sit on his knee for the photographers. They were, they came to believe, just so many props to back up Mayer's fantasy of M-G-M as one big happy family. But exploitation of this kind begins at home, and the M-G-M child stars who want to blame Mayer for their later emotional or professional problems would be better advised to examine the motives of their parents or guardians. Mayer and M-G-M did their best to protect and guide their star children, and if he and his corps of advisers failed, it was definitely not because they took their surrogate duties lightly or irresponsibly. Indeed, like Mayer, many of them were *kindernarr*.

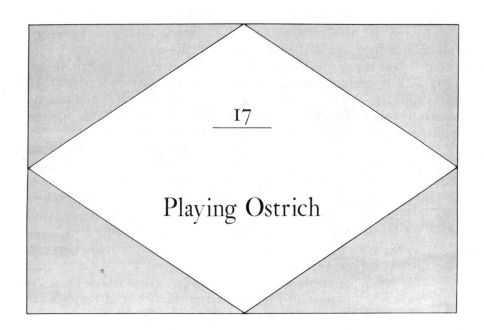

17

Playing Ostrich

One of the pressing problems of the late 1930s for Mayer and the other studio bosses was the sensitive political situation in Europe, and how it should be treated on American screens. As most of the bosses were Jewish (the only major exception being Darryl Zanuck at Fox), Nazi anti-Semitism was a matter of deep concern—Mayer had discussed his distrust of Hitler with Hearst as early as 1932. But since they were first and foremost businessmen whose livelihood depended on manufacturing a consumer product, Mayer and the other moguls had to keep a careful watch on the prevailing mood of the American public. And until late in 1939 that mood was predominately isolationist.

So, by and large, Metro and the other studios steered clear of any controversial subject matter. In doing so, they may have been following guidelines set down by the Roosevelt administration—at least there are unconfirmed reports that the government suggested that Hollywood maintain a neutral position for the time being. But even if the country at large had suddenly capitulated to interventionist fever and Roosevelt had simultaneously switched the red light to green, it is doubtful whether the studios would have rushed into the fray. There was still the foreign market to be considered.

By the late 1930s there were 97,500 movie houses in the world, but only 18,200 were in the United States. Russia took top place with about 35,000; then, after America, came Germany, Great Britain and Italy with roughly 5,000 each; then Spain with just under 3,500. All these countries had their own film industries, but all relied heavily on Hollywood exports, and Hollywood relied heavily on foreign audiences, many films returning a profit only from their international revenues. Germany, in particular, was an enormously lucrative outlet for American producers. Propaganda minister Paul Goebbels, however, scrutinized every picture imported into the country, and the Hollywood studios stayed away from any material that might offend him. To ensure German exhibition of their films, they removed all Semitic-sounding names from their credit lists, even going so far as to provide medical documentation to prove that certain suspect actors were uncircumcised.

This policy of appeasement came under sharp attack from the interventionist press, with Metro bearing the brunt of the censure since Mayer and Schenck supposedly went the furthest in placating Goebbels. But there is no historical evidence to support this allegation. Universal did produce *Little Man, What Now?* (directed by Frank Borzage), a simplistic exploration of the roots of Nazism; and Warners turned out *The Life of Emile Zola*, which exposed French anti-Semitism through the historical perspective of the Dreyfus case. Otherwise there was not much emanating from any of the studios to which Goebbels could take exception.

Metro did take one risk, albeit a slight one. In 1937 the studio bought the film rights to Erich Maria Remarque's *Three Comrades*, a Hemingwayesque portrait of Germany's lost, postwar generation which touched on the struggle between the Nazi and Communist parties for political supremacy. But the novel's social backdrop was less important (at least from Metro's point of view) than its foreground story of a doomed *fraulein* (a tubercular, ethereal counterpart of Sally Bowles) who makes an indelible impression on the three titular comrades. Metro bought it with Joan Crawford and Spencer Tracy·in mind, but by the time it went before the cameras, Margaret Sullavan and Robert Taylor were cast as the leads. Mayer put Joe Mankiewicz in charge of the production, ordering him to suppress as much of the political background as possible. Mankiewicz succeeded so well that only the politically sophisticated could have detected that one of the three comrades was, in fact, a true *tovarich*.

Still very nervous about how the picture would be received overseas, Mayer held a private screening of the first cut for a representative of the German consulate in Los Angeles. His reaction was not favorable, but he suggested that if certain scenes were reshot so that German political unrest was placed on other than Nazi shoulders, all would be well. Mayer asked Mankiewicz to make the necessary changes, but Mankiewicz refused, threatening to talk to the press if he was forced to alter the picture to fit the taste of the German consulate. Mayer backed off, and *Three Comrades* went into release without further revisions. It received excellent reviews and returned a good profit.

Despite this precedent, it would be over a year before Mayer and Metro decided it was safe to take a strong stand against Fascism. By then—the fall of 1939—Germany had declared war on Poland, England and France had declared war on Germany, and the loss of a good portion of the foreign market was a foregone conclusion. There was no reason to continue the policy of appeasement except that many producers felt the American public wouldn't be interested in films dealing with the Fascist menace. But the success of *Three Comrades* and Warner Bros.' *Confessions of a Nazi Spy,* a fictional account of a true-life espionage case, encouraged Mayer to approve production of *The Mortal Storm,* formally announced as "Hollywood's first uncompromising portrait of German life under the Hitler regime."

Today this picture (which features Margaret Sullavan, that quintessential Wasp aristocrat, as a German Jewess) seems quaint and absurdly romantic, but on its opening in June 1940, it was welcomed with superlatives, Metro being heaped with praise for daring to present what *The New York Times* called "a blistering piece of anti-Nazi propaganda."

Much too blistering, as it turned out, for some tastes. The America First association (spearheaded by Charles Lindbergh) became alarmed by the large number of purportedly anti-Nazi films coming out of Hollywood after *The Mortal Storm,* claiming that they were propaganda favoring American involvement in the war. The America Firsters gained the support of Senator Gerald Nye, one of the most powerful and intransigent champions of isolationism. Through Nye's efforts (and, it has been suggested, the efforts of the German consul in Los Angeles and the German ambassador to Washington), the United States Senate appointed a subcommittee to investigate the charges against the film industry.

The committee first met in early 1941 and its hearings dragged on for several months. There was a touch of irony—or absurdity—about the whole affair: for years the studios had been criticized for taking no stand on Fascism; now, they were being chastised for having chosen sides.

Nearly all the studios were on trial—Warners, Twentieth Century–Fox, Metro, Paramount, even Alexander Korda, the British producer then working at United Artists—but the committee was particularly interested in *The Mortal Storm* and another M-G-M production, Mervyn LeRoy's *Escape*, starring Norma Shearer. At Mayer's suggestion, the studios had hired Wendell Willkie as counsel, and Willkie advised Nick Schenck (who represented Loew's–M-G-M) to say that there was no anti-Nazi propaganda in *The Mortal Storm* or *Escape*, that all Metro had been attempting to do in those pictures was provide the American public with "a little additional information on what goes on in Nazi Germany."

Willkie's main line of defense was to prove the studios had taken a neutral position, which by and large was true but was nonetheless difficult to demonstrate since there were no pro-Nazi films to counterbalance the few anti-Nazi films turned out by Hollywood. In the long run, the whole affair was a tempest in a teapot; yes, Hollywood had made some propaganda pictures, but no one could prove that these films had persuaded Americans to switch from isolationism to involvement. On the contrary, most of the propaganda films had been box office duds, including *The Mortal Storm.*

A *Fortune* magazine poll in early 1941 told the Hollywood producers what they already knew—the majority of moviegoing public didn't want to see pictures dealing with the causes or probable consequences of a second world war. *Fortune* also reported that most of the interviewees had chosen Mickey Rooney as their favorite film star, but all things considered, they'd rather stay home and listen to the radio. Around the same time a Gallup Poll relayed the same message: movie attendance had dropped from 85 million in the mid-thirties to 55 million in 1941.

The slump had started late in 1938 when the economy, still nursing itself back to health after the Depression, was hit by a severe recession. The Wall Street index picked up fairly quickly, but film grosses continued to dwindle. Metro, alone among the studios, remained steady. In 1937, M-G-M–Loew's profits amounted to $14.5 million; in 1938 and 1939, almost $10 million; in 1940, when eleven European countries were closed to American films and when both RKO and Twentieth Century–Fox showed losses, it reported a profit of $9 million.

A lot of the profits that kept Metro looking rosy during the dark years of 1939–41 came from *Gone With the Wind*, which wasn't really a bona fide Metro production, though it might have been. Back in 1936, Thalberg had scanned the manuscript of Margaret Mitchell's epic novel, but expressed no interest in acquiring the film rights. He was then working on *The Good Earth*, and was reluctant to take on another epic production. Mayer was more receptive to the book, at least as much of it was included in Kate Corbaley's verbal plot synopsis. As he listened to her summary, he immediately realized that Rhett Butler *was* Clark Gable and that Scarlett O'Hara could be an Academy Award assignment for any number of the company's leading ladies. But Scarlett was a bitch, and he was always against casting his lady stars as bitches. Furthermore, he was concerned about the expense involved in transferring Mitchell's Civil War saga to film. He decided to ask Thalberg's advice.

"Pass on it, Louie," Thalberg said. "Civil War pictures have never made a dime." Obviously Thalberg had forgotten *Birth of a Nation,* but in recent years several Hollywood studios had been burned by Civil War romances, including Metro which lost a bundle on *Operator 13* with Marion Davies. So Mayer accepted Thalberg's decision and passed on *Gone With the Wind.*

The film rights to the novel were eventually purchased by David Selznick, who envisioned it as the supreme achievement of the independent studio he had founded on leaving Metro in 1935. No one thought Selznick would be able to pull it off, including Mayer, who considered this was one of the prime examples of his son-in-law's needing a flywheel: he just didn't have the resources to handle a production of such mammoth scope as *GWTW.* And sure enough, Selznick was soon searching for outside help. First of all, he needed Clark Gable, and to get him he had to bargain with Mayer who was never one to allow family feeling to interfere with business affairs. Gable would be available, Mayer told Selznick, only if *Gone With the Wind* were released through Loew's, Inc. Selznick had no choice but to accept.

A few months later, with cost estimates running sky-high, Selznick was forced to turn again to Mayer, this time with the request for a cash investment. By then, *Gone With the Wind* had become a best seller of fantastic proportions, and Mayer rued the day he had rejected Mitchell's novel. Now he had the opportunity of second-guessing himself. He told Selznick he could have Gable and a check for $1,250,000—something less than a third of the picture's final cost—in exchange for 50 percent of the profits. Selznick agreed.

The deal gave Mayer no artistic control over the production, and he stayed out of the works as much as possible. Consequently, *Gone With the Wind* has to be viewed primarily as a Selznick production and only secondarily as a Metro picture.

Gone With the Wind was, of course, Metro's top grossing release in 1939–40. The runner-up was *Boom Town,* a formula melodrama whose only strength was its stars (Gable, Tracy, Lamarr and Claudette Colbert). Other popular or critical successes of this period included *Goodbye, Mr. Chips,* James Hilton's sentimental story of an English schoolmaster (charmingly played by Robert Donat); Robert Taylor and (on loan from David Selznick) Vivien Leigh in Mervyn LeRoy's World War I tearjerker, *Waterloo Bridge; Broadway Melody of 1940,* starring Eleanor Powell, Fred Astaire and a Cole Porter score; and a financially unsuccessful, but intelligent and winning adaptation of *Pride and Prejudice* with Laurence Olivier and Greer Garson in the leading roles of Darcy and Elizabeth Bennett.

But the pick of the crop was by general consensus *The Philadelphia Story,* another of those pictures which represent the M-G-M style at its poshest. There was praise for everyone involved in the production, especially Katharine Hepburn, who only four years before had been labeled box office poison. At that time, she bought her way out of an RKO contract, and returned to her family home in Connecticut to take stock of her career. While staying in Hartford she was visited by playwright Philip Barry, who outlined two new plays he thought might interest her. One didn't appeal (this was to become *Second Threshold,* produced after Barry's death in 1949), but the other sounded promising. So Barry set about writing *The Philadelphia Story,* with Hepburn specifically in mind.

The Philadelphia Story became a huge hit when it opened on Broadway in February 1939 (some critics declaring it to be Barry's best comedy), and pretty soon the film companies came sniffing around. They were surprised to learn that Hepburn owned the picture rights, and would part with them only if she were to play Tracy Lord in the film version. Warners and Sam Goldwyn both made offers, but specified that they didn't want Hepburn as part of the package: for them, she was still poison. Hepburn wouldn't budge.

Then, about nine months into the Broadway run, Mayer walked into her dressing room at the Shubert Theatre with Norma Shearer on his arm. They congratulated Hepburn on her performance, and Mayer asked if he could meet her the next day. She agreed, though she had a sinking feeling that what he wanted to discuss was Shearer's burning desire to play Tracy on film.

That, however, was not the case. "He was charming," Hepburn recalls. "He started off by recalling Sarah Bernhardt and all the other great actors he had seen or known, obviously moving me up into that category." Then he came to the point: he was ready to buy *Philadelphia Story* with Hepburn as Tracy.

Hepburn was thrilled, but there was one other concession she wanted before reaching an agreement with Metro. "That's wonderful, Mr. Mayer," she said. "But I've been told so many times that I'm box office poison that I feel I have to protect myself, and I'd like to have some of your big stars to play with me."

"Which ones?" he asked.

"Clark Gable and Spencer Tracy," she replied.

The color drained from Mayer's face. "I'll offer it to them, certainly," he said, "but I don't think they'll accept." They did, of course, refuse—*Philadelphia Story* was primarily a vehicle for its female star. Mayer said he could promise her James Stewart "because he is under the kind of contract that requires him to do whatever we ask," but for the other male lead, he had no candidates. "There's no one at the studio, but I'll give you $150,000 and you can get anyone you want."

Hepburn took the money and got Cary Grant, who very nearly stole the movie from his co-stars, though it was James Stewart who was to win the best-actor Oscar over Grant, who wasn't even nominated. Hepburn also lost, to Ginger Rogers for *Kitty Foyle*, a fluke; her only valid competition was Bette Davis in *The Letter.*

Though Hollywood denied Hepburn its ultimate accolade, there was no question that her comeback was a triumph. She was to go on working at Metro for the next decade, though she says there was never an official contract, just a verbal agreement. She came to have great respect for Mayer and he for her.

"I *always* called him Mr. Mayer, never Louie, or L.B.," she recalls. "People say he could be wicked, but he was an angel as far as I was concerned. I was never refused an entrance to his office and he was always receptive to anything I proposed. We were never that close. Occasionally, I went to his house, and he knew that during this period I became a great friend of his daughter, Irene, but I don't think that swayed him one way or the other."

Mayer did not give Hepburn everything she wanted. Shortly after *The Philadelphia Story,* she approached him about filming Eugene O'Neill's *Mourning Becomes Electra* with herself and Greta Garbo in the leading roles. Mayer said he'd look over the script, which meant that he'd have Kate Corbaley tell him the plot. The narration took place before an audience which included Hepburn, Mayer, Eddie Mannix, Bennie Thau and other members of the Metro college of cardinals. As Corbaley reached the conclusion of O'Neill's Freudian epic of adultery, patricide, suicide and latent incest in 1860s New England, an embarrassed silence settled over Mayer's office. Finally one of the lesser cardinals started to giggle. "Jesus, it could break your heart—one disaster after another," he said. "But the biggest disaster would be to film it."

Mayer walked out of the office without comment. Bennie Thau took Hepburn aside and told her to forget about *Electra*. "I don't think Mr. Mayer was shocked by the story," she says, "and I don't think he was worried about censorship problems. That could easily have been taken care of. I think he felt audiences would laugh at it." Which is precisely what had occurred when Metro filmed O'Neill's *Strange Interlude* in 1932.

Hepburn had better luck when she brought Mayer the script of a romantic comedy called *Woman of the Year*, written by two unknown writers, Michael Kanin and Ring Lardner, Jr. Mayer was ready to buy it, but wanted to know who had written it. Hepburn had removed the credit page from the manuscript before sending it to Mayer, guessing he would offer less if he knew the screenwriters had no substantial credits behind them. "I'm sorry, Mr. Mayer," Hepburn said firmly. "I can't tell you."

"You must understand, Miss Hepburn," he replied with equal firmness, "I can't possibly make an offer unless you tell me the name of the author."

"Well, then I'm afraid I'll have to take the script elsewhere," Hepburn countered.

The upshot was that Mayer paid $110,000 for *Woman of the Year* —$100,000 for Kanin and Lardner (at least twice what they could have expected to receive) and $10,000 agent's fee for Hepburn. And as an additional bonus she got Spencer Tracy as co-star. It was inspired casting, the beginning of one of the great star partnerships of Hollywood history.

Hepburn and Tracy kept each other afloat during the 1940s. Some of their films are pretty terrible—*Without Love* and *The Sea of Grass*, for example—and even the best are sustained mainly by their teamwork. Together they were superb, but separately they were often in trouble. Hepburn's films without Tracy in this decade are every bit as bad as those that led to her box office poison label—she's as overwrought and rarified as she had been in the past. And while Tracy made several enormously profitable pictures with other actresses, when he's not playing against Hepburn, he seems disinterested; a monotony creeps into his performances and his celebrated naturalness begins to look like a mannerism.

Howard Strickling says Mayer bent over backwards to keep Hepburn at M-G-M because she kept Tracy happy and under control. And Emily Torchia, Metro's press representative for all Hepburn and Tracy films, says discreetly, "They were easy to work with together; when they were working apart, it wasn't always so easy."

It is true that none of Hepburn's solo outings for Metro made much money (and two or three lost a considerable bankroll), but it's preposterous to believe that Mayer saw her primarily as a nursemaid for Tracy. Admiring her talent and in awe of her acuity as a business-woman, he treated her with a deference few other Metro stars ever received.

On the morning after the first preview of *Woman of the Year*, Hepburn ran into Mayer outside the Thalberg Building. He congratulated her on her performance and on the favorable response of the preview audience. She thanked him, but said she felt the final scene was terribly weak.

"Well," Mayer said, "we can always fix that. Come up with an idea for a new ending and we'll shoot it."

"I think that was a remarkable thing for him to do," Hepburn recalls. "It meant spending a *lot* of money—sets had to be rebuilt, the crew reassembled, but when we did come up with a better ending, he approved it without hesitation. That's one of the reasons I found him such a satisfactory person to deal with. He *adored* the business and he understood it—as much as anyone can understand such a magical and incalculable business. I truly admired him and Sam Goldwyn and Harry Cohn and all those birds. They made the industry what it is . . . or was. It never would have existed without them."

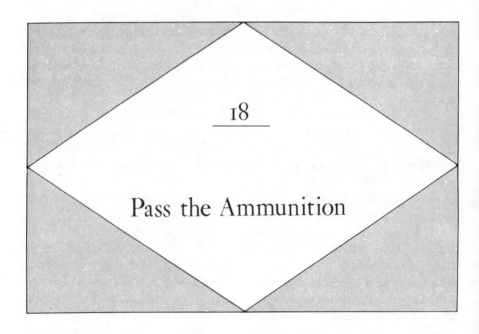

18

Pass the Ammunition

At the start of 1941, Mayer and the other old birds were all feeling their age. The weather was lousy and the economy was worse and every day there was a new headache. Film grosses had declined, not alarmingly so, but there was no indication that an upswing was anywhere in sight. Then, as the crowning blow, came word that the industry was facing what might turn into a major scandal.

In the spring of the year, the U.S. Department of Justice began investigations into the activities of the International Alliance of Theatrical Stage Employees, charging George Browne, a union official, and William Bioff, a Chicago racketeer, with demanding and receiving money to subvert a proposed strike against the studios. Mayer took the stand to testify that Bioff wanted $2 million to call off the strike. Mayer had paid, but only after whittling him down to $50,000. Bioff and Browne were convicted of extortion and sentenced to short prison terms. The studio bosses were all vindicated of any wrongdoing with the exception of Joe Schenck, who was charged with, and pleaded guilty to, perjury. Still, in the public mind, a link had been forged between organized crime and Hollywood, and this Mayer considered to be precisely the kind of publicity the industry must avoid at all costs.

Mayer firmly believed that the industry must always pull together whenever one of its members or institutions came under
attack of any kind, justified or not. Loyalty was all. Therefore, just
as the Browne–Bioff case was winding to a close, he found a new
cause for alarm when he learned that W. R. Hearst was being vilified
in Orson Welles's *Citizen Kane*, which was then in the final editing
stages.

Mayer and Hearst were not as close as they had been when
Marion Davies was the queen of the Metro lot, and during the past
decade they had frequently been on the opposite ends of many political issues. But despite their differences, the two men retained a high
regard for one another—in Mayer's eyes, Hearst would always be a
towering American. In the past he had helped Mayer on innumerable occasions; now Mayer saw the opportunity to return the favor.

The script for *Citizen Kane* was written by a former M-G-M
scenarist, Herman Mankiewicz, who like his younger brother, Joe,
had spent many years at Metro as a screenwriter. A brilliant man of
eccentric temperament, with a heavy drinking problem and a mor-
dant wit, Herman was not the kind of person one would think Mayer
would like, but in fact Mayer did like him, possibly because Mankiewicz backed the studios on several key issues. (He thought most
screenwriters were paid too much, and campaigned vigorously
against the formation of the Screenwriters Guild.) Mankiewicz had
only one trait that disturbed L.B.—he was an inveterate gambler who
never seemed to hit a lucky streak. At least once a month he had to
ask for advances on his salary, and for a long time Mayer okayed
them. But the day arrived when he told Mankiewicz that he had
collected his last loan, and Mankiewicz swore he would never gamble
again.

The next day Mankiewicz was playing poker at the writers' table
in the commissary when he looked up and saw Mayer standing beside
him. Mankiewicz got up from the table, walked to his office, packed
up his pencils and left the lot.

Mankiewicz and his wife Sara (who was a close friend of Irene
Selznick) were frequent guests at San Simeon, and over the years, he
had built up a stockpile of Hearst anecdotes which came in handy
when he started writing *Citizen Kane*. It was this wealth of intimate
detail that made *Kane* an unmistakable portrait of Hearst and not a
conglomerate portrait of various American tycoons, as Welles and
Mankiewicz later claimed. Mayer wasn't fooled by that ruse—as soon
as he saw Herman's name in the credits, he knew Citizen Kane was
really Citizen Hearst.

Citizen Kane was produced by RKO, a studio that had gone

through several financial disasters since its founding in the late twenties and in 1941 was once again in serious trouble. There was no love lost between Mayer and George J. Schaefer, the head of RKO: a few years before, Mayer had asked Schaefer to hire one of his friends for a top position, and Schaefer refused. So at the start of his battle against *Kane*, Mayer directed all his ammunition at RKO and Schaefer.

Though he was general of the campaign, Mayer stayed very much in the background, and plotted with such secrecy that today the veracity of the allegations against Mayer can't be checked with the surviving M-G-M executives. ("I really don't know," says Howard Strickling. "The stories may well be true.") It was Nick Schenck, not Mayer, who first confronted Schaefer. Going straight to the point, Schenck said that if RKO would destroy the negative of *Kane*, M-G-M was prepared to hand the studio a check for $842,000, or about $240,000 more than *Kane*'s production cost.

Schaefer was in a very tight spot. *Kane* had already been rejected by most of the major theatre chains—pressure had been exerted in this direction—and it seemed inevitable that M-G-M's generosity would be gratefully accepted by the studio's board of directors. Still, Schaefer took it on himself to reject the offer, though he guessed that most of the studio bosses had made contributions to Metro's generous check, and that in turning it down, he would be inviting the wrath of the entire industry.

To get *Kane* into distribution, RKO had to rent independently owned theatres in Los Angeles and Chicago for its initial engagements, and by the time it went into national release, the picture was under such a cloud of carefully planted suspicion that despite generally favorable reviews, it did only poor to mediocre business. The box office was also hurt by bad word-of-mouth; the film's multiple-point-of-view narrative confused and irritated audiences.

The peculiar aspect of Hollywood's campaign against *Kane* is why Mayer and the other studio bosses felt they had to defend Hearst, since Hearst had asked for no help and was still powerful enough to defend himself without their support. Possibly Mayer and company found something personally offensive about *Kane*, which was an attack not only on Hearst, but on the entire American power system and on mogulism. Beyond that, they may well have believed, as has often been suggested, that if they did not protest, Hearst could retaliate not only against RKO and Welles, but against Hollywood in general—he knew where all the skeletons were buried and had at his command a widely read columnist, Louella Parsons, who would be delighted to help him dig them up.

Long after *Kane* was in release, Mayer kept up the vendetta against Schaefer, or so Schaefer claims. At a time when his position at RKO was very much in jeopardy, Schaefer learned that rumors branding him an anti-Semite were circulating throughout the industry. Tracking down the source of these rumors, Schaefer discovered they had started with Frank Orsatti—in other words with L. B. Mayer. Whether these slanders originated with Orsatti and Mayer, and whether they played any decisive part in determining Schaefer's fate is debatable, but late in 1942 he was relieved from his post at RKO.

Equally debatable is the allegation that Mayer and other industry bigwigs purposely set out to sabotage Orson Welles's Hollywood career by campaigning against *Kane* during the Academy Award race of 1941. Actually, the film did quite well in the preliminary voting, receiving nine nominations, one less than *How Green Was My Valley,* one more than *Little Foxes,* the other leading contenders for the year. That Welles's masterpiece won in only one category—Herman Mankiewicz for best screenwriting, an award that was widely viewed as a token or favorite-son victory—is less surprising than the multiplicity of its nominations. This becomes clear if the film is viewed in historical perspective. *Kane*'s rococo exuberance, its technical exhibitionism, its innovativeness made it diametrically opposed to the modern school of studio film making. It wouldn't have taken a conspiracy to keep the Academy voters from casting ballots for *Kane* or anyone who participated in its production. Most of them probably sincerely believed that *How Green* or *Little Foxes* or *Sergeant York* (another leading contender of that year) were more worthy of the top honors.

The awards ceremony for 1941 was held in February 1942. For a time, there was talk of cancelling it—the time didn't seem appropriate for a celebration of celluloid glamour—but finally it was decided to go on with the show, albeit with a minimum of fuss and ostentation. Gentlemen were asked to wear suits and the ladies agreed to wear nothing fancier than a cocktail dress.

The reason for this sobriety was, of course, the bombing of Pearl Harbor, which had occurred only three months before. America had immediately declared war on Japan, and four days later, Germany and Italy declared war on America. Parodying one of Mayer's favorite one-liners, Howard Dietz scribbled on his holiday cards, "Well, it's not much of a Christmas, but it's ours." A black joke, perhaps; but for all its flippancy, it expressed the mood of Hollywood—and the country—at the time.

Three weeks later, returning from a nationwide bond tour,

Carole Lombard was killed when her plane crashed in Nevada. She was Hollywood's first war casualty. Clark Gable was devastated by her death—they had been married only twenty-two months—and as soon as he finished shooting *Somewhere I'll Find You* with Lana Turner, he joined the Army Air Corps.

By then, James Stewart and Robert Montgomery were already in uniform. So were Woody Van Dyke and a couple of other Metro directors. Initially Mayer was outraged when his star actors started enlisting or being called by the draft. He argued that the greatest service they could perform for America was to stay out of uniform and keep on making movies, but the men and their draft boards disagreed. Mayer tried to have several of them deferred, but eventually gave in and released them from their contracts for the duration.

Mayer was also disturbed by dire rumors of how the war might affect Hollywood. The government, it was said, was planning to utilize the powers of the Office of War Information to establish a dictatorship over all picture production; film stock was to be rationed and double features banned; no more than five thousand dollars could be spent on the construction of a new set. Of these, only the latter was ever put into effect, and within a brief time, the studios discovered that a little skill and ingenuity reduced the regulation to nothing more than a minor irritant. There was also chatter about a proposed $70,000 ceiling on salaries, but that's all it ever amounted to: chatter.

The studios were eager to do their part for the war effort—cooperation was the best way of avoiding government censorship—but since, as far as America was concerned, the war had barely gotten underway, no one knew exactly what subjects should be treated. It was impossible to show American soldiers in battle because there were as yet no American soldiers at the battlefront. Therefore the studios turned to the events of the previous three years—that period when Europe was at war and America was playing ostrich—for suitable subjects.

Two years before, Metro had bought a novel called *Mrs. Miniver,* written by journalist Jan Struther as a tribute to the courage of average English citizens as they faced the probability of a second European conflict. The book had been bought for a song, and was originally designed as a low-budget "A" production, a possible money-loser, but nonetheless a film that should be made as a public service. With America's entry into the war, Mayer decided to increase the budget and make *Mrs. Miniver* a prestige Metro picture.

Making it a major Metro picture meant casting a major Metro star in the leading role, and that presented Mayer with a thorny problem. Mrs. Miniver was the mother of three children, one fully grown, and no Metro actress was excited by the prospect of taking on such a matronly role. Norma Shearer wouldn't consider it. And Greer Garson, who had just turned thirty-three, wanted no part of it either. So Mayer invited her to his office for one of his pep talks.

Garson was no stranger to these conversations. After her arrival at Metro in 1937, she was shunned by the studio producers who found her too hoity-toity to be real, and Mayer had to tell her that she was creating a bad impression with her English airs. Garson accepted the lecture with grace. She told Mayer she'd put away the white gloves and tone down her teacup manners. His forthrightness inspired her with confidence as to his judgment. Consequently when he insisted *Mrs. Miniver* would do wonders for her career, she made no further fuss about playing the role.

When the film was completed, a print was sent to the White House, and President Roosevelt asked Mayer to rush the picture into release. *Mrs. Miniver,* the president said, would give Americans insight into the demands that would soon be placed on them. Winston Churchill also sent congratulations to Mayer and M-G-M. "*Mrs. Miniver,*" he wrote, "is propaganda worth a hundred battleships."

Mrs. Miniver grossed over $6 million, and became one of the two or three films everyone thinks of whenever World War II movies are mentioned. As Mayer had predicted, it established Garson as one of Metro's top stars and won her the Oscar as best actress of 1942. It was also voted best picture, and brought top honors for Teresa Wright (supporting actress), for director William Wyler, for the scenarists and for cinematographer Joseph Ruttenberg.

Mrs. Miniver conclusively demonstrated that there was a public for war pictures. So M-G-M, along with the other studios, started adding war backgrounds to all the old familiar genres. There were musicals with war settings *(Thousands Cheer, Anchors Aweigh);* comedies with war settings *(The Clock);* glossy women's pictures with war settings *(The White Cliffs of Dover);* fantasies with war settings *(A Guy Named Joe).*

And like the other studios, M-G-M paid tribute to all the branches and subdivisions of the armed forces: *Salute to the Marines; Stand By for Action* (the navy); *Keep Your Powder Dry* (the WACs); *Cry Havoc* (army nurses); *They Were Expendable* (torpedo crews); *Thirty Seconds Over Tokyo* (the air force, specifically General James Doolittle's squadron of Japanese raiders); *Bataan* (an army squadron assigned to the death mission of holding a bridge while General MacArthur made his escape from the Philippines). There were also pictures about Nazi Germany *(The Seventh Cross)*, the Manchurian War *(Dragon Seed)* and the French resistance *(The Cross of Lorraine; Assignment in Brittany)*.

As could be expected, these films varied widely in quality and achieved varying degrees of critical and popular success. But Mayer was proud of them all—they were Metro's contribution to the war effort, and if some lost money, well, everyone was being asked to make sacrifices to protect democracy, human decency and the American way of life.

On the whole, however, there were few sacrificial offerings. Within a year of America's entry into the war, it was evident that the box office slump was over. By the end of 1942, everyone who was not in the army was back at work, earning more money than ever before. And finally, there weren't many varieties of entertainment on which they could spend their money: gas rationing kept nearly everyone close to home, so most people had to choose between the family radio or the neighborhood Bijou. Movie houses were once again filled to bursting. It didn't matter much what they showed or who was in it —people just wanted to spend some of the cash that was weighing down their pockets.

There were a lot of new faces on the screens of the 1940s. In fact, the studio star rosters had not gone through such an upheaval since the advent of sound fourteen years earlier. Half the change came about because of the war; the other half was due to the inevitable march of time.

At Metro, the only male stars of the previous decade who were around during the war years were Spencer Tracy and Walter Pidgeon, both exempt from the draft for reasons of age or health. Taylor, Gable, Stewart, and Robert Montgomery were all in the service by 1943. Lew Ayres, the star of Metro's popular *Doctor Kildare* series, declared himself a conscientious objector ("I'll praise the Lord," he said, "but I'll be damned if I'll pass the ammunition"), and was promptly denounced by the industry press and by Mayer, who announced that Ayres would no longer be working at M-G-M. A short while later the Andy Hardy series came to a temporary halt when Mickey Rooney joined the army.

There was also a mass departure on the part of the ladies. Crawford was about to move to Warners; Shearer was in retirement; Myrna Loy left the screen for war work. And in 1942 Garbo left M-G-M by mutual agreement.

Since the mid-1930s most Garbo films had made money only on their foreign returns. With the closing of the European market, Mayer decided something drastic had to be done to bring Garbo's personality and appearance into line with current American taste. So for *Two-Faced Woman* (1941), a fatuous comedy about a woman who tries to regain her husband's wandering affections by posing as her hotcha twin sister, the actress was redone to resemble a cross between Claudette Colbert and Ann Sheridan. Her hair is restyled to look "oomphy," she dons a form-fitting sweater and a one-piece bathing suit, and introduces a night club audience to the abandoned rhythms of a new Latin dance, "the chica-choca." (Step-kick, step-kick, bump-grind, bump-grind: "that's the chica-choca!")

Garbo went through it without losing all her dignity and individuality, but she looks awfully tired and drawn. At the time of its release, the picture ran into censorship trouble—the idea of a woman trying to seduce her own husband was risqué in 1941—but the brouhaha did nothing to help *Two-Faced Woman* at the box office.

So Mayer invited Garbo to his office for one of his little chats. The gist of the one-sided conversation was that Metro had reluctantly decided not to make any more Garbo films until after the war. The studio was, however, prepared to honor her contract for the duration. Garbo told Mayer to forget it, she didn't want to be paid for duties she hadn't performed. When she left the lot that day, it was an end of an era—the last of the great stars who had started with the company in the silent days was now gone.

In filling up the vacancies left by these departing players, Mayer began by concentrating on the men. Robert Young, who had been around the studio for a long time, was suddenly catapulted into leading roles. Gene Kelly was used in both dramatic and musical roles. James Craig, John Carroll and John Hodiak were tried out (without much success) as Gable substitutes. And such young actors as Van Johnson, Robert Walker, Tom Drake, Peter Lawford and Barry Nelson were all groomed for stardom.

The ladies presented less of a problem. Garson had already inherited the Norma Shearer roles, Hepburn could pinch-hit (and then some) for Loy, and Hedy Lamarr was a passable substitute for Garbo as the studio's leading exotic beauty. (Signe Hasso was also on the sidelines, waiting for a chance to prove that she was the next Swedish sphinx.) Mayer also brought Irene Dunne, one of his favorite actresses, to the studio for two pictures, *A Guy Named Joe* (1943) and *The White Cliffs of Dover* (1944).

Then there was Lana Turner, who had been on the Culver City lot for several years, but emerged as a major star only after the start of World War II. She came to Metro in 1936 under personal contract to Mervyn LeRoy, who decided she would have a better chance at stardom if Metro oversaw her career. During the next five years she went through several physical transformations—her makeup was constantly refined, her hair went from brunette to light brown to red and finally to blonde—as she learned the tricks of the acting trade by appearing in *Hardy* and *Kildare* films. Finally in 1941, Mayer decided she was ready for the showiest of the three leading female roles in *Ziegfeld Girl,* a sepia tinted color, superduper Metro musical.

Turner became a star in the closing scenes of this film, one of the great kitsch sequences of American film making. She plays a show girl who makes it big in the Follies only to lose it all on too much booze and amour. Toward the end of the film, she's lying on her death bed when she learns a new edition of the Follies is opening that very night. An hour later, she's sitting in the mezzanine, listening to the overture, when she's beset by such violent emotions that she dashes from the auditorium, reaching the staircase to the lobby just as the orchestra strikes up *her* song, "You Stepped Out of a Dream." The tune plays Proustian tricks with her mind, and suddenly she's back in the Follies: chin lifted, shoulders squared, tummy sucked in, dragging a fur wrap behind her, she's once again the toast of Broadway until she reaches the bottom step where she collapses, departing this world for that big runway in the sky.

A star exit if there ever was one.

But it was just the beginning for Turner. That same year she was in *Honky Tonk* with Clark Gable—not much of a film, but the chemistry between the stars was all that M-G-M could have hoped for—and the year after that came *Johnny Eager,* an unofficial and uninspired remake of *A Free Soul* in which Turner manages to make Robert Taylor look sexy while she looks like what every G.I. wanted to find in his Christmas package from home.

People started talking about Turner as the new Jean Harlow, but the comparison is misleading. They were both blonde and sexy, but Harlow had rough edges while Turner was soft and velvety —she had a sweet, dimpled smile and a light, slightly petulant voice that had nothing in common with Harlow's raucous vocal delivery. Harlow had real comedic skills; Turner was never to be much of an actress, though she got by as long as she wasn't miscast, as she often was: after *Ziegfeld Girl,* M-G-M kept asking her to impersonate New York debutantes and socialites. Mayer wasn't going to let Metro repeat the mistake that had been made at the start of Harlow's career. Turner was rarely cast as an out-and-out tramp.

Turner's romantic proclivities were to cause Metro a lot of headaches—in 1946 she was to hold up filming of *Green Dolphin Street,* an elaborate and expensive production, while she dallied with Tyrone Power in Acapulco—and from all reports she was never one of L.B.'s favorite stars: he didn't like, in the words of an M-G-M publicist, "hard-core pin-up girls." But she did well by Mayer and Metro, and Mayer and Metro did well by her. Which was one of the things that the studio star system was all about.

Turner was only one of the three Ziegfeld girls in *Ziegfeld Girl*. She is flanked by Hedy Lamarr (whose idea of acting here seems limited to smiling like the Mona Lisa) and Judy Garland, who was Mayer's self-acknowledged "pet." Like Turner, she had been on the Culver lot since the mid-1930s and she had been a semistar since her personal triumph in *The Wizard of Oz* in 1939. When she played Dorothy she was sixteen, an awkward age since she was no longer a child and not yet a woman. M-G-M moved her ahead carefully and cautiously—a little too cautiously for Garland's taste. She resented the fact that in *Ziegfeld Girl*, Lamarr and Turner had all the romantic clinches and big dramatic moments while she worked her butt off to provide this so-called musical with some real musical values. It would be another year before she got her first really grownup role and saw her name alone above a film title: Judy Garland in *For Me and My Gal*.

So much has been written about Garland—of how Ida Koverman brought her to Mayer's attention, of how he and the M-G-M staff groomed her for stardom, of how she almost lost the part in *Oz* to Shirley Temple, of all the later problems, the marriages and divorces, the illnesses and the suicide attempts—that there's little to say here other than to comment briefly on her troubled relationship with Mayer and M-G-M.

In the last years of her life, Garland was to say many unpleasant things about her Hollywood career, and picking up on them, many commentators have accused Mayer and M-G-M of exploiting her as a marketable commodity while ignoring her needs as a human being. Boiled down, the charges go something like this: First, Metro overworked her almost to the point of exhaustion. Second, this arduous schedule forced her to rely heavily on pills. Third, when Mayer was informed that she was under severe mental stress, he thwarted all efforts to help her.

There is evidence to support all these accusations, but each is subject to modification. Garland was not unduly overworked. Between 1940 and 1950 she never made more than three films a year—some of them cameo roles in such all-star musicals as *Thousands Cheer* —which was about the same schedule as Lamarr's, Garson's and Lana Turner's. Turner looked more mature than Garland, but was in fact only two years older. And Margaret O'Brien, who was Judy's junior by fifteen years, kept up the same routine without complaint.

Concerning medication, there can be no doubt that M-G-M did condone pills as part of its diet regime for Garland, knew that she was using pills to put her to sleep at night and pep her up in the morning. And certainly someone at M-G-M should have noticed that the medication was working against her mental and physical well-being long before anyone at the studio chose to recognize her problem. An unwarranted nervousness starts to creep into her screen performances as early as *Meet Me in St. Louis* (1944), and by the time of *The Pirate* (1948), she's visibly strung out, barely in control of her voice and movements, almost anorexic in appearance.

But in Mayer's and Metro's defense, it must be said that in the early forties a considerable portion of the Hollywood elite was popping pills, and almost always with their doctors' approval. At this time, no one suspected that these drugs were anything less than wonderful; no one thought about—or had investigated—the long-range, addictive potential of such pep-up-slim-down-relax medication, especially when consumed in massive doses by someone with a history of emotional instability.

As for charge three: Joseph Mankiewicz, who was romantically involved with Garland around 1942–43, did realize that Judy was walking an emotional tightrope, and got her to agree to seek psychiatric help. Mayer got wind of what was going on and upbraided Mankiewicz, who promptly handed in his resignation as an M-G-M producer.

Though Mayer was not then an advocate of psychotherapy, it was not the kind of treatment prescribed for Garland that disturbed him. What irked him was that Mankiewicz had never consulted him about the problem, and as surrogate father of all M-G-M stars, this was a sin of omission he could not easily forgive.

Mayer always retained a deep affection and keen sense of responsibility for what happened to her, in fact M-G-M often paid her hospital bills. Once he talked to Katharine Hepburn about this concern. "It was one of those times when Judy had, well, kind of tried to kill herself, and Mr. Mayer asked me if I knew her. I said I did, in a tiny bit of a sort of a way, and he said, 'Well, you know, she's made millions of dollars for this studio, and I feel powerless to help her. I was wondering if you could try.' I said I would, and I did what I could, but that's neither here nor there. The point is the genuine distress behind his appeal."

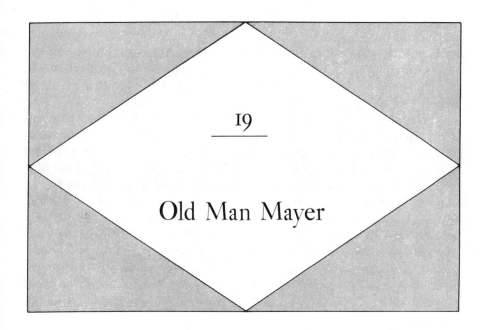

19

Old Man Mayer

As the war was nearing its end, Mayer was reaching a new plateau of public recognition. For years film fans knew him as one of the M's of M-G-M, the business world accepted him as the highest-salaried executive in America, but now he was on his way to achieving legendary status as authors started modeling characters after him. In November 1943 a play called *Get Away Old Man* opened on Broadway, and according to Shubert Alley scuttlebutt, it was a veiled account of William Saroyan's misadventures in Hollywood, with one of the major characters being the spitting image of a certain loud-mouthed, sputtering mogul. Walter Winchell let everyone in on the secret: the old man of Saroyan's title was none other than Mr. M-G-M.

There was more than a little truth to the rumor. Back in 1939, Mayer had been enchanted by Saroyan's first full-length play, *The Time of Your Life,* a jazzy, sentimental paean to the American way of life. Mayer couldn't see it as a movie—there was virtually no plot to speak of—but he could see Saroyan as an M-G-M scriptwriter. He was warned that Saroyan wasn't interested in Hollywood and had turned down several studio offers, but that meant nothing to Mayer. He had a way of getting what he wanted.

Sure enough, Saroyan played hard to get, but when Mayer of-

262 / COCK OF THE WALK

fered him three hundred dollars a week just to come to the studio and look over the business and see if it appealed, Saroyan hopped on the next train to L.A. It sounded like a crazy adventure, and what else is life, Saroyan asks in his plays and short stories, but a series of wondrous, crazy adventures?

Mayer and Saroyan got along beautifully at first. Saroyan had been born in Fresno, California; his parents were humble Armenians; he was largely self-educated; his philosophy of life was folksy-primitive. Out there, he implies, there's a tangled jungle of corruption and evil, but people are intrinsically good and will always be good as long as they are true to the beauty and purity of their inner selves. As this philosophy wasn't all that different from the philosophy behind the Andy Hardy films, it appealed to Mayer. Beyond that, though many of his short stories appeared originally in *The New Yorker,* Saroyan wasn't one of those East Coast writers who immediately took a superior attitude toward Mayer. He didn't take a superior attitude toward anyone, prided himself on being able to talk to anybody.

Still, Saroyan didn't cotton to all of Mayer's ideas—he balked at the suggestion of dramatizing *The Rosary,* a property that Mayer had dreamed of filming ever since the Haverhill days—and for days on end he did nothing but drift around the lot in search of more crazy adventures. Finally, when Mayer began to show signs of impatience, Saroyan sat down and typed out a three-page outline for a film. It was called *The Human Comedy,* and when Kate Corbaley told him its contents, Mayer wept profusely and tried to get in touch with Saroyan to congratulate him. But the writer had gone back to Fresno, where he was developing the outline into a novel.

Mayer was flabbergasted when Saroyan asked $300,000 for his outline, even though (as an afterthought) he said he'd throw in the novel as part of the deal. After a lot of wrangling, Mayer got Saroyan down to $60,000, plus a $1,500 weekly salary while he was being groomed as a producer-director. As part of this apprenticeship, Mayer allowed him to supervise the production of a short film based on one of his stories, *The Good Job.* The picture was such a disaster that it was never released, and after another three months on the lot, Saroyan went back to Fresno to write a play.

The production of *The Human Comedy* proceeded, with Howard Estabrook honing a screenplay from Saroyan's tangled and episodic novel, and with Clarence Brown as director. The final result was a film of which Mayer was inordinately proud; it was, he once said, his favorite film of all time.

"Sentiment is the heart of America," Mayer told Saroyan, and

Saroyan admitted that as he wrote the outline for *Human Comedy,* he kept thinking, "Mayer likes a good cry." Since his taste ran along similar lines, he had no trouble turning out a six-hanky tearjerker.

The Human Comedy got mixed reviews, with the majority of big-city critics dismissing it as superior hokum. Still, it did more for Saroyan's reputation than *Get Away Old Man,* which opened on Broadway about six months later. That play is the story of author Harry Bird, who values himself as the greatest short-story writer in America, and his escapades during his employment at a Hollywood studio headed by Patrick Hammer, a blustering egomaniac. After three acts in which nothing much transpires, Bird goes home to San Francisco to turn out literary masterpieces "that will outshine Henry James and Nathaniel Hawthorne."

Though Bird was played by Richard Widmark, who bore no resemblance to Saroyan, the role was immediately identifiable as self-portraiture, possibly as self-parody. On the other hand, Hammer was played by Ed Begley, who looked a lot like Mayer, but otherwise there was little resemblance between the role and its supposed model: Hammer was just another stereotypic sketch of the Hollywood mogul. Anyway, the last laugh was Mayer's. *Get Away Old Man* closed after thirteen performances, starting off a decline in Saroyan's reputation as a playwright that has never really been checked.

Nothing Saroyan had to say about Hammer/Mayer was so vindictive as the title epithet Old Man—at least from Mayer's point of view. He was then (according to his studio biography) fifty-eight, which placed him (to put it kindly) on the outer edge of middle age. But he felt as feisty as when he was twenty-five, maybe more so. He was, after all, the most powerful czar in the industry, the head of its most glamorous studio, and physically he was, in the words of an Irving Berlin song, fit as a fiddle and ready for love.

His relationship with his wife had become intolerable. Most of the year she was in a sanitarium and when she was at home she was rarely able to go out and only infrequently well enough to entertain at home. Mayer was in an impossible situation—he had a wife who wasn't a wife; a home that wasn't a home—and to relieve the tension, he continued to look for outside comfort. Margaret said nothing, but Mayer nonetheless frequently was overcome by flashes of guilt. Everything his mother had impressed on his young mind about the sanctity of marriage and motherhood, his abiding respect for his wife —this crept up on him, forcing him to admit to himself that he was not the most dutiful of husbands.

The pressure eventually became too much for him. On the eve

of their fortieth wedding anniversary in 1944, Mayer told Maggie that he was moving out. He spent a couple of weeks with Howard Strickling and his wife, Gail, at their ranch in the San Fernando Valley and then rented a house at 910 Benedict Canyon Drive. This was the former Marion Davies dressing room/bungalow which had been carted from Metro to Warners before reaching its final resting place in Beverly Hills. Mayer never had time for redecoration, and a certain unlived-in frigidity about the ambience gave some people the willies, including Jeffrey Selznick, who couldn't understand why Grandpa wanted to live in such "a drafty barn."

Many of Mayer's friends also thought he had taken a wrong turn, though none of them came out and said as much ("not the kind of thing you'd say to L.B."). Why, they wondered, had Mayer chosen to break up a marriage which, while far from ideal, wasn't all that painful either. It is pure conjecture, but there are those who believe Dr. Jessie Marmorston may have played a decisive role in the decision. Mayer first met the good doctor—a handsome, charming and dynamic woman of Russian descent—on the night of Bernie Hyman's death in 1942. Hyman was hosting a dinner party at his home that evening, and Dr. Marmorston had come with Lawrence Weingarten (who had recently separated from his wife, Sylvia Thalberg). She took charge when Hyman was felled by a fatal heart attack, budging not an inch when Mayer came blustering into the house, expecting to be granted total control. "Get out," she commanded. "I don't know who you are, but I'm a doctor. I know what I'm doing and you don't."

That was the unpromising beginning of what was to be a strong and lasting friendship. Like Mayer, Marmorston had come to America as a child, and had suffered innumerable hardships as she worked her way to the top of her profession. This common background gave her an understanding of the psychic forces motivating and bedeviling Mayer. She became his physician, his friend, his confidante and —maybe—his unofficial psychoanalyst. Mayer's decision to leave his wife suggests the influence of an outside force, quite possibly one of those analysts who feel the only way to treat a troubled relationship is to tear it apart. It is also possible that Marmorston saw herself as the next Mrs. Mayer.

Mayer, however, had no immediate intention of marrying Marmorston or anyone else at this time. He never mentioned divorce, but it may have been at the back of his mind, the separation being his first step taken in that direction. For a long time he saw a starlet named Beatrice Roberts, but the precise nature of their relationship is unknown. Then came Ginny Simms, a radio singer who frequently performed with Kay Kyser's band. She was a good-looking woman, but no knock-out; she had a strong voice, but wasn't in the same class with Frances Langford, Helen O'Connell or Helen Forrest. But when Kyser went to Hollywood, she went with him to appear in a few low-grade RKO comedies (*That's Right, You're Wrong* was the most memorable), then moved over to Universal for Abbott and Costello's *Hit the Ice*. Mayer thought Simms showed promise and brought her to Metro in 1944 for a lead role in *Broadway Rhythm*.

In no time at all, he was courting Simms, even went to New York and played stage-door Johnny while she was appearing at the Loew's-owned Capitol Theatre. Much of his wooing was aimed at Simms's mother—he showered as much attention on her as on Ginny, but the plot backfired. Mama Simms melted under all the attention, but her daughter kept her distance. Ginny liked and respected Mayer, but in 1945 she married a nonprofessional and slowly phased herself out of the business.

After Simms came Ann Miller, who was introduced to Mayer by Frank Orsatti, Miller's agent. She was then either nineteen or twenty-five (there is a startling discrepancy about her date of birth) and was a featured player in Columbia "B" pictures with such telltale titles as *Reveille With Beverly*. Like Ginny Simms, Miller had an omnipresent mother who chaperoned her daughter's private meetings with Mayer (home-cooked dinners *en famille*) and who was treated as chivalrously as Mayer had treated Ginny's mother.

Miller claims that Mayer wanted to marry her, but Mayer's friends feel she misinterpreted or exaggerated the seriousness of his intentions. Mayer appreciated the way Miller looked on the dance floor at Ciro's and took a professional interest in her as a possible replacement for Eleanor Powell (who left M-G-M around this time); but when Columbia showed no inclination toward releasing her from her contract, the relationship started petering out. In 1946, Miller married a wealthy playboy and went into retirement. Two years later, when the marriage broke up, she went back to work at M-G-M, playing soubrettes and second leads in some of the company's best musical productions. Mayer bore her no grudge, and Ann might have gone further if she hadn't been in competition with Cyd Charisse, whose legs were every bit as impressive as Miller's and whose balletic technique was more to the taste of the times than the machine-gun tap-dancing that was Miller's specialty.

During their friendship, Miller was thrilled whenever Mayer asked her to visit his ranch at Perris, which he frequently did. He liked entertaining guests at Perris, and every weekend there were a handful of stars roaming the range, highballs in hand, crooning over the elegance and virility of Mayer's thoroughbreds. These afternoon gatherings had a warmth missing from the parties Mayer hosted at the Benedict Canyon house, and some of his long-standing friends felt they compensated for the family feeling lacking in his personal life.

Mayer's relations with members of his family were generally unsteady at this period. He was estranged from his elder sister, Yetta, but on steady and fairly good terms with his younger sister Ida and brother Jerry (who was still working at M-G-M). His daughters had accepted the separation as an inevitability, but Mayer was on poor terms with Edie though he was fond of her children, Barbara and Judith Goetz. In the summer of 1946 Irene and David Selznick separated, and shortly thereafter she left for New York to embark on a career as a Broadway producer. Mayer acted blasé about her departure, but in fact he missed her terribly and frequently went to New York to give her "advice" on her Broadway productions, the first of which was *A Streetcar Named Desire*.

One of the chief pleasures of Mayer's life was his affection for his grandsons, the Selznick boys, Jeffrey and Danny. "Oh my, how he loved them," recalls Mrs. Clarence Brown. "Once I was on the set when Mr. Mayer arrived to show off a birthday gift for one of the boys—a watch, as I remember—and he was glowing with the anticipation of presenting it to him."

The boys usually saw their Grandpa on Sundays, when he would horse around with the kids, almost literally so—he'd get down on all fours, chase them around the room, clacking his teeth like some demented Walt Disney-designed dragon. Occasionally they were invited to screenings at his house. ("I think the only movies Grandpa liked were M-G-M movies," Jeffrey said.) And sometimes they went to the commissary for lunch. Afterwards they would stroll around the lot. "He liked to walk and he walked very fast," Jeffrey recalls. "I had trouble keeping up with him. As we went along, everyone we met tugged their forelock appropriately, and Grandpa would either grunt or say hello, according to his mood. If we passed one of Grandma's relatives, he muttered under his breath, 'That's so-and-so, he's related to your Grandma,' but when we passed one of his relatives, he kept quiet."

The two boys appealed to different sides of their grandfather's personality. Jeffrey shared Mayer's enthusiasm for horses and cars, and it was this bond that formed the major part of their rapport. Danny, on the other hand, "didn't know the front end of a horse from the back, and could have cared less." But he loved movies and Mayer listened to his criticisms of M-G-M films as seriously as he listened to the advice of his college of cardinals. Both Danny and Jeffrey were asked whether they might someday want to take over the studio, and both said no. They wanted to follow in their father's independent footsteps. "This brought on a tirade," Jeffrey recalls. "There were a lot of tirades and lectures, most of which I've forgotten." Later most of the diatribes were to be about politics. Both boys were liberally oriented while Mayer was resolutely right wing.

The sixty-year-old Mayer impressed many people as being a lonely man. It was an elusive feeling, nothing that could be pinpointed, nothing suggested by anything he said or did—maybe it was the idea of him roaming the corridors of that cavernous Marion Davies mansion, as Citizen Kane wanders through Xanadu at the end of the Orson Welles film.

Romantic nonsense, perhaps. Mayer, after all, had a family and friends of all stripes and callings, from the most suspect to the most exalted. All he had to do was pick up the phone and presto! he was talking to Hearst or Henry Ford or K. T. Keller, chairman of the board of the Chrysler Corporation. (Nearly every year Keller sent Mayer a new car, including one of the first Town-and-Country station wagons, complete with a card table built in the back.) And whenever he was in Manhattan, Mayer never failed to visit Francis Cardinal Spellman of New York.

Mayer first met Spellman when the latter, then bishop of Boston, came to Hollywood in the mid-thirties and toured the M-G-M facilities. They hit it off at once. Religious differences aside, they had many things in common—Boston, a passion for baseball and fast cars. Like Mayer, Spellman was a reckless driver who decelerated to sixty when passing a SLOW sign.

Mayer's friendship with Spellman did not endear him to the American Jewish community. He was accused of trying to deemphasize his Jewishness, which was (the story went) also the reason why he dated only Wasp-looking women. (Which is pretty silly. There weren't many Barbra Streisand types floating around Beverly Hills or Hollywood in those days.) Rumors circulated that he had made considerable contributions to the Catholic church and was on the threshold of conversion. But this was not the case. Mayer's religious beliefs were too general to be called anything but ecumenical. He believed in God and country, free enterprise and the Ten Commandments, even the ones he didn't always obey. It's unlikely that he and Spellman ever debated anything more transcendental than the outcome of the next World Series, highly unlikely that Mayer would have bitten at the bait of conversion even if Spellman dangled it before him.

But these friendships with Spellman, Hearst and the Detroit tycoons, while they may have inflated Mayer's vanity, don't seem to have possessed any true sense of intimacy or warmth. His relations with the Orsattis, Dr. Marmorston, his cronies and the M-G-M stars —these, too, are suspect as being too inbred or mutually self-serving to qualify as genuine friendships. As a Casanova, Mayer was something of a fraud; as a paterfamilias, he was alternately pampering and scolding, shifting from one mood to the other at the slightest provocation. He always seemed a little off the beat, not quite at ease, somewhat miscast except when he was behind his U-shaped desk in his third-floor office of the Thalberg Building. Then, and only then, all the disparate roles he wanted to play, all the disparate facets of his personality, came together in a personally rewarding way.

But by the end of the war in 1945 the chair behind that desk was beginning to feel less comfortable than it had four years before. Yes, Mayer was still the highest paid executive in America; yes, M-G-M was still stamped on the public mind as the Tiffany's of studios; and yes, the top Metro productions kept bringing money and heaping up critical raves.

Still, there were indications that everything was not right. The general consensus was that the overall quality of Metro production had started to fall off—the studio was turning out too many films clearly intended as nothing more than filler for the year's schedule. In 1945, Metro-Loew's profits lagged well behind Warners' and Paramount's, and in 1946–47, the net income took another dip, nothing drastic, but enough for Mayer to ponder the situation seriously.

He remained steady and calm, but he knew Schenck's finger was poised over the panic button.

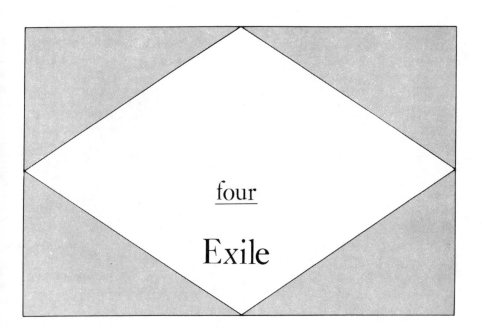

four

Exile

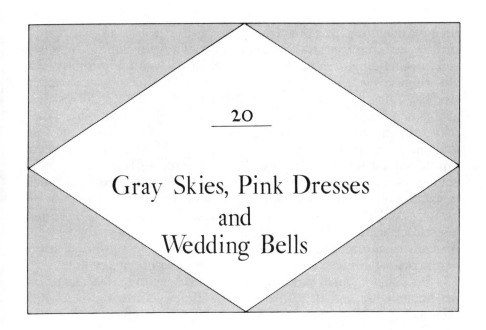

20

Gray Skies, Pink Dresses
and
Wedding Bells

There are several conventional explanations for the crisis that hit the industry in 1947–48, all partly true, all ultimately evasions of the real problem.

The primary factor, according to most commentators, was the Justice Department's investigation of monopolistic charges against the American film industry. After a decade of hearings, U.S. courts ruled between 1946 and 1948 that film studios had violated antitrust regulations and must start divesting themselves of their theatre chains. This meant that the studios would no longer have a ready-at-hand outlet for their product: block booking being outlawed, theatre owners could pick and choose what they wanted, taking a Metro film one week, a Paramount picture the next. But while the long-range effects of this decision were to be shattering, the immediate damage was negligible. The courts gave the studios a lengthy period of time to carry out its order, and through appeals, the studios were able to delay the painful separation for several more years. M-G-M was the last holdout—it wasn't until 1958 that Loew's, Inc. totally severed its production and distribution activities from its exhibition enterprises.

A second group of commentators blame the 1947–48 debacle on television and the moguls' ostrichlike attitude toward the threat of the new medium. And not without reason. It can be argued that if the Mayers, Zanucks and Warners had tried to gain control of television production at the outset, they may have saved the studio system and themselves from extinction. But the TV threat wasn't taken seriously, possibly because the industry had formerly held its own against another upstart—radio—and possibly because an official estimate, but one that admitted to error on the side of generosity, showed that only one household out of 250 had a TV set, most of them purchased by people who wanted a ringside seat at the political conventions of 1948. Once they were over, there was nothing much to watch except wrestling, *Roller Derby* and Dagmar. If people stayed away from the movies, it wasn't because of the allure of TV fare, and it wasn't because of the canasta and gin rummy crazes that swept the country at that time; it was because what was being shown at the neighborhood Bijou wasn't worth the extra effort or gasoline.

But, says a third contingent, they did get into their cars for foreign movies. And they drove home afterward raving over what they had seen. True enough, the great (as well as the shlock) Italian and French neorealistic films hit America at about this time, and critics used them (without discrimination) to score points against American films and their traditional escapism. But outside the big cities and college towns, there was no audience for these films unless, like *Bitter Rice*, they could be promoted as pornographic. The best foreign films appealed mainly to people who rarely went, if ever, to Hollywood movies.

In the late 1940s M-G-M launched an advertising campaign that told film patrons "Movies Are Better Than Ever." The slogan appeared on billboards, in magazines, and at the beginning of previews of coming attractions, but moviegoers wouldn't buy it. And this, far more than TV or the influx of foreign pictures, is the fundamental cause behind the decline at the American box office at that time. M-G-M and the other major studios were no longer turning out movies that appealed to the general public. The moguls and producers once legitimately boasted that they were in tune with the taste and interests of the average filmgoer, but this was no longer true. The old formulas didn't work because they weren't representative of the patterns of American life; no one really believed in them anymore, possibly not even the film makers.

The problem was present long before its effects were felt at the box office. It was already blossoming in *Adventure*, one of Metro's class productions of 1945. This picture (which marked Gable's return from his war duty) uses the standard romantic plot about the tribulations of a seemingly mismatched couple; he's a salty sea captain with a girl in every port; she (Greer Garson) is a spinster librarian who beneath the white gloves is all woman. But this time, it's played for drama, not comedy. Worse yet, there's a subplot about Gable's simple-minded first mate (Thomas Mitchell), who is seeking God's forgiveness for a murder he accidentally committed. The two stories don't mesh, don't illuminate one another, but rather seem to have been arbitrarily joined together only to make a feature-length film. *Adventure* made a lot of money, mainly on the strength of Gable's and Garson's names, but audiences actively loathed it—they hooted and talked back at the screen. The chemistry between the stars just didn't work—every time Garson comes near him, Gable seems to flinch. The film did Gable no harm, but Garson's career went into a sudden and irreversible decline. This was to be the last commercially successful picture she made for M-G-M.

The hollowness, fatigue and sexual fizzle that marked every frame of *Adventure* is symptomatic of many Hollywood pictures of the middle and late forties. As the war ended and men began returning from the battlefronts (and women gave up their wartime jobs to become housewives once again), the prewar patterns of American society seemed to reestablish themselves; but in fact there was a profound change taking place which would not become evident for many years. Accepting surface appearances as fact, American producers went along with the optimistic feeling that everything was soon to be just the way it was before the war, and complacently turned out pictures cut to standard formulas—only to discover that the public, with more to spend than ever before, was spending it on practically everything but the movies.

Whereas in the past movies had been an indoor sport for people of all ages, by the late 1940s, they had become almost exclusively a teen activity. A survey of that period reported that the wide majority of filmgoers were twenty-one or younger. Currently it is fashionable to argue that the studios were slow on picking up the lead given them by the demographers, but this is not true. Many of Hollywood's postwar movies seem deliberately geared toward people whose intelligence was as yet unformed and whose experience of the world was still limited. Certainly it was not true of Metro, where even the most "adult" productions—*The Postman Always Rings Twice,* for example—present lust in a dime-novel fashion that could appear erotic only to the adolescent mind. (Of course, adolescent sexual fantasies lurk within all of us, which perhaps accounts for the enduring fascination this not-so-good movie still has for contemporary audiences.)

But M-G-M had always been heavily into family entertainment, and its most representative pictures during this era were in this vein.

There were the Arthur Freed musicals, though they in time became so fanciful and arty that some of them *(Yolanda and the Thief, The Pirate,* parts of *Ziegfeld Follies)* appealed to a small contingent of window decorators and early devotees of Camp. Then there were the vehicles built around those players who were teen favorites, though few of them were in fact teen-agers—Van Johnson, Peter Lawford, Frank Sinatra, June Allyson, Elizabeth Taylor, Jane Powell and (a little later) Debbie Reynolds. Powell's movies were probably the ones the popcorn-and-petting crowd enjoyed the most—whenever they were watching the screen. She was always taking a cameo-star-studded (Lauritz Melchior, Jose Iturbi, etc.) vacation in Mexico or on a luxury liner, during which she would bully her widowed father or mother into accepting the mate she had chosen for him/her.

Metro's top box office star in this period was Esther Williams, the all American bathing beauty who was bright enough to know she couldn't act and clever enough to share this information with the public. She even swam with tongue in cheek. It's impossible not to like Esther Williams, and thousands of American girls fell in love with her: what Shirley Temple was to tap-dancing, what Sonja Henie was to ice-skating, what Moira Shearer was to ballet in *The Red Shoes,* Williams was to swimming. All over America, girls took to the water, trying vainly to smile and open their eyes as they performed deep-sea sexnastics.

But the Williams aquacades, the Freed musicals and the Allyson-Johnson comedies, bright spots though they were, didn't offset the dimming returns of Metro films, and in 1947 Schenck started pressuring Mayer to get the studio under economic control. Schenck had always wanted to believe that there was too much padding on the Metro payroll, and once profits began to decline, he had legitimate reason for demanding that some of the avoirdupois be stripped away. The dead weight at Metro—the producers who drew large salaries for virtually no work—had become the subject of a joke that made the rounds of the Thalberg Building: "[So-and-so's] only function is to gaze out the window, and if he sees a glacier coming, report it immediately to L.B."

Mayer had already sent out a directive asking all producers to cut the running times and expenses on all future projects. As this was not enough to appease Schenck, he went one step further and reduced the autonomy of the producers' units by placing them under the control of a triumvirate consisting of himself, Eddie Mannix and Bennie Thau, which would have final say over M-G-M production.

The new regime was, however, a half-measure, a reshuffling rather than an overhaul. Mayer remained firmly entrenched in the seat of studio power, though he had to budge a bit to make room for Mannix and Thau. But not that much. Thau and Mannix were Mayer partisans, though they did not fall into the category of yes-men. They spoke their minds, and on several occasions were to disagree with the boss. They weren't intimidated by his vituperative outrages and had learned to manipulate him so skillfully that often they could bring him around to their point of view without his realizing he had shifted position. (Thalberg had displayed a similar knack during the best years of his relationship with Mayer.) Nothing had really changed, but for the time being, Schenck was willing to believe that a profitable alteration had occurred.

One of the reasons for this outward display of solidarity was that M-G-M, along with the other studios, was being attacked by forces which challenged the political allegiance and integrity of the film industry. Starting in 1947, the House Un-American Activities Committee (HUAC) resumed its investigation of allegations that Communist agents had successfully infiltrated the arena of American show business. According to the charges, red agents had succeeded in building up cells of writers, directors and actors who would spread the faith through their contributions to mass-oriented American art —Broadway, movies and radio being the main area of concentration. The indictment was not merely a case of right-wing paranoia, as some historians tend to imply. Show-business cells did exist during the 1930s and 1940s in both New York and Hollywood. But whether the members of these groups ever tried to add a Communist twist to a conventional Hollywood or Broadway or radio plot, whether they succeeded if they did try, and whether their efforts could be construed as subversive—these and other fine points were lost in the hysterical court melodrama that ensued.

One of the earliest of the HUAC sessions centered on *Song of Russia*, a 1944 M-G-M film. Mayer testified that it had been made at the request of (and approved by) the Office of War Information. It contained no propaganda, he said, which was a little white lie. The picture (which was quickly withdrawn from distribution and has rarely been seen since) was obviously made to promote American goodwill toward Russia, a former enemy that had become an Axis ally in the fight against Fascism.

A few weeks later Mayer's testimony was rebutted by Ayn Rand, the author of the 1943 best seller *The Fountainhead*. Rand had worked on and off in Hollywood for over a decade without ever receiving a screen credit. Her novel was based on a personal philosophy she called "individualism," but which many prominent critics were beginning to brand as neofascist. As a native Russian, she was accepted as an expert on Soviet affairs though she had left her homeland in 1926 and had not returned since then.

In her opinion, *Song of Russia* was pure party-line propaganda. The film tells the story of an American conductor (Robert Taylor) whose obsession with Tchaikovsky brings him to Russia where he falls in love with a peasant girl (Susan Peters) just as the world starts preparing for mobilization. According to Rand, the Taylor-Peters union was propagandistic symbolism for a forthcoming alliance between the U.S. and the USSR. She also detected metaphoric implications in a montage sequence, opening with Taylor conducting "The Star-Spangled Banner" and then dissolving to a shot of a mob carrying the red flag. This she found "sickening": it suggested "literally and technically that it is quite all right for the American national anthem to dissolve into the Soviet."

Initially the industry maintained a level attitude toward HUAC —respectful but cool, unperturbed and slightly derisive. But when such widely read columnists as Victor Riesel, Westbrook Pegler, Hedda Hopper and Jimmy Tarantino urged a boycott of "red" actors, and when it became apparent that a considerable portion of the American public—already alarmed at the possibility of the cold war turning hot—were ready to travel in this direction, the calm gave way to anxiety verging on hysteria.

On November 24, 1947, shortly after the notorious ten (a group which included Ring Lardner, Jr., and Dalton Trumbo, both former M-G-M employees) had been cited for contempt after refusing to cooperate with HUAC, representatives of the major studios held a conference at the Waldorf-Astoria in New York. Present that day were Mayer, Mannix and Schenck; Spyros Skouras (Twentieth Century–Fox); Jack Cohn (Columbia); Sam Goldwyn and Walter Wanger (both independents); Dore Schary and Ned Depinet (RKO). There were also a battery of lawyers and, as chairman, Eric Johnston, the president of the Motion Picture Producers Association.

Formerly Johnston had been derisive about the HUAC activities, but now he looked grim. His opening remarks made it clear that the Hollywood ten's lack of cooperation had cast a shadow of doubt over the industry, and that dire steps were needed to counteract this impression. Without saying as much, Johnston kept leading the Waldorf committee to the idea that some kind of punitive action had to be taken against the ten and those who might choose to follow their example. Otherwise, the growing animosity toward the industry would certainly increase.

Eddie Mannix immediately pointed out that there was a California law prohibiting an employer from firing anyone because of his political allegiance. Later this was taken as setting Mannix on the side of the liberals, but probably he was just trying to clarify a legal point. Still, his question opened the way for Wanger, Schary and Goldwyn to launch their defensive attack. And the battle that ensued was perhaps as much personal as it was political. Wanger and Schary had both been employed by M-G-M, one not happily (Wanger), one reasonably so (Schary). Goldwyn was another story. Their simmering hostility, dating back to the days when Goldwyn was peddling Lasky–Famous Artists films and Mayer was an exhibitor-distributor, erupted one afternoon in the thirties when they chased each other around in the locker room of the Hillcrest Country Club, swapping insults and swatting towels at each other's bottoms.

They exchanged snarls once or twice during the Waldorf conference, but neither played a decisive part in drafting the paper which outlined the industry's position against the ten and all other Hollywood employees proven or suspected of being Communist party members or sympathizers. The Waldorf statement left no doubt that the studios would take "positive action" against all "alleged subversive and disloyal elements in Hollywood."

The left-wing and radical press immediately accused the studios with kowtowing submissively before the paranoid whims of HUAC. Mayer was attacked as the most virulent of the Hollywood red-baiters, though this notoriety was largely unwarranted. While there is no doubt that he was in fundamental agreement with the Waldorf statement, he played no major part in formulating it and was no more vindictive than any other studio boss in carrying out its program. The Warner brothers, for example, who were noted Hollywood liberals, were no less severe in executing the Waldorf executionary orders. M-G-M's sacrifices to the blacklist included a few top-notch screenwriters (Donald Ogden Stewart, among others), several up-and-coming directors, a handful of valuable supporting players and a couple of minor stars, the most noteworthy being Betty Garrett.

Few front-rank members of the studio team came under suspicion, the only major exception being Katharine Hepburn. In May 1947, when presidential candidate Henry Wallace (labeled a Communist dupe by conservative muckrakers) was barred from using the Hollywood Bowl for a political address, Hepburn read, at a rally supporting Wallace's constitutional rights, a brief statement, accusing HUAC chairman J. Parnell Thomas of conducting "a smear campaign against all of the motion picture industry." But what Kate said was less important than what she wore, as far as the pro-HUAC press was concerned. "Originally I planned to wear white," Hepburn remembers. "But I decided that would make me look like the dove of peace, so at the last moment I switched to pink. Can you imagine—*pink!* What could I have been thinking of!"

A few days later, when columnists were still talking about Hepburn's pink dress, she came face to face with Mayer on the Metro lot. "He was very upset," she recalls. "He asked me why I hadn't spoken to him about the speech. I said I knew he would tell me to bow out and that I would go ahead anyway, so it seemed pointless. He wasn't really angry—at least he didn't yell or stamp his foot or do any of the things he was supposed to do when he was angry—he just shook his head and looked pained. It wasn't anger so much as disappointment."

When members of his immediate family broke allegiance with his political faith, Mayer was not initially so diffident in expressing his disapproval. Edie and Bill Goetz's liberalism had weakened an already badly strained relationship with Mayer, and the Selznick boys were also to be lectured when they expressed convictions contrary to Grandpa's beliefs. But by the time their mother started campaigning for Adlai Stevenson's presidency, Mayer was in a philosophical mood. "She won't listen, she'll have to learn herself," Mayer said to Jeffrey Selznick. And again, he seemingly spoke more in sorrow than in anger.

Mayer's relations with his family were further strained during this period when his wife, after a three-year separation, finally decided to file for divorce. She presented her decision as an ultimatum: either he came home or he faced the consequences. Probably she would have preferred the former, but he chose the latter. He told Myron Fox, his financial adviser, to give Margaret "anything she wants," or so Fox claimed. Irene Selznick, however, denies Fox's suggestion that a financial settlement was so amicably resolved. She and Edie kept a careful eye on the legal proceedings to make sure their mother got not only what she wanted, but what she deserved.

Eventually a California judge ordered Mayer to settle over $3 million on his wife. She received the Santa Monica house, where she was to live until her death in 1955. She remained pretty much a recluse, though occasionally she'd invite some of the neighborhood children in for popcorn, lemonade and a screening of a new M-G-M film, which her former husband had sent out to the house. At some point before her death she discarded or destroyed the scrapbooks she had kept on the rise of Louis B. Mayer.

To offset the sizable dent the settlement made in his checkbook, Mayer was advised to sell off his stable of horses. There were three auctions, the first and most spectacular taking place in February 1947 when sixty horses were sold at a record $1.5 million. The prize catches included Mayer's favorite, Busher, a thoroughbred he compared in his pep talks to Greer Garson, "a classy filly who ran the track according to orders, and came home with blue ribbons." The subsequent two sales (in 1948 and 1949) garnered Mayer another million. Later the Perris ranch was sold to the Church of Latter-Day Saints for a tidy profit.

While Mayer was busy disposing of the ranch and its livestock, he was also hard at work acquiring a new wife. He was courting Lorena Danker, the pretty, middle-aged widow of Danny Danker, a successful advertising executive. A decade earlier, under the name Lorena Layson, she had appeared as a chorine and bit player in a few Warner Bros. films (her only screen credit was in an obscure 1933 film, *I Loved a Woman*). Now she was the mother of a ten-year-old daughter, Suzanne, and therefore, according to people who placed importance on such things, a more dignified match for Mayer than Ginny Simms or Ann Miller or any of the other girls he had escorted in the past.

He took a definite and immediate liking to Lorena, a natural-born charmer who bent over backwards to make people like her as much as she liked them. She was also a superb dancer, an asset fully appreciated by Mayer who was soon showering Mrs. Danker with gifts and attention. He also enlisted the aid of friends who besieged Lorena with glowing reports of his affections and honorable intentions.

Still the romance did not run smoothly. Lorena was intrigued, but shied away from making the final commitment. And whenever she seemed to capitulate, Mayer had second thoughts about a man of his age embarking on a second marriage. Hedda Hopper went so far as to report that, all rumors to the contrary, Mayer was playing fast and loose with the merry widow's favors. The item infuriated Mayer —he publicly laced into Hopper at a Beverly Hills party, and perhaps to show that under Hedda's hat there was nothing but spite, he stepped up his suit for Lorena's hand. As it happened, she was in a receptive mood. In December 1948, they set a date with the justice of the peace.

Nonetheless the marriage almost failed to come off. Since neither Mayer nor Mrs. Danker wanted any publicity, it was decided they would be married in Yuma, Arizona. Howard Strickling worked out the arrangements—he was an expert at this kind of thing, having arranged a similar "elopement" for Clark Gable and Carole Lombard ten years earlier. The wedding party, which included Strickling and Suzanne Danker, were to fly to Yuma late at night, the wedding would take place early the following morning, and before the Hollywood reporters were ready for their 11 A.M. eye-opener, the newlyweds would be back in California.

But even the plans of Howard Strickling sometimes went astray, and on the night of the flight, a fog closed out the Los Angeles airports. Mayer decided that the trip would have to be delayed for a few days, but Lorena threatened now or never. They took the night train to Yuma.

The wedding party arrived in Arizona a few hours later than scheduled, but otherwise everything went according to plan, with one exception—a gaggle of press gossips were waiting outside the justice of the peace's office after the ceremony. Mayer and party leaped into waiting cars and ripped off, the reporters in pursuit.

The columnists enjoyed themselves the next day, depicting the Mayer wedding as a farce featuring a sexagenarian and a Beverly Hills matron carrying on as though they were the madcap hero and heroine of a screwball comedy. The stories pained his friends and delighted his enemies, who were certain that L.B. was embarking on his second childhood. This was not the kind of publicity Mayer needed, not at this time when rumors were circulating that he was being kicked upstairs at M-G-M. Or worse yet, that there was a movement afoot to get him out of the studio entirely.

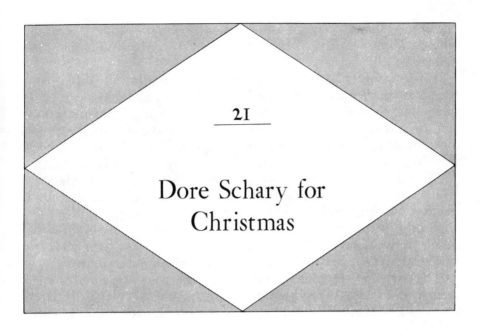

21

Dore Schary for Christmas

The rumors had started several months before Mayer's second marriage. In fact they dated back to the time when Mayer formed his production triumvirate. That reorganization had failed to reverse the declining fortunes of M-G-M, and early in 1948, there were predictions that the studio would end the fiscal year $5 million in the red. That estimate proved conservative—the loss was to be in excess of $6.5 million.

The blame was placed squarely on Mayer's shoulders. At age sixty-three, he was no longer staying in pace with the tastes of contemporary filmgoers. M-G-M kept spinning out sugary family pictures while audiences had started to show a preference for the American brand of neorealism, the gritty *films noirs* and documentary-flavored melodramas—pictures such as *Panic in the Streets, Out of the Past, Kiss of Death, In a Lonely Place*—turned out by Columbia, RKO and Fox. Mayer had nothing but contempt for this kind of picture and for those who acclaimed it as art. "Art!" he snorted. "Kick an old lady down the stairs and then stomp on her face. That's art!"

Well, it may not have been art, but it was boffo box office, and that was something Metro pictures definitely needed. Nick Schenck began pressuring Mayer to find a second Irving Thalberg, someone who could take control of production and bring the studio out of the doldrums.

Surprisingly, Mayer was not averse to the idea. He didn't want to release the reins of control entirely—Schenck had never suggested that—but the pressures of running the studio were getting to him and the possibility of sharing the problems and difficulties with another man was not a disagreeable prospect. Not at a time when he was thinking of remarrying and taking more time to enjoy life.

Finding the right man, however, was not an easy task. Mayer is said to have considered Selznick and Joe Mankiewicz, but knew neither would be interested. Friends say he also thought of Irene—"the only woman I know who could run a studio," he often said—but he never mentioned it to her, though he did offer her a job at the studio when she was thinking of New York and the theatre.

Exactly how he came up with Dore Schary is a subject of controversy. Some claim it was his own brainstorm. Others say it all started with Lillie Messinger, a Hollywood veteran who had worked at RKO and M-G-M in various, overlapping and somewhat amorphous capacities. Mayer respected her enormously, and she shared with Kate Corbaley the Scheherazade honors of telling L.B. the plot of every book or play the studio was thinking of acquiring. Everyone trusted and confided in Messinger, so she knew that Mayer was looking for a new Thalberg and she knew Schary was unhappy at RKO. Playing matchmaker, she called Mayer and said, "Why not Schary?" Mayer replied, "Tell him to call."

Schary confirms that Messinger set up the initial conference between Mayer and himself, but he always believed Schenck was the instigator of that meeting, and that Schenck once admitted that it was he, not Mayer, who had inaugurated Schary's candidacy.

Schary met Mayer at the Benedict Canyon house, which impressed him, like everyone else who entered it for the first time, as being as impersonal as a hotel suite. This was the first time (and apparently one of the last) that Schary had ever been personally entertained by Mayer, but by no means was it the first time they had met. They had worked together in the past with a measure of success and with no hard feelings when eventually they parted company.

In the mid-1930s, Schary had worked as a staff writer at Metro, attracting Mayer's attention with his scripts for *Boys' Town* and *Edison the Man*. In appreciation, Mayer raised Schary's salary from two hundred to two thousand dollars a week, and placed him in charge of a unit producing "important low-budget films." Schary's first production was *Joe Smith, American* (1942), the story of a kidnapped munitions worker who refuses to reveal important government secrets to his Nazi captors. A surprise hit, it was followed by another sleeper, *Journey for Margaret,* which launched Margaret O'Brien as the legitimate heir to Shirley Temple's throne. A year later, the Schary unit came up with a third success, *Lassie Come Home,* featuring two other up-and-coming Metro stars, the transvestite collie (she was really a Laddie) that played the title role and eleven-year-old Elizabeth Taylor.

But after *Lassie,* things took a turn for the worse for Metro's prestige "B" unit. Schary was all het up about something he called *Storm in the West.* It was, according to his outline, the story of Hitler, Churchill, Mussolini and Roosevelt told in the form of (Schary's description) "an American Western epic"; the four powers were to be shown squabbling over the possession of a territory shaped "somewhat like Western Europe." Mayer was understandably less than impressed when he heard Schary's proposal: allegories had never brought in much at the box office, and this particular allegory hardly seemed destined to prove the exception to the rule. Nor was Mayer overjoyed when Schary mentioned that Sinclair Lewis had agreed to write the screenplay. Lewis had made a lot of fuss when M-G-M had shelved its production of *It Can't Happen Here* in 1936, accusing Mayer, Thalberg, the Hays Office and anyone else who came to mind of cowardice and fascist duplicity.

But for all his lack of enthusiasm for Lewis and *Storm in the West,* Mayer did not turn both thumbs down on the project. Schary had done good work for the company, and therefore was entitled to every consideration. Mayer said he'd go along with *Storm in the West* if it was okay with Schenck. But it wasn't okay with Schenck. Schary was so disappointed that he immediately asked for release from his M-G-M contract, and after a few days' delay—obviously he hoped Schary would change his mind—Mayer granted it.

Schary then went to work for David O. Selznick, producing small budget films for Selznick's independent company which then released through RKO. During these years, he developed and produced *I'll Be Seeing You, The Spiral Staircase, The Bachelor and the Bobbysoxer* and *The Farmer's Daughter.* They're not masterpieces, but most are pleasant pictures; they collected some Oscar nominations and one statuette (Loretta Young for *Farmer's Daughter*), and they all made a lot of money. Schary's record was impressive enough to earn him the title of production chief at RKO when that post became vacant in January 1947.

During his first (and, as it turned out, only) year at RKO, Schary oversaw such elaborate productions as *I Remember Mama* as well as such well-crafted, quintessentially "B" films as *Crossfire, The Window* and *The Set-Up,* all three critical and popular successes. These pictures were hailed as the American equivalent of neorealism, and made Schary's name virtually synonymous with social-conscience, message film making.

Schary was a liberal, no doubt about it. At the Waldorf conference, he was one of the minority voices opposing retaliatory measures against those who were placed under HUAC suspicion. Although he had a hand in composing the Waldorf statement, he later refused to carry out the program it presented. He would not fire people because of their political convictions. When the powers above him at RKO did the dirty work for him, Schary considered resigning in protest, but decided he would be more useful by staying on and fighting from within. It was a decision that brought him no friends: militant left-wingers denounced him for taking a compromising stance and the opposite side dismissed him as another noisy liberal.

Schary was having other problems as well. Early in 1948 Howard Hughes bought RKO, and from the outset Schary felt certain he was mismatched with the eccentric billionaire. His anxiety was entirely justified. One of Hughes's first moves was to fire Barbara Bel Geddes, whom Schary had been grooming for stardom; next, he cancelled two of Schary's pet projects, a war film called *Battleground* and an adaptation of *Ivanhoe* (chosen, presumably, because film exposés of anti-Semitism were currently fashionable). Schary promptly tendered his resignation and Hughes accepted it without hesitation.

A few days later Schary was breakfasting with Mayer in Beverly Hills. This meeting still baffles film historians and commentators, who pride themselves on knowing the reason behind every major Hollywood maneuver of the last fifty years. Given Schary's political convictions and his predilection for the American brand of neorealistic film making, it does seem strange that Mayer wanted him as production chief at Metro. Cynics have suggested—and it is a suggestion with wide appeal to Schary-haters—that Mayer chose him because he was certain Schary would fall flat on his face. After that, presumably, Schenck would leave Mayer free to run the studio as he had in the past. But this explanation is too far-fetched to be taken seriously. In the past, he and Schary had had a good, if superficial, relationship, and as for Schary's convictions, those could be brought into line under Mayer's tutelage. Thalberg, after all, originally came to Mayer with some of the political pink still rosy in his cheeks.

Actually, Mayer probably thought Schary could be manipulated to Mayer's advantage in any battle against Schenck. Schenck, who was no more in sympathy with Schary's tastes and convictions than

Mayer, may also have believed that Schary could be counted on as an ally.

Schary, however, showed plenty of pluck when it came to negotiating his contract. Lawyers and agents haggled over clauses for weeks before Schary accepted an agreement that gave him nearly everything he wanted. He had left RKO because he didn't see himself as messenger boy to Howard Hughes, and he wasn't about to move to M-G-M only to play a similar role for Mayer. He wanted assurance that there would be muscle behind his title of vice-president in charge of production, and eventually he was guaranteed final say over choice of stories, stars, writers and directors—in short, total artistic control over the M-G-M product. But it was understood that he was answerable to Schenck and to Mayer, who was still vice-president in charge of the studio, which qualified the force of the guarantee at the outset. Still, Schary got a nice salary—four thousand dollars a week on a seven-year contract, with an additional two thousand weekly deferred until the completion of that contract. There was no profit-sharing arrangement, as there had been for Thalberg.

Schary moved into his third-floor office in the Thalberg Building at the beginning of July 1948. That meant that he would have little influence over the films for the forthcoming fiscal year (1948–49), most of which were already shooting or so close to it that vast alterations would have been too costly. Any changes he wanted to make in the M-G-M program wouldn't be seen until the end of 1949. So Schary started planning for the future. While he was to oversee all Metro productions, he would—like Thalberg—personally supervise the making of a few films each year, and as his first personal production he chose *Battleground,* a fictional replay of the Battle of the Bulge, first developed at RKO and brought to M-G-M (after a cash settlement) as sort of a dowry.

Mayer was no more enthusiastic about *Battleground* than Hughes had been. War films hadn't been grossing much since the end of World War II. At least, not Metro war films. The studio had made a handsome profit on *Homecoming,* but people lined up to see Gable and Turner, not the battle scenes. Even Gable, backed up by Walter Pidgeon, Van Johnson and Brian Donlevy, couldn't make a hit of *Command Decision,* Metro's adaptation of an award-winning play that had run for over a year on Broadway. And earlier, *The Beginning or the End,* M-G-M's ponderous, pseudodocumentary account of the development of the atom bomb, had also failed to make any impact on the critics or the public.

Schary argued that the reason these films misfired was not their subject, but the treatment of that subject, and while Mayer didn't buy that argument, he told Schary to go ahead with *Battleground:* for one reason or another, he was giving a willful employee enough rope to hang himself. Schary brought in an "outsider" to direct—William Wellman, formerly a World War I ace pilot—and cast the film with one Metro star, Van Johnson. The rest of the players were drawn from the M-G-M stock company, with a major part going to James Whitmore, ballyhooed by the studio's publicity department as a second Spencer Tracy. For the only important female role, Schary "discovered" Denise Darcel, whose major talent was her cup size.

The consensus of opinion around the studio was that *Battleground* was destined for disaster, a prospect that filled many hearts with joy. Though the appointment had been sanctioned by Mayer, Schary's production vice-presidency did not sit well with many Metro employees, even those who had no affection or strong feelings for Mayer. Howard Dietz, a Schenck partisan, summed up the opposition's attitude when he scrawled across his 1948 greeting cards: "Watch out, or you'll get Dore Schary for Christmas!"

The prevailing opinion about Schary was that though a nice guy and maybe an effective administrator at RKO, he was a dog-paddler swimming against the currents at M-G-M. He was destined to fail. But then, as Mrs. Howard Strickling recalls, *"Battleground,* alas, was a success." A mediocre film, it nonetheless got good reviews, did well at the box office and received six Academy Award nominations, including best picture, best director and best supporting actor (James Whitmore). It won in only two categories—best screenplay and best cinematography—but the important factor was that M-G-M was now back in the Oscar race after a two-year absence: in 1947 and 1948, the studio had received not a single nomination in any of the major categories.

In the past, when his predictions of failure had turned out to be false, Mayer had been able to take pleasure in seeing himself proven wrong. But not this time. By the time *Battleground* was in release, relations between M-G-M's two vice-presidents had deteriorated to a point where it was impossible for Mayer to rejoice over the acclaim heaped on Schary's first Metro production.

The trouble started over *Quo Vadis?* which had been on Metro's back burner for a number of years. It had often been announced for production, but no one had been able to hone a workable screenplay out of Henryk Sienkiewicz's nearly unreadable novel about Roman emperor Nero and the persecution of the early Christians. The project didn't appeal to Schary who had no appetite for spectacle films, but a treatment prepared by producer Arthur Hornblow and director John Huston was intriguing. Nero was characterized as a proto-

Hitler and his persecution of the Christians was presented as an analogy to the Nazi persecution of the Jews. It was a startling conception, dumb perhaps, but an eye-opener to be sure.

It nearly threw Mayer off his seat. He saw *Quo Vadis?* as a De Millesque mixture of sex, spectacle and last-minute uplift. No, said Mayer. Yes, said Schary. Stalemate. Schenck was called in as arbitrator, and while not thrilled by the Huston-Hornblow treatment, he approved it. Anybody who could get any kind of screenplay out of that turgid novel should be congratulated and encouraged.

So a script was prepared, a cast was sketched in (Gregory Peck, Elizabeth Taylor and in the small role of Saint Peter, the director's father, Walter Huston). The film was to be shot in Rome at the Cinecittà studios, and Eddie Mannix, who was to keep tabs on the production, was already in Italy when things collapsed. Gregory Peck came down with an eye infection. Production had to be postponed beyond the last possible starting date for Huston, who had another commitment. With no star and no director and a partial company on location, *Quo Vadis?* looked like a film that was going nowhere. Then Mayer stepped in. The picture was totally recast (Robert Taylor replaced Peck, Deborah Kerr took over for Taylor). Mervyn LeRoy replaced Huston, and a new screenplay was hastily patched together, with all analogies to Hitler and the Nazis ending on the steno pool floor.

The picture opened to reviews which said in so many words, "What does it matter, you'll go and see it anyway." And people did go to see it. *Quo Vadis?*—Mayer's *Quo Vadis?*—followed *Gone With the Wind* on the list of Metro's top-grossing films.

At about the same time, there was a major disagreement over yet another film, *Red Badge of Courage.* The story of the filming of Stephen Crane's classic Civil War novel has been told so many times—most notably by Lillian Ross in *Picture*—that it hardly needs elaboration. The gist of the matter was that the production, a collaboration between Metro producer Gottfried Reinhardt and director John Huston, gained Schary's support and Schenck's and Mayer's disapproval. But since *Courage* was budgeted economically, they decided to give Schary his way. The result was a *succès d'estime:* critics admired it, but the public showed little interest.

The deterioration of Mayer and Schary's relationship is not, however, adequately explained by these skirmishes over a few films. Nor was it only a question of political incompatibility, though the two men did lock horns over the issue of whether oaths of allegiance should be required of everyone working at the studio. It was more fundamental than this—in a phrase, they were temperamentally mismatched.

Schary was a complaisant man who abhorred all displays of anger or violence, whether verbal or physical; he was overcome by paroxysms of guilt on those rare occasions when he lost control of his own temper. Such a person was not the ideal associate for someone as explosive as Mayer, who believed (if he ever bothered to think about it) that ruthlessness, far from being undesirable, was one of the chief characteristics of every efficient studio boss. Running a Hollywood factory wasn't, after all, a gentleman's sport.

Intermediaries tried to explain this to Schary. Yes, they said, Mayer shouts and calls people ugly names (Schary claims that Mayer once referred to him as a kike); yes, he lops off heads at the slightest provocation. But it meant nothing. The next day the crude epithets were forgotten (at least by Mayer), and the people fired on Tuesday were back on payroll by Friday. It was just L.B.'s way of operating.

Schary understood all this. His father (a New York caterer and resort hotel manager) had been a hothead and bully like Mayer, and since he had learned to handle Papa, Schary was certain he could handle the mogul of M-G-M. Smiling outwardly, but bedrock inside, Schary was ready to stand firm against any hurricane Mayer might unleash in his direction.

This tactic may have worked with Papa Schary, but it didn't go down with Mayer, who found it infuriating. Comparing Schary to Thalberg, he said that Irving and he used to bat things around and eventually come up with something that both could live with, but Schary didn't argue, wouldn't discuss; he just stated his case, waltzed out of the office and rarely had anything further to say except to ask Schenck to referee. Go-betweens urged Schary to be more attentive to Mayer's objections and suggestions (even if the attention was merely sham), but Schary was proud of his integrity—a personal quality visible mainly to himself—and refused to stoop to such subterfuge.

Schary's slighting treatment of Mayer did not sit well with Metro old-timers. He was viewed as prissy and foolishly idealistic and incompetent, a silly stooge who screened M-G-M rough cuts at home and allowed his daughters to decide what changes should be made in the final editing. Although a competent writer, producer and minor executive, Schary was outside his class as Metro's production vice-president. He never realized that he was no more than a straw man in the battle between Mayer and Schenck for studio supremacy.

The possibility of a direct conflict became almost inevitable early in 1951. Several studio executives' contracts were up for renewal, and as a bonus for good performance, Mayer suggested that they be given the option to buy Loew's stock at a reduced rate. A memo to this effect was sent to Schenck, who did not respond. Schary may or may not have been included in Mayer's list of worthies, but apparently he was. Still, a few weeks later, when Schenck and Schary were vacationing in Florida, Schenck told Schary about the option but made no mention of Mayer, except to say that when and if Mayer resigned his position, Schary would automatically become head of production and head of studio at M-G-M.

A few days later, Loew's New York office announced that several M-G-M executives (including Schary) would be granted profit-sharing options as would several East Coast Loew's–M-G-M executives. The West Coast names were those sanctioned by Mayer; the others were Schenck's idea, and the addition made a subtle point: the East Coast (financial) office was now on equal footing with the West Coast ("creative") operation. What bothered Mayer about the announcement was not, however, this equalization of the balance of powers, but that Schenck had not consulted him before releasing the announcement and that the statement made no mention of his name. The impression created was that of Schenck as a bountiful lord doling out gifts to his dutiful servants.

Mayer flew into one of his imperial rages. Schenck assured him that the omission of his name was carelessness, not deliberate oversight, but Mayer suspected that Schenck and Schary were in cahoots to phase him out and to gain control of the studio for themselves. One day while Schary was in his office, he came out with this allegation while talking on the phone with Bob Rubin. It was a tactless remark to make in front of Schary, and possibly Mayer may have lost his head in a fit of anger. It is also possible that he was testing Schary, wanted to take him by surprise and see how he would react.

Schary was nonplussed. He insists that this was his first inkling of any animosity between Mayer and Schenck. If this is true, he must have been extraordinarily obtuse.

What had always been an open secret in the industry became public knowledge a few weeks later. While talking to Thomas Brady, a *New York Times* reporter, Mayer spoke intemperately on a broad range of topics, including "dirty actors" (meaning, one supposes, Marlon Brando and his tribe of imitators), the New York office and Loew's stockholders. There was even a faint hint that he might resign out of sheer disgust. When Mayer saw his statements in print, he was outraged, as were Schenck, his New York office, the dirty actors and Loew's stockholders—a public exposure of the division in the ranks of Loew's could be very detrimental to its continuing economical recovery. Mayer had Brady called on the carpet, but eventually he admitted to saying the things quoted in the article, though out of context they sounded much harsher than he had intended.

Hard feelings continued to pile up until one day, again on the phone, this time talking to Schenck, Mayer blurted out, "It's either me or Schary." Schenck said nothing then, but a few days later in a letter he replied that, all things considered, it would have to be Schary. He enumerated his reasons for this decision, and they were impeccable: In the brief time he had been in charge of production, Schary had vastly improved the quality and profits of the M-G-M product. Of the fifteen top-grossing M-G-M films made (prior to 1952), five had been produced under the Schary regime—*Quo Vadis?* (number 2), *Ivanhoe* (3), *Show Boat* (8), *Annie Get Your Gun* (10) and *The Great Caruso* (12).

In Mayer's defense it could be argued that in the same period, Schary turned out *The Next Voice You Hear* and *It's a Big Country*, two fiascos that would be outstanding candidates for anyone's list of the ten worst films ever made. Similarly, it could be said that *Quo Vadis?* was made according to Mayer's specifications, not Schary's, and that the remaining four Schary hits represent no break with or advance over the artistic policy of the preceding Mayer regime. *Show Boat* and *Annie* came out of the Freed unit, which had been Mayer's creation and remained his very pampered pet; *Caruso* starred Mario Lanza, who had been "discovered" by Ida Koverman and thereby qualified as a Mayer protégé. *Father of the Bride*, another highly successful Metro film of this period and one in which Schary took exceptional pride, probably would not have been made without Mayer's support. Schary had fallen in love with Edward Streeter's novel, but the rights were so expensive he had all but abandoned the idea of turning it into a film. Mayer told him that if he really wanted to do it, he should forget the cost and forge ahead.

But such arguments are tenuous, while profits and awards are concrete. Schenck had facts, figures and business logic on his side when he made his decision. After reading the letter, Mayer passed it in disgust to a group of faithful cohorts, including Strickling, Mannix and Louis Sidney (Mannix's right-hand man). As expected, they were horrified by Schenck's curt dismissal of the man who was responsible for making Metro the studio of Hollywood studios.

Undoubtedly Schenck could have handled the situation with more diplomacy. Mayer occasionally spoke of retirement, and while he may have been only half-serious when he did so, he could perhaps have been persuaded to spend his remaining working years in some honorary post. (Later, Paramount, faced with a similar situation, was to nudge its patriarch, Adolph Zukor, into a dignified, semi-emeritus position.) But Mayer was as responsible as Schenck for what happened: he made a direct challenge—"Schary or me"—in a situation where delicate negotiations were in order. Delicacy, however, had never been Mayer's strong point, and under different circumstances, he might well have approved of Schenck's action. He once told Schary that unpleasant business (dismissal, for instance) should be carried out as swiftly and (if necessary) as cold-bloodedly as possible.

And Mayer did, in fact, accept Schenck's decision in this fashion. He didn't argue or try to weasel out of his ultimatum. He sat down and wrote a letter of resignation, effective August 31, 1951.

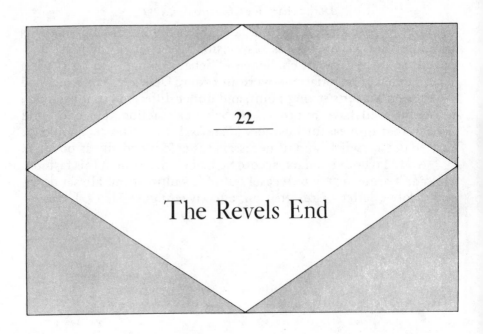

22

The Revels End

There was to be a prolonged period of intricate negotiations over the settlement of Mayer's contract. Most of the haggling concerned his 10 percent interest in the residual rights of all films produced by M-G-M since 1924, a matter of some financial consequence now that the television networks were leasing old Hollywood pictures for late-night exhibition. Several outsiders offered to buy out Mayer's interests, but eventually he sold the rights back to the studio for $2 million, only a fraction of what he would have realized when the M-G-M films were finally released to TV a few years later. He understood that if he held out, he could probably have gotten much more, but in 1951, all he wanted was to get his money out of the enemy camp.

Though the first announcements of Mayer's departure from M-G-M brought predictions that he would retire from active participation in the industry, Mayer immediately made it clear that this was not to be the case. While retirement had held a momentary attraction a few years before, it no longer seemed so entrancing: he was not going to fade out of the business under a cloud of forced resignation. He announced his plan to enter independent production with one or both of two projects he was developing—either an adaptation of the biblical story of Joseph and his brethren or *Blossom Time,* Sigmund Romberg's 1921 operetta based on the life of Franz Schubert. Neither project aroused much enthusiasm. Even Mayer's friends considered them too old-fashioned for modern taste, and none of the major studios expressed any interest in forming an affiliation with Mayer.

For a time there were rumors that he would become head of Warner Bros. He had the support of a group of businessmen who planned a takeover of the studio, but the takeover never came off. So for over a year Mayer bided his time. Loretta and he had recently moved into a relatively modest house in Bel Air (if any house in Bel Air can accurately be described as modest) where they entertained infrequently, watched television and just puttered around like any normal, well-off Southern California couple. Mayer worked on a new hobby, a collection of Grandma Moses paintings; returned to an old one, horse breeding, though in a much smaller way; and dabbled in real estate, buying property in both California and Florida. But to make it clear that he wasn't quietly phasing himself out of the industry, in early 1952 he acquired the film rights to the Alan Jay Lerner–Frederick Loewe musical *Paint Your Wagon.*

The rights came high, too high, according to insiders who considered the deal another indication of Mayer's obsolescence. *Paint Your Wagon* eked out a modest Broadway run, but it was never much of a critical or popular success—a good score was almost cancelled out by a very weak book—and there wasn't much Hollywood interest in the property until Paramount decided that, with some revising, it might serve as a Bing Crosby vehicle. And probably Paramount would have been able to obtain the rights at a very modest fee, if Mayer had not taken a fancy to the show and started overbidding. Eventually Paramount dropped out of the race and Mayer got the property at a price that was, according to Lerner, much more than M-G-M had paid for *Brigadoon,* a smash Broadway hit.

Such extravagance was, in the view of the industry savants, just another indication of how far out of step Mayer was with the economic realities of current-day Hollywood. He was paying too much for an indifferent property that he had no prospects of ever getting on the screen. But then it seemed as though Mayer would have the last laugh. He got his chance at a comeback not through one of the established Hollywood companies, but through a new organization, Cinerama.

In October 1952, this company exhibited in New York its first release, *This Is Cinerama,* a feature-length travelog which demonstrated a new and potentially revolutionary screen technique. Cinerama was a gigantic wide-screen process capable of creating the illusion of a third dimension. Wide screens and 3-D were then much discussed as the ultimate secret weapon against TV, but like so many desperate measures—color and sound, for instance—the need for innovation had taken precedence over the need for further refinement of a technique that was still in only a rudimentary stage of development. The curved Cinerama screen had two plainly visible seams that broke the visual image into a sort of triptych, the sections of which were not always evenly matched. And the three-dimensional effect came and went—strong in some sequences, nonexistent in others.

The public, however, wasn't disturbed by these technical imperfections, and neither was Mayer, who bubbled with enthusiasm after seeing *This Is Cinerama* at the Broadway Theatre in November 1952. He had come to New York as the guest of Lowell Thomas and Dudley Roberts, leading officials of the Cinerama Corporation, who were interested in bringing Mayer into the company in some executive capacity. Mayer's excitement led to his appointment as position of chairman of the board at a thousand-dollar-a-week salary. In addition to his salary, he received a liberal expense account and the right to buy Cinerama stock at well below the market price. It was also agreed that Cinerama would purchase any or all of the three screen properties Mayer controlled, with *Paint Your Wagon* announced as the company's first fiction film production.

Mayer was to supervise the development of the project. He envisioned Spencer Tracy in the leading role, and to prepare the script he hired John Lee Mahin, an M-G-M veteran who had worked on two of Tracy's biggest hits, *Captains Courageous* and *Boom Town*, and who was also one of Mayer's favorite screenwriters. Mahin was to collaborate with Alan Jay Lerner, the author of the musical's original book and lyrics.

Lerner was another Mayer favorite, though he himself didn't realize it at the time. They had first met in 1945 when (at Mayer's insistence) M-G-M became a silent backer of one of the first Lerner and Loewe musicals, *The Day Before Spring*. In exchange for the investment, M-G-M got the screen rights to the musical, but it was only a modest success and the studio eventually shelved the property. Lerner, however, became one of the fixtures of the Freed unit, writing a number of prominent M-G-M pictures, including *Royal Wedding* and *An American in Paris*. The latter was in production at the time that the Schenck-Mayer crisis reached its denouement, and Mayer's support during this grisly period is undoubtedly one of the reasons why Lerner is today a Mayer fan.

Lerner's script for *American in Paris* had been designed to climax in an extended ballet set to George Gershwin's jazz tone poem. By early January 1951, everything except the ballet had been shot and the footage had been assembled into a rough cut. After viewing the material, the New York office decided the film was in near perfect shape—just a little tidying up here, a little excising there, but forget the ballet, which was budgeted at over $400,000. Freed didn't want to forget the ballet, neither did Lerner, and Mayer stood firmly behind them. There were lots of phone calls between the East and West coasts, but one of Mayer's final acts before leaving the studio was, according to Lerner, "getting an okay for the ballet. That's the way the picture got done. Later Dore Schary intentionally or unintentionally took credit for that, but Mayer did it. I saw *American in Paris* recently and it hasn't aged awfully well, but I don't think it would be anything at all without the ballet."

It was not, however, until *Paint Your Wagon* that their association started in earnest. Usually they met for breakfast at Mayer's Bel Air home. "He loved his breakfast meetings," Lerner recalls. "And very funny breakfasts they were, I must say. Also very informative breakfasts. I learned a lot about the picture business during those early morning hours."

At one of the sessions, Mayer told Lerner that he was going to be his next Irving Thalberg. "I was stunned. . . . Why he ever thought that, I'll never know. I had no interest. I explained that I really wanted to write plays and while I liked writing screenplays, I was. basically a playwright. But nothing I said seemed to register. 'Yes, yes,' he said and then went on talking as though I had never opened my mouth."

Mayer occasionally gave vent to his rage at what had happened at M-G-M, at Schary or Schenck. Lerner was sympathetic. "I didn't know all the ins and outs, but I thought he had gotten a raw deal, and I thought he was fascinating. I loved his panache. I've always been taken by people like that, people like Mayer and Coco Chanel who operate in the grand manner. They are very much themselves, which is more than most people are today, despite this vaunted psychological era we're living in.

"He could be very charming, when he wanted to be. He could be boring, naturally, because he talked and you had to listen. He could be very funny. Sometimes unintentionally so. One day, he was glancing through *The Hollywood Reporter* and he came across an item about Dore Schary. Occidental College, or some such place, had given Schary some kind of humanitarian award, and Mayer shoved the paper across the table, and yelled, 'Look at that! Veterans need lumber for housing and that prick Schary is collecting wooden plaques!' ''

Before Lerner finished the first draft of the screenplay, Mayer had broken ties with Cinerama. The company was in financial trouble even before Mayer had joined it as chairman of the board. Launching its first production (which had been extensively and expensively advertised) and furnishing a few theatres with the equipment to exhibit it had left Cinerama in a financially embarrassed condition. The first profits, while considerable, couldn't keep up with the money going out of the company for further expansion, and with several other wide-screen processes coming onto the market, none of them quite as grandiose as Cinerama but several of them more practical and technically viable, Lowell and Roberts were hard pressed to find additional capitalization. As board chairman, Mayer became embroiled in these problems, but they held no real interest for him. What he wanted was to oversee the production of Cinerama movies—he wanted to be a showman, not a financial adviser. He wasn't prepared to put any of his money in the company, as Thomas and Roberts projected he would, though he did help in raising outside financing. Once economics started taking precedence over production matters, Mayer decided to leave, and the parting proved to be a reasonably amiable corporate divorce.

No one was ever to discover a way of utilizing the ungainly Cinerama process as more than an occasional road-show novelty, but Mayer's failure was regarded as another indication of his dwindling powers. After the break, he disappeared from the pages of *Variety* and the other industry sheets. It was more or less assumed that he had gone into retirement, fading away with the industry's other old soldiers who hadn't the good taste to die before they became obsolete.

The bitterness Mayer experienced on being pushed out of Metro now began to grow and fester. But for the time being there was nothing much he could do beyond fingering the sore. So he prowled around the Bel Air house, adding new Grandmas to his Moses collection, bullied his relatives, kept tabs on what was happening at M-G-M through his spies at the studio, watched TV, shopped for fresh vegetables at the Farmer's Market, went to Santa Anita or Hollywood Park every day during the season, entertained now and again.

Lorena and he had now become particularly close with director Clarence Brown and his fourth wife, Marion. This was hardly a new friendship—Brown spent most of his years as a director (1920–52) at M-G-M, and though during that period there had been prickly patches and scurrilous name-calling skirmishes, Brown had a genuine admiration for Mayer which was fully reciprocated. Brown was one of the few Metro directors Mayer leaned sideways to accommodate. In 1948, when the studio was already feeling financially pinched, Brown approached Mayer about filming Faulkner's *Intruder in the Dust.* "He was ready to throw me off the lot just for suggesting it," Brown remembers, "but I had been through the Atlanta race riots when I was sixteen, and this was a picture I had to make. So I kept after him. I wasn't going to back off just 'cause Mayer dumped on the idea." Brown's persistence wore down Mayer's resistance. "I don't like it, Clarence, but if that's what you really want to do, go ahead." *Intruder in the Dust* was a low-budget picture and it never returned a penny to the studio, but it was one of the most critically acclaimed of all M-G-M films of the late 1940s, far superior to the Schary socially conscious productions of the same period.

Brown left M-G-M only a few months after Mayer. His swan song was *Plymouth Adventure,* one of Schary's personal productions, an account of the Pilgrim fathers and their *Mayflower* voyage. Opening nationally on Thanksgiving Day, it was a turkey, and Brown, then sixty-two, decided to call it a day. He didn't like Schary and wasn't interested in free-lancing or moving to another studio. "I left Metro, and never went back, turned my rump on the whole damned thing."

Mayer and Brown became much closer after leaving the studio. "During those last five years, I don't think there was a day when we didn't see each other or talk or something. He was the closest friend I ever had." Like so many of Mayer's friends, Myron Fox and Strickling included, Brown was a track fanatic, and when the ponies were running, they spent practically every afternoon at Santa Anita. And one year Brown and his wife joined forces with L.B. and Lorena for a Grand Tour of Europe.

"That was one peculiar trip" Brown recalls. "I had to handle him like a child. I made all the arrangements and took charge of the tickets and all that crap. Whenever I had to leave him alone in a railroad station or air terminal, I'd say, 'Now, Louie, stay right here and don't move until I come back,' and he wouldn't budge. Once Loretta and Marion suggested they get some coffee, but he said, 'No, Clarence told me to stay here.'"

Though a shadow of senility hovers over this anecdote, that is certainly not the impression Brown wanted to convey. Mayer was accustomed to having Strickling's special service department take care of all the aggravating, petty details that are the blight of any vacation. And he believed only one person should control travel arrangements—the followers should be docile about obeying the leader's instructions. Mayer was still healthy and his mind was sharp as a tack, though his judgment was not as acute as before.

Brown was one of many friends who felt Mayer was foolish to get involved in the internecine warfare that disrupted M-G-M during the mid-fifties. But the bitterness within Mayer needed an outlet and led him into the first and, as it turned out, final misadventure of an otherwise masterly minded career.

The trouble at M-G-M was really a continuation of the problems that had led to Mayer's resignation. Once he was gone, Schenck had instituted a number of money-saving operations, including drastic cuts in production costs, salaries and personnel. Fewer films were made each year, and soon the M-G-M firmament of stars started looking less and less like the Milky Way. Between 1952 and 1954, George Murphy, Clark Gable, Greer Garson, Esther Williams, Van Johnson, Mario Lanza, Deborah Kerr, Kathryn Grayson, Lionel Barrymore and Spencer Tracy left the studio either voluntarily or because their options were allowed to lapse. The directorial and writing staff was similarly pared down. But these economies failed to impress Loew's—M-G-M stockholders, who watched anxiously as the annual profits began to decline at the end of the 1953–54 fiscal period.

Schenck had made a tactical error. In dismissing Mayer, he had done away with a convenient scapegoat and set himself up as a direct target for corporate discontent. And it was not long before bricks were thrown in his direction. There were three major areas of vulnerability. First, Schenck's pay cuts had stopped at the top echelon —he and the other big M-G-M and Loew's executives earned as much as ever. Second, he was guilty of nepotism, and third, he wasn't keeping up with the times. He wouldn't, for instance, sanction percentage deals with star actors, a practice that was becoming increasingly prevalent in the post–World War II era.

Undoubtedly, Mayer backed Schenck on most of these issues. He too practiced nepotism; he had never, in periods of crisis, cut his own or his cardinals' salaries; he was adamantly against profit-sharing arrangements with actors. It was no secret that he vehemently disapproved when his son-in-law, Bill Goetz, made one of the first of these deals with James Stewart.

But while he was in agreement with Schenck on these points, he was appalled (and also possibly not at all displeased) at the deterioration of the studio since his departure. For which, of course, he held Schenck responsible. And for which he hoped Schenck would get his comeuppance.

The day of reckoning occurred in December 1955. Under pressure, Schenck resigned the position of chairman of the board. It was passed on to Arthur Loew, the son of the company founder, Marcus Loew. For many years the younger Loew had headed the company's foreign operations, an important post and one that he handled skillfully but one that also kept him distant from the personality conflicts that erupted all too frequently within the organization. He didn't really want the presidency, and accepted it only when it became clear that no other candidate would be acceptable to all parties involved in the decision.

Loew's appointment was not, however, the occasion for hosannas and hoopla celebration. From the day he took office, it was rumored that Schenck had sanctioned Loew only because he thought he could manipulate him. Loew knew of the gossip, ignored it for almost a year, but then, dissatisfied and disgusted, he chose to resign.

It was at this point that Mayer set out on his great misadventure. The ground plan was already mapped out—watching the crumbling of the Loew's–M-G-M empire from his Bel Air home, Mayer had been stealthily charting the paths that might return him to power. A year or so earlier he had welcomed into his circle of friends a young television producer, Stanley Meyer, who had accumulated a small fortune from the *Dragnet* series and was looking around for some new and exciting way to make a second killing. He talked about this to Mayer (who was to become the godfather of Meyer's son, Peter, who was to use L.B. as the subject of a master's thesis at Yale). Mayer proposed that he apply his money and time to a takeover of Loew's, Inc.–Metro.

There is an alternate version of the story that says Meyer was the mastermind of the plot, and L.B., having nothing to lose, went along with him. Certainly it is true that Meyer did most of the preliminary footwork. He discovered that Joseph Tomlinson, a Canadian financier, owned 180,000 shares of Loew's common stock, the biggest block controlled by any single individual, and through sweat, persistence and expensive dinners, it was he who convinced Tomlinson to join the rebellion against Loew's–M-G-M.

Meanwhile, in New York, Schenck, as board chairman, was searching high and low for a replacement for Loew. Candidates were proposed and discarded, until finally in despiration Schenck turned to Joseph Vogel, the head of the Loew's theatre chain. Vogel had never been a Schenck supporter, and got the job as the last resort. Schenck was not overly fond of Vogel, and whatever friendly feelings they may have harbored for each other quickly evaporated. After Vogel's appointment, Schenck was overheard shouting at the new Loew's president, "I'm going to live to piss on your grave."

One of Vogel's first acts was to fire Dore Schary, whose production record in the past two years had been poor. Vogel's action was not unwarranted, but Schary's dismissal was another indication that the company was in a sorry state of corporate disarray. The time had come for the Mayer-Meyer-Tomlinson coalition to swing into action.

The battle that ensued was long, complicated, ugly and finally tedious to anyone not fascinated by the machinations of corporate power play. Since the details of the plan have been extensively covered in several books, no more need be said than the plan almost succeeded, probably would have succeeded if Mayer had not unexpectedly expressed reservations about assuming the presidency of Loew's, Inc.

What caused him to back off at the last minute? There are several possible explanations. First, he may have known that nothing he could do would restore M-G-M to its former glory. The studio system was crumbling, and there was little he could do to reassemble the pieces. Irene Selznick remembers that her father had forecast everything that would come. There would be chaos, fruitless and costly battles among the three branches of the industry; there would be no organization, no overall design, no company esprit, no pride, no sense of leadership.

Everything Mayer had predicted was coming true, and it seems likely that he was astute enough to realize that neither he nor anyone could reverse the tide. Furthermore the presidency of Loew's, Inc. was not a post he had ever hankered for. In the past he had often said he wouldn't take Schenck's job for love or money. He couldn't picture himself sitting in New York, courting stockholders, worrying over daily receipts, virtually isolated from the creative side of film making. Apparently for a time he chose to forget his distaste, but then, when the job was practically in the bag, he remembered and pushed it aside.

Then, too, it's possible that even if he had wanted the job, he may have realized that he no longer possessed the physical stamina to carry it out. During the weeks while the coup was being plotted, he had frequently complained of feeling peckish, but scoffed when Lorena and several friends urged him to have a checkup. There was nothing seriously wrong with him, he insisted. Still, in early August 1957 he did agree to enter Stanford University Hospital near San Francisco for a complete physical examination. When it was over, the doctors told him he was suffering from a minor blood disease. He was never told he was dying of leukemia.

He returned to his Bel Air home in September, but a few days later his condition worsened and he was taken to the Medical Center of the University of California in Los Angeles. His good friend Dr.

Jessie Marmorston was in constant attendance. Irene Selznick flew in from New York, stayed for a few days, then returned to the East Coast, thereby keeping up the pretense that there was nothing seriously wrong with her father.

Danny Selznick wonders whether L.B. was ever aware that he was dying. "I think Grandpa believed he had beaten the odds against death," he said. "I think he believed in his own immortality." And at first Mayer was in constant high spirits. He joked around with the steady stream of visitors who came to call, cross-examining his old studio buddies about what was going on at M-G-M and keeping a critical eye on the performances of his nurses. One day, while Clarence Brown was visiting, the flow of his intravenous feeder became irregular. "He knew exactly how much he was supposed to get, had it down to the minute, and when the stuff started blocking up or coming too freely (I don't remember which) he got very angry. Rang for the nurse and gave her hell. It was kind of funny and also very moving. He was a dying man, but there he was still trying to run things, still bossing people around. Only now the only people he could boss were a bunch of twitty nurses."

But his condition deteriorated rapidly. Soon he was listless, expressing little interest when told the Meyer-Tomlinson coup, without Mayer as the kingpin, had failed to come off; barely listening when Howard Strickling told him the latest gossip from M-G-M. Informed that the end was near, Irene Selznick rushed to Los Angeles.

She and Lorena were at his bedside when, a few minutes after midnight on October 29, 1957, Louis Burt Mayer died.

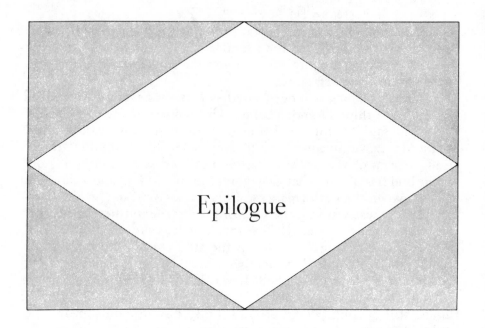

Epilogue

"If my father had died, like Zukor, at over a hundred, things might have been different," remarked Irene Selznick. She was referring to Adolph Zukor, Paramount's founding father, who died at the age of 104 in 1977. "Zukor managed to outlive all his enemies, so when he died, there was barely anyone around to remember how rough and ruthless he could be."

Zukor also happened to die at a time when every second person seemed to be drooling with nostalgia over the good old Hollywood days. Mayer, on the other hand, died at a time when *mogul* was a dirty word and the studio system was under attack as philistine and artistically corrupt.

Consequently, the reports of his death, while front-page news, were somewhat restrained in their evaluation of his achievements. Empty seats were strikingly visible during the funeral service at a temple on Wilshire Boulevard. Irene Selznick put herself in charge of these final rites. Jeanette MacDonald opened the ceremony by singing "Ah, Sweet Mystery of Life." Then, following the Kaddish, Spencer Tracy read the eulogy, written by David O. Selznick with help from John Mahin and Carey Wilson, Mayer's two favorite screenwriters. Later, someone joked that in typical M-G-M fashion, Mayer's final tribute was a collaborative effort.

Nine days later—November 11, 1957—Mayer's will was made public. His estate was valued at about $7.5 million, which was considerably less than expected. Mayer had often implied that he was as rich as Croesus, and when this proved not to be so, many expectant heirs were disappointed. In some cases, disappointment soured into resentment, particularly on the part of Dr. Marmorston, who became distraught when she learned she wasn't mentioned in the will, and the Cummings family, who expected more than they got.

He left $750,000 and the Bel Air house to Lorena; to Irene Selznick and Lorena's daughter, Suzanne, he left $500,000 each; Jeffrey and Daniel Selznick each received trust funds of $250,000. Howard Strickling and Myron Fox each received $50,000, and Mayer's sister, Ida Cummings, got a small gift. But no other members of the family were mentioned, and Edith was specifically disinherited: "I have given them [referring to Edie and her children] extremely substantial assistance during my lifetime."

This display of ill will toward Edie was the culmination of a bitterness dating back for over a year. Mayer knew he was responsible for putting his son-in-law on the Hollywood map and was first hurt, then embittered when Goetz failed to show respect. Rumors filtered back to him about how the Goetzes amused their guests with anecdotes about L.B.'s idiosyncrasies. Mayer pointed out that the Goetz's luxurious life-style was at odds with their ultraliberal political convictions. He became enraged when Goetz sponsored a Los Angeles cocktail party for Adlai Stevenson with Dore Schary as his co-host—support for Stevenson he might have forgiven, but playing buddies with Schary was another matter. The estrangement deeply distressed Edie, and though Lorena tried to bring father and daughter together, there was no reconciliation before Mayer's death. Edith attended the funeral services; Goetz did not.

But the disinheritance of Edie Goetz was not the only surprise in Mayer's will. Even more startling was that the major portion of the estate went to the Louis B. Mayer Foundation, a charitable institution that was unknown to the public. Mayer had never been renowned for his charitable instincts; on the contrary, he was reputed to react violently whenever the subject of philanthropy was mentioned in his presence. And, there were no specifications as to how the money should be used, except that a major portion should be utilized for medical purposes. Details were left to the discretion of the board of directors—Lorena Danker Mayer, Myron Fox and Gerald Mayer, one of L.B.'s nephews.

Unfortunately the board—whose membership has shifted several times over the years—and the Mayer family have never seen eye to eye on how the money should be spent. One faction, spearheaded by Danny Selznick, has fought for a small allowance for research projects in film history. The other side, headed by (until his recent death) Myron Fox and Howard Strickling, regard allocations of this kind as frivolous. This group prides itself on the foundation's generous grants for medical equipment and hospital wings, all impressively recorded in handsome, elegantly bound scrapbooks, which are brought out like holy relics for visitors to the foundation offices on Wilshire Boulevard.

M-G-M paid no special tribute to Mayer at the time of his death. Even before he died, the studio made an official practice of overlooking his contribution to its corporate history, a policy which continues to the present—characteristically, M-G-M's two major productions of the late seventies, the nostalgia-happy *That's Entertainment* compilation films, made only fleeting mention of Mayer. This upset Mayer's friends, and it was distasteful, but what can be expected of a studio that had stooped to sucking the marrow from the bones of its past glory?

The studio had put itself on lean rations by the early 1960s. By then, Robert Taylor, Elizabeth Taylor, Lana Turner, June Allyson, Ava Gardner and Debbie Reynolds had left the lot, and the studio's stellar system now sparkled only when a visiting star dropped by for a picture or two. By the late sixties, there was no one lunching in the commissary except transients working on TV productions shooting on one of the sound stages Metro rented to make ends meet. The city that had once been M-G-M was now virtually a ghost town. In the seventies, the studio started selling off its acreage and put up its prop and wardrobe department for auction, and gowns once worn by Judy Garland and Greer Garson now were sported by drag queens (who, incidentally, cherish and preserve them as Metro in this declining period had never done). Next, the company dissolved its distribution networks and started to release through United Artists. In recent years, M-G-M has gone the Walt Disney route, and instead of making movies, is concentrating on building pleasure palaces for children of all ages, namely its Grand Hotels in Las Vegas and Reno.

The course of M-G-M history is not so different from the history of other studios, only M-G-M hit bottom faster and stayed there longer than the others. As of this writing, things are looking up—so they say. David Begelman, production chief at M-G-M (after being pushed out of a similar job at Columbia for pleading *nolo contendere* to a charge of embezzling $40,000 of company funds), has promised that he will return M-G-M to its former glory as a major studio. Other studio heads are making similar sounds: productivity will be increased, they say; actors will be developed and given multipicture deals; the studio system will blossom again. But they are talking about twelve to fourteen pictures a year, which isn't much of a harvest compared to the old studio-system yield.

The predictions of a second coming are based on a belief in the enormous potential of the technology—pay-TV, videocassettes and other electronic wonders, which, it is predicted, will double or triple the audience for movies. In the future, if the prediction holds true, there will be a triple, sometimes overlapping, public for films; there will be (1) those who go to theatres to see films, (2) those who watch them at home on network or cable television, and (3) those who buy cassettes of their favorite films as part of a permanent library. And this enormous audience will increase revenues, which will allow for greater productivity. It will, according to blueprint, allow producers to make films that have limited appeal to audiences number 1 or 2, but could return a profit from sales to audience number 3.

All of which sounds sterile and pretty grim to those of us who grew up in the Bijou and candy-bar era of moviegoing. There's something depressing about imagining a family rummaging through their cassette library to decide on, what? Maybe *The Exorcist* or *Jaws* or a Barbra Streisand classic. At the time of the paperback revolution in publishing, it was predicted that soon the American unlettered would be hooked on Henry James, but today most subway readers are passing the time with *Princess Daisy*, not *Daisy Miller*.

But one can't hang back, one has to forge ahead with the times. And movies, like that other fabulous invalid, the theatre, will get yet another second wind and revive. But the next life won't be the same as the one before. There won't be a second coming of the studio system.

Louis Jouvet, the great French actor and director, once said that every society deserves the art it gets. There is an ominous ring to this, but behind it lies a simplistic observation: society is the true creator of any art form. If this is so, and it does seem particularly applicable to the popular arts, then there would be no way to bring back the studio system without recreating the conditions, concerns and people who played a part in its evolution. Which is an impossibility. Today we have fine actors and box office bonanzas (like *Kramer Vs. Kramer*) and executives like Begelman and Sherry Lansing and Ray Stark, but we don't have Garbo or Gable or nice night-out films (like *Penny Serenade*) or moguls like Selznick, Thalberg, Goldwyn or Mayer.

"There'll never be another Louis Mayer," says Alan Jay Lerner. "He was of a different stripe from any of the other studio bosses I've dealt with. For instance, Jack Warner simply disregarded contracts and obligations. Mayer never did that. If he said this is what you will get, that was what you got. With Warner, there was a verbal agreement that the 'Get Me to the Church' sequence of *My Fair Lady* would be shot in London—we were to do location work in all the great pubs of England—but Warner decided to forget he had made that agreement. That would never have happened with Mr. Mayer. He never backed away from anything. . . .

"One Ivy League type who was writing a thesis on M-G-M came to me and said, 'Why was Louis B. Mayer such a villain?' And I said, 'First of all, this man wasn't a villain. If you want a villain, go look at the head of ITT or General Motors or the head of whatever . . . just because Mayer stepped on some toes or because he browbeat some actresses into playing parts they didn't want to do, or because there was a certain amount of conniving around—this made him a villain? Then, God help us all. Mr. Mayer was a great showman, and he loved and believed in what he was doing. He created something that was unique and which is wonderful and of lasting value."

To which one can only add, Amen.

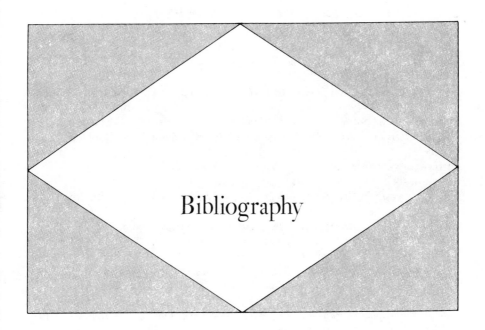

Bibliography

AGEE, JAMES. *Agee On Film.* New York: McDowell, Obolensky, 1958.

ARDMORE, JANE. *The Self-Enchanted, Mae Murray: Image of an Era.* New York: McGraw-Hill, Inc., 1959.

BAINBRIDGE, JOHN. *Garbo.* Garden City, New York: Doubleday & Co., 1955.

BEEKMAN, EDWARD O. *The Lady and the Law, The Remarkable Story of Fanny Holtzmann.* Boston: Little, Brown & Co., 1976.

BEHLMER, RUDY, ed. *Memo from David O. Selznick.* New York: Viking Press, 1972.

BEHRMAN, S.N. *People in a Diary.* Boston: Little, Brown & Co., 1972.

BENTLEY, ERIC, ed. *Thirty Years of Treason, Excerpts from Hearings Before the House Committee on Un-American Activities.* New York: Viking Press, 1971.

BLESH, RUDI. *Keaton.* New York: Macmillan, 1966.

BODEEN, DEWITT. *From Hollywood.* New York: A.S. Barnes & Co., 1976.

BROWNLOW, KEVIN. *The Parade's Gone By.* New York: Alfred A. Knopf, 1968.

———, and KOBAL, JOHN. *Hollywood, The Pioneers.* New York: Alfred A. Knopf, 1979.

CHAPLIN, CHARLES. *My Autobiography.* New York: Simon & Schuster, 1964.

CHIERICHETTI, DAVID. *Hollywood Costume Design.* New York: Harmony Books, 1976.

CORLISS, RICHARD. *Greta Garbo.* New York: Pyramid Publications, 1974.

CROWTHER, BOSLEY. *Hollywood Rajah, The Life and Times of Louis B. Mayer.* New York: Henry Holt, 1960.

———. *The Lion's Share.* New York: E. P. Dutton, 1957.

DAVIES, MARION. *The Times We Had.* New York: Bobbs-Merrill Co., 1975.

DE MILLE, CECIL B. *The Autobiography of Cecil B. De Mille.* Englewood Cliffs, New Jersey: Prentice-Hall, 1959.

DIETZ, HOWARD. *Dancing in the Dark.* New York: Quadrangle, 1974.

EAMES, JOHN DOUGLAS. *The MGM Story.* New York: Crown Publishers, Inc., 1976.

FINCH, CHRISTOPHER. *Rainbow, The Stormy Life of Judy Garland.* New York: Grosset & Dunlap, 1975.

————, and ROSENKRANTZ, LINDA. *Gone Hollywood.* Garden City, New York: Doubleday & Co., 1979.

FLAMINI, ROLAND. *Scarlett, Rhett and a Cast of Thousands.* New York: Macmillan, 1975.

FORDIN, HUGH. *The World of Entertainment.* Garden City, New York: Doubleday & Co., 1975.

FOWLER, GENE. *Good Night, Sweet Prince.* New York: Viking Press, 1943.

FRANK, GEROLD. *Judy.* New York: Harper & Row, 1975.

GARNETT, TAY. *Light Your Torches and Pull up Your Tights.* New York: Arlington House, 1973.

GEIST, KENNETH L. *Pictures Will Talk.* New York: Charles Scribner's Sons, 1978.

GRIFFITH, RICHARD. *The Movie Stars.* Garden City, New York: Doubleday & Co., 1970.

————, and MAYER, ARTHUR. *The Movies.* New York: Simon & Schuster, 1957.

GUILES, FRED LAWRENCE. *Marion Davies.* New York: McGraw-Hill, Inc., 1972.

HAMPTON, BENJAMIN B. *A History of the Movies.* New York: Arno Press, 1970.

HARMETZ, ALJEAN. *The Making of The Wizard of Oz.* New York: Alfred A. Knopf, 1977.

HARRIS, LEON. *Upton Sinclair, American Rebel.* New York: Thomas Y. Crowell Co., 1975.

HARVEY, STEPHEN. *Joan Crawford.* New York: Pyramid Publications, 1974.

HECHT, BEN. *Charlie, the Improbable Life and Times of Charles MacArthur.* New York: Harper, 1957.

HOPPER, HEDDA. *From Under My Hat.* Garden City, New York: Doubleday & Co., 1952.

HOWE, IRVING. *World of Our Fathers.* New York: Harcourt, Brace, 1976.

HUFF, THEODORE. *Charlie Chaplin.* New York: Henry Schuman, 1951.

JACOBS, LEWIS. *The Rise of the American Film.* New York: Harcourt, Brace, 1959.

JOHNSTON, ALVA. *The Great Goldwyn.* New York: Random House, 1937.

KEATON, BUSTER, and SAMUELS, CHARLES. *My Wonderful World of Slapstick.* Garden City, New York: Doubleday & Co., 1960.

KOBAL, JOHN. *Gotta Sing Gotta Dance.* London: Hamlyn, 1970.

LAHUE, KALTON C. *Continued Next Week.* Norman: University of Oklahoma Press, 1964.

LAMBERT, GAVIN. *The Making of Gone With the Wind.* Boston: Little, Brown & Co., 1973.

LEROY, MERVYN, and KLEINER, DICK. *Take One.* New York: Hawthorn Books, 1975.

MACGOWAN, KENNETH. *Behind the Screen.* New York: Delacorte Press, 1965.

MARION, FRANCES. *Off With Their Heads.* New York: Macmillan, 1972.

MARX, SAMUEL. *Mayer and Thalberg, The Make-Believe Saints.* New York: Random House, 1975.

MILLER, ANN, and BROWNING, NORMA LEE. *Miller's High Life.* Garden City, New York: Doubleday & Co., 1972.

MINNELLI, VINCENTE, and ARCE, HECTOR. *I Remember It Well.* Garden City, New York: Doubleday & Co., 1974.

OPPENHEIMER, GEORGE. *The View from the Sixties.* New York: David McKay Company, 1966.

PARISH, JAMES ROBERT. *The Jeanette MacDonald Story.* New York: Mason/Charter, 1976.

————, and BOWERS, RONALD L. *The MGM Stock Company.* New Rochelle, New York: Arlington House, 1973.

RAMSAYE, TERRY. *A Million and One Nights.* New York: Simon & Schuster, 1964.

ROSE, HELEN. *Just Make Them Beautiful.* Santa Monica, Calif.: Deanes-Landman, 1976.

ROSENBERG, BERNARD, and SILVERSTEIN, HARRY. *The Real Tinsel.* New York: Macmillan, 1970.

ROSS, LILLIAN. *Picture.* Garden City, New York: Doubleday & Co., 1952.

RUSSELL, ROSALIND, and CHASE, CHRIS. *Life Is a Banquet.* New York: Random House, 1977.

SCHARY, DORE. *Heyday.* Boston: Little, Brown & Co., 1979.

SINCLAIR, UPTON. *Upton Sinclair Presents William Fox.* Los Angeles: Sinclair Press, 1933.

STEWART, DONALD OGDEN. *By a Stroke of Luck.* New York and London: Paddington Press Ltd., 1975.

SWANBERG, W.A. *Citizen Hearst.* New York: Charles Scribner's Sons, 1969.

SWINDELL, LARRY. *Spencer Tracy.* New York: World Publishing Co., 1969.

THOMAS, BOB. *Thalberg, Life and Legend.* Garden City, New York: Doubleday & Co., 1969.

TORNABEE, LYN. *Long Live the King.* New York: G.P. Putnam's Sons, 1976.

VALENTINO, LOU. *The Films of Lana Turner.* Secaucus, New Jersey: Citadel, 1976.

VIDOR, KING. *A Tree Is a Tree.* New York: Harcourt, Brace, 1952.

VIERTEL, SALKA. *The Kindness of Strangers.* New York: Holt, Rinehart & Winston, 1969.

WILSON, ROBERT, ed. *The Film Criticism of Otis Ferguson.* Philadelphia: Temple University Press, 1971.

YOUNG, CHRISTOPHER. *The Films of Hedy Lamarr.* Secaucus, New Jersey: Citadel, 1978.

ZOLOTOW, MAURICE. *Stagestruck: The Romance of Alfred Lunt and Lynn Fontanne.* New York: Harcourt, Brace & World, 1964.

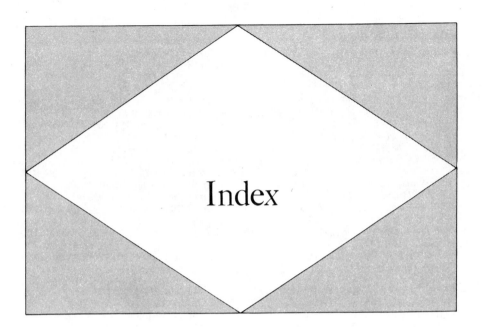

Index